SOVIET SOCIETY UNDER PERESTROIKA

Completely revised edition

David Lane

WITHDRAWN

London and New York

First published 1990 by HarperCollins*Academic*
New Edition published in 1991

Revised Edition published 1992
by Routledge
11 New Fetter Lane, London EC4P 4EE

Simultaneously published in the USA and Canada
by Routledge
a division of Routledge, Chapman and Hall, Inc.
29 West 35th Street, New York, NY 10001

Typeset in 10 on 12 point Times by Setrite Typesetters Ltd
and printed and bound in Great Britain by
Biddles Ltd, Guildford and King's Lynn

British Library Cataloguing in Publication Data

Lane, David Stuart
  Soviet society under perestroika.
  1. Soviet Union. Society. Political aspects
  I. Title
  947.08'5'4

ISBN 0−415−07600−5

Library of Congress Cataloging in Publication Data
has been applied for

ISBN 0−415−07600−5

CONTENTS

Part One

THE POLITICAL AND ECONOMIC FRAMEWORK

Part Two

SOCIAL CLASSES AND GROUPS

Part Four

CONCLUSIONS

LIST OF TABLES

LIST OF FIGURES

PREFACE

It has been twenty years since the first edition of *Politics and Society in the USSR* was published. That book was innovative because it was one of the first books to use data, inexact and inadequate as they were, that had been collected by Soviet social scientists. In the early 1970s the study of class, nationalities, and pressure groups in the political process was regarded as marginal by most and even irrelevant by some Western commentators who in their demonic black art of kremlinology focused narrowly on the "outputs" of the political system. Like Soviet political writers, Western scholars emphasized the differences between Soviet communism and Western society: the polarities of democracy and control, civil society and the state, liberty and equality, individualism and collectivism, welfare and exploitation were at the fore in the analysts' preoccupations with their rival claims of the superiority of capitalism or communism respectively. My own attempt to define the USSR as a species of industrial society was not popular with the established opinion-makers in either the Soviet or the Anglo-Saxon academic establishments. The boon of an expansion in the study of political science and sociology and a growing interest in socialist countries (often precipitated by a thirst to "know the enemy"), however, ensured the book's success and replacement by a two volume work in 1985.

In 1991 the specter of communism in the West has changed completely. It is symbolic that President Gorbachev is feted in Western capitals: he has been given a state welcome by Queen Elizabeth II, and he had a tumultuous reception in West Germany. The repudiation of Marxism-Leninism, the collapse of the Communist Party of the Soviet Union and creation of a new Union of Sovereign States in the autumn of 1991, has led Western writers to pontificate on the end of the epoch of socialism started in 1917. Soviet writing about the USSR has experienced a parallel shift. If ideologists were previously concerned with the "export of revolution" from the USSR, now they are preoccupied with the import of Western artifacts and ways of doing things. The emphasis is to stress the "common European heritage" of the Soviet Union and the advanced Western nations. Soviet writings are replete with more popular Western approaches to their own society. Conflict, totalitarian control, interest groups, ethnic and generational forms of identity, and the role of the market are prevalent in Soviet writings.

This book concentrates on the changes that have taken place in the USSR under the leadership of Gorbachev and attempts to give the reader an introduction to the problems confronting the reform leadership and the ways in which they are being addressed. The narrative is informed by current thinking in sociology and political science. There are many books on perestroika and Soviet society. What, then, is novel about this one? The approach I have adopted is sociological and this involves considering society as a total entity with interacting parts, hence the political impacts on the social and economic, which in turn affect politics. While it has been impossible to include the whole web of social interactions in this book, those aspects of society studied here are interdependent. Part 1 examines the economic and political developments, Part 2 looks at the changing character of classes and gender, ethnic and generational groups, and part 3 explores forms of social control — education, ritual, the media, and the provision of welfare.

Since the first edition of this book was published, the rate of change has significantly increased. The Communist Party of the Soviet Union gave up its legitimate monopoly of political power and competing parties and groups entered the political market. A new form of government was initiated: presidential power. This gave the first head of state (Gorbachev) powers comparable to those of the tsars. The Party has lost its monopoly of power to new parties and political groups. Gorbachev survived a coup d'etat, but conceded political power to his rival, Eltsin. Internal conflicts have escalated: between nations and ethnic groups, between parties, between individual leaders, between traditional ideologists steeped in Marxism—Leninism and those favoring a Western market-type system with private ownership and competition. The country has appeared to be facing an economic collapse as it moved from a centrally controlled economy to one with market competition; economic growth declined. Disintegration and dislocation characterized the transitional period. The Soviet Union's position as a world power was put in question: the previous client states of Eastern Europe became independent, with non-communist governments. The messianic claims of world communism have been buried. These developments are reflected in the much revised chapters in Part 1 and in chapter 6. The appended Constitution has also been updated.

The events of August 1991 have clearly focused the contradictions of

Soviet society under perestroika. The leaders and supporters of the failed coup sought to reassert some of the traditional values, whereas the victorious leaders of the democratic movement advocated a rapid move to a market system, a confederation of sovereign states and the destruction of the Communist Party. The implications of these events are as momentous as the October Revolution itself and can only briefly be indicated in this book. What I attempt to show is that these developments were part of a cumulative process of change and development.

I hope the book will appeal to teachers and students alike who are concerned with comparative politics, and political sociology, as well as those studying Soviet politics and society. Other readers interested in the evolution of Soviet society and socialism will also be able to benefit from reading the book.

I have not been able to include an historical component and this, together with international affairs, will have to be provided by other books. A number of original sources have been reproduced that detail points which cannot be made in the text. The references have been kept to a minimum in the text as I have found that few students use them and many are put off by what appears to be academic heavy baggage. Bibliographies of the most important European language works and articles cited in the text are included at the end of each major section. Russian language sources have been excluded.

I am indebted to many people who have stimulated me in the writing of this book. I am happy to acknowledge the support given by the Sociology and Peace Studies Departments at Cornell University. I am grateful to Jackie Johnson of the CREES Library, Birmingham, for her help in securing Soviet literature, to two anonymous referees whose comments enabled me greatly to improve the text. My thanks to Charles Jenkins, Christel Lane, Christopher Lane, and Sheila Marnie for reading and commenting on some of the chapters and to Valya Hine, C. M. Davis and Gordon Hyde for advice on many points.

Acknowledgement for permission to reprint copyright material is made to: Oxford University Press, Ellen Mickiewicz, *Split Signals: Television and Politics in the Soviet Union* (1988), p. 109 and to BBC Monitoring, Summary of World Broadcasts, "Eltsin's Election Address", USSR, SU 0421, C 1, 30 March 1989 and "Manifesto of Nina Andreeva", USSR, SU 0126 B/1–6, 15 April 1988, CPSU Programme Statement, SU/0821. C2/1: 20 July 1990; Draft Union Treaty (revised 23 July 1991) SU/1152.C1: 16 August 1991.

David Lane
Faculty of Social and
Political Sciences, University of Cambridge, England

Chapter 1

CHANGING CONCEPTIONS OF SOVIET SOCIETY

Since its foundation the Soviet Union has been considered by most people in the West to be a major adversary to our conceptions of a democratic state and society. Following the temporary alliance between the Allies during the Second World War, Western governments have regarded the Soviet Union and the Warsaw Pact countries as pursuing policies inimical to the interests of Western states. The West has not only regarded their foreign policies as hostile, but also has viewed their internal political and social organization as illegitimate. Such political conflict in the international sphere has created an environment in which the social and political systems of the major adversaries have been stereotyped in the popular imagination. The image of Soviet society in the eyes of people outside the USSR has been one of an illegitimate totalitarian society in which individual rights have been sacrificed to meet the needs of an all-powerful totalitarian state. George Orwell's novels *Animal Farm* and *1984*, have been powerful symbolic representations of the fate of the masses in socialist states.

This book will subject such popular conceptions to critical scrutiny. Under the leadership of Gorbachev a new turn has taken place in Soviet policies. Many of the old ways of doing things have been questioned; radical attempts for reform (*perestroika*) have been made. In the pages that follow, the impact of the reforms on the structure of Soviet society will be analyzed. Following a discussion of the reform strategy of Gorbachev, its economic and political implications, we shall consider the relationships between the major social groups (classes and nationalities), forms of social welfare and control (education and the family) and the processes of social change (the mass media and the rise of independent groups). By analyzing the social context in which Soviet politics takes place — the ways that politics constrains the social system and vice versa — we shall understand better the changes and challenges the USSR faces.

In the first instance I shall outline some of the assumptions that people have, or the expectations they entertain, about the nature of communist (or as I define them, state socialist) societies. Moreover, one cannot study data in an ideological vacuum; one's perceptions are influenced by assumptions taken from one's own society, its history and values. These preconceptions affect the ways that we interpret foreign societies, especially in the context of international competition. We may define two worldviews of the USSR that were current in the West before the advent of perestroika: the benign and the malevolent.

THE IMAGE OF THE SOVIET UNION: BENIGN

The polarity of antagonism between East and West as outlined above is an oversimplification, and the image of the Soviet Union as destructive of human rights is one-sided. The Russian Revolution and the Soviet system that emerged from it have been, and are, greeted with acclaim by many in the West. Rather than mere hostility, there has always been ambivalence to the Soviet Union in the West.

Many socialists and liberally minded people in the West saw the Russian Revolution as ushering in a new society that represented an alternative in advance of capitalism. Born in the genocide of the trenches of the First World War and followed by the poverty of the Great Depression of the 1920s, the revolution was regarded as the beginning of a new world order that would put an end to the uncertainty of the market, the irrationality of competition that gives rise, on the one side, to a system of inequality and poverty, and on the other, riches and domination. In the West communism has not only appealed to the underdogs — who would have most to gain materially from systemic change — but also to the idealists and intellectuals who regard socialism as a form of society superior to capitalism and who condemn the class-ridden rapacious Western imperialist powers. The imagery of such thinkers is symbolized not by the malevolent utopia of George Orwell but by the benevolent one of Aldous Huxley's *Brave New world*.

Supporters of communism have in mind a society based on conscious human control. To meet human needs, the spontaneity and uncertainty of market competitive relations in superseded by planning, while production of commodities for profit is replaced by the administrative allocation of goods and services. Marx's assumption that under socialism the labor process would not be determined by exchange but "in accordance with a definite social plan" has been widely accepted by critics of capitalism. Competition is to be replaced by cooperation in a classless society. Equality (social, economic, and political) is a watchword of a socialist society in which the pathologies of capitalism — greed, exploitation, and domination — would wither away. These assumptions concerning what socialism ought to be have been conflated into a stereotype of what the USSR became.

The reality of the Soviet Union, moreover, has always belied its claims to rationality, order, benevolence, planning, and equality. Nevertheless, "progressive" writers who have supported the Soviet Union have adopted the mantle of apologists. The Soviet Union, they claim, inherited an economic and political base that did not provide the necessary conditions for a planned and equal society. Tsarist Russia was one of the poorest countries in Europe and its political culture was not initially conducive to political participation. Perhaps more important, these writers assert that the presence of a hostile world environment in the form of predatory capitalist states has caused the malformations of the socialist states. Soviet socialism was born imperfect, and it would remain flawed as long as the contradictions of capitalism continue in the West.

This position, in turn, has legitimated practices that in themselves were foreign to the structure of socialism — a strong state with a large military and a secret police, institutional forms of inequality, and internal pathologies, such as crime, exploitation, and prejudice.

Despite such imperfections in the USSR, its supporters claim it had superior institutional arrangements: the supremacy of plan over market, the priority of collective over private interest, and the absence of conflicting social classes. The achievements of the socialist order, they contend, include constant economic growth, full employment, comprehensive welfare, and relative social equality.

THE IMAGE OF THE SOVIET UNION: MALEVOLENT

With the exception of certain periods during the Second World War, the weight of Western opinion has been opposed to this charitable view of Soviet society. Ideologically, Western opponents have deplored the destruction of individual human liberty. Freedom is held to be an integral value of democracy and the Western way of life because it promotes the development of the human will and spirit. Freedom, from this standpoint, is the absence of constraint, freedom allows the internal striving of the individual to flourish to fulfill human needs. Individuals, it is contended, have inalienable rights, which are manifested in the ownership of property and in the unconstrained formation of ideas, beliefs, associations and groups, and in the sanctity of the family. Only individuals have interests and their unfettered expression leads to human emancipation and progress. Such were the values of the French and American revolutions. The interaction of individual rights is furthered through the market in the economy and the parliamentary or representative state in politics. Both institutions create an environment in which individual freedom is promoted whilst the minimum constraints of freedom necessary to enhance collective welfare are secured.

This worldview gives rise to a perspective on socialist states that is quite apart from that held by "progressives." The essence of state socialism, opponents point out, is replacing self-motivation and individual interest by a collectivist state. Such a state is external to the individual and acts as a constraint on the person. Socialist society as such is inimical to freedom, human liberation, and progress in general because freedom is sacrificed for equality. The individual has no rights. Whereas the state in liberal democracies promotes minimal interference with the activity of the individual, the Soviet state espouses complete control: because planning is a collective effort that requires the subjugation of the market and individual enterprise, the state invades the privacy of civil society.

The institutions of state socialism, then, deprive the individual of rights: ownership of property is denied, a free market is replaced by government regulation, individual associations are limited to what the state thinks fit, and political parties and trade unions, which would express individual interests, are suppressed. People are isolated and become actors in a "mass society" — they are unable to express their spontaneity and humanity through spontaneous interaction with other people. Instead of the state expressing individuals' interests, associations perform the state's interest.

Totalitarianism is the concept that sums up Western democratic opposition to the sociopolitical order of state socialism. Contrasted to pluralistic Western societies, totalitarian societies allow no autonomous associations or institutions and those that are authorized are state managed. The essence of the totalitarian approach is the absence of any distinction between the state and civil society. The state reaches down into the very pores of society.

The description of totalitarianism is best known by the six-point definition concocted by the American writers C. J. Friedrich and Z. K. Brzezinski in 1956: an official ideology, a single mass party, a system of terroristic police, a monopoly of control of mass communication, a monopoly of all means of armed combat, and the control and direction of the economy. Collective control is assured because a single dominant political party has a monopoly on political power. The party's values are derived from an all-embracing ideology — Marxism-Leninism — that concentrates all activities on the achievement of a "utopian" society, communism. Only modern technology, it is claimed, gives the possibility for such ubiquitous forms of control.

Moreover, the activity of the totalitarian state is malevolent: it exploits the individual while the political elite pursues its own interest and dominates the masses. Such domination is secured not only by coercion — through the apparatus of the political police — but also by manipulation — through the ideology that is secured by a monopoly on the means of mass communication. The planning of the economy entails the bureaucratic coordination of all kinds of activities — education, wages, social insurance, and welfare — and thus not only does the state suppress the spontaneity of individuals and groups but it also does not meet consumer demands. State socialist societies are, according to this viewpoint, modern forms of tyranny that differ from those of the past by the extent of political control and, paradoxically perhaps, by virtue of the willingness of the masses actively to support the system.

It is my own view that neither of the above stereotyped positions captures the reality of the contemporary Soviet Union, though both say something important about the nature of the modern world. The totalitarian model never comes to grips with the fact that under Stalin and until relatively recently the Soviet Union was largely a rural society and thus the "technologically" conditioned means of control must be doubted. Traditional mores and ways of doing things are in practice very resistant to change. It must be conceded, however, that the Soviet state under Stalin and his successors did have and still has a wide range of activities under its control — much more so than in the pluralistic West. Under Gorbachev, however, this has been changing. The totalitarian model is static: it does not allow for significant change in society that would arise from the social structure, that is, from groups or interests. There has been a tendency to dismiss any developments (economic, political, social) as not "really" or "in essence" changing anything; and the process of change and political transformation which led to the coup of August 1991 has been overlooked.

Analysis of the Soviet Union must be made in an historical perspective and one must be aware of its changing ideology and structure, its leading personalities and ambitions, as well as the changing world systems in which it operates. By analogy, the United States and Britain have had transformed world roles in the twentieth century. Their internal social structures and political processes have evolved from Roosevelt to Reagan and from Lloyd George to Thatcher. So, too, one must recognize that the Soviet Union under Stalin, Khrushchev, Brezhnev, Gorbachev and Eltsin is distinctive. The USSR must be conceptualized as a changing and developing society. The grand sweep of political ideology whether it be totalitarian or communist does not grasp the reality of social transformation under state socialism.

FROM KHRUSHCHEV TO GORBACHEV: THE CHANGING NATURE OF SOVIET POLITICS

It must be emphasized from the outset that the Soviet Union under Gorbachev has undergone radical changes that make many of the characteristics of earlier periods obsolete. The policies ushered in by Gorbachev (like the short-lived ones of Dubcek in Czechoslovakia, twenty years earlier) have cast in doubt the validity of the antinomy between capitalism and communism and the associated competing organizing principles of

1953	Death of Stalin.
1956	Twentieth Congress of the Communist Party of the Soviet Union (CPSU): Khrushchev exposes Stalin's excesses.
1961	New Program of the CPSU adopted at the Twenty-second Party Congress.
1964	Brezhnev and Kosygin come to power.
1982	Andropov comes to power.
1984	Chernenko comes to power.
1985	Gorbachev comes to power.
1986	Twenty-seventh Congress of the CPSU. Program of the CPSU revised.
1988	Nineteenth Conference of the Communist Party of the Soviet Union.
1989	USSR Congress of People's Deputies elected.
1990	Party plenum relinquishes monopoly of power by CPSU.
1990	Non-communist governments elected in some republics.
1990	Presidential power declared.
1991	Referendum on Union Treaty.
1991	Attempted coup fails, Eltsin asserts authority.
1991	Union of Soviet Socialist Republics disintegrates, new Union of Sovereign States created.
1991	Baltic states recognized as independent.
1991	Communist Party of Soviet Union destatized and banned in some republics; Gorbachev resigns as General Secretary.

Figure 1.1 Some Important Dates in Recent Soviet History

planning and market, private and public, individual and collective. A look at the political, economic, and ideological developments between the leadership of Khrushchev and that of Gorbachev will provide a foundation for understanding the changing nature of the goals of Soviet communism. Two major watersheds in recent Soviet history may be distinguished: Khrushchev's Program of the CPSU (Communist Party of the Soviet Union) and its revised version brought out under Gorbachev. For important dates in recent Soviet history see Figure 1.1.

The Program of the CPSU adopted at the Twenty-second Party Congress on 18 October 1961, reflected the optimism and confidence of the political leadership under Khrushchev. The Program asserted that the world socialist system would triumph given the cumulative "crisis of world capitalism." It was proclaimed that within twenty years the Soviet economy would catch up with the standard of living of the United States. This goal would be ensured by the advantages of state ownership, central planning, and Communist Party leadership based on Leninist principles. The 1961 Program marked, in its own words, the beginning of a period of "full-scale communist construction."

Almost a quarter of a century later on 25 February 1986, Gorbachev presided over another version of the Party Program at the Twenty-seventh Party Congress. This time the tone was more cautious. In his introductory remarks, after praising previous Soviet achievements, he said, "the leadership considers its duty to tell the Party and the people honestly and frankly about the deficiencies in our political and practical activities and the unfavorable tendencies in the economy and the social and moral sphere." The claims of the revised Party Program of 1986 are more modest. There are no references to the attainment of communism. If a fundamentalist regards Khrushchev as wanting to dig a grave for capitalism, Gorbachev may be said to have been doing the same for the traditional Soviet concept of communism. Ideologically, the Party's Revised Program made no reference to the attainment of communism, to the expansion of collective forms of welfare outside the price system, nor did it refer to the withering away of the state.

The problems of socialist construction became the center of the Party's attention. As Gorbachev emphasized in January 1987 at a Plenum of the Communist Party, "No accomplishment, even the most impressive ones, must obscure either contradictions in the development of society or our mistakes or failings." Furthermore, Gorbachev's speech at the Twenty-seventh Party Congress was in many ways a more fundamental critique of the deficiencies of Soviet society than was Khrushchev's secret speech in which the cult of personality of Stalin was denounced. Khrushchev offered few structural criticisms of Soviet society whereas Gorbachev provided a critique of the state system and its methods of bureaucratic control, and he outlined inadequacies in the nature of the economic and political systems.

In a speech at the Twenty-seventh Party Congress, Gorbachev defined in Marxist phraseology four major contradictions within the system: a contradiction between the way work is organized and carried out, and what is needed to operate a modern economy; a contradiction between the form of ownership under socialism and the way that management and control are performed; a contradiction between the commodities that are produced and the money that is available to distribute them to consumers; and a contradiction between the centralization of the economy and the need to give economic units independence to organize things efficiently. As Gorbachev put it, there is a "lack of correspondence between productive forces and productive relations, between socialist property and the economic forces of its implementation, in the relations between goods and money and in the combination of centralization and independence of economic organizations" (February 1986).

Internal Economic Developments

Among the many objective reasons for this change of emphasis, Khrushchev's economic aims did not materialize. Over a long period, the expectations generated in the 1960s were not fulfilled. Considering the goals of the Party Program of 1961 against achievements reached in 1980, real conditions fell considerably short of anticipations. National income was 36 percent less than the long-term plan, gross agricultural production was 56 percent short, electric power was 57 percent down, and grain production fell 39 percent below the estimate. The quality and regularity of food delivered to the urban areas was inadequate. This does not mean that there were no improvements: compared to the 1960 levels, the actual level of national income had risen 320 percent, gross agricultural production had risen 65 percent, electric power 470 percent, and grain production 141 percent. Standards had improved, but they had not improved enough to meet the high expectations engendered by the political leadership of Khrushchev.

This process of underfulfillment of plans continued in the early 1980s. Economic indicators comparing objectives and achievements of the Eleventh Five Year Plan (1981–85) were underfulfilled, particularly in agriculture (plan 13 percent, actual 6 percent) industrial productivity (plan 23 percent, actual 17 percent). Nevertheless, by the mid-1980s conditions had improved and it cannot be doubted that standards had been rising. In industry as a whole the work week has shortened from 47.8 hours in 1955 to 40.5 in 1985, and the average number of holidays rose from 18.5 in 1958 to 22 in 1983. The index of consumption (a measure of the standard of living) had risen from 100 in 1970 to 176 in 1981 (and remained the same in 1982); it rose to 189 in 1984 and 196 in 1985. Even according to estimates made by the Central Intelligence Agency of the United States, the USSR had an annual rise in gross national product of from 2 percent to 2.5 percent in the early 1980s. A later revised CIA figure put the latter figure at 1.9 percent. Of Western European states, according to the organization for Economic Cooperation and Development (OECD), this record was matched only by Ireland in the 1980–85 period; the Federal Republic of Germany had an average rate increase of 1.3 percent and Britain 1.2 percent.

While Brezhnev was consoled by the steady though slow rate of progress, Gorbachev and many others were not. Moreover, the Soviet Union has experienced a long-term decline in its rate of economic growth. Official figures show a reduction in growth rates; the average increase in produced national income was 8.9 percent for 1966–70; 6.3 percent for 1971–75; 4.7 percent for 1976–80; and 4.0 percent for 1981–83. Economic growth in the 1980s was further negatively influenced by the decline in the growth of the working population, its shift to the non-Slavic East, and by an increase of the economically dependent population, for example, those in old age. The defense burden was immense. It is confidently estimated in the West that Soviet defense spending was some 15 percent of its gross national product compared to only 7 percent of that of the United States. (In 1989 Gorbachev conceded that defense accounted for 15.6 percent of the total budget.)

World Politics and Economics

The Soviet Union's problems, furthermore, had not been confined to internal economic ones. On the international front the Soviet Union's military position became much stronger vis-à-vis the United States during the period after Khrushchev, but under Brezhnev the policy of peaceful coexistence and detente was in crisis. The Soviet Union since the end of the Second World War had steadily lost its hegemony over the world communist movement. It had conceded ideological leadership: some of the sacred assumptions of Marxism-Leninism, central planning, and collectivism, were shrouded in doubt. Those assumptions have been cast aside by movements ranging from Eurocommunism to economic reform programs in China and Hungary. And the Soviet mold of socialism had

been openly challenged by diverse forces such as the Czechoslovak Reform
Movement and the Solidarity movement in Poland.

The current international economic and political system is of a qualitatively different type than the system in which the Soviet command
economy developed under Stalin. The Soviet model of growth has appealed
to relatively underdeveloped countries. The centralization of political
and economic control facilitated the allocation of resources necessary to
create an industrial society. The technological hardware of the advanced
countries was relatively easily transferred and adopted by the underdeveloped ones. Full employment and a relatively equal society in terms of
consumption was a major appeal to observers in the West and the growth
rates of the economy compared well during times of depression.

Since the end of the Second World War, the world economy has
changed fundamentally. The advent of high technology, the rise of the
service industries in the West, the dependency on scientific advance for
the achievement of state defense and economic growth has put a greater
store on internal innovation and dynamism. The world economy has seen
the rise of new economies in Southeast Asia as well as technological
progress in the advanced Western societies. The Soviet model has failed
in this international competition. The technological gap, particularly in
the evolving weaponry of the United States, has been a cause for concern
in the USSR. Rising Japanese economic power has brought it into contention with the USSR as the world's second largest producer of economic
wealth.

Advanced technology itself has brought the image of the advanced
capitalist countries into the USSR. Communication is international in
scope and contact with the West has "contaminated" the Soviet public.
The population has developed a consumer mentality and the intelligentsia
a yearning for liberalism, democracy and civil society.

This, then, was the political and economic legacy inherited by Gorbachev.
It was one of frustration on the part of the political leadership and the
Soviet people as a whole. While the USSR remained a major world
power claiming a quantitative gross national product second only to that
of the United States, the country had experienced a cumulative decline:
political, economic, and ideological.

CONTRADICTIONS UNDER SOCIALISM

Gorbachev's answer to the malaise facing the Soviet Union has been
policy of *uskorenie*, meaning acceleration or rapid growth. It has been a
general strategy involving "a new quality of growth: the all-round intensi-

fication of production on the basis of scientific and technical progress, a structural reshaping of the economy and efficient forms of managing and stimulating labor."

The means to achieve such acceleration mark a radical break from previous thinking and practice. "Perestroika" is the term used to describe the process of change. It may be translated as restructuring, or radical reform, or even revolutionary transition. Perestroika is significant because it is a comprehensive and theoretically based policy of change. Reforms, it may be argued, were undertaken under Khrushchev, Kosygin, and Brezhnev, but they tended to be piecemeal rather than systemic; these leaders assumed that the underlying political and economic structures devised under Stalin were essentially sound and needed improvement to correct distortions in their administration rather than radical reform. The process of perestroika must be considered a different phenomenon. The reforms have been comprehensive in scope, politically radical, executed with positive skill, and have enjoyed, at least as principles, widespread support. Underlying the process of perestroika is a major theoretical reappraisal and critique of social relations in the USSR that has provided the basis for the working out of a comprehensive reform program.

Soviet thinking has undergone a revision in its focus on the various forms of incompatibilities, tensions, and conflicts generated in society. In Soviet phraseology, there has been a redefinition of the nature of "contradictions" under socialism. "Contradictions" is a concept that describes any incompatibility, tension, or conflict between people, groups, or institutions. In Marxist theory, antagonistic contradictions involve irreconcilable conflicts of interests; under capitalism, for instance, that between the proletariat and the bourgeoisie. Such contradictions are resolved, not by compromise or accommodation of mutually opposed positions, but by a change of state. The antagonistic interests under capitalism are abolished through a movement, by a revolution, that ushers in socialism. In contrast to capitalism, however, contradictions under socialism may be resolved peacefully, with mutual goodwill, through common understanding and good leadership. To distinguish these contradictions from those under capitalism, they are termed "nonantagonistic."

Under Stalin and during the period from Khrushchev to Chernenko, the leadership held that under Soviet socialism the "fundamental interests" of state and society coincided. The social order was one of social harmony and conformity. The conflicts that arose were incompatibilities rooted in the nonantagonistic contradictions between the "survivals of capitalism" and the emergent social formation of socialism. Incompatibilities had their source in backwardness — the idiocy of traditional peasant life, the superstition of religion — or were the direct negative influence of the capitalist West (through malevolent propaganda and sabotage). Leaders held that with the maturation of the Soviet economy and with the growing strength of socialist states in the world political order, such antagonisms would sharply decrease, though the Soviet state would have to continue until capitalism had been finally buried.

The need for state power is a contradiction under socialism, for Marxists conceive of the state as an expression of a ruling class. Under socialism the need for a state is justified by the necessity of maintaining vigilance against an external class enemy in the shape of the hostile capitalist states. As Khrushchev envisaged it, in the future the internal role of the state would "wither away."

Internal policy operated through compromise designed to promote and solidify internal social harmony. Under Brezhnev, a "social contract" between leaders, government, and people developed. The political leadership provided a framework of stability and peace. The government apparatus was secure under the traditional forms of central planning. The working class enjoyed full employment, an undemanding work environment, and a steady but slow amelioration of pay and conditions. There was a liberalization of conditions for the intelligentsia: within restricted circles discussion was not curbed. (Many of the policies adopted by Gorbachev were worked out by reform-minded intellectuals under Brezhnev.) When reforms were suggested, they were experimented with but when problems or resistance arose, reforms were quietly dropped. These are the roots of what is now called the "period of stagnation."

The cumulative economic, political, and international decline of the Soviet Union under Brezhnev led to a reassessment of the assumptions on which policy was based. This thinking is epitomized in the "Novosibirsk document" attributed to a leading Soviet sociologist, T. Zaslavskaya, and circulated in the USSR in 1983. Contradictions under socialism were indeed nonantagonistic — they did not have the explosive character of class conflict under capitalism, but they were less benign than the incumbent leadership assumed for two reasons. First, they originated not just in the "left-overs" of capitalism but in the structure of Soviet socialist society itself, which generated group and class interests. Second, such interests gave rise to contradictions, conflicts, and antagonisms between groups.

Zaslavskaya contended that the antagonisms between groups are at the heart of the malaise of Soviet society and they account for the deceleration of growth and the lack of dynamism. Furthermore, the political leadership under Brezhnev was a source of contradiction in that it perpetuated bureaucratic forms that acted as a brake on the development of productive forces. Production relations (the system of economic management and political control) were in conflict with the potentialities of the productive forces. This conflict, in turn, led to "stagnation" — the retardation of economic development, corruption, a decline of socialist morality, public apathy, and alienation.

The recognition that contradictions are built into socialism gave rise to the conception of a society with policy preferences linked to individuals and the positions they occupy and the privileges they enjoy. "Interests" then are at the center of contemporary Soviet political analysis. At the February 1988 Plenum of the Central Committee, Soviet society was defined in terms of a "plurality" of opposing "interests and views." According to this reassessment, various vested interests and groups at the heart of the political system have prevented development; they are a brake or a fetter on the development of productive forces. They were legitimated by the cult of personality under Brezhnev and administered by the apparatus of government and Party. To break out of the vicious circle of complacency, decline, and stagnation, the mechanisms that perpetuate them have to be replaced and those individuals and vested interests who benefit must be removed. The conflict between "reformers" and "traditionalists" which cumulated in 1991 was part of the dynamic of perestroika which had been legitimated by Gorbachev.

PERESTROIKA: GORBACHEV'S REFORM STRATEGY

Perestroika (restructuring or radical reform) has been a set of tactics aimed at resolving contradictions. Rather than a set of policies, perestroika is an attitude or approach to politics and society. Its major components, illustrated in Figure 1.2, are explained below to give the reader an overview, and in later chapters we shall take up its component parts in more detail.

Perestroika involves four mobilizing strategies:

- Individual (and group) self-interest (including *khozraschet*)
- Public criticism (*glasnost'*)
- Democracy (*demokratiya, demokratizatsiya, plyuralizm*)
- Law and control

Self-interest is a mobilizing principle. The underlying assumption of perestroika is that if self-interest is allowed to take its course, higher ~~goal~~ levels of economic and political efficiency are achieved. While self-interest and economic accounting had been espoused even under Stalin, their role now is much more important than in the past. *Khozraschet* involves

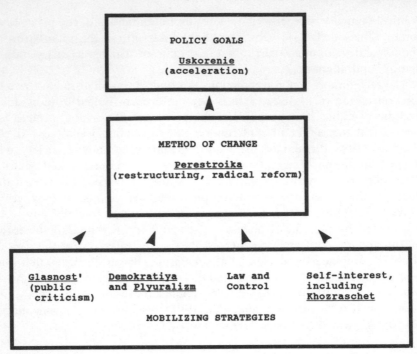

Figure 1.2 Gorbachev's Reform Strategy

economic accountability and independence (literally, it means autonomous profit and loss accounting). It may apply to individuals (they should be given initiative and rewarded for what they do), institutions (enterprises should be given greater independence over production and rewarded or penalized for their efforts), even regions of the country are encouraged to manage their own affairs. The important shift in the organizing principles of Soviet society involves changing from an administered model — in which the public interest is determined centrally by the authorities — to a system wherein individuals and groups are allowed to express their own interests. It entails markets to contain these interests.

Glasnost' means public criticism and access to information. It legitimates the articulation of individual group interests and the answerability of decision-makers to criticism; and thus involves greater individual and group autonomy. The mass media, rather than being merely a conduit for the transmission of government policy, has the responsibility to articulate a spontaneously expressed range of views. Thus glasnost' entails a pluralism (*plyuralizm*) of points of view rather than the previously centralized and controlled media.

Demokratiya (democracy) and *demokratizatsiya* (democratization) involve a transformation in participation in decision making. The process of transition to "democracy" is "democratization." The objective is to place more authority with the rank-and-file citizen or member of a collectivity or group. A thorough restructuring of the apparatus of the state will devolve power to the government apparatus (the Soviets) and place a limitation on the centralized role of the Party. *Demokratiya* seeks to involve the masses in a more positive way in public affairs and in so doing to restrict the power of the political leadership. A *plyuralizm* of interests is to be encouraged. Hence democratization is an important mechanism to combat traditional interests that maintain the status quo and was thought to be a necessary condition to ensure the acceleration of economic development, *uskorenie.*

The principles of discipline and control originated with Andropov (the short-lived leader of the USSR who preceded Gorbachev). Their objective was to strengthen commitment and obedience to socialist laws, while opposing corruption and administrative privilege. In the early days of perestroika Andropov's principles led to administrative measures against malingerers and an alcoholism campaign. With the advent of perestroika the notion of law and control means that the Soviet Union is moving toward a legally constituted state. Prescribed laws intended to guarantee civil rights to the population are to define the legal operation of the state. As Gorbachev put it at the Nineteenth Party Conference in June 1988, "the process of the consistent democratization of Soviet society should complete the creation of a socialist state governed by the rule of law." A major shift in the relationship between the individual and society should provide citizens with rights, although they will also be constrained by law. Before 1991, laws were shaped by the Party and the state enforced laws which defined the context in which individuals and groups enjoyed rights (see Figure 1.2).

At first sight, there appears to have been an odd combination of traditional concepts (law and control) and a more open market orientated approach with concern for democracy, pluralism, and public criticism. There are two explanations for this paradox. First, the significance of stressing law and order and the drive against corruption was an attempt to strengthen the integrity of Soviet society. The aim was to provide a framework of morality, discipline, and rules enforced by law, which was an attempt to move to a legal-rational type of society. If market relations and private trade are to develop, it is necessary to have effective legal control.

Second, democracy was in essence a form of control from below. The objective of the reform leadership is to appeal over the heads of the bureaucracy and middle management to the rank and file: using lower levels in the power structure as levers of change is the strategy for overcoming inertia and maladministration. The arrows in Figure 1.2 illustrate that policy goals are achieved from below, rather than from the top down. A policy involving a shift of power away from the centrally controlled bureaucracy to lower levels gives people a greater chance to participate. It legitimates the articulation of group and individual interests. The introduction of competitive elections put pressure on incumbents of political position to become more responsive to the demands of the people they represent.

The boundaries of democracy, glasnost', and financial autonomy, as we shall discuss later, have not yet been fully worked out. In my view, the leadership adopted this strategy as a device to precipitate change, to involve the public in new policies, and to weaken forces opposed to the new incumbent political elite under Gorbachev. This has led to greater participation, a more open exchange of information and "plyuralizm" (that is, a limited form of group autonomy). In the early days of perestroika, the leadership sought to contain criticism within the parameters of Party control, but forces unleashed by the reform movement became uncontrollable and exerted interests inimical to Gorbachev's command.

Perestroika has undergone changes through time. First, it involved a psychological campaign to alert the public to the need for change, to raise levels of consciousness, to overcome inertia and moral turpitude. Various antialcoholism, anticorruption, antimalingering campaigns were started, and claims were made to institute socialist "justice."

Second, a vigorous personnel (or cadres) policy was instituted that sought to install "from the top and from below" people in authority who supported the new policy.

Third, a new style in leadership was initiated. This has been more direct, honest, and open, and has involved public participation and debate. It has led to direct open communication with the West, and in practice to a more American presidential style for Mr. Gorbachev (and the cultivation of a First Lady role for Mrs. Gorbachev).

Fourth, a comprehensive set of interrelated reforms has been introduced. These have ranged over the industrial enterprise, health, electoral and mass media practice, the rule of law, individual and group rights, education, the organization of the economy, and government and foreign affairs.

Fifth, the fundamental objective of the attainment of communism has been repudiated; any remaining concern with a struggle against capitalism has been dropped. As Gorbachev put it in February 1987: "Our desire to make our own country better will hurt no one, with the world only gaining from this." Social development takes priority over class interests.

Sixth, perestroika involves a view of the interdependence of the capitalist and socialist systems. They cannot develop separately or even in parallel. The two systems interact within one framework. For progress on both sides, cooperation and mutual trust is essential. This has involved a major change in foreign policy. There has been a genuine movement toward disarmament and a reduction in international tension. The Soviet government has also allowed the states of Eastern Europe to adopt anti-communist governments; a process spectacularly repeated in August 1991 in the USSR itself.

Seventh, the general principle that underpins these changes has been to allow the articulation of interests by individuals and groups and resolving them through political exchange. A pluralistic and interest-driven social and political system has been added to the existing centralized forms of political control. This has created its own form of tension. This principle involves relying on markets in politics (more competition through elections) and in economics (prices are intended to reflect supply and demand).

Finally, the reform policy led to a major attack on the interests of the incumbents of state and Party positions which provoked resistance. To fuel the process of reform, the leadership allowed popular movements to multiply. They grew in strength and authority. The desired questioning of people in authority became an undesired confrontation with authority and Soviet and communist institutions and ways of doing things. An intended plurality of views became an unintended plurality of organizations and parties. The hegemony of the Party and the injunction of "discipline and control" was lost.

INSTABILITY AND POLITICAL CONTROL

To what extent will the changes which have been introduced under Gorbachev lead to a fundamental readjustment in the nature of Soviet society? Is the initially grudging acceptance and later admiration of Gorbachev in the West an indication of a profound convergence with capitalism? Are the proposals operational within the context of Soviet society? The following chapters will consider these questions in more detail.

All societies hold some tenets as sacred: in the West the underlying values of individualism, the market (in economics and politics), rights, and private property underpin the political system. What are the sacred components of Soviet society? In a February 1988 speech to the Central Committee Plenum, Gorbachev emphasized that the USSR is "not departing by one

step from socialism, from Marxism-Leninism." For Gorbachev, the essence
of socialism lies

> in establishing the power of the working people and giving priority to the good
> of the individual, the working class and all the people. Ultimately socialism's
> task is to put an end to the social alienation of the individual which is
> characteristic of the exploitative society, alienation from power, from the
> means of production, from the results of labor and from spiritual assets.

In an economic sense, the foundations of socialism lie not only in state
ownership, but also in other forms of cooperative and individual economic
activity. Under perestroika central planning has had to take place in the
context of economic incentives for growth and has had to overcome
individual alienation. The centrally directed and authoritarian political
system, argue the reformers, is no longer appropriate for the kind of
social structure that has developed in the USSR in the past twenty years.
By making the political system more open and responsive, Gorbachev
hoped that alienation (in the sense of disenchantment with conditions and
processes) would be overcome. Enhanced forms of participation, moreover, were also the means by which *uskorenie* could be achieved: the
forthcoming higher quality of political input would lead not only to a
more legitimate political system but also to more efficient decision making.

As the Soviet Union entered the 1990s, this optimistic scenario faded
and was replaced by anarchy. Economic performance did not improve;
the idea of *acceleration* was forgotten. In 1990, gross national product
decreased by 2 percent. In the first five months of 1990, 100,000 persons
per day on average were absent from work as a result of national strife.
Starvation appeared a possibility in the winter of 1990/91: Western food
aid was delivered from Germany, the European Economic Community
and the United States. The promised marketization led to profiteering.
Open inflation was spurred by the government meeting price hikes with
higher wages. Perestroika did not achieve acceleration but economic
deceleration, social despair and political instability.

The economic policy of reform contained a duality between market and
plan. Gorbachev wanted to maintain both. Initially, there were significant
limits on the development of private property and on the market as a
determinant of economic activity. The direction of investment, it was
intended, would be largely determined by the central planners, rather
than through decisions of a stock exchange or industrial combines and
banks. (There were no plans for the institution of a stock exchange.)
However, the more radical reformers faced with growing economic decline
cast doubts upon the need for such central controls over major economic
decisions. Private property was also considered by more radical reformers

to be necessary for the development of market relations as well as being a major support to the growth of civil society.

Democratization went much further than the reform leadership of Gorbachev had intended. As Party Secretary and Politburo member V.A.Medvedev had put it: "Socialism must create a political system which takes account of ... the multitude of interests and aspirations of all social groups and communities of people. What is meant, of course, are healthy, economically and morally substantiated interests which do not run counter to our system." At the Nineteenth Congress of the Communist Party of the Soviet Union (1988) it was made clear that no competing political parties would be allowed. While other groups or interests may legitimately be formed, the Communist Party should maintain its monopoly of *political* organization. This proved unrealistic. Gorbachev's powers were more constitutional than real.

Here then we may pinpoint a contradiction in the strategy of perestroika between Party hegemony and the freedom to form associations in civil society. This was resolved in the direction of the strengthening of the latter. The pent-up forces of opposition grouped around People's Fronts led to resistance and confrontation to the Communist Party. These interests were manifestly against the system identified with Gorbachev.

At the Nineteenth Party Conference, Gorbachev noted the ways that the political system had become subjected to "serious deformations" and had led to "repressions and lawlessness" under Stalin. Stalin was considered an opponent of socialism. But was not Soviet society created by Stalin and, if so, then was not Soviet *socialism* discredited? With the desacralization of the Soviet past, the symbolism of the Revolution was destroyed: its values and traditions were discredited. In the search for a new identity, for new forms of cohesion and solidarity, the peoples of the Soviet Union turned to traditional values and beliefs — of nationalism and religion. A new framework for the relationship between the government of the USSR and the republics (such as the RSFSR and Georgia) had to be worked out.

The upshot of reform by the beginning of the 1990s was that perestroika had gone much further than the political leaders around Gorbachev had intended and its critics in the West had supposed was possible. The Party had relinquished its constitutional monopoly of political power and the Constitution recognized the rights of other parties to compete for political power. Traditional Marxism-Leninism, with its goal of a proletarian world order and a classless political order, with a Communist Party ruled through democratic-centralism, was replaced by a socialist perspective. The Party retained a vanguard role but in an attenuated form and its policy was more in keeping with Western social-democratic parties aspiring to a welfare state in a mixed economy. The dislocation and fragmentation of the Soviet Union led to major changes in the form of government. Presidential power was declared. Gorbachev was effectively the chief of the executive, legislative arms of government, and retained the chief post in the Communist Party of the Soviet Union.

The underlying legitimacy of the system had been destroyed. The Party had been weakened, if not smashed. The performance of the economy declined disastrously in 1991: Western estimates put inflation at 140 percent and unemployment at 10 percent, and gross national product declined by 15 percent. The legitimacy of the Soviet government was challenged by the republics. Boris Eltsin evolved as a potent leader of an anti-communist Russian Republic; the Baltic states appealed for international recognition as independent states.

The traditional forces in Soviet society tried to halt the twin processes of democratization and political collapse. On 19 August 1991, a state of emergency was declared. Gorbachev was placed under house arrest. For three days in August the fate of the USSR was in the balance. But the coup collapsed. Rallying the forces of reform, Eltsin held out in the government buildings of the Russian Republic. The military and security forces were unable to assert their power and the leaders of the coup gave up.

Remarkable constitutional changes followed. Eltsin emerged as a moral victor. Gorbachev was reinstated as President and dismissed his own government ministers. The Communist Party was declared illegal in Russia and other republics and was dissolved; Gorbachev resigned as General Secretary. The Baltic states were recognized as independent by Gorbachev. Many of the powers of the USSR government were transferred to the republics, all of whom by September 1991 had declared independence. As statues of Lenin and other communist dignitaries were destroyed, communist power was toppled. The contradictions of perestroika were resolved; the traditional system of Party control, central planning and Soviet socialism were abandoned. Finally, the USSR as a centralized state collapsed and was replaced by a Union of Sovereign States in which the locus of political power shifted to the republics.

Part One

THE POLITICAL AND ECONOMIC FRAMEWORK

Chapter 2

KHOZRASCHET

Managing the Economy

We noted in the first chapter that relative economic decline was one of the main factors that impelled the reform program initiated by the Soviet leadership under Gorbachev. Change of the economic mechanism is intrinsically bound up with the political system — with the way that the Soviet Union is governed — and cannot be separated from the structures that constitute the Soviet state. This is the case because in the economic system developed under and since Stalin property is owned by the state; planning encompasses the totality of economic activities — there has been relatively little "private enterprise" (an important exception has been agriculture); and the political apparatus actively intervenes in the operation of the economy to secure political objectives.

The significance of these points will become clearer if we consider by way of comparison the organization of a Western capitalist economy. The reader will bear in mind that this is a somewhat simplified account, but it will serve to highlight some of the main differences between a capitalist economy and the traditional "command" or "administered" economy. Following this discussion we shall turn to a consideration of the economic reforms taking place under Gorbachev and the difficulties posed by the transition to a market economy.

THE CAPITALIST ECONOMY: AN OVERVIEW

A distinctive feature of contemporary Western capitalist society is that the government exercises a controlling influence over the economy. Government plays an important role in shaping the levels of investment;

government expenditure (particularly defense spending) and taxation influence the value of money; welfare, education, and security programs as well as "nationalized industries" provide citizens with goods and services; control of the exchange rate of currency and legal enactments directly influence the level of competition with foreigners. Legislation actively shapes the market conditions under which production and trade take place — various minimum wage, antitrust and antimonopoly legislation are important examples.

But the government's activities are limited: private enterprise and initiative governs by far the bulk of economic activity, even in the welfare states of Western Europe. Not only the large corporations, such as Ford Motor Company or Imperial Chemical Industries, but all retail trade from Macy's to the local restaurant or pub is privately owned and managed. This demarcation between state and economy has important implications for politics. The state has a limited responsibility; it is not held responsible for the collapse of businesses and the ensuing ruin of entrepreneurs and the unemployment of redundant labor, though to be sure the modern capitalist state attempts to alleviate the poverty and distress that may ensue from the operation of the market. The state may also directly intervene to subsidize or even buy up businesses whose collapse may threaten national integrity.

Under capitalism the objective of business is to make a profit. If companies fail to do so, they become bankrupt, the shareholders lose their money, and the employees lose their jobs. To make profits, sales of commodities and services must be secured. The price must be right and the goods or service must be purchased. Hence, meeting consumer demand is crucial. This process is linked to the motivating principle of making money: workers need money to live, employers measure profit by the surplus between revenue from sales and costs (materials, rent, interest, wages). The economic mechanism of capitalism is summarized in Figure 2.1.

The social process of production illustrated in Figure 2.1 may be summarized as follows:

- The worker sells labor for wages. The objective is to obtain money to buy goods and services.
- The capitalist/entrepreneur invests money in a product with the objective of making a profit.
- Both the employees' needs for commodities and the capitalists' objective of profit are met through the market.
- Commodities are sold at a price determined by what buyers are prepared to pay and sellers are willing to produce.

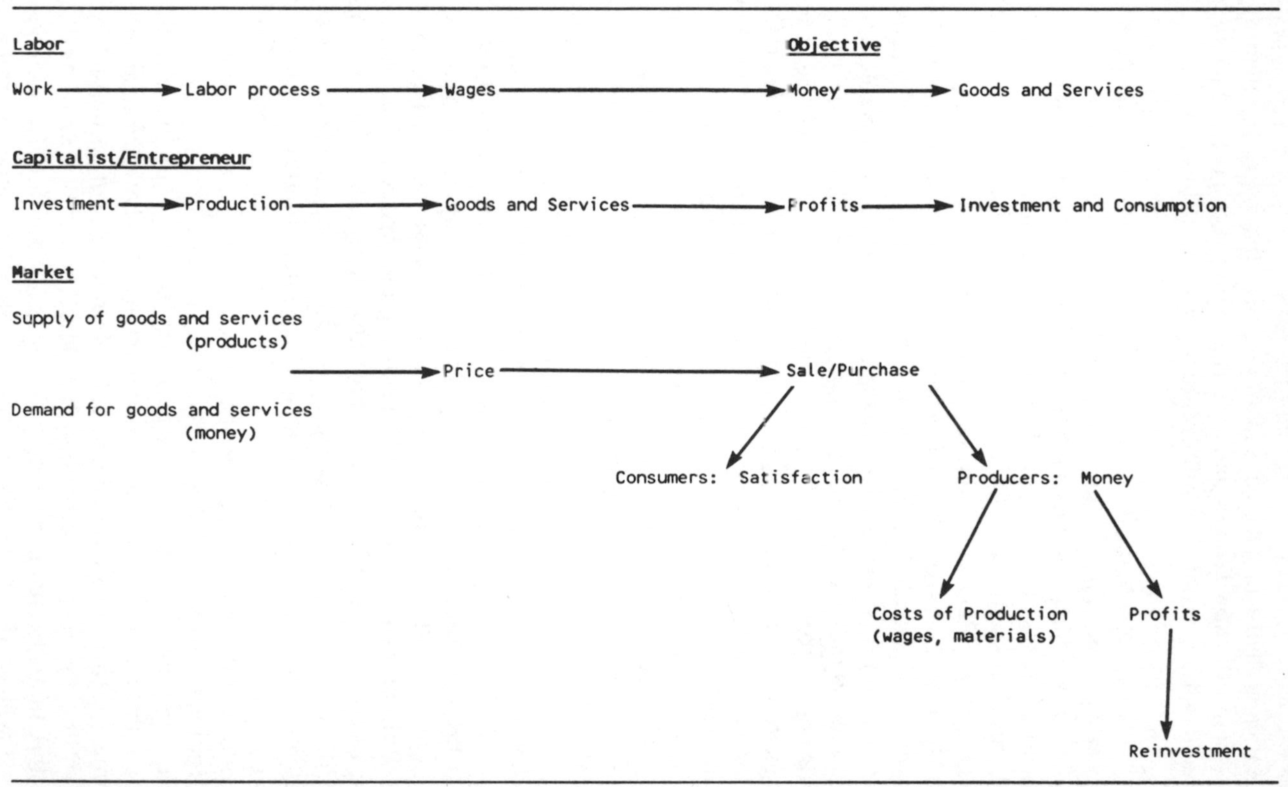

Labor
Objective
Work
Labor process
Wages
Money
Goods and Services
Capitalist/Entrepreneur
Investment
Production
Goods and Services
Profits
Investment and Consumption
Market
Supply of goods and services (products)
Demand for goods and services (money)
Price
Sale/Purchase
Consumers: Satisfaction
Producers: Money
Costs of Production (wages, materials)
Profits
Reinvestment

Figure 2.1 The Economic Mechanism of Capitalism

- Consumers try to allocate their money to maximize their level of satisfaction.
- Unless capitalists can achieve a money return that is greater than the costs of production (wages and materials and other costs) then they will not make a profit and will eventually go out of business.

Through the dynamic of capitalism, capitalists make products that people will buy and produce them at the lowest possible cost in order to maximize profit. The government provides a framework to achieve such objectives. The cheapest means of making products involves keeping wages as low as possible and inventing methods of production (including management) that will lead to efficient production. If profits are not made, further accumulation in terms of capital investment will not take place, unless lenders can be persuaded that profits are likely in the future. In practice various distortions of the market take place that lead to imperfections: some producers may have a monopoly position and earn monopoly profits that prevent newcomers from entering the market, in which case the government has to step in to ensure competition. Also, advertising influences the goods that people may buy. Consumers and employees are not equal in their market relations with producers and employers.

The motivating principle of capitalism is making money on the part of the capitalist and entrepreneur. To do so, their business must be cost-effective and meet a consumer demand. The entrepreneur's product must compete with other goods. Similarly, employees must secure employment that provides them the income they need to live.

In Western capitalism, the economic system is legitimated by the production of the commodities that people want (or can afford to buy) through the operation of the price system. The constant interaction of supply and demand gives rise to new businesses and the satisfaction of wants. Entrepreneurs react to the needs of the market. The market system, of course, also has its social shortfalls: the needs of the rich are met at the cost of the poor, the unemployed, the old, and the feckless. The distribution of wealth and income under capitalism does not promote the equal satisfaction of needs of all members of society. Moreover, the separation of state and economic activity makes this system of distribution quite legitimate, so far as the government is concerned.

While state and charitable welfare is available for the needy, life without money is inconceivable under capitalism. What, then, are the comparable forms of motivation and control under Soviet socialism? We consider first the form of economy that developed under Stalin in the 1930s and that characterized the evolution of state socialist societies. Then we will go on to discuss the reforms that have been introduced under Gorbachev.

THE SOVIET PLANNED ECONOMY BEFORE PERESTROIKA: AN OVERVIEW

A major difference between capitalist and state socialist societies is that under socialism, with some notable exceptions, all economic activity — production, distribution, and exchange — is under state ownership and control. The government makes detailed decisions about investment, consumption, prices, and incomes.

The socialist equivalent of the capitalist corporation is the government ministry and its productive subdivisions. Until the advent of perestroika, local shops and restaurants were subordinate to a government (or local government) agency. These organizations do not compete to make a profit; there is no risk of them going out of business; the wages of the employees (as the security of their jobs) are guaranteed by the state. An analogy with the armed forces in the West is apposite: all members of the army are state employees funded by the government, and the services of the armed forces are not subject to market competition.

Unlike capitalism, then, there is no division between state and economy. The state assumes the responsibility for economic welfare in its broadest terms. The activity of production enterprises as much as the level of employment and rate of growth is the responsibility of the government. An important political consequence follows from this. When times are good, the government claims responsibility for the people's economic growth and prosperity and the leaders bask in reflected glory. In times of adversity, however, the Party/government leadership is held responsible — poor harvests, natural disasters, and an unfavorable change in the terms of trade are all blamed on the political leadership.

Marxist Ideology

The system of state ownership and control is founded on Marxism, which claims that political power and exploitation are rooted in private ownership of the means of production. With the October Revolution of 1917 the expropriation of private ownership became the path to real democracy and the empowerment of the working class.

Traditionally, Marxists have shared a deep suspicion if not an outright opposition to the market. They believe that the market is not only uneven or unequal in the relationship between buyers and sellers of commodities, but also that the exchange involves "exploitation." For Marxists the market may be defined as the mechanism through which labor power is exploited because the worker's labor creates a profit for the entrepreneur and shareholder. In so doing, capitalist exploitation gives rise to anarchy in production. It leads to slumps and to unemployment, which in turn gives rise to poverty. These ideas have been propagated in the Soviet Union since the time of the October Revolution, and among many strata of the population there is a strong antipathy to the introduction of market relations.

The traditional Marxist standpoint also criticizes the process of mass consumption itself: under capitalism there is a "fetishism" of commodity production. Goods are not produced to meet human needs, but to make a profit: the operation of the mass media and the domination of advertising lead to the production of goods that do not provide psychic satisfaction to the individual. While even the rich may amass an abundance of consumption goods, these goods do not give satisfaction on a human scale. The individual is alienated from the artifacts of capitalism and the endemic competition that pits person against person, company against company, country against country and leads to spiritual, moral, and political poverty — set in a world of plenty. In place of the consumer economy Marxists have advocated a planned economy which they believe will serve the interests of the people.

While Marxists agree that "public ownership" must replace private ownership, there has always been debate about how public ownership should be controlled and how the economy should be ordered and organized — how in practice the general interests can be furthered by a system of planning. Recognizing the evils of capitalism is one matter, but agreeing on how to improve on its system of production and exchange is another. The Soviet system has adopted a form of state ownership and control. The bare bones of this structure, which originated under Stalin in the 1930s, is illustrated in Figure 2.2.

As there is no free market, a government planning agency with the status of a state committee, *Gosplan* (literally, state plan) attempts to organize the economy. It has been assisted by other state committees (such as those on prices, procurement of materials, science, and technology). "Branch ministries" were formed to organize the production of a given industry. There were branch ministries, for example, in coal, electronics, fish, food, gas, machine tools, petroleum, power and electrification — a list that includes all manufacture, commerce, and exchange. Agriculture is also subject to such a planned output system, save that collective farmers have always been able to sell on the collective farm market produce mainly from their private plots; prices here were (and still are) determined by what people will pay and are two to three times those in the shops selling price-controlled agricultural produce.

The central planners attempted to arrange administratively the "inputs" to enterprises (the amount of steel to be delivered to an auto plant, its total wages bill, the wage scales on which the employees are to be paid)

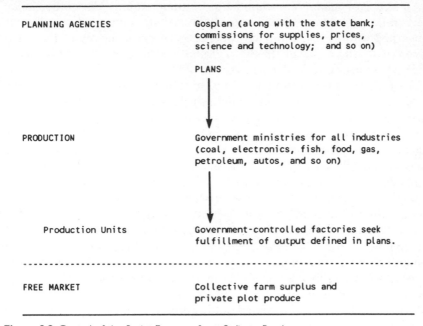

Figure 2.2 Control of the Soviet Economy from Stalin to Brezhnev

and also to fix the outputs (the number and type of cars produced, their prices, and to whom they should be delivered).

Money as a medium of exchange was (and still is) retained; goods are not formally rationed or directly distributed to consumers. Instead, consumers purchase goods that are available in the shops. There is a quasi-market because prices do not respond to demand and production does not respond to shortage. Output and prices are determined administratively. The prices of consumer goods are fixed in relation to their cost of production plus a margin. The State Price Committee (*Goskomtsen*) has set prices: the numbers involved are gigantic — there are some 200 million prices and a further 200,000 new prices have to be set annually. These prices do not reflect what they could fetch in the market. Many goods remain unsold, while for others there is a great shortage. If there is a shortage, people have to wait in line and when things sell out some people just have to go without. Commodities are rationed on a first-come/first-served basis, rather than by price. Soviet street scenes are characterized by lines of people waiting to buy "deficit" products.

All this is a mammoth administrative undertaking. Under Brezhnev there were around a hundred ministries, departments, and committees concerned with the planning and operation of the economy at the "All-Union" (or federal) level. In the national republics of the USSR, there were 800 ministries and departments in 1986.

The process of production and consumption as it has developed essentially from the early 1930s under Stalin's rule is summarized in Figure 2.3. As in the capitalist system, labor is employed and paid a wage. The objective of work, however, is not solely to earn money. Money has less salience than in the United States and other capitalist countries because many commodities are provided in kind and many goods and services are available at very low prices that do not reflect their market price. For example, a metro ride in Moscow between any two stops on the underground costs only about 5 cents (about 7 British pence); the monthly charge for house central heating is only a few dollars and is paid as part of the rent — a sum that has not changed since the 1920s. There is a comprehensive system of social security and many services are outside the price system and allocated on the basis of need or position. (This will be discussed further in chapters 5 and 10.)

Production has not been carried out for profit. Resources were allocated by *Gosplan* to ministries to fulfill plans, which in turn are carried out by factories or "enterprises." Each production unit has a plan — to produce so many cars, or in universities, so many students, or in conservatories, so many musicians — there was even a plan for the different kinds of circus performers required.

Goods and services have to be produced, but selling them has not been a criterion of success. In practice, the planning system gives people what it wants to produce, but the needs of people are incompletely fulfilled. Consumers have to take what comes out of the system even if the material and human products do not meet their needs. This has led to the criticism that the planners have exercised a "dictatorship over needs."

Ministries pay production units for goods that are produced — rather than for goods that are sold. Many services are provided outside the price system for direct consumption. Housing is allocated to employees of enterprises, medical and educational services are available, in theory, on the basis of need. Even places in holiday resorts are distributed according to an administrative procedure: trade unions have so many places and will distribute them according to work record or level of activism; favoritism and corruption may lead to the allocation of facilities to those who have not earned them. The deficits of goods and the administrative distributive network mean that money is not a universal medium of exchange as it is under capitalism.

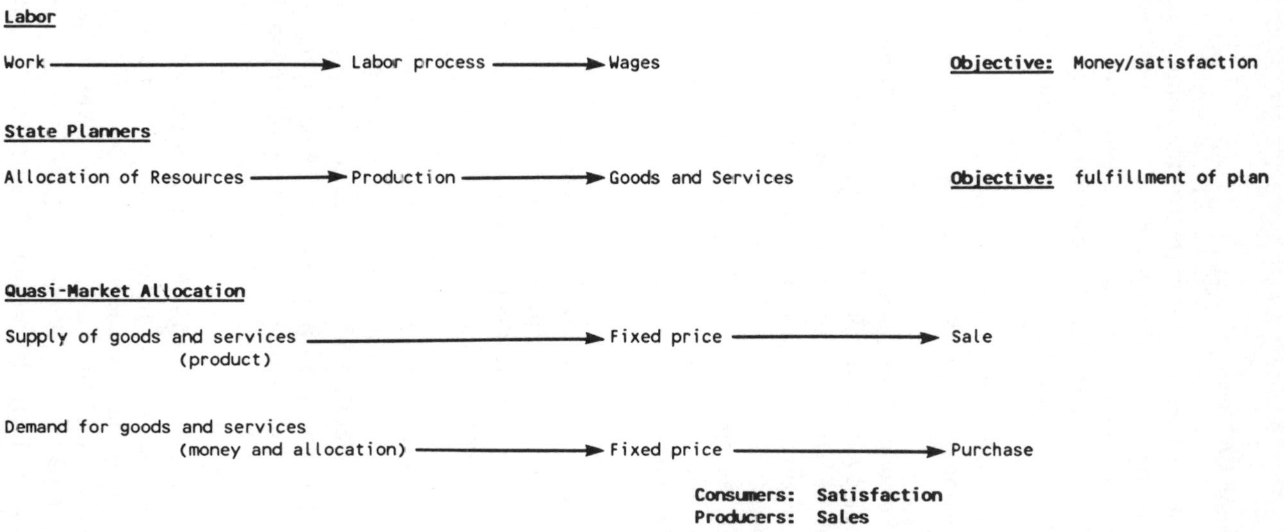

Labor

Work ———— Labor process ————▶ Wages   **Objective:** Money/satisfaction

State Planners

Allocation of Resources ————▶ Production ————▶ Goods and Services   **Objective:** fulfillment of plan

Quasi-Market Allocation

Supply of goods and services ————▶ Fixed price ————▶ Sale
(product)

Demand for goods and services ————▶ Fixed price ————▶ Purchase
(money and allocation)

    Consumers: Satisfaction
    Producers: Sales

Figure 2.3 The Economic Mechanism of Traditional Soviet Planning

REPERCUSSIONS OF THE SOVIET SYSTEM OF PLANNED ECONOMY

A Full-Employment Economy

In the USSR and state socialist societies (before the political and economic reforms) there has been an interdependence of polity and economy. Political priorities have determined economic provision and have given rise to what may be described as a "low-pay full-employment economy."

Rapid industrialization in the interwar period wedded to the Marxist-Leninist insistence that labor fulfills human needs has created conditions for a full-employment economy. Western and Soviet specialists concur that the Soviet economy employs a very high proportion of the labor force — probably the highest yet known in human history. In the late 1980s, labor participation rates have been around 88 percent for both men and women; in 1980, for people in their thirties, 97.6 percent of men and 92.7 percent of women were employed (this includes women on maternity leave). Figures for industrialized capitalist countries are also in the 90 percent range for males in their thirties, but the percentages are much lower — in the 50 percent to 60 percent bracket — for women. Soviet female employees are employed full time, whereas in capitalist countries a sizeable proportion — between 25 percent and 30 percent — are part-timers.

Such high labor participation rates do not preclude involuntary unemployment. The absence of mass unemployment in the USSR since 1931 has led to the discontinuation of the collection of comprehensive unemployment statistics. In the early 1980s frictional unemployment averaged twenty-five to thirty days between jobs. The proportion of the work force changing jobs creates an average turnover of 19 percent for the USSR annually. A rate of frictional unemployment of between 1.3 percent and 1.5 percent can be confidently estimated (before perestroika).

There is also considerable underemployment, especially in the rural areas of rapid population growth in Central Asia. Here women (and increasingly young men) are occupied on private plots and in the domestic economy. In the Central Asian republics the labor participation rate is approximately 10 percent lower than the average for the USSR, and significant pockets of unemployment have always existed.

For a number of reasons, which have to do with the peculiarities of the labor market, there has been less labor mobility both between jobs and geographically in the USSR than in the West, even during periods of full employment. First, there has been a lack of wage incentives for mobility in the USSR. Until the advent of Gorbachev's leadership, differentials were relatively low (see chapter 5). Second, jobs have not been advertised on a national basis, and promotion has been arranged administratively within institutions. Third, given the general shortage and cheapness of labor, enterprises have hoarded workers — there have been no competitive forces compelling factories to reduce their labor force. Fourth, the enterprises believed that labor turnover was bad for production — retraining new workers has a disruptive effect. Penalties have been exacted against those who changed jobs — they lost holiday entitlement, for instance. Fifth, workers found that the factory provided many of their social and welfare facilities: housing, sports, leisure, holidays, food supplies, child care, medical facilities, evening classes are all part of the factory *kollektiv* (collective). The trade unions' task has been to keep the worker contented and to hold personnel in the plant. Finally, the high female participation rate makes the husband/wife pair the unit of the labor market. Women appreciate their jobs from a social as well as a financial point of view, and this militates against occupational mobility involving a geographical move.

Inefficiency in the Utilization of Labor

While capitalist systems give rise to structured unemployment caused by a shortage of jobs in relation to the supply of labor, in state socialist systems inefficiency is created by a surplus of jobs in relation to the number of workers. At the same time labor is underutilized and underemployed in the urban-industrial areas; there is also significant underemployment of labor in the rural areas of Central Asia.

Underemployment means conditions in which workers are paid for jobs but their labor is not efficiently used — they may be idle for all or part of the time or their level of skill may be higher than the job requires. The Soviet economy is often characterized as one of labor shortage and labor underutilization. Vacancies in the USSR regularly exceed two million, which includes an annual addition of about 750,000 new jobs. For 1980, when the employed work force was 112 million, this vacancy figure represents some 2 percent of the work force. Moreover, there are various forms of underemployment, principally people are idle or inefficient for much of the time on the job. Analyses conducted in the USSR show that Soviet plants use from 30 percent to 50 percent more workers than comparable plants abroad and that in imported manufacturing units as many as 1.5 times more operatives are employed, 3.5 times as many engineering, technical, and administrative staff, and 8 times as many auxiliary workers. Surveys have indicated that from 15 percent to 20 percent of the work force is often underutilized because of poor organization. Labor reserves are useful because they allow enterprises to make up for shortages and bottlenecks, and to substitute for capital.

Labor productivity is not only lower than in Western capitalist countries, but the growth in labor productivity fell from 139 percent in the period 1966–70, to 125 percent in the period 1971–75 and 117 percent in the period 1976–80. The regime of "soft" labor discipline and the strong bargaining position of labor are results of a full-employment economy.

From an individual and a political point of view, full employment has many advantages: it promotes social and political stability; the population may have a low standard of living, but it is not subject to uncertainty; and people are occupied in useful, or at least harmless, activities; crime is minimized. The other side of the coin is that the social conviviality of the workplace may go on at the cost of economic efficiency.

The Shortage Economy

The effects of a low-paid and (over)full-employment economy have been generalized under the term "shortage economy" by a Hungarian economist, Kornai. The effects of the labor shortage are the loosening of labor discipline, the deterioration of work quality, and the lessening of workers' diligence. The security of employment gives rise to irresponsibility in anyone susceptible to it. Absenteeism only exacerbates the shortage. Output becomes erratic and supply of commodities and services falls short of demand. Shortage characterizes the wholesale market. Shortage of supplies, materials, and services, in turn, leads to slackness on the job, creating "storming" when those goods and services become available. The efficiency of the economy is thus seriously undermined, labor productivity falls, innovation is not encouraged, and economic growth declines. This cycle has serious consequences for social stability and national security, for the economy is unable to meet the population's aspirations for a rising standard of living.

Here, then, is the dilemma for a socialist welfare policy: the provision of full employment provides security, but an unintended consequence is that the attendant poor motivation and poor quality of work reduce the ability of the economy to create surplus and growth. This dilemma has led, in the USSR and other socialist states, to demands for reforms — not just by right-wing "capitalist restorationists," but by many strata of the population whose consumption aspirations are underfulfilled.

The economic and political reforms of the Gorbachev leadership have sought to improve the economic mechanism in order to increase labor productivity within the context of a full-employment economy. The intertwining of economics and politics has led to the realization that political as well as economic reform is necessary.

THE ECONOMY AND POLITICAL REFORM

Because the economic and political are interwoven in socialist societies, economic change cannot be accomplished without political change. The novelty of Gorbachev's policy is the recognition that the interrelationship between economic and political forces has led to stagnation. In his speech to the Party Plenum on ideology in February 1988, Gorbachev spoke of how development was hampered by "the administrative decree system of management which grew up in the 1930s, the bureaucratic, dogmatic and voluntarist distortions, tyranny and in the late 1970s and early 1980s lack of initiative and retarding phenomena leading to stagnation."

In order to understand the Soviet political system and the changes introduced by Gorbachev, it is necessary to consider the ways that the Soviet state system was organized before 1991. There were three major institutions: the executive or government (Councils of Ministers),* elected legislatures (Soviets); and a political leadership (the Communist Party of the USSR). In this chapter we shall consider the executive, which controls the economy; in the next we shall turn to the Soviets and the Communist Party. Since the reforms of Gorbachev other parties and groups have grown which now play an important role in politics — these are considered below, in chapter 4.

The Government Structure before 1991: The Council of Ministers

The Soviet economy has been incorporated into the Soviet system of government. The student has to make a mental leap to conceptualize the scope of the Council of Ministers, or Soviet government. It oversees the management, organization, and development of the whole economy in its internal and external workings. By external, one means not only control of the exchange rate of Soviet currency, but also the supervision and channeling of foreign contracts (imports and exports of commodities). In addition to its economic roles, the government also has the traditional responsibilities of Western governments: defense, internal security, public works, education, and welfare.

The Soviet economy is the largest in the world after the United States and has a larger employed work force. The Soviet Union has the biggest

---

* Its name was changed to the Cabinet of Ministers in a reform of December 1990 — it is described below. Following the coup of August 1991 this in turn was abolished and replaced by a State Council — see below.

single health service employing the world's largest contingent of doctors (in 1987 the health service had in all 7 million employees), and its armed forces have the greatest number of full time personnel (in 1987 there were 5.2 million in the Soviet forces, compared to 3.2 in the Chinese forces and 2.1 active in the United States). Hence the Soviet bureaucracy is enormous in size.

Before Gorbachev, the economy and other instruments of administration were centralized. There were three types of ministry. First, the All-Union ministries covered activities throughout the USSR: ministers in Moscow were responsible for the detailed organization of output, for example, in production branches of ministries located in, say, Riga or Erevan. Second, the Union-Republican ministries involved a two-tier system with the central administration operating through ministries in the republics. Finally, republican ministries had authority only in a given republic. By volume of production in 1987, the industrial undertakings of the All-Union ministries accounted for 61 percent of output; Union-Republican ministries 33 percent and Republican 6 percent. Hence the All-Union ministries (ruled from Moscow through the government of the USSR) have enormous power and exert control over enterprises located in the republics: sovereignty over these resources has become a major bone of contention between the center and republics in the early 1990s. The structure is illustrated in Figure 2.4.

The All-Union law passed in April 1990 gave the government of the USSR the major role in economic affairs, including: jurisdiction over the functioning of the all-union market, the tax system, the budget, economic development, pricing policy including finance, credit and a unified money supply, environment, communication and information systems, investment policy, science and technology, employment, public education, health and culture, minimum payrates, foreign economic policy, customs, boundaries of economic zones, state foreign loans, protection of economic interests of the USSR, statistics and accounting, patents, weights and measures and weather services.

The essence of the stagnation in the system of state economic management was that the planning mechanisms were not responsive to what people wanted. The administration of industry was inert. Industrial discipline was lacking; workers and employees lacked incentives. The industrial ministries acted as independent, autonomous bodies, becoming laws unto themselves. They were able to write their own plans. Each ministry could act relatively independently, and they would often deceive the central planners about their real economic resources. Plans would be fulfilled in a routine and bureaucratic fashion with little concern for quality.

The chiefs of these bodies had immense political power. The institutions

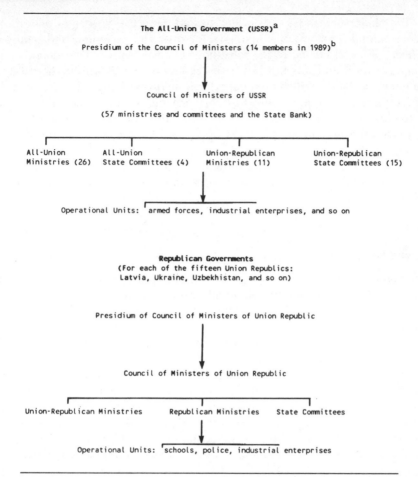

The All-Union Government (USSR)[a]

Presidium of the Council of Ministers (14 members in 1989)[b]

Council of Ministers of USSR

(57 ministries and committees and the State Bank)

| All-Union Ministries (26) | All-Union State Committees (4) | Union-Republican Ministries (11) | Union-Republican State Committees (15) |

Operational Units: armed forces, industrial enterprises, and so on

Republican Governments
(For each of the fifteen Union Republics:
Latvia, Ukraine, Uzbekhistan, and so on)

Presidium of Council of Ministers of Union Republic

Council of Ministers of Union Republic

| Union-Republican Ministries | Republican Ministries | State Committees |

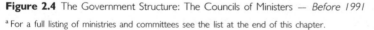

Operational Units: schools, police, industrial enterprises

Figure 2.4 The Government Structure: The Councils of Ministers — *Before 1991*

[a] For a full listing of ministries and committees see the list at the end of this chapter.

responsible for oversight of the ministries — *Gosplan* and the elected bodies, the Soviets — were weak. The administrative system lacked the discipline of the market that prevails under capitalism. The consequences, from an economic point of view, were inertia and lack of innovation, and from a political standpoint, the growth of a power bloc of *apparatchiks*, or state bureaucrats. The widespread shortages and inefficiencies led to corruption, illegal trading, and moral degeneracy. Reform of the economy, Gorbachev has emphasized, is "the decisive sphere of the life of society" (January Party Plenum 1987).

The leadership under Gorbachev has adopted two strategies to reform the economic system: the first is reform of the economic mechanism, which will be discussed in the remainder of this chapter. The second is to democratize political control over the economy, which will be the subject of the next chapter. Such political reform involves giving greater power to the organs of popular control — the Soviets — and recalibrating the activities of the Party and its apparatus. In this context, the posts (plural because they operate at the level of the All-Union and the Republican level) of President have been created, enhancing the authority of the elected Soviets over the government executive and Party bureaucracy. These developments involve a greater independence of the economic from the political.

Economic Reforms

Discussion of economic reform in the Soviet Union is not new. Khrushchev attempted to break up the economic bureaucracies by setting up over a hundred regional economic councils and giving them power over many economic activities on a regional basis. His scheme was short-lived, however, and the Soviet system was reconstituted under Kosygin on a centralized basis as described above.

The objectives of the reforms under Gorbachev have been to reduce the "overcentralization" of the economic mechanism; to use the market to establish prices and money as incentives for producers, workers, and consumers; and to retain the benefits of planning — rational forms of investment and a full-employment economy. To obtain these objectives Gorbachev initiated economic reforms that may be summarized as follows:

- the growth and legitimation of market transactions
- an increase in private and cooperative trade
- greater authority to production units
- adoption of the accounting principle of *khozraschet* (which requires units to balance their income and expenditures).

These measures have involved a lessening of the powers of the economic ministries and central control, more uncertainty for managers and workers, and greater use of money as a stimulus. The enterprise has been given greater autonomy over its own affairs, but it has had to work within the confines of a plan handed down by the central authorities. Prices, except in the cooperative and private-initiative sectors, are not subject to the forces of supply and demand but are fixed administratively. (Eventually prices, it is envisaged, will come under market influence.)

The reforms introduced involve weakening the power of the industrial ministries. This involves the development of other forms of property and market relationships. Laws have been passed giving individuals and "cooperatives" rights to private trade: they have legal rights over what produce they sell and buy. Employment of hired labor (at least in any significant quantity) is prohibited, hence the system tends to encourage family units. Certain kinds of activity are also proscribed (such as general education films and videos, and television transmissions).

The number of cooperatives has risen considerably since the mid-1980s, and by 1988 there were a total of 19,539 units in operation with 245,700 people working in them. There were another 369,400 people working on their own account: in handicraft trades (60.2 percent), services (26.8 percent), social-cultural (for example, medical, 4.7 percent), and artistic (1.0 percent). By 1 April 1989 the cooperative sector had grown considerably: there were 99,300 registered cooperatives employing 1.951 million people. By the beginning of 1991, the number of cooperatives in goods and the provision of services had risen to 260,000 and employment in them had reached 6.2 million. The number of people employed in them, however, was relatively modest compared to the total number of Soviet manual and nonmanual workers — 118.6 million in 1987. The increase in the number of cooperatives has brought much illegal economic activity into the taxable category: tax rates range from 30 percent (for incomes between 500 and 700 rubles per month) to 90 percent for incomes over

Reform of the Economic Administration

The reform administration under Gorbachev has aimed to limit the power of the centralized ministries, a policy that has involved major changes. First, the powers of the ministries have been curbed: "financial autonomy" is being given to production enterprises to encourage economic rather than administrative relations. Second, greater autonomy is to be devolved to the republics. The executive of the Cabinet of Ministers of the USSR will continue to control the economic regulation of the economy and other state objectives (defense and foreign affairs). From December 1990 to 19 August 1991, the President was chief executive and the Cabinet of Ministers (chosen by the President) worked under him.

The number of republican ministries was reduced from 800 to 600 in March 1989 and over 1,000 main directories and directorates were abolished. In 1989 it was reported that the number of staff in apparatuses of ministries, committees, and departments had declined between 1985 and 1988 by 543,000, a decline of 33.5 percent. Nine All-Union ministries and departments were closed down by March 1989, and at the first meeting of the reorganized Supreme Soviet in June of that year (which will be discussed in detail in the next chapter) Prime Minister Ryzhkov announced that the economic Union-Republic ministries would be abolished and their activities transferred to the republics. Furthermore, the number of All-Union ministries and committees was reduced. The number of ministries dealing with industry, building, transport, agriculture, and defense was reduced from fifty to thirty-two. In addition, twenty-five committees, bureaus, and ministries dealing with control and other matters of state (finance, foreign affairs, prices, economic reform, and so on) were constituted.

All-Union ministries were organized under the Cabinet of Ministers of the USSR. Such ministries and committees operated directly throughout the whole of the USSR, and Union-Republican ones function through the Union Republics. *Gosplan* and the KGB were among the fifteen important Union-Republican state committees. (A listing of these institutions, in 1991 is appended.) A parallel system of administration had been established in each of the fifteen Union Republics (equivalents to the states in the United States).

We may note here that the attempt to shift the balance of power away from the ministries and the center to the market and the republics has created many problems in the period of transition. The bodies charged with economic policy and control in the republics have adopted policies at variance with the USSR government and there has been a protracted period of conflict about areas of jurisdiction and economic policy. The process of change has sharpened the interests of officials in the state bureaucracy who have resisted reorganization. Differences have become manifest between the center (the All-Union ministries) and the periphery (the republics) over areas of competence and power. Republican and local Soviets have decreed that assets in their territory belong to them. In the Ukraine in February 1991 a commission was set up to supervise the transfer of mines from the USSR coal and metallurgy industries to republican ownership. Following the coup in August 1991, Eltsin declared All-Union property located in the Russian republic to be under his command. The uncertainty introduced by marketization has unsettled lower-level officials and workers. The move to a market price system has exacerbated shortages as consumers have hoarded supplies before expected price increases.

Increasing Productivity: Incentives for Enterprises and Workers

To reduce the detailed administrative control of enterprises, the reform strategy calls for the use of "economic" criteria: the principle of *khozraschet* has been adopted. *Khozraschet* is the idea of autonomous financial accounting: each accounting unit must balance its own books. By 1 January 1988 55 percent of enterprises in industry had gone over to *khozraschet*; a year later, all enterprises were required to do so. Production units have initiative to determine the ways that planned targets are met, and they also have incentives to market output produced over the target defined in the plan. The idea is that the center will allocate to enterprises realistic targets for output, increases in labor productivity, and product quality. The objective is to increase economic efficiency by encouraging and rewarding increases in productivity at the point of production.

Exchanges between individuals and institutions will be influenced more by individual and group self-interest; money will become a much more important medium in the economy, as is illustrated in Figure 2.5.

Gosplan, at the top of the diagram, is assisted by various other planning committees (on prices, procurement of materials), and formulates plans. Each ministry (each industry) has a plan, which indicates its quantitative production goals (so many cars to be made, houses to be built). These plans are "disaggregated" to give each production enterprise a plan. In practice the enterprise negotiates targets with the ministry. The agreed plan contains inputs (so much steel, a budget for wages) and the state orders, which detail production targets (so many completed cars, houses) that have to be met.

In the past the plan for the enterprise detailed the total output. Enterprises were paid if the output targets were reached. Under the current scheme surpluses over the targets defined in the plan can be sold, and the profits will accrue to the enterprise. Profits may be used to finance new investment or may be distributed as wages to employees. This principle is applied to production enterprises, work units, and even to research institutes that have to meet their costs from the sale of their research — if they cannot sell their research they will close. This procedure pushes decision making and authority away from the center to the point of production. All economic units should gain financially if they increase productivity.

Under Gorbachev much more has been left to the discretion of the enterprise: it can contract with its consumers and supply their orders. Nevertheless, prices and many key inputs to the enterprise are defined in the plan. State orders, contracts to supply the superior ministry, will

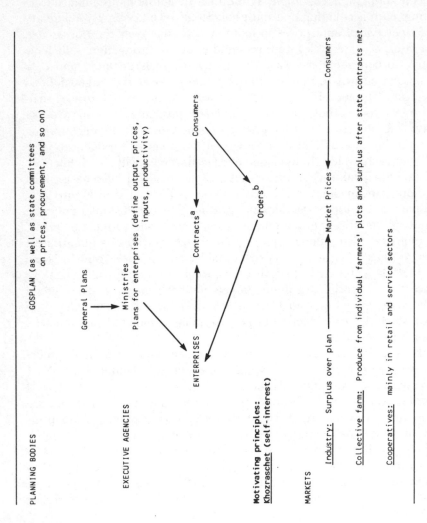

PLANNING BODIES   GOSPLAN (as well as state committees
                       on prices, procurement, and so on)

                       General Plans

EXECUTIVE AGENCIES   Ministries
                       Plans for enterprises (define output, prices,
                       inputs, productivity)

                                                    Consumers

                                         Contracts[a]   Orders[b]

ENTERPRISES

Motivating principles:
Khozraschet (self-interest)

MARKETS

Industry: Surplus over plan → Market Prices → Consumers

Collective farm: Produce from individual farmers' plots and surplus after state contracts met

Cooperatives: mainly in retail and service sectors

Figure 2.5 Central Planning under Gorbachev

[a] Negotiated prices.
[b] Prices and outputs defined in plan.

continue for some time; they provide a fall-back for the enterprise and for the economy as a whole, ensuring that essential defense contracts, or food supplies, for instance, are maintained. The intention, however, is for orders to be contracted "horizontally," to consumers directly. In this way production should meet what consumers really need, rather than what is stipulated in the plan.

This strategy has some important consequences if pushed to its logical conclusion. Enterprises that do not cover their costs will become bankrupt and go out of business. The strong will thrive. Wages in efficient enterprises will rise. Those in uncompetitive ones will decline; some members of the labor force may even become unemployed.

In an attempt to strengthen the links between employees and the enterprise, it was agreed in 1988 that securities (or shares) could be sold to members of enterprises (if sanctioned by the government). It was argued that this would overcome working people's alienation from state property and draw personal savings into production in a democratic way. The issue of securities was also legitimate as one element of a socialist market. By 1991, embryo stock exchanges had been set up, though their scope was limited.

The reforms of the late 1980s directly addressed the working class. Gorbachev has widened the "brigade system" and instituted an enterprise law to give workers a greater role in the factory. The brigade system involves a group of workers fulfilling a contract for an output target, given certain inputs (in materials and wages), and if it overfulfills the set target, the members of the brigade share the surplus among themselves; they also have a certain freedom collectively to determine relative wages for members of the brigade. The system includes incentives to "free labor" (create redundancies, layoffs), thereby lowering labor costs and increasing productivity. The social pressure of the brigade, it is believed, will positively influence the slower, careless, and undisciplined workers. Furthermore, the brigade will not only have a financial interest in declaring redundancies, but will make labor layoffs more acceptable to the work force as a whole. The economic mechanism will have an influence that is independent of the state.

Introducing the Market System to the Socialist Economy

The provision of a consumer market is crucial to the success of the proposed reforms. The stimulus of money is only operative if there are artifacts to buy, or things to invest in. A consumer mentality is a necessary condition for a market-generated and acquisitive society. Aganbegyan has put it as follows: "The whole transformation is directed towards ful-filling the needs of the consumer. The reform in prices, financing, and banks; the shift from central supply to industry; the return, in the future, to a convertible ruble; and all technical renovation and regeneration is directed towards this aim." The Soviet leadership now takes the world market seriously and their objective is to make Soviet manufactured goods competitive in the world economy.

The market under socialism has a new respectability. Politburo member Yakovlev in a speech in 1988 pointed out that:

> The development of the socialist market is one of the roads leading to the combining of interests and to the shaping of the ideology of the good socialist manager ... The market is made socialist or capitalist not by the move-ment of commodities, capital, or even the work force, but by the social context of the processes which accompany it ... The dividing line ... lies in defining the place of people in society and whether they are using the market for the ultimate goals of society or as a source of profit.

Here Yakovlev is distinguishing between a capitalist and a socialist market. The latter is constrained by the ownership of the major productive forces by the state and the prohibition of the extraction of profit.

The political leadership has encouraged the use of the market as a mechanism to reconcile demand and supply. As the market gets under way, surpluses will be earned that can be used to purchase other inputs, and products may then be sold at prices fixed by supply and demand. This strategy gives a greater role to consumers and entails greater flexi-bility and responsiveness of prices and wages. Over time, prices as a whole will come to their market level. It is believed that this will give consumers a greater stake in the reform. The other side to prices "find-ing their own level" is that they certainly will rise, leading to price inflation, which will cause those on low incomes or pensions to suffer. An envir-onment of rising prices creates uncertainty, demands for higher wages, and social unrest.

While prices and output will for the foreseeable future be given in the factory's plan — determined by the central planners — surpluses may be traded freely and prices of such commodities will be determined by supply and demand, while key levels of production will be maintained by "state orders." The market already includes the produce of individual farmers' plots and the cooperative and individual traders' activity. All prices currently set by supply and demand are higher than state prices and lead to price inflation.

Enterprises have financial incentives to exceed the plan targets and to economize on labor and material costs. There should be no incentive to hoard labor or to underutilize resources. Furthermore, production establishments should institute and maintain contracts from wholesalers or retailers. The demand for an enterprise's output will be reflected in the number of contracts it fulfills, and this will be taken account of in the allocation of resources, at the next round, by the planners. Hence, the system of central planning remains and elements of consumer demand influence the allocation of resources. It is also intended that the proportion of state orders will decline as the reform grows in momentum. In 1989 state orders ranged from 25 percent of output in machine tools to 59 percent in the fuel and energy sector. In the future it is anticipated that from 50 percent to 70 percent of the output of enterprises will be derived from orders from customers. Of particular importance in the procurement of customers is that many enterprises may trade directly with foreign companies, and joint ventures are being encouraged with Western firms. The economic system is rapidly moving to a mixed economy.

While the system weakens the ministries and planning apparatus, many of the features of the centrally planned system have been retained. The market does not determine, except in a marginal way, the direction and rate of investment. Prices are still for the most part set administratively. It is intended that the State Committee on Prices will eventually only control some 10 percent of production prices, but these could exert a major influence over the cost structure of the whole economy. The negative effects of the market have not been allowed to occur — at least not yet. Gorbachev, when asked about unemployment, has categorically said that it will not be countenanced as a form of discipline for labor. The bankruptcy of enterprises and the laying off of workers is not contemplated without the agreement of the trade union council or committee. But the USSR State Committee for Labor and Social Issues has estimated that overemployment in Soviet enterprises ranges from 10 percent to 20 percent of the work force, and a more efficient use of labor on purely economic grounds would lead to from three million to three and a half million layoffs during the current five year plan. Severe layoffs are unlikely given the ideological and organizational context in which the Soviet enterprise is embedded. In 1988 labor employed in the state sector declined by more than a million, but much of this loss was taken up by an increase of employees in the cooperative and individual labor sector.

By the early 1990s, unemployment had increased, though its extent is not accurately measured: in 1991 following the political unrest and economic dislocation, unemployment soared and is reliably estimated at 10 percent and short-time working caused by lack of supplies is widespread.

Agriculture

Agriculture is a major source of weakness in the Soviet economy. Under the administrative or command system there are three types of farming units: state farms, which are organized by a ministry and operate to fulfill a plan; collective farms, which are run collectively by farmers who legally own the produce of the farm (but not the land); and private plots, the produce of which may be used for consumption or for sale on the market (prices here are fixed by supply and demand).

Agriculture has provided sufficient food to maintain the population, but the quality and availability of foods has been below people's expectations. Part of the problem has been the rapid urbanization of the Soviet Union — between 1950 and 1980 the urban population rose from 39 to 63 percent of the total population, an increase of 97 million people. Because movement to the towns is associated with rising living standards, it is possible that the quality of consumption actually declined, as agriculture did not keep up with the demand. For 1985, for instance, the Soviet economist Alexander Zaichenko has calculated that the con-

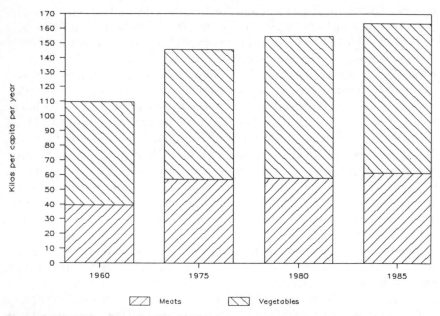

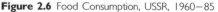 Meats   Vegetables

Figure 2.6 Food Consumption, USSR, 1960–85

Source: Based on data, from Hans Aage, "Consumption, Income, Distribution, and Incentives," in *The Soviet Economy: A New Course?* (Brussels: NATO, 1987), 47–70.

sumption of meat was (on average) 62 kilograms in the USSR — about half the U.S. figure. The provision of adequate food supply is crucial for the stability and success of current policy. As Gorbachev put it at a Party Plenum in March 1989:

> Great concern over [food supply has been] raised at recent Party report-back and election meetings and conferences ... The real situation is such that we are experiencing shortages of farm produce. The state has to buy large quantities of grain, meat, fruit, vegetables, sugar, vegetable oil and some other produce abroad. We are still behind developed countries, big and small, in productivity, yield capacity of fields and livestock productivity and in the diversity and quality of foodstuffs. The gap is widening rather than narrowing. The shortage of food creates social tension and generates not merely criticism but actual discontent on the part of the people ... So far, we have been unable to find a cardinal solution to the food problem despite the fact that this is a country which possesses such great potential.

Food consumption has risen steadily since 1960 as shown in Figure 2.6. Figure 2.7 shows comparative food intake for the USSR, the United States, the United Kingdom, and Italy. Bearing in mind that consumers

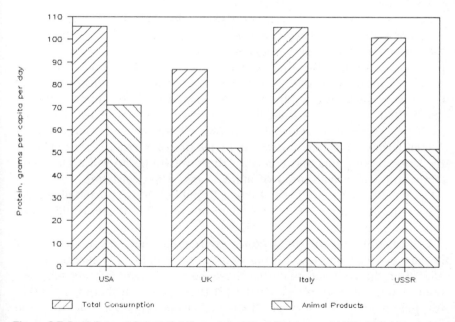

Figure 2.7 Food Consumption, United States, Italy, United Kingdom, and USSR, 1983–84
Source: Based on data from Aage (NATO, 1987).

in the advanced Western countries (especially in the United States) are continually reminded by health experts that they eat too much meat and insufficient vegetables, Soviet food consumption is not as out of line as is often asserted; indeed it is comparable in quantity, though not quality, to the average diet in Italy. Many of the problems stem from poor distribution and wastage of supplies. Transport, storage and refrigeration facilities are very rudimentary.

For agriculture the reform strategy attempts to inject an element of private enterprise to increase output through the leasing of land and the use of a quasi-family contract system. As Gorbachev put it in March 1989, "The essence of economic change in the countryside has to consist of granting farmers broad opportunities for displaying independence, enterprise and initiative." Work groups within state and collective farms have been encouraged to lease land and equipment and to farm it on a contract basis. The collective or state farm is given a plan and farmers are required to fulfill it as efficiently as they can. This can be done if families or other work groups organize production on plots leased to them by the farm. Leases may be arranged for periods from five to fifty years; it will also be possible to transfer leases to members of families who have worked the land. In 1990, in many republics legislation was passed which allowed for private ownership of land. In the Russian Republic, for instance, in December 1990, it was enacted that land could be bought and sold through the local Soviet of People's Deputies, with the proviso that such land could not be further bought and sold for a period of ten years. But the legislature of the USSR did not adopt this measure. In January 1991, Gorbachev issued a decree instructing the executive committees of republics and local Soviets to create a special "land fund" constituted from unused and surplus land which could be available for lease, cooperatives, private allotments and building. Inefficient farms could be transferred to lessors or peasant farms. Unlike the situation in China and Hungary, there was to be no widescale decollectivization or privatization of state farms. This legislation was somewhat at odds with that of the Russian Republic and is an example of the ways that the policy of the government of the USSR was in conflict with that of the republics.

Lessees are paid for the produce contracted; they receive no money if they produce nothing. Surpluses may be traded at a market price, and after the contract quantities have been fulfilled, farmers may use their facilities as they please (that is, if they think that there is a market for melons, they can cultivate them, even if melons do not figure in the farm's plan). The results have not been encouraging: for the first nine months of 1990, statistics show that meat and fish production declined and despite a record harvest other food commodities available only increased by a few percentage points. An increase in money supply (discussed further below) led to massive price hikes for food sold in the (free) collective farm market: for the first six months of 1990 food prices were 18 percent higher than for the comparable period in 1989; and collective farm meat was 30 percent higher in price for the first nine months of 1990 compared to the first nine months of 1989. The rise in money incomes led to acute shortages in the state shops; queuing was widespread and many areas restricted sales to local residents. In 1990 retail prices rose considerably with meat and bread doubling in price.

THE EFFECTS OF THE REFORMS

The Soviet economy grew 5 percent from 1987 to 1988, compared with a 4 percent average growth from 1981 to 1985. (These data, again, remind one that the growth of the Soviet national product compared well with that of major Western industrial countries in the early 1980s.) Labor productivity increased 5.1 percent compared to 3.1 percent, respectively. Wages rose 7 percent for manual and nonmanual workers in 1988 over 1987; however, per capita real income rose only 3.5 percent in this same period. By 1990, however, the Soviet economy was characterized by increasing dislocation. The old command system was being dismantled but a new one was not in place. The major indicators for economic development were all negative. For 1990, gross national product *fell* by 2 percent (compared to the previous year) and labor productivity was down by 3 percent. The national debt rose to 550 billion rubles. In 1991, Western specialists estimated that GNP decreased by 15 percent.

Oleg Bogomolov, director of the Institute of the Economics of the World Socialist System, has anticipated that the budget deficit will come to 11 percent of the gross domestic product. This compares, for instance, with the American deficit of 3−4 percent. As Bogomolov in 1989 has put it:

> Under our conditions, inflation is manifested not so much in price rises as in shortages, the disappearance of essential goods and the disruption of the market. This is accompanied by speculation, bribery, the bribing of officials responsible for the distribution of goods in short supply (corruption) and the emergence of organized crime.

Price inflation in the late 1980s rose significantly: from an average of 5.7 percent for the period 1981−85 to 7.4 percent in 1987, 8.4 percent in 1988 to 10 percent in 1990. In 1991, economic and political dislocation and an increase in money supply led to inflation estimated in the West to be as much as 140 percent. A consequence has been inflated prices in the collective farm market and the decline of the ruble as a medium of exchange and the increased use of foreign currency and cigarettes.

The disruption of the central planning system led enterprises not to deliver output; one quarter failed to meet their contractual commitments. In the consumption sector the amount of goods not received according to contract increased fourfold between 1989 and 1990. Greater uncertainty, despondency and falling morale characterized the Soviet economy. Many supplies were withheld and bartered for goods. This was to the advantage of food-producing areas, but to the dismay of areas concerned with defense industries. The shortages of consumer goods led local authorities to forbid sales to non-local people. This led to retaliation: rural areas withheld sales to urban areas, thus causing even greater disruption. Labor discipline worsened and absenteeism from work spiraled. In 1989 alone, according to Soviet figures, 44 million working days were lost through infractions of labor discipline. Exports declined by 12 percent and the earning of foreign currency fell. Chaos, uncertainty and decline typified the Soviet economy. In these conditions Gorbachev was confronted by demands, not to bolster the planned economy, but to reform more radically.

The Shatalin 500 Day Program and Gorbachev's Economic Program

In the fall of 1990, Stanislav Shatalin's "500 Day Program" advocated a rapid transition to a market economy. During the first 100 days the major industrial (All-Union) ministries located in Moscow would be privatized by way of auctions and would be converted into joint stock or private companies. During the next 150 days, privatization of smaller enterprises would take place at a republican level. During this period, price controls would be abolished at republican levels. In the following 150 days, the plan anticipates that 30 percent of industry would be privately owned, as would 50 percent of transport and building and 60 percent of services. Unemployment would begin to bite but would be minimized by the growth of private enterprise. In the final 100 days a free market in labor would be set up. Currently, the movement of labor is controlled by the issue of residence permits, which limits mobility and the consequent demand for housing. These would be abolished. Free trade with other countries would be permitted (subject to republican tariffs) and it is contemplated that the Soviet economy would be able to compete on the world market.

Gorbachev initially warmed to this plan, which was enthusiastically supported by Eltsin. However, Gorbachev and his advisers in the USSR government finally rejected the plan, for two reasons. First, the timescale was regarded as unrealistic. The necessary conditions of a market had not been created and it was thought the precarious economy would collapse and lead to further social unrest. Second, the plan gave too much power to the individual republics. The All-Union government would be severely weakened as the republican governments would be given control over natural resources and the major industrial ministries would be privatized.

In October 1990, the leadership's reform program was published. Its objective was to move to a market-type economy combining state and private property — a "mixed economy". "The transition to the market does not contradict our people's socialist choice. Only the market, combined with the humanist orientation of all society, is capable of ensuring the satisfaction of people's needs, the fair distribution of wealth, social rights and guarantees of citizens, and the strengthening of freedom and democracy" (Presidential Statement October 1990). It envisaged an eighteen month to two year timescale and its implementation would vary according to local conditions in the fifteen national republics (and autonomous republics). The program would be dependent on the completion of a union treaty between the republics and the USSR which would set the framework for economic and political relations.

The early period of preparation would be concerned with the stabilization of the monetary system and the value of the ruble. Gorbachev stressed the need to create the condition for the operation of a market economy: the control of inflation through the money supply. A financial legal structure in which enterprises have responsibility for profit and loss is also necessary. This involves the creation of a "system of commodity and stock exchanges, commercial banks, a broad network of wholesale trade enterprises ..." (Gorbachev's speech to Supreme Soviet USSR, 19 October 1990). A new framework of social security is to be set up. Enterprise and work are encouraged and social assistance is to be limited to the "socially vulnerable strata". The market will create labor layoffs which will need different kinds of security support (for instance, unemployment compensation) than existed under the command system.

The transition to market consumer prices will be gradual and state-controlled prices will apply for the period of transition (presumably two years). People on fixed incomes (pensioners, state employees) will be index-linked. There will be a step-by-step movement to the convertibility of the ruble. The transition is dependent on working out how a market on an All-Union basis will operate. The decentralization, noted above, has led to the breaking of central authority. Until the political relations are settled between the parts of the USSR, Gorbachev argues, a market reform cannot be carried out.

The Coup of August 1991

The compromise position of Gorbachev, fuelled by the collapse of the economy and increasing civil strife, was too much for the leaders of the government bureaucracy which led the coup against Gorbachev. Their policy was to restrict the growth of the market and privatization. However, the policy of the more radical reformers who took power through Eltsin after the failure of the coup in August 1991 was to move more rapidly to the market and privatization.

In the aftermath of the coup important changes in the organization of the economy took place. The Cabinet of Ministers formed by Gorbachev has been abolished. Most of the All-Union ministries have been split up and hived off to the republics. Only a few major ministries remain including foreign affairs, internal security, and defence. The new structures are summarized in Fig. 2.8.

During the transitionary period following the coup of 1991 the precise details of the ministerial set-up have to be worked out. It is clear, however, that the powers of the center have been severely curtailed. It will coordinate the relations between the republics constituting the union. The republics will have greater control of the enterprises within them and a rapid movement to privatization in some of them may be expected.

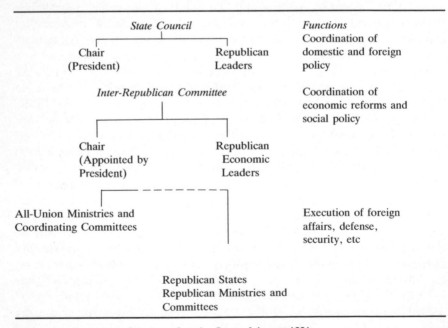

Figure 2.8 Government Structure after the Coup of August 1991

CONCLUSION: AFTER THE COUP OF AUGUST 1991

In the introduction we noted that the Soviet economy has experienced falling rates of economic growth and levels of productivity, and it has not been able to satisfy consumer demand. Economic reform is a major objective of the Soviet leadership. The main changes introduced involve economic organization: an increase in the number of cooperative and individual private producers, decentralization of planning giving production units greater discretion over details of production and limited market relationships with consumers, and the introduction of leasing in agriculture.

Major forms of decentralization and privatization of state property have been envisaged by the Gorbachev leadership, but by 1991 have not been put into operation. The reforms have maintained many of the components of the traditional system — public ownership, central control of most prices and investment — and have continued to stipulate certain planned indicators for enterprises. Market elements, processes of self-financing, and self-interest have been introduced to encourage efficiency. Whereas under the traditional system, the market was considered irrational and unjust, it is now regarded as a major tool in the allocation of resources.

The major problem facing the reform leadership is how to reconcile the new economic mechanisms with the traditional objectives of the Soviet state without suffering a loss of political legitimacy. The retention of "state orders" is one strategy to ease the transition, but there is a danger that they may become institutionalized. The movement to a price system that equilibrates supply and demand would lead to higher prices and inflation, and in the labor market to unemployment. Rising unemployment, decline in production and rampant inflation have led to political instability in 1991.

There is much scope in a mixed economy, as the study of Western capitalism shows. The market can be consistent with weak state penetration of the economy as in the United States (and increasingly in the United Kingdom) or with the efficient welfare state and interventionist policies of the Scandinavian countries or West Germany. There is no theoretical reason why the USSR cannot combine full employment with a greater use of the market, although all experience to date leads one to believe that income differentials and unemployment will increase.

It has been argued that economic reform is dependent on political reform. Both kinds of reform are causally related because the Soviet Union has been an administered economy. As we noted above, effective ownership and control has been located in industrial ministries headed by ministers and operating on a bureaucratic basis. Politics has controlled economics, unlike under capitalism, where it is the other way round. Acceleration of the economy can only occur if the political obstacles to economic reform can be removed. In principle the leadership of the Soviet Union has accepted such a strategy. In practice, however, Gorbachev has found inordinate difficulties in moving forward. If the All-Union industries are privatized or decentralized, the power of the All-Union government (that of the USSR) will be seriously weakened and the defense capacity as well as the credibility of the President will be undermined.

The first five years of perestroika in the field of economics have been fraught with difficulties. Acceleration has not been achieved; on the contrary, economic growth has declined. In 1991, Gorbachev faced crises: the system of planning had been disrupted and the market was not working; shortages were exacerbated, inflation was rife, discipline was weak. The problems of introducing an infrastructure for a market system — private ownership, a price mechanism, exchanges for commodities and stocks, an enterprise culture, norms governing exchange between republics, agreement on the need for a single currency, the extent and form of government intervention — had proved intractable. The government and President Gorbachev faced growing criticism. While the policy of marketization and a movement to a mixed economy was not in doubt, the means to implement it and the timing of a move forward threatened the continuation of the Soviet government.

Gorbachev vacillated between the old and the new system: he was the target of the reformers' criticism for not moving fast enough, and Eltsin called for his resignation. The leaders of the August 1991 coup believed he was disrupting the economy and society and were supported by Gorbachev's own Cabinet of Ministers — elected by him only months previously and all summarily dismissed following his reinstatement after the coup.

At this stage we turn to consider the system of industrial administration as it is located in the apparatus of the government. We shall then be in a position to understand more clearly why economic reform is bound up with the reform of the political mechanism. We shall also learn that perestroika is much more than a mechanism that promotes economic change: it has broadened into a political and social movement.

APPENDIX: GORBACHEV'S MINISTRIES AND STATE COMMITTEES (1991)

USSR All-Union Ministries

Ministry of the Aircraft Industry,
Ministry of Motor Vehicle and Agricultural Machine Building,
Ministry of Nuclear Power Generation and the Nuclear Industry,
Ministry of Foreign Economic Relations,
Ministry of Economics and Forecasting,
Ministry of Geology,
Ministry of Civil Aviation,
Ministry of the Material Resources,
Ministry of Metallurgy,
Ministry of the Merchant Marine,
Ministry of the Oil and Gas Industry,
Ministry of the Defense Industry,
Ministry of Defense,
Ministry of General Machine Building,
Ministry of Railways,
Ministry of the Radio Industry,
Ministry of the Fisheries Industry,
Ministry of the Use of Natural Resources and Environmental Protection,
Ministry of the Shipbuilding Industry,
Ministry of Transport Construction,
Ministry of Labour and Social Questions,
Ministry of the Coal Industry,
Ministry of the Chemical and Oil Refining Industry,
Ministry of the Electronics Industry,
Ministry of the Electrical Equipment Industry and Instrument Making.

USSR Union Republic Ministries

Ministry of Internal Affairs,
Ministry of Health,
Ministry of Foreign Affairs,
Ministry of Culture,
Ministry of the Agriculture and Food,
Ministry of Installation and Special Construction Work,
Ministry of Communications,
Ministry of Trade,
Ministry of Finance,
Ministry of Power and Electrification,
Ministry of Justice.

USSR All-Union State Committees

USSR State Committee for Science and Technology,
USSR State Committee for the Procurement of Food Resources,
USSR State Committee for Machine Building,
USSR State Committee for National Questions.

USSR Union Republic State Committees

USSR State Committee for Construction and Investment,
USSR State Committee for Chemistry and Biotechnology,
USSR State Committee for Statistics,
USSR State Committee for Public Education,
USSR State Committee for Forests,
USSR Committee for State Security.

Commissions

State Military-Industrial Commission,
State Fuel and Energy Commission,
State Commission for Emergencies.

Interrepublican Organs

Union-Republican Currency Committee,
State Council for Economic Reform,
Heads of Republican, Governments (15).

Chapter 3

DEMOKRATIZATSIYA
From Partocracy to Presidency

The main point, comrades . . . is that at a certain stage, the political system . . . was subjected to serious deformations. . . . The command-administrative methods of management that developed in those years had a pernicious effect on various aspects of the development of our society . . .

The existing political system proved incapable of protecting us from the growth of stagnant phenomena in economic and social life in recent decades . . . The ever-greater concentration of economic-management functions in the hands of the Party and political leadership became typical . . .

During the period of stagnation, the managerial apparatus, which had grown to almost 100 Union and 800 Republican ministries and departments, to all intents and purposes began to dictate its will in the economy and in politics. It was departments and other managerial structures that had charge of the execution of adopted decisions, and through their actions or inaction, they determined what would be and what would not be. The Soviets, and in many respects the Party agencies as well, proved unable to control the pressure of departmental interests . . .

It is in this ossified system of power, in its form of command and structure of control mechanisms, that the fundamental problems of restructuring are grounded today.

M. S. Gorbachev's report to the Nineteenth Party Conference, 29 June 1988

Soviet leadership under Gorbachev has considered that the existing forms of control of the government apparatus have been ineffective and inefficient. The industrial ministries have developed into self-regulating bodies that tend to be inert and resistant of outside control. How then is the government apparatus controlled? How can it be considered to be a form of government that executes the will of the people? Gorbachev is reputed to have quoted John Stuart Mill's opinion of the Russian Empire: "The Tsar himself is powerless against the bureaucratic bodies: he can send any of them to Siberia, but he cannot govern without them, or against their will. On every decree of his they have a tacit veto, by merely refraining from carrying it into effect" (quotation attributed to Gorbachev on his meeting with Soviet writers in June 1986).

It is in this context that democratization of the apparatus is intended to break up the control of these administrative elites and vested interests. Greater decentralization, an enhancement of the market's role, and a movement of decision making downward, as in *khozraschet*, noted previously, are economic devices that may be used to limit the power of the bureaucracy. In addition, we must consider other parts of the political

Table 3.1.
Major Institutions of Soviet Politics

A   Before 1990
THE COMMUNIST PARTY OF THE SOVIET UNION (CPSU)
  Function: To provide political leadership

THE LEGISLATURE — THE SOVIETS OF PEOPLE'S DEPUTIES (THE SOVIETS)
  Function: To enact laws

THE GOVERNMENT — (Until December 1990) THE COUNCIL OF MINISTERS
  Function: To execute laws and administer public affairs

B   From January to August 1991

THE PRESIDENCY
  Functions: To provide political leadership, enact and execute laws and administer public affairs

THE GOVERNMENT — THE CABINET OF MINISTERS (chaired by the President)
  Functions: To execute laws

THE LEGISLATURE — THE SOVIETS OF PEOPLE'S DEPUTIES (THE SOVIETS)
  Functions: To enact laws and to endorse the actions of the President and his Cabinet

THE COMMUNIST PARTY OF THE SOVIET UNION (CPSU) AND OTHER PARTIES AND ASSOCIATIONS
  Functions: To articulate and aggregate interests and to recruit leaders

---

system to evaluate whether the reform movement can succeed where the tsars failed. Before 1990, there were three major institutions of power in the contemporary Soviet Union (see Table 3.1.). The executive — the system of ministries and state committees — was discussed in chapter 2. Here we consider how the elected legislature or Soviets (the legislative part of Soviet government), the Communist Party of the Soviet Union, and the presidency have been reformed under perestroika.

Until 1990, according to the Constitution of the USSR, legitimate power was wielded by a system of parliaments, called Soviets, and this power was exercised in the presence of the Communist Party of the Soviet Union (CPSU) which was "the leading and guiding force of Soviet society and the nucleus of its political system, of all state and public organizations" (Article 6). In March and December 1990, important changes took place which amended this clause from the Constitution and recognized the rights of other groups to organize and campaign for office. The office of President responsible to the Supreme Soviet was created in March and significantly strengthened in December. This system had hardly begun to operate when the attempted coup occurred in August 1991. Following it, further changes were made which are discussed at the end of this chapter.

REPRESENTATIVE INSTITUTIONS: THE SOVIETS

Soviets have been elected at three main levels: (1) the Supreme Soviet of the USSR, headed by the President; (2) the Supreme Soviets of the Republics, 15 in all; and (3) the local Soviets, with over 50,000 separate units. The first level has been that of the USSR as a whole, or in Soviet terms, All-Union level, at which the Supreme Soviet of the USSR has been constituted; it is analogous to the Congress of the United States. Second, there have been fifteen Republican (e.g., Latvia, Ukraine) legislatures — called Union-Republics — that have their own Supreme Soviets. Third, there are Soviets that have been operating at the local level — for example, Soviets of the city of Leningrad, of the village of Kutuzov — and include over 2,000 city councils and over 50,000 village councils. Only the first two levels concern us here. Such bodies are elected and in turn elect organs that exercise authority over the executive, which was discussed in the previous chapter.

Under Stalin elements of the state bureaucracy — the ministries and committees, particularly the internal security organs, the KGB — became important sources of power. As integrated, professionally run organizations with powerful financial means and organizational facilities, they were virtually outside popular control, by either the Party or the popularly elected parliamentary organs, the Soviets. The reasons for this are complex.

The Soviets were ineffective because they were weak in personnel and had no independent financial means or powers. The deputies were part-time politicians with full-time jobs, and the Soviets met only for a few days on two occasions per year. Furthermore, signs of dissent by the deputies were regarded as weakening the consensus on which Soviet society was based. In a period of nation building under Stalin, any sign of division was considered to undermine the foundations of Soviet power. Rather than openness and public criticism, obedience and solidarity were required of deputies. Elections were important in reaffirming the allegiance of the people to Soviet power, rather than as articulating different political positions and criticism of the political leadership or of its policies.

The leadership under Gorbachev in the autumn of 1988 instituted a major reform of the system of Soviets, which is predicated on his much-uttered statement that the Soviets must be revitalized to act as the mainstay of the political system. The reform was based on the assumption that there is a pluralism of interests in Soviet society. The articulation of a plurality of views is the objective of the constitutional arrangements. Also, as many of the established political interests were responsible for the stagnation of the Brezhnev period, they are being brought to account and made responsible for their actions. Hence the ministerial apparatus — the executive arm of the government — has been undermined. The institution of law (the expression of the legislature) rather than political position (derived from position in the bureaucracy) is to be a governing principle of the Soviet order. The powers of the Soviets and their political authority will be enhanced if they are popularly elected.

The important constitutional point about the Soviets is that, at least in theory, they always have had the legitimate right to control the executive, and its various subdivisions. In practice, however, the Soviets have been very weak bodies and have not had the political clout to do so.

Between 1989 and 1990, Gorbachev strengthened the Soviets and also initiated the post (occupied by himself) of President. During this time, however, executive authority was exceedingly weakened and the USSR drifted towards anarchy and civil strife. John Stuart Mill's prognosis of the weakness of the tsars' power must have come home to President Gorbachev as effective government proved unattainable. In December 1990, the President's powers were dramatically strengthened. He instituted a Cabinet of Ministers under his leadership and abolished the Council of Ministers (of which he was not a member). (See Appendix to chapter 2 above.)

REFORM OF THE SOVIETS PRIOR TO THE COUP

The reforms operative since 1989 described here have attempted to give the Soviets more power over the executive arm of government. The electoral mechanism of the Supreme Soviet as constituted under Gorbachev is shown in Figure 3.1.

At the apex of the system of power is the presidency, introduced in 1990, which will be discussed at the end of this chapter. The President (Gorbachev) was elected directly by the Congress of People's Deputies, though in future elections, according to the Constitution, direct, universal and secret ballot will be the form of vote — as in the United States.

The Presidium of the USSR Supreme Soviet is an executive body of the Supreme Soviet. It is composed of leading members of the Supreme Soviet: the chairperson and first deputy chairperson of the Supreme Soviet, the chairperson of the Central Electoral Commission, and fifteen representatives of the Union Republics, who were chosen by assemblies of deputies from the republics and endorsed by the Congress of People's

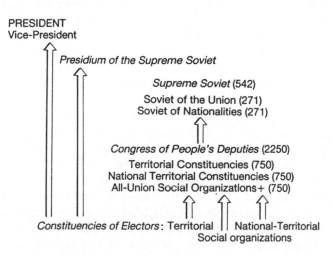

PRESIDENT
Vice-President

Presidium of the Supreme Soviet

Supreme Soviet (542)
Soviet of the Union (271)
Soviet of Nationalities (271)

Congress of People's Deputies (2250)
Territorial Constituencies (750)
National Territorial Constituencies (750)
All-Union Social Organizations+ (750)

Constituencies of Electors: Territorial || National-Territorial
Social organizations

+ This constituency has been abolished from 1990 and in subsequent elections to the USSR Congress will not operate. In the 1989 election it was constituted as follows:
All-Union social organizations: CPSU 100 deputies, USSR trade unions 100, Young Communist League 75, women's councils under the Soviet Women's Committee 75, war and labor veterans 75, associations of scientific employees (academy institutions, Society of inventors and rationalizers) 75, creative unions (Architects, Designers, Journalists, Cinematographers, Composers, Writers, Theatre Workers, Artists) 75, other legally constituted social organizations with all-unions status 75.

Figure 3.1 Supreme Legislative Bodies of the USSR

Deputies. In addition there are ex-officio members including the following: the chairpersons of the two houses of the Supreme Soviet (the Union and the Nationalities); fifteen deputy chairpersons of the USSR Supreme Soviet, who are chairpersons of the Union Republican Supreme Soviets; the chairperson of the USSR People's Control Commission; and the chairpersons of the permanent commissions of the committees of the Supreme Soviet.

The Supreme Soviet is the chief legislative body of the Soviet Union. It is elected by the Congress of People's Deputies, and has 542 members. The Supreme Soviet is composed of two chambers: the Soviet (sometimes called in English, the Council) of the Union and the Soviet of Nationalities. These are equal in number of members and equal in rights. The Supreme Soviet is elected by the members of the Congress of People's Deputies. A fifth of the members retires each year and their places are taken on the results of elections conducted in the Congress of People's Deputies.

The Soviet of the Union is elected "taking into account the number of voters in the Union Republic or region" (Constitution of the USSR, Article 111, see Appendix 1 for full details). The Soviet of Nationalities is "elected from among the USSR people's deputies from the national-territorial constituencies and the USSR people's deputies from the social organizations in accordance with the following norms: eleven from each union republic, four deputies from each autonomous republic, two deputies from each autonomous oblast, and one deputy from each autonomous okrug."

Like the Congress in the United States or Parliament in the United Kingdom, the Supreme Soviet is a body in continuous session; it passes the laws and acts as a monitoring body over the Cabinet of Ministers (the executive arm of government). The Supreme Soviet oversees the working of the government, within the confines of Soviet law. It appoints the chairperson of the Cabinet of Ministers, ratifies its composition or changes in it, approves the composition of the USSR Defense Council, ensures the legality of legislative regulations, and submits long-term plans to the Congress of People's Deputies. The Supreme Soviet can repeal decrees and resolutions of the Presidium of the USSR Supreme Soviet, orders of the chairperson of the Supreme Soviet and resolutions of the Cabinet, and it monitors the conduct of presidential power.

Commissions and Committees of the Supreme Soviet
Under the Supreme Soviet are fourteen committees of the Supreme Soviet and eight standing commissions of its two chambers. Like legislative committees in Western states, these deal with various details of legislation and aspects of public affairs. Some 800 members of the Congress of

People's Deputies sit on these commissions. Full members are selected from the deputies of the Supreme Soviet but others may participate as nonvoting members; they have a right to information and documentation.

The USSR Congress of People's Deputies is composed of 2,250 deputies. 750 are elected from electoral districts from territorial constituencies of an equal number of voters; 750 are from national-territorial constituencies (32 from each Union Republic, 11 from each autonomous republic, 5 from each autonomous *oblast*, and 1 from each autonomous *okrug*); 750 are from All-Union social organizations — the Communist Party, the Young Communist League, the trade unions, and other recognized groupings such as associations of veterans or women (see Figure 3.1). This body meets only twice per year to conduct elections of the Supreme Soviet and other bodies and to discuss "basic guidelines of USSR domestic and foreign policy" for the ratification of long-term state plans and programs and other business. This system of election follows that of the United States in that the representatives of territorial districts — like the House of Representatives — are elected according to population density, and the national-territorial constituencies arc chosen by geographical area (like the U.S. Senate). The election of the deputies to the All-Union social organizations has no parallel in the United States or Britain.

Just under one quarter (24 percent) of the deputies are elected to the Supreme Soviet. Deputies may stand for election to the chamber that is appropriate to the constituency from which they were originally elected. For example, a deputy elected in a national-territorial constituency can only be elected to the Soviet of Nationalities. However, deputies elected into the public organizations' constituencies may stand for election for either of the two chambers.

People's deputies not elected to the Supreme Soviet may serve on its commissions or committees with rights to vote. Such deputies are also able to participate in the sessions of the Supreme Soviet and have a right to documents and papers of the Supreme Soviet.

The reform of the Soviets reflects the pluralism of Soviet society. The constituency of social organizations leads to the direct representation of interest groups; the election of delegates is determined by the organization itself. In the 1989 elections for the Congress of People's Deputies, the Presidium of some organizations chose the delegates; others chose a number of candidates who subsequently were elected by the members of the organizations. The elections frequently are contested; this gives greater answerability on the part of deputies to their constituents.

The permanently staffed Supreme Soviet (and local Soviets) may strengthen their control over the executive. Members of the Cabinet may not hold a seat in the Supreme Soviet. (This policy does not exclude the holders of other posts in the Party, the Young Communist League, or trade unions from membership.)

The place of the Communist Party of the Soviet Union in the Supreme Soviet was secured through a procedure in which the relevant party secretary is "recommended for" and then wins the election for chairperson of the Soviet. This procedure occurs at all levels of the Soviets. In this way, the Party's general secretary (Gorbachev) became the head of state. The election for such posts will be contested. Moreover, the person elected must secure over 50 percent of the votes, so nomination does not guarantee election. The Party also has 100 members whom it directly elected in the Social Organizations constituency of the Congress of People's Deputies, and there are another 75 members allocated directly to the Young Communist League, or *Komsomol* (see Figure 3.1, note). This electoral procedure clearly favored the Party.

The Supreme Soviet in October 1989 deleted clauses from the constitution pertaining to the election of social constituencies. At future elections all deputies will be directly elected. The formation in 1989 and the legalization in 1990 of parties other than the Communist Party further weakened its authority. In contested elections held in the republics, Communists lost their seats and in many republics non-communist (and anti-communist) majorities were elected. We shall turn to this below.

THE ELECTORAL PROCESS

A major arena in which the policy of *demokratizatsiya* (democratization) is being effected is in the electoral process. In politics, elections are the market in operation; they bring into contact the suppliers of policies — the politicians — and those who consume them — the citizens. In Western states, elections are often regarded as the essence of democracy. In a pluralist society, any group may articulate its policy and stand for public office.

The context in which elections are held, of course, limits their effectiveness and the extent to which groups can canvass their policies and have a chance of winning. It is expensive to campaign, to stand for election, to organize the vote, and to communicate one's program. The electoral system often stipulates conditions for entering the electoral arena, and small parties lacking rich backers are often disadvantaged. Nevertheless, elections at least provide some form of political accountability for those with political office while they ensure that minor and major issues are subject to political debate.

Marxist-Leninists have always been dubious about, if not downright hostile to, the legitimacy of the electoral process as it operates under capitalism. Rather than a clash of fundamental political platforms, of debate in which the elector in casting a vote has political sovereignty, Marxists have stressed the social-economic context in which Party competition takes place, contending that parties represent classes which are the major foci of interest. Under capitalism, the exploited classes and under-privileged groups are at a severe disadvantage: the financial and ideological apparatus of the capitalistic state precludes such parties from presenting their position effectively. (In some cases, as in West Germany and in Northern Ireland, some opposition parties have been proscribed as unconstitutional.)

From this viewpoint, the electoral struggle in capitalist states is often between different factions of the ruling class that represent competing groups (large against small business, creditors and debtors, industry and agriculture, national versus international interests). Furthermore, electoral competition can only take place within the rules of the game, and parties seeking a revolutionary transformation are precluded or severely weakened by the state apparatus.

Given these assumptions about the political process, the leaders of the Communist Party of the Soviet Union have claimed a monopoly of political organization: competing parties have been banned. Parties, it was asserted, would undermine the unity of a socialist society; a competitive electoral process would ideologically weaken communism.

The reform leadership under Gorbachev has modified some of these assumptions. Rather than being the vehicle of socialism, the political leadership of Brezhnev had been a brake on the expression of interests and views and hampered the development of a socialist consciousness. Apathy and alienation have grown under this Soviet form of rule. In this context, democratization of a more pluralistic kind, which takes account of the multiple interests and views in socialist society, has been envisaged. The political institutions under democratization must allow for the expression of such interests.

> The main thing, comrades, is democratization. This is a decisive means of achieving the aims of perestroika. Democratization accords with the very essence of the Leninist concept of socialism. ... The entire party must have a clear understanding that only through democratization is it possible to involve the human factor to the full in the profound transformations of all aspects of society's life, in the real processes of management and self-management. Only through democratization and glasnost' can an end be put to the deep-rooted apathy and a powerful boost be given to the working people's sociopolitical activeness. Only through the committed and conscious participation of the working people themselves in all of society's affairs is it possible to realize socialism's humane goals. [Gorbachev, in a speech before the Central Party Plenum on Ideology, 18 February 1988]

In the absence of competing political parties in the past, it was thought that the deputies elected to serve on the Soviets should be in proportion to the social composition of the population in order to secure representation of different social groups in Soviet society. For this reason it was arranged that the constituent Soviets had certain proportions of women, manual workers, collective farmers, ethnic groups, and members of the Young Communist League. This is a system of representation by social characteristics. Choice of candidates would have disturbed the symmetry of this procedure. Hence, candidates were presented for election after careful evaluation by electoral commissions that were charged with the selection of candidates.

Candidates could not be elected unless they received at least 50 percent of the vote (some did not do so). Starting in 1987 experiments with multiple candidates were instigated in the local elections of that year (more than one candidate stood in about 1 percent of the constituencies); this was generalized in the electoral law of December 1988 and put into effect in the election of March 1989.

The Electoral Process Adopted from March 1989

The description that follows refers to the elections to the Parliament of the USSR. Electoral procedures for the republics are defined in their constitutions and differ in some respects. The law specified that nominations for election to the Soviets could be made by organizations or by electors at public meetings. In the territorial and national constituencies for the election to the Congress of People's Deputies in 1989, 7,500 people were nominated for 1,500 seats.

Nominees had to have programs and show evidence of support. (See the Reading at the end of this chapter for the Election Platform of Boris Eltsin, the victorious candidate in the Moscow national constituency, as it appeared in *Moskovskaya Pravda* on 21 March 1989.) Nominees must have the support of an institution or group (e.g., a Party, Komsomol, or trade union committee, or an association, such as the Soviet Peace Committee) as was the case before 1989. However, the new electoral law allows nominations from meetings of electors. Yet not all of those nominated in 1989 became candidates.

Electoral commissions were set up for each constituency, and they had the responsibility to ensure that the nominations were properly constituted and that frivolous applicants were rejected. Often nominees were unable to find a sufficient number of supporters to meet the legal requirements;

they had to achieve more than 50 percent of the registered electors attending a nomination meeting, which has a quorum if 500 voters attend. (For details, see Law on Election of People's Deputies.) Meetings were badly organized. Many prominent people, such as the editor of *Ogonek*, Vitaliy Korotich, fell foul of these requirements and did not succeed in becoming candidates at this stage. In total 2,850 candidates stood for election to 1,500 seats.

If more than two candidates are nominated, the electoral commission meets to discuss procedure and to see whether nominating organizations may be prepared to drop candidates or have them excluded by a vote of the nominating commission. The practice of the electoral commissions varied in the 1989 elections: in the Baltic republics very few nominations were excluded and ballot papers had from five to ten names. In other areas, such as the Ukraine and the Russian Republic, electoral commissions sometimes asked nominees to withdraw and only allowed one candidate to be registered. In some cases demonstrations followed the rejection of popular local candidates by the electoral commission. One of the major reasons advanced for renouncing candidates is that too many candidates could split the vote and would make the voting procedure complex — in some cases in 1989 there were over 20 nominees — and lead to an inconclusive result necessitating another election.

Registered candidates campaign for support. They are able to draw on staff provided by the election committee. The upshot of this phase of the election campaign in the March 1989 election to the Congress of People's Deputies was that in 399 territorial and national constituencies there was only one candidate (26.6 percent of the constituencies). In the social organizations constituency 871 candidates ran for 750 seats.

The social background of candidates differed considerably from the previous system of social selection. The number of women, young people, collective farmers, and manual workers offered for election fell. This is illustrated in the second column of Table 3.2, which shows the nominated and elected candidates in 1989 and only the latter in 1984 (see also Figure 3.2).

This tendency continued in the elections to the Supreme Soviet in 1989. Table 3.3 (see also Figure 3.3) compares the social composition of the 1984 Supreme Soviet with that of the 1989. Note the dramatic fall in the number of manual workers, collective farmers, and unskilled manual workers in contrast to the rise of professionals and lower management. The decline in the top and middle bureaucracy and management may be accounted for by the absence of government ministers, who are unable to participate in the activities of the legislature. Party functionaries and office holders in the Soviets are eligible for election.

Table 3.2
Social Background of Nominated Candidates and Elected Deputies in 1989, and Elected Deputies in 1984 (percentage of total)

	Elected 1984	Nominated 1989	Elected 1989
Women	32.8	15.8	17.1
Manual workers	35.2	23.7	18.6
Collective farmers	16.1	9.0	11.2
Party members	71.4	—	87.6

Table 3.3
Social Composition of USSR Supreme Soviet in 1984 and 1989 (in percentages)

	1984	1989	1989 (n)
Top leadership	1.5	0.2	1
Top/middle bureaucracy, management*	40	32.8	178
Lower-level management	6.6	35.3	191
Manual workers, collective farmers, unskilled nonmanuals	45.9	18.3	99
Professionals	6	12.5	68
Others	0	0.9	5
Total	100	100	542

Source: Izvestiya, 6 May 1989; *Moscow News*, 16 April 1989.
* Party leaders of republics, central committee members, government ministers (1984), leaders of Supreme Soviets in republics, military leaders, educational chiefs.

We noted above that in addition to the public elections for the two constituencies of the Congress of People's Deputies, a third curia included social organizations. In this case, the selection of candidates was left to the organization concerned. Here, however, only 871 candidates were registered for the 750 seats. The social background of the candidates was largely middle class and professional. Some three quarters of the candidates had higher education and one-third a degree and academic title.

The respective governing councils of the social constituencies selected the deputies and asked for endorsement from the membership (sometimes exclusively defined). In the case of the 100 seats allocated to the Communist Party of the Soviet Union, for example, an enlarged Central Committee (including first secretaries from Union Republics and regions and areas and second secretaries of central committees of Union Republics, chairpersons of the presidiums of the Supreme Soviet and Councils of ministers

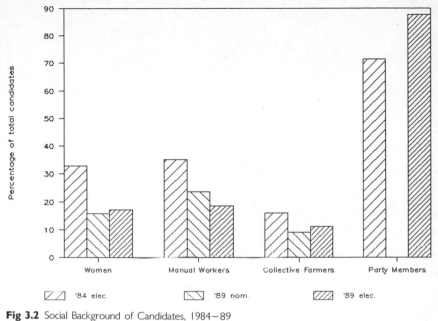

Fig 3.2 Social Background of Candidates, 1984—89

Source: Izvestiya, 6 May 1989; *Moscow News*, 16 April 1989.

of the Union Republics and ministers and leaders of central departments and organizations and commanders of military districts) voted on 100 candidates *chosen by the Politburo* from 312 nominations. These candidates included the Party elite.

This procedure precluded a possible embarrassing rebuff for unpopular members of the top leadership. Study of the voting, moreover, showed some dissent on the part of the members of the enlarged Central Committee. Out of a total of 641 votes cast, Gorbachev had 12 against, at the top of the negative votes was Party Secretary and Politburo member Ligachev with 78; the liberal member of the Politburo and Party Secretary, Yakovlev, followed with 59; and a number of prominent intellectuals were given the thumbs down (Ulyanov, chairman of the board of RSFSR [the Russian Republic] Theater Workers, had 47 against, and Abalkin, the director of the Institute of Economics of the USSR Academy of Sciences, 32 against). It seems likely that if a competitive vote had been held some leading heads may have rolled. Democratization was not only called for in the Soviets but also in the ruling Party. The procedures adopted by the Central Committee could be criticized on the grounds of being against the spirit of *demokratizatsiya*.

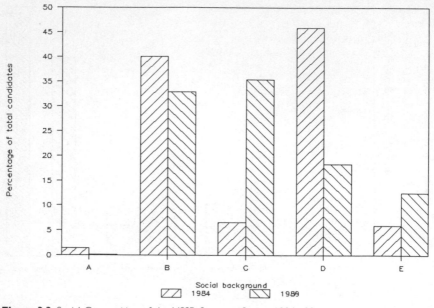

Figure 3.3 Social Composition of the USSR Supreme Soviet, 1984—89

Source: Izvestiya, 6 May 1989; *Moscow News*, 16 April 1989.
Key: A = Top Leadership; B = Top/Middle Bureaucracy and Management; C = Lower Level Management;
D = Manual Workers, Collective Farmers, and Unskilled Nonmanual Workers; E = Professionals.

In October 1989, at a meeting of the Supreme Soviet of the USSR, it was resolved that the form of election from social organizations be discontinued. In future elections all deputies will be elected directly by popular vote. Hence, the reader should bear in mind that in the republican and local government elections held between December 1989 and March 1990, all deputies were elected on the basis of territorial electoral constituencies. At the same meeting of the Supreme Soviet, it was decided to allow union and autonomous republics to determine whether or not their presidents should be elected by direct popular vote.

In the elections for the twenty-five seats allocated to the Academy of Sciences, an enlarged meeting of the Presidium, only eight of the candidates put before the 900 voting members of the Academy received the required 50 percent of the votes. A new round of elections had to take place in April 1989.

The results of the elections in the All-Union social organizations ensured that 732 people were elected at the first stage: only in five associations did 18 deputies not receive a sufficient number of votes.

In the elections for the territorial and nationalities constituencies in March 1989 voting ranged from 80 to 85 percent of the registered voters. At the first round of elections, out of the 2,250 seats in the Congress of People's Deputies, 1,958 were filled, leaving 292 vacancies — 18 in social organizations, mentioned above, 160 in territorial constituencies, and 114 in national-territorial ones.

Places were not filled because candidates did not receive sufficient votes. Even in constituencies with one candidate, the rule that an elected deputy had to receive more than 50 percent of the votes had a telling effect. In 168 constituencies where only one or two candidates were on the ballot a sufficient majority was not received; therefore, the full election procedure was held again, and candidates had to be renominated. In 68 constituencies where there were three or more candidates and the top one did not receive the necessary 50 percent, the two candidates that topped the poll could contest the election a second time.

There were some notable rejections: the Mayor of Moscow was defeated, as were First Party Secretaries in Kiev and Leningrad (the latter received only 15 percent of the vote); First Secretary of the Leningrad Oblast Party Committee and candidate member of the Politburo Yuri Solovev failed to retain his post (as a sole candidate he received only 44.8 percent of the vote). Deposed Politburo member and ex-Moscow Party chief Boris Eltsin was elected with a massive majority over the rival candidate who was sponsored by the Party committee (see also the discussion in chapter 9). In all forty Party functionaries of upper and middle rank were not elected. Some, but by no means all, of the defeated Party leaders were asked to resign their Party posts for failing to secure the public support — though this is not obligatory and practice varies depending on the circumstances and the persons involved. Decisions about defeated Party candidates are decided locally. For example, both Yuri Solovev, First Secretary of the Leningrad Oblast Party Committee, and Konstantin Masik, First Secretary of the Kiev City Party Committee, resigned following their failure to win their respective elections.

As noted previously, there were also important changes in the social composition of the elected personnel. The share of workers among the deputies fell from 35.2 percent to 18.6 percent; collective farmers received only 11.2 percent (compared with 16.1 percent; women had 17.1 percent of the seats (compared with 32.8 percent). (See Table 3.2 and Figure 3.2, which compare the membership of the deputies to the Supreme Soviet in 1984 with those of the Congress of People's Deputies in 1989.) In contrast, the number of deputies from the professional classes with higher education rose: the number of journalists increased from seven in the previous Supreme Soviet to sixty.

Another important change was that the representatives of government bodies (chiefs of ministries, state committees) declined because the law precluded their standing for office; the number of Party government and trade union officials on a republican and regional level increased. The number of Party members elected was 87.6 percent — which represents a rise in Party density from 71.4 percent in 1984.

Functions of the Congress of People's Deputies in the Electoral Process

The Congress of People's Deputies elects the USSR Supreme Soviet and its chairperson, the USSR Committee for Supervision of the Constitution. It ratifies the appointment of the Chairperson of the USSR Supreme Court, the USSR Procurator General and the USSR Supreme Arbitration Court and a number of other posts (see Article 108 of the Constitution, which appears in the Appendix).

In the March 1989 elections for the chairperson of the Supreme Soviet, three people were nominated: Gorbachev, Eltsin, and Obolensky (a delegate from Leningrad). Eltsin declined to stand for election, a decision that was put to the conference and accepted — fourteen people voting against and one abstaining. Obolensky had nominated himself so as to set a precedent for holding an election. His nomination did not go forward, however. A majority of the members of the Congress voted against his name being put on the ballot paper (voting was 1,415 against, 689 for, and 33 abstentions). Consequently, 2,123 deputies voted for Gorbachev and 87 against. As noted previously, it is Soviet practice for a vote to take place, even if only one candidate is nominated, but the nominee must win more than 50 percent of the votes.

In the elections to the Supreme Soviet, there was little voting on the floor of the Congress. Territorial delegations met before and during the Congress and drew up lists of candidates. For the Soviet of Nationalities, only one Republic (the RSFSR) had more candidates than seats (272 for 271 places). Eltsin had insisted on standing, though he had not found favor in the list of nominees. Although he was not elected, Eltsin did receive more than 50 percent of the votes, but he was at the bottom of the poll. It was pointed out that the six million electors of the Moscow area (an electorate larger than many of the national republics) had no representative in the Soviet of Nationalities. The upshot was that one of the elected members from the RSFSR (Kazannik, a lecturer from Omsk University) stood down on the condition that Eltsin take his place. When Kazannik withdrew his candidacy and it was accepted by the Congress, Eltsin was automatically elected as he had received more than 50 percent of the votes — and he did not have to submit to an election, which he might well have lost.

In the Soviet of the Union, areas returned lists of nominations that tallied with the number of seats within those areas. The exception was Moscow, where 55 candidates were nominated for 29 place. Here notable reformers were overwhelmingly defeated: Zaslavskaya, the prominent sociologist (591 votes for and 1,558 against); Gavril Popov, an economist and fervent advocate of Eltsin at the Congress (1,007 votes for and 1,131 against, a result accorded with applause).

Despite the defeat of some notable reformers, this electoral process provided an opportunity for candidates with a wider spectrum of views to be elected than previously, and some were not approved by the Party apparatus. After these elections, further developments involved the growth of competing parties and defeats for the CPSU; a plurality of views led to a plurality of political associations — embryo political parties. Before considering these processes, we examine how reform affected the evolving role of the Soviet Party itself.

THE COMMUNIST PARTY

One of the traditional characteristics of modern communist states was that they were led by a Communist Party organized along Leninist lines. Such parties were of a new type. Unlike Western democratic parties, which work in the context of a multiparty political system and whose main function is to contest for the privilege of controlling the government, Marxist-Leninist parties in communist states consider themselves to be class parties. They are the political arm of the working class, its vanguard. Marxist-Leninist parties were set up to achieve the overthrow of capitalism and to rule on behalf of the working class. It is important to grasp the fact that traditionally Soviet communists have legitimated the monopoly of political organization by the Communist Party in class terms. Political parties were considered to be the expression of classes: as the Soviet Union is a unitary class society having only a working class, other political parties were not legitimate — their existence would undermine the foundation of the social order.

To further the vanguard role of the Communist Party, a unique type of organizational structure has been devised: democratic centralism. This involved the election of bodies from the bottom up and control from the top down. Marxist-Leninist parties are disciplined parties: members are obliged to follow the Party line and to support it. As parties that have carried out a revolution, they are centralized and factions are banned; consensus rather than conflict and dissent is favored. Such accord should be achieved by democratic discussion and debate, with rights to all members to participate and air their views. There has always been a tension between the democratic and the centralist elements in this doctrine. Under Stalin, centralism became dominant.

At the Nineteenth Party Conference, Gorbachev complained that democratic centralism had been "largely replaced by bureaucratic centralism." Gorbachev emphasized a more pluralistic approach.

> Under the one-party system that historically came about and became established in our country, we need a constantly operating mechanism for the comparison of views and for criticism and self-criticism in the Party and in society in conditions of growing democratization ... This is how the essence of inner-Party democracy was understood by V. I. Lenin ... who was resolutely opposed to the persecution of Party comrades for thinking differently. (Gorbachev, Nineteenth Party Conference, 29 July 1988)

Unlike in the past when executive officers of the Party were selected by the Party apparatus and put before the membership for approval, Gorbachev advocated (1) nomination of more candidates than offices and (2) secret-ballot elections. Officials should be subject to election on their merits and in appropriate circumstances had to be ratified through elections (as described earlier) instead of (as previously) through appointment by higher bodies. As in the elections to the Soviets, the principle of social representation — percentages of women, youth, and manual workers — that determined the composition of new members has been abolished. Leading officials, including the general and first secretaries, are limited to two five-year periods of office.

The earlier ideas of Gorbachev were to enhance the authority of the Party and to use the Soviets as conduits through which Party policy would be channelled. As Gorbachev put it when discussing the "improvements in the organization of power" at the Nineteenth Party Conference, "The Party's policies — economic, social, nationalities — should be conducted above all through the Soviets of People's Deputies as the agencies of people's rule."

A major function of the Party has been to provide political leadership in it widest sense. It traditionally sought not only to guide but to monopolize the direction of political change. In 1988, Gorbachev still believed that the Party should maintain its supremacy and leadership; it should retain its traditional role of defining the values of society and stipulating the legitimate relationship between individuals and property. Gorbachev wanted to establish a more authoritative and responsive form of Party rule. The intention of the reform leadership was to maintain and even enhance the authority of the Communist Party within a new, more democratic framework of public responsibility. A "plurality of views" could flourish in a one-Party state.

As the editor of *Pravda* in June 1988 has put it: "We have to understand once and for all that in a socialist society there are no political grounds, no social reasons, for the creation of a new, different political party, still less for the creation of some kind of body of control above the party."

At the Nineteenth Party Conference Gorbachev explicitly ruled out a multi-party system and the creation of "opposition parties".

> [R]ecently we have several times encountered attempts to use democratic rights for antidemocratic purposes. Some people believe that all questions can be resolved in this way — from redrawing boundaries to creating opposition parties. The CPSU Central Committee believes that such abuses of democratization are fundamentally at variance with the aims of restructuring and are contrary to the interests of the people [Prolonged applause].

Gorbachev and other progressive Party leaders had already conceded that the constitutional role of the Party had to change. An article in *Kommunist*, the theoretical journal of the CPSU, in 1989 had argued for a revision of Article 6 taking account of the constitution of a democratic state. The "political fate" of the Party would be decided by the people through elections.

Political pressures on Gorbachev (particularly the de facto rise of parties in the Baltic and elsewhere), moreover, were decisive in persuading him to recognize that the traditional form of Party authority could not endure. At the February 1990 plenum, the Party agreed to relinquish its de jure monopoly of political organization. Following discussion at the Congress of People's Deputies and the Supreme Soviet of the USSR, clause 6 of the Constitution of the USSR was amended to:

> The Communist Party of the Soviet Union and other political parties, as well as trade union, youth and other social organizations and mass movements, participate in the formulation of the policy of the Soviet state and in the administration of state and social affairs through their representatives elected to the Soviets of people's deputies and in other ways.

In the early 1990s, the leadership of the Party under Gorbachev moved decisively away from its traditional organizational and ideological stance. In the statement of the Party's program adopted at the Twenty-eighth

Congress in 1990, only the "legacy of Marx, Engels and Lenin freed from dogmatic interpretation" was recognized. (This is the only reference to these thinkers in the Program Statement which is appended at the end of the chapter.) Little of the traditional essence of Marxism—Leninism has been preserved. The organizational form associated with Soviet-type societies has been abandoned: "The CPSU resolutely rejects democratic centralism as it evolved in conditions of the administrative-command system and rigid centralization and defends democratic principles — electability and interchangeability, glasnost' and accountability, sub-ordination of the minority to the majority and a minority's right to uphold its views, including the party mass media organs." However, the concept has not been completely overthrown. Article 6 of the Party rules ratified at the same congress states: "The CPSU lives and operates on the basis of ideological community and Party comradeship, of the principle of democratic centralism which ensures self-management in party life, the combination of the interests of the Party and individual communists and the power of the Party masses with conscious discipline."

The Party's definition of itself is social-democratic. Its Program Statement, adopted at the Twenty-eighth Party Congress in 1990, was subtitled: "Towards a Humane, Democratic Socialism". The following extract from this document epitomizes its outlook:

> The CPSU is a Party with a socialist option and a communist outlook. We regard this prospect as the natural, historical thrust of the development of civilization. Its social ideal absorbs the humanist principles of human culture, the age-old striving for a better life and social justice.
>
> In our understanding humane, democratic socialism means a society in which:
> humankind is the aim of social development;
> living and working conditions for people are worthy of contemporary civilization;
> man's alienation from political power and the material and spiritual values created by him are overcome and his active involvement in social processes is assured;
> the transformation of working people into the masters of production, the strong motivation of highly productive labor, and the best conditions for the progress of production forces and the rational use of nature are ensured on the basis of diverse forms of ownership and economic management;
> social justice and the social protection of working people are guaranteed — the sovereign will of the people is the sole source of power;
> the state, which is subordinate to society, guarantees the protection of the rights, freedoms, honor and dignity of people regardless of social position, sex, age, national affiliation or religion;
> there is free competition and cooperation between all socio-political forces

operating within the framework of the law. This is a society which consistently advocates peaceful and equitable cooperation among the peoples and respect for the rights of every people to determine their own fate.

Political Recruitment

Like Western political parties, the CPSU has had a crucial role in the allocation of personnel to leading positions. As there has been no private enterprise, it has exerted influence over the selection of staff to fill positions in the government apparatus. It has done this through a system know as the *nomenklatura* — a list of appointments which have to be vetted by the Party. The Party also has had oversight over the affairs of state: a parallel organization of Party committees and groups have been set up to exercise tutelage over executive government bodies. In the past, moreover, the Party apparatus had become intertwined with the apparatus of the government. Rather than being an agent of the people, it has been an instrument of the apparatus.

Gorbachev attempted to revitalize the process of selection and renewal of officials. The principle of glasnost' was to make officials directly responsible to the public. His earlier intentions were to maintain Party hegemony though public approval of nominations. After March 1990, Gorbachev was elected President and he retained his position as General Secretary of the Party. This principle was followed at other levels as well. Appropriate Party chiefs (first secretaries) should be recommended chairpersons of the legislative bodies (that is, Soviets in the republics and in local government).

> While heading the Soviet and their presidiums, they will very vigorously promote the improvement of all aspects of the activity of the bodies of popular representation. ... If the first secretary of a Party committee is elected chairperson of a Soviet, this will raise the Soviet's prestige, enhance monitoring over the activity of the executive committee and its chairperson ... On the other hand, comrades, the recommendations of Party leaders for posts as chairpersons of Soviets will put them under more effective monitoring by the working people, since elections at the sessions will be held by secret ballot. ... Of course, there may be instances in which the recommended candidacy of a Party secretary is not supported by deputies. Then, naturally, both the Party committee and the Communists will have to draw the appropriate conclusions. (Gorbachev, Report to Nineteenth Party Congress 28 June 1988)

The sting in the last sentence was to have far greater effect than Gorbachev had anticipated. The elections of March 1989 to the Supreme

Soviet led to many Party officials being defeated. They fell to other candidates or failed to receive the requisite number of votes. Their non-election was considered a vote of non-confidence: some were asked to resign from their posts.

Such non-elections gathered momentum later in 1989 and 1990. Rather than the electoral process being concerned with the legitimacy of individual communists, the Party leadership itself was to become the subject of appraisal. Before turning to this phenomenon, to complete our description of the Party we may consider its structural forms.

The Structure of the Communist Party of the USSR

The Party structure may be considered in two parts: the Party membership and its mass activity, and the Party *apparat*, or administration. A simplified version of the Party's structure is shown in Figure 3.4. This is divided into three streams: the executive (the Party's administrative arm, or *apparat*); its policy-making bodies; and its representative or deliberative bodies. On the right-hand side of the figure is the deliberative institution that consists of the representative bodies of the Party. These are composed of rank-and-file Party members (though they include Party officials). Within the units, the day-to-day activity of the Party is pursued, and at the higher reaches, Party policy is decided.

At the bottom right of the figure, are the basic units or branches of the Party: there were nearly 442,000 of these with a total of 19.4 million members in 1989. The branches elect members to the town, district, or rural conferences in the locality; these conferences in turn elect executive committees that oversee local government organs. This procedure continues up to the republican levels, execpt in the Russian Republic (RSFSR), where there is no republican Party organization. The apex of the Party, the Central Committee, is a crucial body. These deliberative bodies have not been effective bodies for the working out of decisions, for they are often large and unwieldy and meet infrequently.

Various subcommittees and bureaus are set up and are shown in the middle of Figure 3.4. The most important of these is the Politburo elected by the Central Committee. There are Politburos in all the republics including the Russian Republic (RSFSR), which, however, has only had its own Party organization (the Russian Communist Party) since June 1990.

Before Gorbachev's reforms of 1990, the Politburo was composed of around a dozen members, and it operated rather like the cabinet in British politics. It was the top policy-making body of the Soviet Union. It must be pointed out that there is an important difference here compared

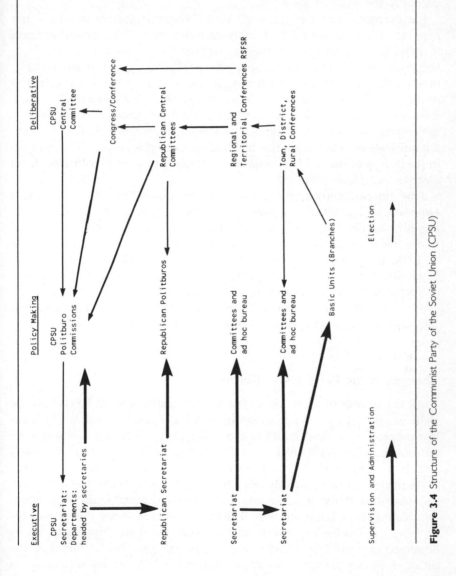

Figure 3.4 Structure of the Communist Party of the Soviet Union (CPSU)

to the structure of politics in Western states: the chief political body has been a *Party* institution, not a government one. Members of the Politburo were the chief government ministers and the leading people in the Parliament. As mentioned earlier, its chief (the General Secretary) is still currently the head of state.

Furthermore, the Party has its own executive apparatus: the Party *apparat*. It is a series of departments each dealing with aspects of political activity. It is serviced by a full-time staff (hence the term *apparatchiks* — those who work in the apparatus). The executive apparatus has complemented the state structure by having departments for the major activities of the government. The departments change over time, and in 1989 there were nine: Party work and personnel, ideology, socioeconomic policy, agriculture, defense, government and legal, international, general, and administration. The secretariat has had tremendous power; its personnel or cadres department has been responsible for placing officials in all elective and Party posts.

This system, known as the *nomenklatura*, has been modified under Gorbachev. The process of *samoupravlenie* (self-government) has led to organizations making their own appointments. We have noted too the way that popular elections act as a check on this procedure. Since the autumn of 1988, six policy commissions have been subordinated to the Central Committee: Party issues and personnel, ideology, social and economic policy, agriculture, international policy, and legal problems. These bodies contain people who are not full-time Party officials. It is intended that they will play a greater role in the formation of policy.

Changes in the Party under Gorbachev

Until the advent of Gorbachev, Party organizations at all levels had the right to control the organizations in which they were located. Such organizations, for their part, often found the Party to be a useful source of patronage: it provided links with other higher bodies, and the local Party secretary could often be relied on to help to secure resources.

As the reader may have already inferred, the complexity and overlap of organizations (Party, government, Soviets) has led to ambiguity, indecision, and confusion in administration. The system also requires a large number of officials. Gorbachev has tried to divest the Party apparatus of its administrative role in industry and in government. As he put it at the meeting of the Supreme Soviet in November 1988 in his discussion of constitutional reform:

A clear-cut separation of functions of the Party and local government bodies is essential precisely for both the Party and the Soviets to be able to perform their role effectively in the political system. . . . Measures have been elaborated and began to be implemented to stop the duplication of state functions by Party organizations at all levels up to the discharge of the functions of political leadership.

Changes are apparent in the composition of the Central Committee, with a declining proportion of leaders from the Party *apparat*: their share has fallen from 43.6 percent in 1981 to 33.9 percent in 1989, and a smaller reduction occurred for government officials. Membership of the Central Committee has widened considerably with greater representation of the diplomatic corps, the intelligentsia, mass organizations, and rank-and-file workers (see Figure 3.5).

The position of the top leadership has also been significantly altered. At the Twenty-eighth Conference of the Party in July 1990 many important

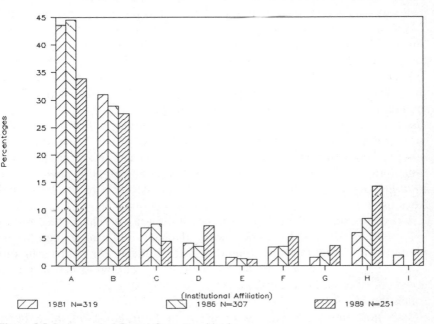

Figure 3.5 Background of Central Committee Members

Source: Based on data from Teague, 1989, p.4.
Key: A = Party Apparatus; B = State and Government Apparatus; C = Military; D = Diplomacy; E = KGB; F = Scientific and Cultural Elite; G = Mass Organizations; H = Workers and Peasants; I = Others.

changes were made. The Politburo has been significantly downgraded and is no longer a major determinant of state policy. It does not include the leading personnel of government, but includes the fifteen first secretaries of all the Republican Parties, the Secretary of the Moscow City Committee, the Chairman of the All-Union Central Council of Trade Unions (Gennadi Yanaev, who later in 1990 became Vice-President) and the editors of *Pravda* (the Party newspaper) and *Krestyanka* (a paper concerned with women in the countryside), the latter giving the first female member since Furtseva left in 1961. The Politburo does not include the chief members of the Cabinet of Ministers and legislative bodies of the Soviets. Before Gorbachev, the Politburo met weekly and provided the political leadership for the country; in its new form it meets only monthly. It is more an advisory body like the executive committees of ruling parties in Western societies. The authority of the President is derived from the Supreme Soviet and the Congress of People's Deputies.

The General Secretary of the Party is elected directly by the Party Congress, not — as in the past — by the Central Committee. In 1990 the post was contested: Gorbachev was elected, receiving 3,411 votes against 1,116 cast for his opponent. Direct election strengthens the General Secretary's position against any threatened coup by the Central Committee (as happened under Khrushchev). The position of General Secretary is less powerful than hitherto. From 1990, the position of President is the supreme post: he has his own advisers, independent of the Party apparatus — again shifting power away from the Party apparatus. (See discussion of the presidency, below.) However, the political base of the present President (Gorbachev) remains in the Party. This brings the Party more in line with Western parliamentary-type parties, which perform the function of political recruitment. The General Secretary is now assisted by a Deputy who performs the routine administration of the Party and frees the top person for state political roles.

The composition of the Central Committee was also changed considerably in 1990. Here 412 members were elected — 112 more than for its predecessor — and these no longer include all the major political figures from the government and legislature. The Party secretariat has also been downgraded to an organization concerned with Party matters, rather than ruling the country.

The most important change occurred in February 1990, at a Party plenum when its de jure monopoly of political power was relinquished. The leadership called for "a political dialogue and cooperation with everyone who favours the renewal of socialist society". In practice the Party leadership recognized the rights of other associations, groups and *parties* to formulate alternative policies. Within the Party, factions have arisen and the previous monolithic unity has disintegrated. Moreover, formulating policies in the context of democratization called for putting them into operation. From 1990, the Party lost its own self-legitimacy over its monopoly of political power.

The Communist Party was hailed by Lenin as one of "a new type". It was the vanguard of the working class. Its ideology, practices and personnel have ruled and have been defining characteristics of communist states. Gorbachev's policies have changed the way that the vanguard operates and considerably reduced its functions. The *apparat* of the Party no longer determines policy; central control has been displaced by a heterogeneous number of groups and interests within the Party, many of which, after 1990, have broken away from it and have formed independent parties. The Communist Party of the Soviet Union has lost its prime de jure position: presidential power is influenced by other groups and parties and the powers of the President are legitimated by the legislature (the Supreme Soviet of the USSR). Marxism−Leninism as it had developed from Stalin to Brezhnev provided a political spine through Soviet society. Under Gorbachev, it seeks to provide a vanguard role in quite a different way. Gorbachev, in November 1990, when addressing a Moscow Party Conference reiterated the Party's role:

> Our role is a vanguard one, and I shall not renounce it, and I shall never agree with the other concept that we should be a parliamentary party, a party of some kind of political club. ... [W]e should remain a serious party, we now occupy a ruling position and we should do everything to ensure that this position is preserved, and that we use this in the interests of moving the country within the framework of a socialist choice to new horizons.

Prior to the coup attempt of August 1991, the Communist Party, was still an important force: it remained a well-organized political party spanning the whole of the USSR, it had a large membership and had at its command a range of personnel and material resources which outstripped those of other parties and groups. It maintained an important role in political recruitment. The major leaders of the USSR have evolved within and owed allegiance to CPSU. (The position in the republics is somewhat different.)

THE PRESIDENCY OF THE USSR

The decline of the Communist Party of the Soviet Union as the "nucleus of the Soviet political system" has left a vacuum in that system. The

Communist Party lost its constitutional right to a monopoly of power and a presidential system was created. This had been discussed for some time in the Soviet press. Fedor Burlatski, for instance, in *Literaturnaya gazeta* in June 1988, had advocated the election of a President in a direct country-wide secret ballot:

> Experience has demonstrated that the mechanism whereby the leader of the country is elected by the Politburo of the CPSU has serious shortcomings. Otherwise it is impossible to explain how leaders like L. I. Brezhnev and K. U. Chernenko could have found themselves at the head of our great power in a most difficult period of world history.

In keeping with the philosophy of pluralism and democratization, the presidency would encourage the development of civil society, and could make the head of state more publicly accountable to the Supreme Soviet. As Burlatski suggested, a popularly elected President (as in the United States) would enhance his (or her) authority. More pressing reasons in the spring of 1990 were to be found in the political problems facing Gorbachev as the leader of the movement for reform. The economy was failing and opposition to marketization was strong. Gorbachev's power base was in the Party. As we noted above, his election to the Congress of People's Deputies was a result of direct Party nomination. While the CPSU had been severely weakened under the reform program it still had considerable influence and a sizeable organization. It could organize against Gorbachev (as it had done against Khrushchev) and oust him and replace him with a person more inclined to the traditional system. A formal position of President would strengthen his hand and it would enhance his powers to act over the bureaucracy — in both the state and Party apparatuses.

More immediate issues were the trend to anarchy and ungovernability in the country. As the First Secretary of the Leningrad district Party Committee put it in *Pravda* on 7 February 1990.

> The destabilization of the situation in the political and economic sphere is increasing every day. ... There are many reasons for this, but the most important is that the mechanism of executive power has broken down completely. The governability of the state is rapidly declining. The ministries are in a state of utter paralysis. The present local Soviets do not yet possess the necessary competence or authoritative powers, either legally or in practice. At the same time a systematic process of distancing the Party from the leadership is taking place.

Changes made to the Constitution of the USSR in March 1990 formalized the position of President, who is secretly elected on the basis of universal franchise. This is for a period of five years and may be extended by election for a second period (see Article 127 of the Constitution reprinted in the Appendix below). However, direct election was not carried out in 1990, owing to the urgency of political reform, and in March Gorbachev was formally elected President by the Congress of People's Deputies of the USSR: he received 1,329 votes (59.06 percent of the total possible vote); 495 voted against and the remainder either did not vote or were absent. Gorbachev still remained as General Secretary of the CPSU — a post he retained after his election by the Twenty-eighth Conference of the CPSU.

The President's powers include the right to declare and conduct war. He can impose martial law or declare a state of emergency in parts of the USSR. He may issue decrees (bypassing the Supreme Soviet) within the law and he may veto laws of the Supreme Soviet. However, the President's powers are curbed: he cannot remove the Chairperson of the Supreme Court; to declare a state of emergency in a republic the President must have the consent of the republic concerned or if not receive a two-thirds majority support of the members of the USSR Supreme Soviet; any Supreme Soviet legislation vetoed by the President may be upheld by a further two-thirds majority of its members.

In March 1990, two presidential consultative bodies were also set up — the Federation Council and the Presidential Council — thought the latter was to be short-lived. The President's powers were strengthened even more between March 1990 and January 1991. In September 1990, the Supreme Soviet gave the President the power to issue decrees on the financial system, the maintenance of law and order, property rights, prices and the budget. The major restraint is that the decrees have to be within the law of the USSR. Oversight is carried out here by the USSR Committee for Supervision of the Constitution. The President is not outside the law. In September, the Committee declared unconstitutional Gorbachev's decree removing the right to allow rallies in central Moscow from the city Soviet and giving it to the government. In February 1991, it considered the legality of Gorbachev's decree authorizing joint patrols of police and army. It seems unlikely that it will intervene effectively in the control of presidential power.

In December 1990, the Presidential Council and the Council of Ministers were abolished and three bodies coming under the control of the President were constituted. Rather than being consultative bodies, these have executive powers. They are the Federation Council (already formed in the spring), the USSR Cabinet of Ministers, and the Security Council. In addition, the post of Vice-President was created (see Figure 3.6). As noted above, the current President (Gorbachev) remains the chief

PRESIDENT (Assisted by Vice-President)

USSR Cabinet of Ministers	Federation Council	Security Council
	CHAIRED BY	
The President	The President	The President
	COMPOSITION	
Prime Minister plus 62 leading Ministers and other top officials	Top state officials from republics and other important federal units (including Presidents)	Chiefs of Defense Internal and Foreign Affairs KGB
	MAJOR FUNCTIONS	
Control over economy	Control over republics and federal units	Control over forces of coercion

Figure 3.6 Presidential Power before the Coup of August 1991

executive of the Communist Party of the Soviet Union and presides over its Politburo.

The reasons for the greater power accruing to the President have been spelled out by Gorbachev in his opening speech to the USSR Congress of People's Deputies in December 1990:

> The current situation in the country is a difficult one. Processes of crisis are continuing to build up for the time being in the economy, in the social and political spheres and especially in inter-ethnic relations. Stability and order have been undermined. ...
>
> There is great alarm in society both about today and the future. Dissatisfaction is increasing with the way the central, republican and local bodies of authority, especially the bodies of executive authority, are functioning in this situation. ...
>
> Comrades, the most essential thing now is to overcome the crisis, is to restore order to the country. This boils down to the matter of power. If there is firm power, discipline, control over the implementation of decisions, then we will be able to get a normal supply of foodstuffs going, to curb criminals and to stop inter-ethnic hostility. ...
>
> I mean a power functioning on the basis of law and capable of ensuring stability and civic peace and of overcoming the crisis situation, within the framework of legality. ...

I see the tasks of presidential power in defending citizens' rights, the honor and dignity of every person, the normal functioning of the constitutional system and state institutions. It is precisely for the sake of these objectives that strong executive power is needed at all levels, from the head of state down to the executive committees in town and country.

The powers of the three presidential committees are comprehensive and through them the President intends to implement his decrees. The Federation Council, composed of the chief state officials (Presidents) from the Republics (and on occasion other federal units), is mainly concerned with activities of an All-Union nature and with policies concerning preservation of the federation. Its aim is to strengthen interaction between the constituent parts of the Soviet Union and to act as a legitimate force to provide cohesion in the interest of the whole of the union.

The USSR Cabinet of Ministers replaces the Council of Ministers of the USSR. Its meetings are chaired by the President who selects it. In February 1991 it was reported that the cabinet had 55 members (including a Prime Minister): with seven other full members to be appointed. It is responsible to the President and to the Supreme Soviet which by vote ratifies its composition. The objective here is for the President to use the leading officials of the executive to carry out his economic policy. Its remit comprehensively covers the activities of the government of the USSR: financial policy, currency, budget, All-Union economic programs, developmental funds and catastrophes; food, health, education, research, foreign policy, foreign economic activity of the republics, protection of property and the rights and freedoms of citizens.

The Security Council is chaired by the President. It is responsible for defense, the maintenance of stability and order in society. It includes economic and ecological security, dealing with the consequences of natural disasters. Its members include the ministers of defense, internal and foreign affairs, and the chief of the KGB (State security). Its major objective is to enforce All-Union laws against defiant republics and local Soviets. It will enforce the laws of the Union when they are in conflict with other laws.

These developments have put the President in a dominant position. Since 1990, he has been aided by a Vice-President to whom he may delegate his powers. (The Vice-President is nominated by the President and ratified by the Congress of People's Deputies.) Following the changes enacted in December 1990, the President has had under his command the chief executives who legally should carry out his decrees. Also, it should not be forgotten, he has continued to hold the senior position (General Secretary) in the CPSU, which, despite its decline since the introduction of perestroika, was until August 1991 the single most powerful political force in the USSR. The President has the legitimate right to declare a state of emergency in any part of the USSR and to rule there directly. The major restraint on presidential power is that it has to operate within the laws of the USSR. Effectively, the President has wrested power from the secretariat of the Communist Party of the USSR and the Supreme Soviet of the USSR. This has led to widely voiced accusations that he has been usurping power and that the situation has the makings of a dictatorship.

The governance of the Soviet Union has undergone a major transformation: from Lenin to Brezhnev it was a Partocracy; in the period of perestroika it has moved through a quasi-parliamentary system to a presidency. Even more remarkable has been the context in which the government and political leaders have operated. Independent political movements and groups have appeared on the political scene and not only contend for power but confront the political leadership. These developments are indications of the development of a civil society, which will be the topic of the next chapter.

THE COUP OF AUGUST 1991 AND ITS REPERCUSSIONS

On 19 August 1991, the developments we have described were brought to a sudden halt. The following statement was broadcast:

> In view of Mikhail Sergeevich Gorbachev's inability, for health reasons, to perform the duties of the USSR President and of the transfer of the USSR President's power ... to the USSR Vice-President, Gennady Ivanovich Yanaev, ... we resolve: 1. to adopt the most decisive measures to prevent society from sliding into national catastrophe and ensure law and order, to declare a state of emergency in some parts of the Soviet Union for six months from 0400 Moscow time on 19 August; 2. to establish that the constitution of the USSR has unconditional priority throughout the territory of the USSR; [and] 3. to form a State Committee for the State of Emergency [SCSE] in the USSR to run the country and effectively exercise the state-of-emergency regime.

The declaration was signed by six leading government statesmen: none had a position in the Party apparatus. Formally, they were the most powerful men in the USSR: the vice-president of the USSR, the Prime Minister, the chief of the KGB, the Interior Minister, the chief of the Military-Industrial complex, the head of the Food industries and the president of the association of state industries. (The vice-president, Yanaev, had been in the Politburo when elected, but later resigned.)

It subsequently transpired that Gorbachev was placed under house arrest. The political objective of the plotters was to ban the opposition and to govern the society along more traditional lines. Only approved newspapers were allowed to be published and the Committee took control of the media. Tanks patrolled the streets of Moscow. Presidential power and democratic processes were suspended. Mill's prognosis had rebounded on Gorbachev with a vengeance. The men he had only months previously selected to carry out his policy were against him. Further, it was reported that his Cabinet of Ministers had also supported the state of emergency.

The main opposition to the coup was master-minded by Boris Eltsin, the President of the Russian Republic. He ordered that all members of the Internal Affairs Ministry, the Committee of State Security (KGB) and the Defence Ministry should obey the orders of the RSFSR President (himself) and RSFSR institutions. By an irony of history, Eltsin, who had been excluded from the Politburo by Gorbachev and had become one of his major critics, now found himself defending the Constitution and the legitimacy of Presidential power.

The leaders of the coup were unable to assert their power against Eltsin whose supporters took over the RSFSR government buildings in Moscow. Eltsin had substantial popular support and the new leadership was unwilling or unable to take punitive measures to crush popular opposition. After three days the leaders gave up. Gorbachev was returned from his house arrest. The coup leaders were arrested and charged with treason.

But now the political situation had changed. Eltsin was widely regarded as the saviour of the Constitution. Gorbachev was significantly weakened politically. His chosen government and right hand man, Yanaev, had opposed him. While the conspirators were not Party functionaries, they were senior Party members. The Party's Politburo had not lead popular opposition to the illegal detention of the General-Secretary. This (rightly or wrongly) implicated the Party in the plot. The "conservatives" (those wanting to preserve elements of the traditional system) emerged from the plot disgraced and discredited. On the other hand, the reformers had gained the initiative psychologically, morally and politically. Not only had they defeated an illegal coup, but in doing so had received acclaim and recognition from the Western states.

Thus fortified. Eltsin took the initiative. He demanded and achieved significant political changes. These were all calculated to shift the balance of power away from the government of the USSR to the Republics. The following are the major changes:

1. The Communist Party was destatized. The formation of groups in government organizations (such as the security and armed forces) was banned. For the part it played in the coup it was made un-

constitutional in the Russian and some other Republics. Gorbachev resigned as General-Secretary. Effectively the Party was destroyed as an organized force. Party offices were closed, its property was seized, and its members left in droves. Gorbachev lost his political base.

2. The power of the republics was enhanced. Eltsin's Russian Republic, and later Gorbachev on behalf of the USSR, recognized the independence of the Baltic states. All republics made declarations of sovereignty and declared their independence.

3. Presidential power was weakened. Property of the All-Union ministries on Russian soil was nationalized by a decree by Eltsin during the state of emergency and subsequently condoned by Gorbachev.

4. The power of the All-Union government was broken. For their support of the coup, all the members of the Cabinet of Ministers were dismissed by Gorbachev and a new structure of government was devised (see above chapter 2).

5. Radical reform was now a major goal of the government and institutions were set up to achieve a rapid move to a market economy.

6. The final nails were buried in the coffin of the command economy and Party hegemony. Symbolically, the public symbols of the revolution were repudiated. Statues of Lenin and other leaders were pulled down, the Lenin Museum was closed and Leningrad reverted in name to St Petersburgh.

7. At the subsequent Congress of People's Deputies, the form of state changed significantly, the Union of Soviet Socialist Republics was superseded by a Union of Sovereign States. These events signalled a major break with the past of the USSR and its revolutionary legacy.

We noted above that the political developments under perestroika had led to instability which Gorbachev had sought to control through his assumption of Presidential power. However, the aftermath of the coup led to further instability and to the lack of an effective political power.

An extraordinary Congress of the Council of People's Deputies was convened and abolished itself. As a transitionary measure, before the signing of a Union treaty (see below chapter 6), a new constellation of state forces was hurriedly assembled. The control of the economy has been outlined above in chapter 2. The legislative organs are shown in Figure 3.7.

The Soviet of Republics is composed of 20 deputies from each Union Republic delegated by the Supreme Soviet of the Republic. An exception is made for the Russian Republic which has 52 deputies to reflect its size. The Soviet of the Union consists of groups of deputies from the republics

Supreme Soviet:

	Composition:	Functions:
1. Council of Republics	deputies delegated from supreme soviets of these republics.	Organization and work of republican bodies. Ratifies international treaties of USSR.
2. Council of the Union	Constituted by population as previously	"Rights and freedoms" of USSR citizens.

Figure 3.7 Legislative Organs of State Power: September 1991

made up in accordance with the existing quotas which reflect population density. The total number will depend on the number of republics which join the Union.

These developments effectively have ended the USSR as a federative state. Following the meeting of the Congress of People's deputies, the state will be more of a confederation and has been referred to as a Union of Sovereign States. The republics will define the conditions under which they will join the Union which will be concerned with a limited number of functions: among the most important being foreign affairs, defense, internal security, energy and science, and possibly money supply for the union. Different forms of association are possible: some states (such as Byelorussia) having close political associations, others (possibly Armenia) would maintain strong economic ties.

SUMMARY OF CHANGES

A. Prior to August 1991
1. The Politburo was no longer the supreme political body in the USSR. Its members and the secretariat of the Party did not attempt to rule the country but functioned in an advisory capacity in the government system. Political recruitment was a major activity of the Party and brings it more in line with Western parties working in a pluralist context.
2. The head of state was the President of the USSR. Policy formation has shifted from the Party secretariat and the Politburo to the President. Gorbachev, as President, has retained the chief position in the Communist Party of the Soviet Union (its General Secretaryship). This symbolizes the shift from the leadership of the Soviet Union identifying with the *Communist* Party to its representing a

sovereign state. In future elections, the President is to be directly elected.

3. In the economic order the Party has lost direct influence. There was more reliance on the market and greater use of economic rather than administrative levers. Under Gorbachev there is developing a greater formal division between the economic and the political — as in Western capitalist states.

4. The increasing ungovernability of the Soviet Union at the turn of the decade led to the President assuming greater powers. By 1991, he had under him three executive committees (Federation Council, Cabinet and Security Council) giving comprehensive legal control of the government. He retained the top executive post in the Communist Party of the Soviet Union. This gave him more *legitimate power* than that afforded to any other leader of the Soviet state.

5. *Demokratizatsiya* has created a more pluralistic political environment which has overshadowed the Party organizations, reduced their political space and led to the rise of other political centers of power.

B. *After the coup of 1991*
1. The CPSU and the All-Union powers of the KBG (state security) have been destroyed.
2. The powers of the Union have been minimized.
3. The Union republics have assumed major economic and political powers.
4. The power of the President of the USSR has been eroded.
5. State government has assumed the character of a Union of Sovereign States in which the state republics (especially the Russian Republic) play a major role.
6. Political instability and the absence of authoritative political channels are a characteristic of the evolving political system.

READINGS TO CHAPTER 3

Eltsin's Election Platform (21 March 1989)
Moskovskaya Pravda, 21 March 1989
Source: BBC World Broadcasts, SU 0421 CI, 30 March 1989.

The country's supreme legislative body must express the people's will in the resolution of all fundamental matters and must prevent the adoption of unnecessary and at times even harmful decisions and resolutions. All government, political and public organisations without exception, including the party, must be legislatively accountable to it.

It is necessary to introduce a practice whereby central bodies report to the Congress of People's Deputies and the USSR Supreme Soviet.

The current law on elections is not genuinely democratic. Elections of deputies and chairmen of soviets at all levels must be universal, direct, equal, secret and always competitive [Russian: sostyazatelnyy], including the election of the Chairman of the USSR Supreme Soviet.

It is necessary to create a state-legal mechanism ruling out relapses into authoritarian forms of rule, voluntarism and a personality cult.

It is necessary to struggle against the existing elitist bureaucratic stratum via the transfer of power to elected bodies and the decentralisation of political, economic and cultural life.

Legislation must not be anonymous: every draft law and amendment must be attributed to its authors, and authors must be responsible for it.

A people's deputy must have the right to demand referendums on the most important issues of state life (the building and use of the armed forces, priority avenues of economic and social policy, construction of nuclear power stations and so on).

Concern for man is the main objective of socialism. It is necessary to give even greater priority to a strong social policy and to concentrate all efforts along the three most important avenues: supply of foodstuffs and industrial goods; the services sphere; housing. Larger sums must be appropriated for the solution of these tasks, including by means of reduced appropriations for the defence and other sectors. The implementation of a series of space programmes ought to be postponed for five to seven years. This will make it possible to substantially enhance Soviet people's living standards within two to three years.

Priority in social policy must be given to the socially least protected members of society: low-income families, pensioners, women and the disabled.

Bearing in mind the unjustified stratification of the population according to property criteria, it is necessary to intensify the struggle for social and moral justice. It is necessary to aim for equal opportunities for all citizens — from the worker to the head of state — as regards the acquisition of foodstuffs, industrial goods and services and the receiving of education and medical services. The fourth directorate of the USSR Ministry of Health, which today serves the leaders, should be reorientated to meet the needs of society's socially least protected members. The sundry special rations and special distribution centres must be eliminated. The sole incentive for good work ought to be the rouble, with indentical purchasing power for all strata of society.

Only an efficient economy can provide a lasting foundation for a strong social policy. There is a need for a clear-cut scientific programme to improve the economy's health as soon as possible.

Within the framework of this programme — the slogan "Land to the peasants!" must be implemented. Land must be transferred under long-term leases. People must choose for themselves the forms of economic management;

— there must be a sharp reduction in the number of ministries and departments and their apparatus must be gradually transferred to full economic accountability. Enterprises must be given an opportunity to withdraw freely from ministries and the right to engage in autonomous economic activity;

— there ought to be a 40% reduction in appropriations for industrial construction and they ought to be excluded from the budget as lacking commodity backing. This ought to result in a sharp reduction of the state's internal debt and stabilisation of the rouble's exchange rate.

The solution of economic and social problems is possible only under further development of democracy. Mass media must be given greater independence and a law on the press ought to be adopted defining the duties of press, radio and television workers and protecting their rights. Mass media must depend not on groups of people but on society.

Serious attention must be given to relations between nationalities. All USSR peoples must have de facto economic, political and cultural autonomy.

I share people's anxiety over the acuteness of the ecological problem. It is necessary to adopt a law on ecological responsibility. An ecological map of the country must be drawn up, and an end must be put to industrial construction in regions under ecological pressure, including Moscow.

A number of legislative acts on young people ought to be adopted. Agreement in principle must be given to the possibility of alternative young people's organisations being created.

Restructuring and democratisation must bring revolutionary changes in our society and the struggle for them ought to be waged in revolutionary fashion.

CPSU Programme Statement, July 1990

STATEMENT ADOPTED BY CPSU CONGRESS

'Pravda' second edition 15 July 1990

Text of "28th CPSU Congress Programme Statement: Towards a humane, democratic socialism"

I THE CRISIS IN SOCIETY AND THE PARTY'S STRATEGIC GOALS

Assessment of the Current Period

Perestroyka marked the beginning of democratic changes in the country's life. For all the contradictory nature of the processes of social development, the people are being spiritually and politically emancipated, people are acquiring civic and national dignity and taking on the affairs of society and the state. The myths that obscured consciousness and prevented a vision of the way forward are collapsing. The barriers that separated the country from the outside world are being removed. Preconditions for extricating society from the crisis in which it has found itself are being created step by step, in an acute struggle between the old and the new.

The congress considers that the deep-rooted sources of the crisis lie not in the decline of the very idea of socialism, but in the deformations that this idea suffered in the past. Statisation of all aspects of social life and dictatorship by the party-state elite on behalf of the proletariat brought about new forms of man's alienation from ownership and power and led to tyranny and lawlessness. The natural environment was rapaciously exploited. Dogmatism prevailed, giving rise to intolerance of dissent. A scornful attitude toward the peoples' cultural and historical values and intellectual wealth was inculcated. The world was regarded as the arena of implacable confrontation between social systems.

Distortions of the principles of socialism during the period between the 1930s and 1950s created difficult problems in our country's development and, in the second half of the 20th century, when a major shift developed in the life of all mankind owing to the scientific and technical revolution, the authoritarian-bureaucratic system proved completely incapable of bringing the country into the mainstream of world civilisation.

Nevertheless the urgent need for radical change was ignored for a long time. The resolution of the pressing historical conflict was artificially checked by a structure of party-state power cut off from the people.

Perestroyka marked a radical shift toward a policy of renewal and of freeing the country from social forms alien to socialism. But it also revealed that the simultaneous transformation of all spheres in the life of a vast state with a population of almost 300 million is exceptionally complex. What is more, some decisions and actions by the party's and the country's leadership over the last few years have proved to be inadequately worked out, inconsistent, and, in a number of cases, simply mistaken. Miscalculations in investment and export and import policy, in combating unearned income, and in carrying out the anti-alcohol campaign and distortions in the organisation of the co-operative movement had adverse consequences.

The old economic mechanism is being dismantled, and the new one has yet to be created. Control of the money supply and the market situation has been lost to a considerable extent. The creation of a legal base for the impending economic and political transformations has been excessively protracted. The country is rocked by inter-ethnic conflicts. The prestige of the state power has declined. Spiritual and moral values are being eroded and there is a growing wave of violence and crime.

The Central Committee and the Politburo have quite often lagged behind the development of events and operated by means of trial and error when adopting and implementing decisions and reforming the CPSU itself.

The party is living through a complex, crucial period. The renunciation of the former role played by the nucleus of the administrative-command system and its acquisition of the qualities of a socio-political organisation are accompanied by the painful exacerbation of contradictions, the decline of many party organisations' activeness, the polarisation of opinions and positions and growing criticism of the party.

A rapid process of forming sundry socio-political groups and movements is under way in the country.

The conservative-dogmatic current whose representatives see the policy of renewal as an encroachment on the principles of socialism and are preaching a return to authoritarianism has become more active. It objectively attracts that section of the bureaucratic structures which is incapable of restructuring itself, which sees society's democratisation as a threat to its political influence and social status and which is therefore doing its utmost to try to freeze the processes of change.

Movements that reject the socialist option and campaign for the unrestricted transfer of social ownership and for the complete commercialisation of education, health care, science and culture are gaining momentum. Monarchist and even fascist extremists have made their presence felt.

Social democratic currents of diverse hues have become a noticeable phenomenon in the country's socio-political life.

Without breaking with the idea of socialism and retaining its commitment to social security for the population, the social democratic current often lays the stress on mechanical imitation of contemporary socio-economic structures in developed industrial states without consideration of our country's specific features; many of its representatives refuse to consider Marxism as their ideological base.

National movements in which chauvinist and nationalistic sentiments are manifested increasingly actively alongside democratic trends have gained considerable scope. Setting some nations against others and promoting slogans of separatism and "national exclusiveness", they often turn out to be mouthpieces for the interests of old or new anti-democratic groups yearning for power.

Democratic perestroyka forces oriented on the socialist option and represented by most CPSU members and many organisations that express the political and vocational interests of the working class, the peasantry, the intelligentsia, young people, servicemen and veterans are to be found at the centre of the political spectrum taking shape in the country.

At a time of political instability which could result in social and economic chaos, the Communist Party sees its task as becoming the party of civic accord and ensuring constructive co-operation among various socio-political forces interested in escaping from the crisis and achieving a democratic reorganisation of society, so as to unite, support and defend all who through their honest labour have created, are creating, or will create the people's prosperity and spiritual values. It counters those forces that would like to turn society back — to a bourgeois system or barrack usages — and to incite anarchy and civic confrontation and the division of nations and peoples. The congress considers that a consistent course of renewing the social system within the framework of the socialist option is the foundation of the contemporary strategy of advance towards a prosperous and free society and the tactics for extrication from the crisis.

What Kind of Society Are We Striving Towards?

The essence of the perestroyka policy resides in the transition from an authoritarian-bureaucratic system to a society of humane, democratic socialism. This — although difficult — is the only correct way to a dignified life, to the realisation of the country's material and spiritual potential. While severing links with all that is alien to socialism, the CPSU rejects the denial of the ideals of October and the nihilistic attitude towards the Soviet people's revolutionary gains. It is necessary to clearly distinguish in our country's past between, on the one hand, phenomena engendered by Stalinism and stagnation and, on the other, the real achievements of the USSR's peoples. The party gives due credit to the constructive labour and self-sacrifice of all generations of the working class, peasantry and intelligentsia and to their heroic endeavours in the name of the homeland.

We hold sacred the memory of the people's sacrifices during the years of most rigorous ordeals.

The CPSU advocates a creative approach to the theory and practice of socialism and their development through constructive analysis of the historical experience of the 20th century and the legacy of Marx, Engels and Lenin freed from dogmatic interpretation. We deem it necessary to utilise the best achievements of human reason and the experience accumulated in the world of effective economic management, the solution of social problems and the development of democratic institutions.

The CPSU is a party with a socialist option and a communist outlook. We regard this prospect as the natural, historical thrust of the development of civilisation. Its social ideal absorbs the humanist principles of human culture, the age-old striving for a better life and social justice.

In our understanding humane, democratic socialism means a society in which:

— man is the aim of social development;

living and working conditions for him are worthy of contemporary civilisation;

man's alienation from political power and the material and spiritual values created by him are overcome and his active involvement in social processes is assured;

— the transformation of working people into the masters of production, the strong motivation of highly productive labour, and the best conditions for the progress of production forces and the rational use of nature are ensured on the basis of diverse forms of ownership and economic management;

social justice and the social protection of working people are guaranteed — the sovereign will of the people is the sole source of power;

the state, which is subordinate to society, guarantees the protection of the rights, freedoms, honour, and dignity of people regardless of social position, sex, age, national affiliation or religion;

there is free competition and co-operation between all socio-political forces operating within the framework of the law.

This is a society which consistently advocates peaceful and equitable co-operation among the peoples and respect for the rights of every people to determine their own fate.

II   CPSU ACTION PROGRAMME

The implementation of the CPSU's programme goals requires the implementation of both emergency anti-crisis measures and the implementation of a long-term policy to comprehensively transform society. The CPSU will strive to achieve these goals by political methods and by the deliberate and co-ordinated actions of communists, including those working in soviets and other state organs and social organisations and by using its constitutional right of legislative initiative and winning the trust of the masses.

Emergency Measures for Extrication From the Crisis

The party puts forward the following as IMMEDIATE TASKS:

First. The elaboration this year of a new treaty on the union of republics as sovereign states on a strictly voluntary basis of mutual benefit and freedom of national self-determination; a treaty which takes account of both the specific features and requirements of the republics, and the interests of the union as a whole.

Second. To carry out in the socio-economic sphere within 18—24 months: — the normalisation of the consumer market, above all the market in food, by the very rapid reorientation of the economy towards the consumer sector, the all-round development of entrepreneurial initiative, procurements of imported goods, and the maintenance of fixed prices for a series of essential commodities during the transition to free price formation; — the stabilisation of money supply by the pursuit of financial and credit reform, the distribution of shares among the population, the selling off of surplus stocks of material resources, the sale of housing, increasing interest on the population's bank deposits, the granting of loans against the future sale of goods and reduction of the state budget deficit to a minimum; — additional funding of urgent socio-economic tasks by means of sensible cutbacks in defence spending, ineffective capital investments, and expenditure on maintaining the managerial apparatus and the regulation of foreign economic ties.

Third. The resolute intensification of discipline and law and order and the intensification of the struggle against crime and of crime prevention. The use of all available resources — economic, political and legal — to combat the shadow economy. The urgent adoption of laws to provide legal foundation for the implementation of the emergency measures to overcome the crisis and the development of mechanisms for their implementation.

For Freedom and People's Well-Being

The party regards the ensuring of worthy living conditions for Soviet man as the central, strategic task of its policy.

CIVIL RIGHTS AND FREEDOMS. The party advocates:
— the implementation of human rights at the level of internationally recognised norms.

LABOUR AND WELL-BEING. Honest labour is the basis of the well-being of society and each individual. The party advocates:
— guarantees of the right to work, the provision of fair payment for end results without any restrictions; the elimination of levelling, dependence and the eradication of illegal income and privileges.

SOCIAL GUARANTEES. The party proposes:
— creating an integral social-state system of social protection and material support for low-income and large families, ensuring that the level of pay, pensions and allowances is no lower than the subsistence level.

EDUCATION, SCIENCE AND CULTURE. The CPSU considers the development of education, science and culture as a priority area of its policy. By protecting creative freedoms, the party will uphold the highest humanitarian values. It is opposed to bureaucratic administration of the spiritual sphere and the wholesale transfer of culture, art and education to a purely commercial footing.

For An Effective Economy

The creation of a reliable basis for social progress demands the democratisation of economic relations by genuinely emancipating people's initiative and practical activity and bringing incentives for highly productive labour into play. This is the essence of the programme proposed by the CPSU for perestroika in the economic system.

BECOMING THE MASTER AND REVIVING INDUSTRIOUSNESS. The party considers it necessary to create conditions for the formation and development of diverse and equal forms of ownership, their integration and free competition among them:

— state ownership (all-union, republican, municipal) must be transformed from formal, bureaucratic ownership into social ownership controlled by working people themselves on the basis of existing legislation. Working people's collectives are to be granted the right to lease state enterprises and property and acquire industrial, trade and services sphere facilities; use is to be made of the joint-stock form of enterprise organisation; — it is necessary to develop various types of co-operative ownership, ownership by public organisations and mixed forms of ownership;

— private labour ownership, which could improve the lives of the people, must have a place in the system of forms of ownership.

The CPSU is against total denationalisation or the imposition of any forms of ownership.

TOWARDS A REGULATED MARKET. The market economy is an alternative to the outmoded administrative-command system of management of the national economy. Advocating a phased transition to the market, the CPSU deems it is necessary to:

— accelerate the elaboration of legislative and legal norms and mechanisms ensuring a switch to a market economy;

— grant enterprises and all commodity producers, regardless of their forms of ownership, autonomy and free enterprise and to promote the development of healthy and honest competition among them; and to separate the functions of state management from direct economic activity;

— implement demonopolisation of production, banking and insurance, trade and scientific development; give support to the development of a network of small and medium-size enterprises;

— gear the state regulation of market relations to the protection of citizens' social rights, carry out major structural transformations in the national economy and the scientific-technical and ecological programmes, and safeguard the country's interests in the system of world economic links. Preserve state management of major transport networks, communications, the power industry, and defence

complex enterprises within the framework of a single market on the basis of financial autonomy principles and work collectives' self-management;
— switch, in the planning system, to the elaboration of strategic outlook plans for economic development and targeted state programmes, to indirect regulation of the economy through state orders, pricing, depreciation and customs policy, taxes, interest on credit and so on;
— ensure the switch to a convertible rouble and to an economy that is open to the world market, the creation of favourable conditions for enterprises' foreign economic activity and the involvement of foreign capital to ensure the earliest possible introduction of progressive technologies and supplies to the market.

MARKET AND PROTECTION MECHANISMS. In view of the fact that the switch to the market is not an end in itself but a means of solving social problems, and in view of the possible adverse consequences of this switch, the CPSU proposes:
— compensating the populace for losses due to the revision of retail prices of goods and services; introducing a flexible system for indexing the population's monetary incomes and increasing them depending on the growth of consumer prices;
— creating an effective mechanism for maintaining employment, for finding jobs and for vocational retraining; compensation payments during the period of temporary unemployment, retraining and acquisition of new skills;
— ensuring social and state monitoring of the observance of laws regulating market relations.

AGRARIAN POLICY. In it the party proceeds on the basis of the following principles:
— supporting the soviets' right to own land and the state, collective and individual farms' right to use and manage land;
— ensuring equal economic relations between town and countryside;
— ruling out any kind of dictate and bureaucratic rule in all that pertains to land management and relying on the peasant's free choice; ensuring equal opportunities for the development both of social farming — collective farm and state farm — and of newly established individual, family and lease farming;
— ensuring the priority development of the agro-industrial complex's material-technical base in the light of the requirements of all forms of economic management;
— enabling every rural inhabitant and anyone wishing to live and work in the countryside to set up his own home and farm holding; improving the social infrastructure of the countryside and making work on the land socially attractive and economically effective.

Towards Genuine People's Power

THE CIVIL SOCIETY AND THE LAW-GOVERNED STATE. The party consistently advocates:
— the formation of a civil society in which man does not exist for the sake of the state but the state for the sake of man; and all social groups and communities have a legally-guaranteed right and actual opportunity to express and defend their own interests;

— the strengthening of the law-governed state which excludes the dictatorship of any class, party, grouping or managerial bureaucracy and ensures access for all citizens to involvement in state and public affairs and to the holding of any post; the state and its citizens are connected by mutual responsibility, given the unconditional supremacy of democratically adopted law and the equality of all before the law;

— the free competition of socio-political organisations within a constitutional framework;

— the embodiment of the principles of universal, equal and direct suffrage.

We understand democracy not only as rights and freedoms but also as the civil responsibility, strict observance of laws and self-control which are organically linked with them.

SEPARATION OF POWERS into legislative, executive and judicial will create guarantees against the usurpation of unlimited authority and abuse of power and will enable spheres of competence and responsibility to be clearly demarcated.

The Country's Security

As long as the danger of armed conflicts exists, the country needs reliable defence. The party considers it necessary:

— to implement a military reform based on the new defensive doctrine and the principle of reasonable sufficiency and on the priority of qualitative parameters in military building.

While remaining under modern conditions a vitally necessary institution for defending the constitutional system and maintaining public order, internal affairs and state security bodies must act strictly within the framework of the law and under the control of representative bodies of power. It is necessary to raise the standard of professional training and improve material support for law-enforcement body personnel.

Towards a Renewed Union of Sovereign Republics

FOR A VOLUNTARY UNION OF PEOPLES. The CPSU believes that the development of centrifugal trends can be prevented only on the basis of the democratisation of relations among the peoples and the national-state formations of the USSR and the successful development of the economy of all regions and a single, union-wide market. The party proceeds from recognition of the nations' right to self-determination, even including secession, but does not confuse the right to secede from the USSR with the expediency of such secession and believes that, proceeding from the interests of the country's peoples themselves and the trend of world processes toward integration, it is necessary to preserve the integrity of the renewed union as a dynamic multinational state. The CPSU favours the friendship and international unity of all the nations and ethnic groups of the country.

The party will pursue the line of strengthening the sovereignty of union republics. It proposes political and legal diversity in ties between the republics themselves and with the union as a whole and diversity in their economic relations on the basis of enterprises' economic independence.

HUMAN RIGHTS AND THE RIGHTS OF NATIONS. The CPSU comes out: — for the expansion of the rights of nations while recognising the priority and the strict and unconditional safeguarding of the rights of each person;

— against the existence of any legal norms and laws which allow inequality among citizens on ethnic grounds, and for full freedom of choice in individual national self-determination;

— for respect for the cultural traditions and interests of all ethnic-national groups of the population when adopting the republics' legal norms and laws.

Towards Mankind's Peaceful Development

The party believes that the USSR's foreign policy strategy should be based on the ideas of peace, co-operation, collaboration, progress and humanity; and should contribute in every way possible to the processes of our internal perestroyka and ensure international stability.

FOREIGN POLICY GUIDELINES. With a view to strengthening world security, the party advocates:

— energetic continuation of the successfully launched demilitarisation of international relations; the reduction of arms and armed forces to the limits of reasonable defence sufficiency; the total exclusion of the use and threat of force from world practice; the further lowering and then the complete surmounting of military confrontation;

— the creation of global and regional security structures on the basis of a balance of the interests of all sides to prevent conflicts and international instability;

— the underpinning of relations among states with a legal base guaranteeing freedom of socio-political choice, sovereignty and independence and the development of co-operation and partnership with all countries of the world;

— the further normalisation of Soviet-US relations and their channelling towards a constructive partnership; enterprising participation in the all-European process and the overcoming of the historical split in Europe; the development of new forms of political and economic co-operation with the countries of Eastern Europe; comprehensive consolidation of positive trends in relations with the PRC; an active policy in the Asia-Pacific region with a view to turning it into a zone of peace and co-operation; participation in the political settlement of regional conflicts; collaboration with the Non-Aligned Movement and co-operation with developing countries.

TOWARDS A NEW QUALITY OF INTERNATIONAL CO-OPERATION. The party considers the pooling of efforts of all members of the international community in resolving common problems facing mankind to be vitally necessary.

The Renewal of the Party

As the nucleus of the administrative edict system for many long years, the party itself was subject to serious deformation. Over-centralisation and the suppression of critical thought had a pernicious effect on relations within the party. Tremendous damage was done by the ideological and moral degeneration of a number of party leaders.

The congress notes that the CPSU as the ruling party bears political and moral responsibility for the situation that developed in the country, and it has itself talked candidly about the mistakes made by the country's party and state leadership and condemned the Stalin-era crimes and the flagrant violations of human rights. But the congress resolutely opposes blanket accusations against honest communists of both past and present generations. Millions of communists served the people selflessly, worked whole-heartedly, and fought courageously for the homeland's freedom and independence. There have always been progressive forces at work within the CPSU, and it is they who inspired and have led society's restructuring.

The CPSU resolutely repudiates political and ideological monopolism and the supplanting of state and economic management bodies. The dynamics of the changes dictate the acceleration of the CPSU's transformation into a true political party expressing and defending the fundamental interests of the working class, peasantry and intelligentsia and operating within the framework of a civil society.

The Party's Role in Society

The CPSU is a political organisation which, by its practical activity and its constructive approach to the solution of the problems of society's development, will uphold the right to political leadership in free competition with other socio-political forces.

The party performs the following functions:

THEORETICAL. On the basis of a scientific analysis of objective trends in society's development, a theoretical evaluation of its prospects, and an elucidation and consideration of the interests of different social groups, it elaborates the strategy and tactics of socialist renewal and socio-economic, political and other programmes.

IDEOLOGICAL. The party defends its philosophy and moral values, propagates its programme goals and policy and draws citizens to the side of and into the ranks of the CPSU.

POLITICAL. The CPSU performs daily work among the masses and in work collectives, organises co-operation with social organisations and movements, campaigns in elections for seats in bodies of power at all levels and, if victorious, forms the corresponding executive bodies, carries out parliamentary activity and implements its pre-election programme.

ORGANISATIONAL. The CPSU conducts organisational work to implement its programme guidelines and decisions. The party renounces formalism and the nomenklatura-based approach in cadre work. The authority for taking cadre decisions in bodies of state power and administration belongs to those bodies and within the party itself is transferred from superior bodies to party organisations and all communists.

In present-day conditions, it is necessary to form in soviets at all levels party groups and inter-party blocs, and communists must be guided by the will of their voters and the CPSU's programme goals when participating in those groups or blocs.

Democratisation of the Party

Without the most thorough democratisation of intra-party relations, the CPSU will not be able to perform its role in society.

The CPSU resolutely rejects democratic centralism as it evolved in conditions of the administrative-command system and rigid centralisation and defends democratic principles — electability and interchangeability, glasnost and accountability, subordination of the minority to the majority and a minority's right to uphold its views, including in the party mass media organs.

Democratisation in the party presumes participation by all its members and structures in shaping CPSU policy by means of partywide and regional discussions and referendums; the right of individual communists and groups to express their views in platforms; collectiveness and openness in the work of all party bodies and freedom of criticism. The profound restructuring of intra-party relations and the party's activity is designed to ensure the democratic unity of CPSU ranks and to prevent a factional schism. An important factor in the renewal of the CPSU is the recruitment of fresh forces and the rejuvenation of cadres.

The CPSU's base is its primary organisations. Autonomously and in the light of specific conditions they determine the tasks and forms of activity, structure and numerical size of their bodies and apparatus, the periodicity of and procedure for holding meetings and political actions and they have the final right of admission to the CPSU. Decisions made by them within the framework of powers vested in them by the CPSU Statutes may not be revoked by higher bodies.

The territorial and production principle of party building needs adjustment. While retaining party organisations in production and other collectives, it is necessary, in the light of the increased significance of the pre-election struggle waged among the population in local neighbourhoods, to emphasise the development of powerful and active primary territorial organisations. A CPSU member has the right to choose the primary organisation — production, territorial or both — in which he will work. Freedom to create and act within horizontal structures — party clubs, councils of party organisations' secretaries and other special interest, professional and other associations — is guaranteed.

The congress does not consider it right to deprive communists in the army, the KGB or the MVD of the right to party membership and the creation of party organisations or to other forms of political activity. However, these organisations must be separate from state and administrative bodies, including military-political bodies, responsible for the moral and political education of armed forces, MVD and KGB personnel.

The congress advocates the election of party committee secretaries and party forum delegates by direct and, as a rule, multi-candidate elections through secret ballot and with the free nomination of candidates. The actual election procedure shall be determined by communists.

Party control must also be democratic. The central, republic, kray, oblast, okrug, town and rayon control bodies are elected autonomously, are independent of party committees and are accountable only to the congresses and conferences which elected them.

To resolve its set tasks an elective party body forms, within its budget limitations, an apparatus to perform organisational and consultative functions.

AUTONOMY and UNITY. In the process of the USSR's renewal, the autonomy of union republic communist parties, which is dialectically combined with the unity of the party on the basis of the fundamental principles of the CPSU Programme and Rules, must be ensured. They elaborate their own programmes and normative documents in accordance with which they themselves resolve political, organisational, cadre, publishing and financial and economic questions, pursue a party line in the sphere of state building and the socio-economic and cultural development of the republics, and form ties with other parties and social movements, including those abroad. The leaders of union republican communist parties are members of the Politburo of the CPSU Central Committee. In the event of disagreement with a decision by the party's central leading bodies, a republican communist party central committee has the right to demand the discussion of the question at a CPSU Central Committee plenum or combined plenum of the Central Committee and CPSU Central Control Commission.

The Party and Social Organisations

The CPSU seeks co-operation with movements and organisations of a socialist orientation and dialogue and equal partnership with all progressive ideological-political currents. The party is ready to create political blocs with them.

CPSU members take part in mass movements which act within the framework of the law. However, the party considers it impermissible for communists to belong to other parties or to organisations which propound chauvinism, nationalism, racism or anti-socialist ideas.

The CPSU will promote the rebirth of worker and peasant movements and development of social activeness among the intelligentsia.

The CPSU welcomes the renewal of trade unions and supports their desire to work actively in the interests of working people and the defence of their rights and freedoms.

The CPSU regards the All-Union Komsomol as an autonomous socio-political communist organisation of young people and expects it to take direct part in the elaboration and implementation of party policy. Party and Komsomol organisations must learn how to form their relations as political allies. It is necessary to treat the emergence of new youth organisations with understanding, to promote the molding of their socialist and general humanist thrust and to instil in young people a sense of involvement in the people's destiny. The CPSU directs all its organisations resolutely towards young people's problems. This is also dictated by the interests of the party itself: Without young people it will have no future.

Those are the CPSU's conceptual and theoretical standpoints and political goals by which communists, party organisations and party organs are to be guided in their practical work until the adoption of a new CPSU Programme. The congress hopes that they will be supported by all democratic forces in the country advocating perestroyka and the renewal of our society.

Source:
BBC World Broadcasts SU/0821/C21   20 July 1990

Chapter 4

PLYURALIZM
Toward Civil Society?

Western societies are often defined as democratic not only in terms of the elective process and the competition of political parties, but also because there is a division between state and society that allows for the association of individuals independent of the state. Such groupings may be spontaneous and occasional — joining a chess club or a mothers' association — or may take a political form — a campaign for the rights of veterans of Vietnam. The essence of a civil society is the right to free association of individuals; and the acid test of the vitality of civil society is the toleration of dissent and the creation of independent political parties that may compete for power.

In Western societies for hundreds of years human rights in politics have enabled people to have freedom of thought and expression. Such freedoms have been linked to the freedom to express religious views, a right that has been won after long struggles against religious persecution. Americans are particularly concerned with the right to express individual views: an important element in the founding of the North American colonies was the desire by many of the early settlers to escape from religious persecution in Europe.

By the twentieth century in Western industrial countries free association and dissent had been institutionalized: individuals, groups, and political parties were able to coexist and articulate their own interests within the law. A democratic infrastructure had been created in which individuals were able to associate independently of the state and had the right to campaign to change laws enacted by the government. The rights of association, the right to campaign on the one hand, and the responsiveness of the government to the needs of the people on the other are important ingredients of a democratic society. This process of exchange and the relative autonomy of individual and group activities give rise to civil society.

But often even in Western societies some groups cast doubts about the effectiveness of the arrangements of civil society. Radicals often complain that their ability to capture mass support for their policies is constrained by the sociopolitical environment and that their claims for reform are often marginalized by the media and the operation of the political system. Mass protests that act as safety valves to allow the manifestation of dissent are permitted. Views on major issues, such as unemployment, poverty in the Third World, or nuclear disarmament, are acknowledged by the political elites while the message is politely ignored. Hence, from this point of view, the distinction between civil society and the state is largely an artificial one. The free association of civil society is constrained by the state and is limited to those groups that are essentially apolitical. The capitalist state, it is further asserted, through its taxing, legal, and penal systems and through the security services effectively eliminates individuals and groups that are in disagreement with the dominant values when those individuals and groups become a real political threat to the integrity of the state. Nevertheless, it is correctly contended that in modern Western societies there are important areas of social relations that stand between the economy and the state and that are relatively independent of them.

SOVIET COLLECTIVISM AND DISSENT

In the Soviet Union there have been weak or nonexistent boundaries between state and society. The state has claimed authority in areas of life that are private in Western states and that are part of civil society. Russian and Soviet ideals have glorified the collective; both the Russian Orthodox Church and the Communist Party have stressed, for different reasons, the primacy of the collective. Thomas Cushman (1988) has argued that *kollektivnost'* (collectivism) is "the dominant normative ideal in both Russia and the Soviet Union." Individualism has not had the same salience as a value either in prerevolutionary Russia or during the period of socialist revolution. Individualism was a creed bound up with the rise of Protestantism, the Renaissance, and the rise of capitalism. All of these movements had little impact on Russia.

The attitude of the Soviet authorities to the suppression of interests in civil society has been derived from the creed of collectivism. The traditional line of argument as it has developed since the time of Stalin is as follows:

the Party articulates the will of the people; the Revolution, Lenin, and the Soviet state are sacred. Opposition to the Party and to its policies is disloyalty — it is harmful to the general interest of the working class and to the triumph of world communism. Individual and group rights by definition weaken the solidarity of the collectivity and are socially divisive. An analogy may be made to the attitude of Western governments during wartime when human rights are suppressed in the interest of national security.

Collectivism in the USSR has led to the politicization of a wide range of behavior and institutions and has also led to the state defining an extensive range of behavior as political dissent. Hough (1979) has critically described Western interpretations of Soviet dissent, "People striving to achieve personal goals are engaged in dissent; consumerism is dissent; proposals to increase the use of market mechanisms are dissent; a failure to work conscientiously is dissent; the advocacy of efficiency and professionalism is 'an obviously dissident ideology.'"

We might narrow this all-inclusive approach to dissent by listing three components in the definition of dissent. First, dissenters have espoused values that are in disagreement with the regime. Second, dissent is a demand that is expressed outside the formal political arrangements of the state. Third, the political authorities consider dissent to be a threat to the legitimacy and process of the socialist regime.

These three defining characteristics have given rise not only to widespread suppression but also to arbitrary suppression of dissenting views and to the reprimand of groups that express opposition in the USSR. Since the death of Stalin there has been a gradual redefinition of what constitutes dissent and what may legitimately be the concern of private citizens in civil society. A comparison of the definition and suppression of dissent before Gorbachev came to power with the stance on dissent afterwards will demonstrate the evolution taking place in Soviet society.

Suppression of Dissent Before Gorbachev

Khrushchev, who liberalized the system in many ways, strongly opposed ideological deviance: "Anyone who advocates the idea of political coexistence in the sphere of ideology is, objectively speaking, sliding down to positions of anti-communism." People articulating antistate activity, "slandering the Soviet regime," could be punished by imprisonment for from six months to seven years and also by exile for from two to five years. As a punishment for "ideological subversion," for instance, Solzhenitsyn was deported, the writers Sinyavski and Daniel were sentenced to five and seven years, respectively, in a labor camp. Penal sanctions were enacted against people advocating national and religious beliefs thought to be incompatible with the Soviet order, though the state claimed at the same time that national and religious rights were guaranteed under the Constitution. Other subversives were deprived of liberty for advocating "bourgeois" liberal rights and for criticisms of the regime that included positive evaluation of the West.

Such penal activity was paralleled by the procedure of "hospitalization." When it was thought that a court would not convict an accused person, forced hospitalization was utilized as a means of detaining people. The police called for the psychiatric diagnosis of dissenters, and people allegedly suffering from paranoia or more usually, schizophrenia, were hospitalized. It is notoriously difficult to determine whether psychiatry is misused in any society; there seems little doubt, however, that misuse took place in the USSR and that many people were wrongly diagnosed. Bloch and Reddaway (1978: 258) have documented 210 cases of such wrongful hospitalization between 1962 and 1976 (fifteen new cases per year), although other estimates are higher. This kind of suppression of the individual through internal exile, imprisonment, and hospitalization has been a major cause of tension in East-West relations.

Aims of the Dissident Movement

The "dissident movement," as it became known, had two major objectives: the institutionalization of law (often the enforcement of Soviet laws in the face of lawlessness by the authorities), and the autonomy of individuals and groups in a civil society not subject to state interference. Despite harassment and imprisonment the dissident movement began to grow in size in the 1960s. There was a Human Rights Movement and a Democratic Movement whose major activity was the publication of illegal literature — *samizdat*; forty periodicals were published between 1960 and 1980. Nationalist and religious groups advocating their particular rights were also formed. These were the antecedents of the unofficial independent groups that have flourished under Gorbachev.

Sakharov in his book *Reflections on Progress, Co-existence and Intellectual Freedom* (1968) advocated that "socialism and capitalism are capable of long-term development, borrowing positive elements from each other and actually coming closer to each other in a number of essential aspects." Such intellectual currents of the dissident movement advocated civil rights under a changed Soviet system, the abolition of censorship, the amnesty of political prisoners, the creation of legal procedures, and the condemnation of Stalin.

Sakharov called for economic, political, and social pluralism: autonomy for factories freed from state tutelage, partial denationalization of state property, partial decollectivization, the freedom for workers to strike, legal guarantees for individual rights, the rights of republics to secede from the USSR, a multiparty system, the convertibility of the ruble, and the abolition of the foreign trade monopoly by the government (Sakharov 1968: 10, 101−2). In 1980 Sakharov was sent into "administrative exile" without due process of law. Most of the points in his program, however, have been adopted by Gorbachev and the reform movement under perestroika. In the late 1980s he became a leading figure in the Congress of People's Deputies and in political life in general.

PERESTROIKA AND CIVIL SOCIETY

Perestroika seeks to change the orientations of people. The political leadership has attempted to move from a collectivist and unitary set of motivating principles to individualistic and pluralistic ones. The notion of civil society has not been explicitly used by the Soviet leadership, though it has been by the radical democratic forces. Articles in the press refer to "informal or independent initiatives" as the development of aspects of "civil society" (*grazhdanskoe obshchestvo*; see *Kommunist*, the official journal of the CPSU, No. 9, June 1988: 95−106). The notion of "socialist pluralism," which involves rights being devolved to individuals and groups rather than remaining enshrined in collectivities, has been utilized and replaced or at least modified the principle of *kollektivnost*.

In 1988 Party Secretary and Politburo member V. A. Medvedev (whose main responsibility at that time was ideology), defined the

> fundamental political principle of socialism [as] full power by the working people and their practical participation in all state and local affairs at both central and local level. . . . This means that socialism must create a political system which would take into account the real structure of society and the multitude of interests and aspirations of all social groups and communities of people. (*Pravda*, 4 October 1988)

Medvedev then went on to define what he meant by socialist pluralism:

> First the shaping and improvement of a ramified network, a system of organizations, associations and institutions which would appropriately and flexibly express their multitude of social interests. Second, consistent modification of the party's functions and methods of activity along the avenue of its profound democratization. And third, implementation of the idea of a

socialist law-governed state, consolidation of the legal foundations of all social life and assertion of lofty legal, political and general culture.

The process of law and the adherence to legal codes would replace politics as an arbiter between state and society and between individuals and groups.

Much that was sacred and associated with the Soviet regime has been rejected and considered, in Medvedev's words, as "dogmatic interpretations of Leninism."

There are, however, limitations on the pluralistic nature of contemporary Soviet society. Gorbachev at a meeting of the Central Committee on 8 January 1988, discussed the limits on socialist democracy as follows: "We are for openness without reservations, without limitations. But for openness in the interests of socialism. ... if openness, criticism and democracy are in the interests of socialism, in the interests of the people, then they have no limits." Medvedev elaborates somewhat when he points out: "What is meant are healthy, economically and morally sub-stantiated interests which do not run counter to our system."

The Communist Party from this viewpoint should maintain a monopoly on political organization in the state apparatus. Medvedev pointed out "In its relations with public organization, the Party respects their right to have their own opinion, to uphold their own position and to protect their own interests. In these conditions, there is absolutely no sense at all in artificially creating other parties as opponents of CPSU policy." But the development of other de facto parties forced the leadership to concede the right for other parties to organize. The Platform of the February Plenum 1990 made clear that "the procedure for their formation will be established by law and reflected in the USSR Constitution".

This new approach to society has transformed the position of dissent and dissenters in the Soviet Union. The underlying change has been the recognition of interests with autonomy in civil society. The state has relinquished its right to control many personal activities. The principle of glasnost' has led to the encouragement of public criticism rather than its suppression. "Informal" groups have been encouraged. Many voluntary (obshchestvennye) organizations, such as Friendship Societies with Foreign Countries, Leagues of Inventors and Innovators, have existed for a long time. The difference under perestroika is that the informal groups are no longer under the direct tutelage of the authorities; they are not controlled by organizations such as the trade unions, the Komsomol, or the Party.

The position on dissent has changed qualitatively. Political prisoners have been pardoned and released. Sakharov, the leading civil rights campaigner, was not only allowed back in Moscow, but was publicly welcomed by Gorbachev and has become a public crusader for Gorbachev's policies and perestroika. Many previous dissidents have been given compensation and restored to their jobs. Lev Kamenev, Zinoviev, and Nikolay Bukharin were rehabilitated in 1988 and the latter had the Soviet press carry notices commemorating the hundredth anniversary of his birth. (Of the leaders of the Party at the time of the Revolution, before 1991 only Trotsky remained in official disgrace.)

There has been greater emigration of dissatisfied citizens — Jews and Germans in particular, have been allowed to leave the country. The Crimean Tatars have been given the right to return to the Crimea. (They were forcibly transported to Soviet Central Asia during World War II.)

The churches have been given greater freedom and autonomy in keeping with the division of state and church and the freedom of conscience proclaimed in the Soviet Constitution. The thousandth anniversary of the adoption of Christianity in Russia was publicly acclaimed in 1988. Many buildings have been returned to the Orthodox Church including the Holy Danilov monastery in Moscow. New congregations have been registered with the authorities, which reflects a widening of interest and confidence on the part of believers. The 600th anniversary of the Lithuanian Catholic Church and mass was celebrated in the reopened cathedral in Vilnius.

There has been a complete reversal on the position of Stalin and Stalinism. Rather than being a legitimate and positive form of political leadership and activity, Stalinism has been decried and rejected by the political leadership. Roy Medvedev, the Soviet historian, has appeared on Soviet television and was interviewed about his book that condemned Stalin (17 June 1988). Other Western critics, such as Robert Conquest, have been given much coverage in the Soviet press. People who suffered under the arbitrary power and lawlessness of Stalin and other Soviet leaders have been restored to their rightful positions in society. The Memorial Society has been founded to promote the recognition of the victims of Stalin and Stalinism. A week's commemoration of Stalin's victims was held in Moscow in November 1988, and models of a memorial to be built to those who suffered at his hands were put on display.

The leadership of Gorbachev has emphasized the role of law and legality, which will be strengthened constitutionally to prevent a recurrence of the lawlessness that has occurred in the past. Many previously dissident activities have become normalized. Illegal hospitalization has been outlawed by the political leadership. The Ministry of Internal Affairs (responsible for the ordinary police, the MVD) and the committee for state security (the security police, KGB) have been the subject of investigative journalism as well as the subject of Procuracy investigators (the body responsible for legal enforcement). The former chief of the

MVD (Nikolay Shchelokov) committed suicide after being arrested and his former deputy, Yuri Churbanov (Brezhnev's son-in-law) was tried and sentenced for corruption. In 1988 the head of the KGB, Viktor Chebrikov, pledged that his organization worked within the law and distanced himself from the excesses of the Stalin period.

The Growth of Informal Organizations

Of the 30,000 "informal organizations" reported by *Pravda* in November 1987, many interest groups have an accepted presence under perestroika, including instrumentalist self-interest promotional groups, leisure and consumer associations, and those with ideal or value orientations.

Self-interest groups include such associations as the Initiative Group to Defend the Rights of the Disabled; an unofficial trade union called Public Initiative for Perestroika formed by transport workers in Lipetsk in 1988 who rejected their own official union; circles of veterans from Afghanistan, described later; spontaneous assemblies of workers and employees who have carried out collective action against their employers (strikes of bus drivers and library staff have been reported in the Soviet press). Various cooperatives engaging in retail trade and services could be included in this category. All these associations have the common characteristic of coming together to further their self-interest.

The second type of association may be termed independent or grass roots (*samodeyatelnye*) initiative groups. They form local clubs for children with problems, support museums, and consider town planning problems. They organize sports and leisure activities, such as theater groups, poetry readings, and discussions. Environmentalist groups are important in this category — they oppose poaching and protect the countryside against the effects of pollution. Among these are a number of associations that are officially backed, but are organized and increasingly financed independently, including the Lenin Children's Fund and the Soviet Cultural Fund. As their titles indicate, they support projects for deserving children's causes and in support of independent artistic and cultural activities.

The third type of association, which sometimes has political objectives, often develops out of the previously mentioned circles. In their attempts to acquire independent action such groups come into conflict with the authorities and become more politicized. Many of these have become transformed into political parties in 1991 (see below, pp. 121–6). The "Greens" in the Baltic republics link industrial pollution to economic exploitation and consider nuclear power (and nuclear armaments) as political phenomena requiring political change. Air and water pollution are regarded as serious health risks that can only be eliminated by local public action, which makes entering into a political struggle with the authorities inevitable.

A Green perspective may also lead to opposition to some of the tenets of the reform movement. For instance, a letter in *Sovetskaya Rossiya* (7 August 1988) criticized the market as a mechanism, and particularly found fault with reformer economist Abalkin's approach.

> In the Komi republic forests are being barbarically cut down, to such an extent that there is a danger that only empty land will remain there. In many industrial centers you can't breathe because of the harmful emissions from the enterprises. Why is this happening? Because it is economically beneficial. ... What we need ... is a program to save the country, revive the wastelands, clean up the poisoned rivers, plant forests to replace those that have been predatorily destroyed, ensure the country's technological, economic and political independence, and eradicate the cultural and spiritual-moral decline among broad strata of the people ... in a word, a program of great works which would motivate the people and spur them to unprecedented accomplishments.

Another example of the politicization that may take place in initiative groups is the case of the Memorial Society. This began as a movement to draw attention to the needs of victims of Stalinism; but the group's plans to build a memorial to the victims brought them into confrontation with the Ministry of Culture.

People's Fronts are the most important development of this value-oriented social movement. The common political platform of the People's Fronts has been greater sovereignty for the national republics, more control over locally generated resources, enhancement of the vernacular language to the status of official language, restrictions on immigration, and censure on the Stalinist past. These associations originally sought to work within the context of a reformed Soviet state, and are discussed in more detail in chapter 6.

Other groups aspired to systemic changes and particularly the rise of a multiparty system. In 1987 the Inter-National Committee in Defense of Political Prisoners was formed by Ukrainian and Armenian ex-political prisoners. In 1988 this group was enlarged to form a "Co-ordinating Committee of Patriotic Movements of the Peoples of the USSR" composed of representatives of nationalist groups from the Ukraine, Lithuania, Estonia, Latvia, Georgia, and Armenia. It advocated greater rights for the non-Russian republics and had an objective of forming a joint platform against Soviet rule.

The Democratic Union was founded in May 1988 from more than a hundred representatives of various informal groups. Before its inception, some of its spokespersons envisaged a democratic union of informal groups composed of individual members and groups that would be an association of mainly noncommunist members who embraced a wide spectrum of thought. According to one of its leaders, Boris Kurashvili, it was envisaged as "a mass sociopolitical organization." It became much more than that. Its objectives were to "set up a political organization in opposition to the totalitarian structure," according to its first bulletin. Its aims inlcuded the establishment of a parliamentary system with competing political parties and civil rights. The leading role of the Communist Party would be abolished, as would the "ideology of Leninism"; the KGB and military service would also have to go.

A Western type of system with private property, trade unions, and a free press would be established. The Union's leadership declared the Baltic republics "occupied" by the Soviet Union and called for them to be given their freedom. It aspired to become an opposition party and claimed a membership in forty-eight cities. This association has formed the basis for a more radical critique of Gorbachev and his leadership and grew into a political party as discussed below.

Towards the other end of the Soviet political spectrum in the Russian republic is *Pamyat'*, which was formed in 1980 with the aim of maintaining Russian culture, particularly old buildings and monuments. It developed into a Russian nationalist organization with right-wing tendencies and eventually adopted the name Pamyat National Patriotic Front. In the autumn of 1988, the organization had branches in thirty towns. It has anti-Semitic tendencies and is opposed to other nationalities of the USSR. Many people consider *Pamyat'* a rallying point for the counter-reform movement. This view has been forcibly put by the Russian emigré writer Alexander Yanov in his article "Russian Nationalism as the Ideology of Counter-Reform" in *Russian Nationalism Today* (1988: 43–52). *Pamyat'* opposes the Westernization aspects of the reform movement, which range from rock music to the market system, considers Stalinism an "historical necessity," and seeks to utilize Russian nationalism as an ideology counter to perestroika. It condemns the press from a right-wing position.

Even more extreme right-wing organizations have developed. Neo-Nazi circles have sprung up in many Soviet cities (Leningrad, Moscow, and Murmansk) as well as in the Baltic republics and the Ukraine. They advocate a type of Russian fascism. Many Soviet youth are attracted to the strong leadership and the opposition to communism and capitalism that Hitler is said to have espoused. Such groups trail the Nazi flag and consecrate Soviet memorials to the Second World War dead. Groups like the Black Hundreds who committed pogroms (organized massacres) against the Jews in prerevolutionary Russia have surfaced under perestroika. In Estonia a National Fascist Party has been reported and leaflets have been distributed — leading to arrests — that "contain slander about socialism and other assessments which do not correspond with reality."

PERESTROIKA AND THE LIMITS OF SOCIALIST PLURALISM

Just as law and custom define the limits of group activities in the West, so, too, the Soviet authorities under Gorbachev have been redefining the permissible level of dissent under perestroika. The objective has been to allow dissent and criticism without undermining the integrity of the Soviet state and it is likely that some of the more politically oriented groups mentioned above will with the passage of time be repressed. Party Secretary and Politburo member V. M. Chebrikov in February 1989 pointed to the way that some informal associations "are doing considerable harm. ... Coming under the influence of extremist leaders, they embark on a path of antisocial and illegal activity. ... There are also frankly antisocialist elements which are attempting to create political structures opposed to the CPSU. We must, of course, react to such attempts and actions." On the other side, some of the more liberal leaders of perestroika have advocated freedom for such groups.

Not all associations and demonstrations have been permitted under *demokratizatsiya*. In November 1988 it was reported that in Moscow alone in the first ten months of the year, 640 attempts to hold meetings had not been sanctioned by the police — the chief of Moscow police said they were "provocative" and "anti-Soviet." Arrests of two members of the Democratic Union, it was reported, had been made while the group demonstrated in Pushkin Square in 1988. But the situation has radicalized since then. The growth of independent political groups and de facto parties has been a victory for democratization. While the Secretary of the Estonian Communist Party, Vaino Valyas, has publicly called for the creation of Estonian citizenship and the republic's right to restrict immigration, he has maintained that changes should be carried out under the leadership of the Communist Party. As we shall consider in the chapter on nationalities, in practice the national front organizations in the Baltic republics and elsewhere have operated as parties in the sense that they have a political platform and campaign for public office.

The creation of parties on a nationalist basis have lead to demands for secession from the USSR by dissatisfied national minorities. Demands for secession that have been advocated under the cloak of the People's Front in Estonia have been deplored by the local Party organization.

Public demonstrations in favor of national interests have gone unchallenged in some republics, particularly in the Baltic and the Caucasus, but in other areas, such as the Ukraine, "traditional methods" of repression have broken up demonstrations. Nevertheless, demonstrations took place in the Ukraine and Belorussia in 1989. In Azerbaidzhan in 1990, local nationalists openly campaigned against Soviet power. By 1991, with the growth of political parties (discussed at the end of this chapter), opposition to the CPSU and the domination of the government of the USSR, led by President Gorbachev, has exploded. Communists supporting the CPSU have been defeated in local elections and non-Communist governments have been formed in the Baltic Republics, Moldavia, Armenia, the Russian Republic (RSFSR) and Georgia. Following the unsuccessful coup in August 1991, the party has been banned and its property confiscated.

The Nina Andreeva Affair

One of the more enlightening episodes that illustrates the limits of the development of civil society is to be found in the discussion surrounding a letter that appeared in the leading Soviet newspaper, *Sovetskaya Rossiya* (13 March 1988, see the reading appended to this chapter). The Nina Andreeva affair illustrates that under perestroika those groups that support the processes of the Stalinist period are considered to be engaging in dissent. Such views have become reprehensible to the reform leadership, and such opposition has found itself ideologically constrained.

The author of the article, Nina Andreeva, a lecturer at the Leningrad Lensovet Technological Institute, while ostensibly supporting perestroika and Gorbachev, criticizes as nonsocialist and anti-Soviet many of the liberal developments taking place under the guise of glasnost'. She conjoins topics "prompted by Western radio stations" and the ideas of Soviet reformers "who are shaky in their concepts of the essence of socialism." She singles out "A multiparty system, freedom of religious propaganda, emigration to live abroad, the right to broad discussion of sexual problems in the press, the need to decentralize the leadership of culture, abolition of compulsory military service."

She goes on to emphasize the need for a "class-based vision of the world and an understanding of the links between universal and class interests." Such a vision, she argues, is incompatible with the "political anecdotes, base gossip, and controversial fantasies which one often encounters today" — referring to stories about Stalin's guilt, repression, and censorship. She criticizes the plays of Shatrov, which decry the achievements of the building of socialism, deny the validity of the dictatorship of the proletariat, and mock its leaders. Shatrov deviates from the tenets of socialist realism, for instance, by showing Lenin kneeling before Trotsky.

Andreeva also reprimands the press for a one-sided and critical treatment of events in Soviet history and calls for the more traditional Party position "to uphold the honor and dignity of the trailblazers of socialism" in defense of socialism. She alleges that attacks on the state have their base in a "social substratum." She refers to an alliance between a progressive intelligentsia and the political leadership, and she condemns the champions of "left-wing liberal socialism." The other "tower" of criticism is the "ideologists of 'peasant socialism' who wish a return to a prerevolutionary state of agriculture" and who share "an uncritical perception of mystical religious Russian philosophy ... and an unwillingness to perceive the postrevolutionary stratification of the peasantry and the revolutionary role of the working class."

She denounces the rise of many informal organizations and associations, the politicization of which is "on the basis of a by no means socialist pluralism." She emphasizes the leading role of the Party and the working class in the building of socialism and restructuring and calls for a reassertion of socialist ideology "guided by our Marxist-Leninist principles" in the face of nonsocialist pluralist tendencies.

Andreeva nowhere rejects explicitly the ideas of perestroika; indeed in several places she refers to Gorbachev in support of her position. What appears at first sight to be a mild reassessment of glasnost' and perestroika led to much opposition and condemnation in the Soviet media.

Following Andreeva's article, the official Party and government central press (the leading papers, *Pravda* and *Izvestiya*) was silent until 5 April 1988. Until that time, her article was reprinted in many papers, and photocopied sheets were made available at meetings. Conferences were organized to discuss the article and one was shown on television. No one criticized the letter because many thought that it indicated a change in direction by the political leadership. It was later alleged that many in the apparatus regarded the article as their *Manifesto*.

The line taken in an editorial in *Pravda* (5 April 1988), and which may be considered the official position, was that the article by Andreeva was anti-perestroika. The editorial in *Pravda* argued that before Gorbachev came to power, the country was in a "pre-crisis situation." The old methods and style of leadership had failed dismally. "Authoritarian methods, unthinking execution of orders, bureaucratism, the absence of control, corruption, extortion, and petit bourgeois degeneration flourished." The article went on to say that the essence of socialism had nothing to do with old authoritarian methods, with dogmatism and deviations from the principles of socialism, and it accused Andreeva's position of showing a false patriotism and "whitewashing the past"; it justified "political deformations and crimes against socialism."

Pravda criticized the Andreeva article for using "bourgeois sources" (positive statements made by Churchill about Stalin) to justify its case against the current position taken by the Party. *Pravda* reiterated that Stalin was guilty of mass repression and lawlessness and emphasized the need for openness: "nothing is absolute or sacred." It reaffirmed the unity of the intelligentsia and proletariat that the article sought to fragment. While stating that there are no forbidden subjects, *Pravda* criticized *Sovetskaya Rossiya* for publishing the article — by implication, the editor lacked a sense of responsibility, as the piece "departed from the principle of perestroika." This *Pravda* leader established a boundary of glasnost': — the defense of Stalinist ways, of previously established dogmatics, could not be defended in the public media. The media were to reflect current Party policy and its definition of perestroika. The revolutionary principles of restructuring were "more openness, more democracy and more socialism."

For some time following this editorial, nothing appeared in *Pravda* in support of Andreeva. Apart from reporting a number of hostile telephone calls, all coverage of her position was of a negative kind, and many letters and excerpts (prominently featured in half-page displays) supported the *Pravda* editorial: many readers expressed their "profound satisfaction" and "enormous gratitude." As for *Sovetskaya Rossiya*, on 15 April it again returned to Andreeva's polemic.

> The editorial board of *Sovetskaya Rossiya* discussed the [*Pravda*] article. . . . at a meeting and fully agreed with the critical assessments, propositions and conclusions contained therein. It was acknowledged that, during the preparation for the press of the letter "I Cannot Forego Principles," sufficient responsibility and careful consideration were not displayed, and there was an inadequate understanding of the fact that it would lead all of us away from the revolutionary renewal of society on the basis of democracy and openness.

Eleven letters were published on the same page: all in support of *Pravda's* line and none in favor of Andreeva's sentiments. There followed numerous discussions on both radio and television programs. It is notable here that no speaker argued on Andreeva's behalf.

Andreeva is reported as saying to the Yugoslav paper, *Vjesnik*, that she received 3,000 letters, 90 percent supporting her position, and in six months 500 people visited from other towns. Andreeva has stuck to her guns. Gorbachev in an aside at the Nineteenth Party Conference stated that she had sent a letter that would be read by members of the Presidium, but its contents and Andreeva's position were not divulged to the conference.

Such an absence of discussion in the main outlets such as *Pravda*, however, may have worked to Andreeva's favor, giving her position official condemnation. In the summer of 1989 she published another article, this time in *Molodaya Gvardiya* (No. 7). Here she criticized more explicitly developments under perestroika. She argued that democracy and glasnost' have to be limited and demanded the "resolute and consistent parting of the ways with those who are not taking the socialist path with the people."

Andreeva has been publicly joined in her criticisms by the late editor of the Party's journal, *Kommunist*, Richard Kosolapov. In *Moskovskaya Pravda* (2 August 1989) he suggested a purge of the Party apparatus and a limit to the period of office of the General Secretary of the Central Committee — presumably to limit Gorbachev's personal power. O. Kazarov (writing in *Sotsialisticheskaya Industriya*, 6 August 1989) also criticizes Gorbachev's views that the Party is lagging behind in the process of perestroika.

Common themes in this critique are: loss of communist ideals furthered by reliance on the market and private enterprise in the form of cooperatives, the activism of "informal groups," which undermine social solidarity and subvert the defense mentality, a belief that the center under Gorbachev has been acting without consulting the Party, that perestroika is presiding over a redistribution of authority from the working class to the intelligentsia. The more emphatic features of this position are that the mass media should be censored and act only in the interests of the socialist state. The proclamation of nationalist tendencies must be prevented, the egalitarian structure of the society must be defended, and the rise of private enterprise under the guise of cooperatives must be stopped. Such arguments were supported by the leaders of the unsuccessful coup of August 1991.

In 1989, too, a mass movement, the Russian United Workers' Front, was founded with working class support and sustained many of these ideas. The Front will be discussed further in chapter 5, which deals with the working class.

The Rise of Opposition Parties

While the traditional position of orthodox communists is encapsulated by Andreeva's views and is a threat to Gorbachev's political leadership from the "right", from the late 1980s Gorbachev and his supporters have been confronted by another challenge from the more liberal reformist groups.

These advocate a more radical policy and accuse the leadership of not moving fast enough and compromising with communist orthodoxy.

As noted above, the formation of separate parties had been proscribed by the CPSU until 1990. Until then the various People's (or Popular) Fronts in the republics, which will be discussed below (see chapter 6) had in effect become alternative parties and were a threat to the hegemony of the CPSU. They were, however, localized and did not have All-Union status. The Fronts had and have a program and campaign for election to state bodies. In the elections to the Supreme Soviet of the USSR in March 1989, the reform movement in Lithuania (Sajudis) won 31 of the republic's 42 seats, in Latvia 25 of the 29 candidates supported by the People's Front were elected and in Estonia 15 of the 21 seats went to candidates of the People's Front. Since 1989, in the elections in the republics, non-communist or anti-communist groups, fronts or platforms have won majorities and formed governments in the republics of the Baltic states, Georgia, Moldavia and the Russian Republic; also many city Soviets (notably Moscow and Leningrad) have elected a political leadership hostile in many respects to Gorbachev and the CPSU. They have advocated policies in opposition to those of the government of the USSR, headed by Gorbachev. All these Soviets, in one form or other, have advocated political independence or sovereignty from the USSR. These developments signify the growth of a multi-party system in the USSR.

On 16 October 1990, *Pravda* reported that there were 11,000 unsponsored organizations and 20 political parties in operation. Parties in the early 1990s are at an elemental stage of development. They hardly measure up to Edmund Burke's definition of groups of people united on some principle on which they are all agreed. The so-called parties are often loose associations of people who know against what or whom they are opposed than like-minded political activists.

The Law on Public Associations approved by the Supreme Soviet of the USSR in October 1990 gave legal recognition to a multi-party system. Political associations have to be registered with the Ministry of Justice and registration may be refused to organizations seeking the overthrow of the constitutional order by force or advocating the violation by force of the territorial unity of the USSR or of any republic.

These associations might be grouped into the following broad categories:

1. People's Fronts exist in all the Union republics and most of the autonomous republics. In the Russian Republic, over a hundred Fronts have been organized in major cities. These groups are extremely variegated in political complexion. Appended to chapter 6

below is the Charter of the Estonian People's Front; the Baltic republics follow this model. They emphasize local autonomy, sovereignty and independence. In the Russian Republic Fronts vary enormously. The Russian People's Front, for example, is strongly anti-Communist and reveres all things Russian — from the monarchy to the Orthodox Church. At the other end of the political spectrum are the "Inter" (internationalist) Fronts. They are often supported by Russian minorities in the non-Russian republics (particularly in the Baltics); a large proportion of these groups are working class — reflecting the composition of the immigrant population in these areas. They support a strong center and the continuation of the USSR and are opposed to local nationalist movements for independence.

2. Economistic interest groups and movements have grown up in the late 1990s. Some have been founded on the strike committees which have arisen in many areas. These are trade union-type organizations which have campaigned for the improvement of workers' conditions. By February 1990, the Association of Trade Unions in the USSR claimed 36 organizations, with a membership of 20,000. They have opposed the existing "official" Party and trade union organizations. They are analogous to the early Solidarity movement in Poland, though they lack its religious flavor. Another such formation is the trade union for members of the armed forces (*Shchit*). It campaigns for servicemen's rights and for veterans of wars (particularly in Afghanistan). The Scientific Industrial Union of the USSR was initiated in Moscow in June 1990 by members of the Council of People's Deputies of the USSR. In composition it includes individuals and groups (foreigners may also join). About forty associations, enterprises and organizations in addition to the people's deputies took part. The Union enhances the rights and interests of industry and scientific provision under the new economic system and it seeks to further rights of property in a market system.

3. Idealist groups are founded on some patriotic or moral principle. The *Pamyat'* society is an association which is pro-Russian and strongly anti-semitic. The *Memorial* society has members who are united in their opposition to the horrors of the Stalinist period. They campaign in support of its victims, to whom they have erected monuments. Church groups (such as the Ukrainian Catholics) defend Church interests and agitate politically for greater religious freedom. The Green movement is also vigorous. Its activities range from anti-pollution campaigns (particularly over Lake Baikal) to anti-nuclear (and anti-war) groups. These "idealist" groups verge on the political.

4. Self-defined political parties began to displace the more "pressure-group" bodies described above in the 1990s, though many existed before then. A lot of them stemmed from factions which have split off from the Communist Party of the Soviet Union. In many republics, the Communist Party split into two: one loyal to Moscow, the other with allegiance to the titular republic. A major boost was given to the formation of independent parties by the declaration of the CPSU (and consequent changes to the Constitution) to concede its organizational monopoly and to allow the formation of other political parties. This led to the breakup of the Communist Party itself and the splitting from the party of different political groups. These have been particularly notable in Moscow and Leningrad, where they have beaten the Communist Party in elections and control these local Soviets.

The Democratic Platform was composed of members (now many ex-members) of the CPSU, its leaders including Eltsin and Popov — President of the Russian Republic and Mayor of Moscow respectively. Many of this tendency left the CPSU during the Twenty-eighth Party Congress in 1990 and in November 1991 formed, with others, a separate political Party called the Republican Party of Russia ("Russia" indicating that it operates within the RSFSR). Its policy is in support of a market economy, individual rights and "social protection of every citizen in the republic". It advocates the restoration of sovereignty to Russia. Similar in ideology is the Social Democratic Party of Russia, formed in May 1990. Its guiding principles are "freedom, equality and solidarity". In addition to these somewhat ambiguous principles, the party supports private enterprise, a regulated market and the privatization of state-owned assets. In the autumn of 1990, these two parties discussed merging.

The Marxist Platform occupies the more traditional leftist territory of opposition to private ownership and support for state control and planning. Finally, there is a more orthodox bloc called The Union for Leninism and Communist Ideals, whose membership includes Nina Andreeva. (See her "platform" appended below.)

The Liberal-Democratic Party of the Soviet Union (LDP) had its first congress in March 1990. According to its Chairperson it "upholds the liberal traditions of the Cadets (Constitutional Democrats), the Octobrists and the Trudoviks (pre-revolutionary parties). ... We want to be a European, industrial society. ... Through we consider that part of the economy should be state-run, we favor private ownership, a free market and free enterprise. Any regulation should be carried out through taxation" (*Moscow News*, No. 17, 1990). The party's social base is among non-manual workers and it claimed 4,000 members in May 1990.

The Democratic Party of Russia (DPR) was founded in May 1990. It is strongly anti-communist. Its ideology is "To proceed from the Universal Declaration of Human Rights, Andrei Sakharov's draft of the Constitution and the program of the Democratic Russia bloc. ... The DPR will work to overcome the remnants of totalitarianism and make the Russian Federation into a sovereign, democratic and economically strong Republic. ... The Party supports local self-government, national and cultural autonomy, a market economy and private ownership." In May 1990, it claimed groups in 130 regions of the USSR. The *Shchit* and *Memorial* groups are collective members. (See account in *Moscow News*, No. 21, 1990.)

The Democratic Russia movement is a powerful umbrella organization. It is a loose constellation of groups opposed to the leadership of Gorbachev and seeks more radical reform. By the middle of 1990, its members had succeeded in winning majorities in the Congress of the RSFSR and the city Soviets of Moscow and Leningrad. At its congress in October 1990, 1,181 delegates attended from 71 areas. It included representatives from nine political parties and nineteen associations (such as the Democratic Party and groups under it noted above). It seeks to bring together anti-communist democratic organizations under one anti-communist liberal-democratic banner. It supports the rights of republics to leave the USSR and in effect advocates the dissolution of the Union. It advocates a much faster course of economic reform, as advocated by the government of the Russian Republic (under Eltsin) in 1991. It seeks to depoliticize the armed forces, the security forces and the procuracy. It vigorously opposes the *apparat* of the CPSU and since 1990 the leadership of Gorbachev. It strongly supports a market economy, privatization of state property and private property.

The Russian Christian Democratic Movement (RCDM, the Kadets) was founded in April 1990. Its professed ideology is anti-communist, Christian and pro-"enlightened patriotism" (Spokesperson interviewed in *Moscow News*, No. 21, 1990: 6). It seeks to re-establish the pre-revolutionary order which passed away in February 1917. Christian values are taken from Russian Orthodox culture. Groups associated with it include individuals who were engaged previously in *samizdat* publications, Christian clubs, Orthodox associations and charitable centers. Its main support lies in Moscow and Leningrad and it claimed 15,000 members in June 1990.

The Rus Party (also called the Civic Association for a Sovereign

Rus) was founded in Leningrad in 1988. Its aims are "The restoration of Russian national self-consciousness. Presidential Republic of Rus and self-government of autonomous national groups with the RSFSR." It had a membership of about 100 in June 1990.

The Free Labour Party was founded in December 1990. Its political stance is "anti-communism and economic liberalism". It supports a mixed economy, different forms of property and entrepreneurial activity. It cooperates with the "independent trade unions". Its membership was 1,085 in December 1990 — a third being self-employed professionals and the remainder members of cooperatives and business persons.

The constituent congress of the Peasant (*krest'yanski*) Union took place in June 1990. It was attended by 1,718 representatives from nine union republics. These were countryfolk, collective and state farmers, rural specialists (teachers, vets) and workers in rural industries such as food processing. Its aims are to improve conditions in the rural economy and life in general in the countryside. The Union supports the constitution of the USSR and seeks to work through it.

The opposition parties in the USSR differ somewhat from those in Eastern Europe. There many of the leaders came from outside the formal apparatus of power. In the Soviet Union, very few have been associated with the dissident movement. Many of the dissidents were allowed to leave the country for the West, whereas in Eastern Europe they stayed in their own country. The Communist Party of the Soviet Union was, as some Western writers assumed, a heterogeneous body composed of politically motivated activists. As the system has become liberalized, it has split into factions and parties. The parties are at an early stage of formation, their ideologies and membership are in flux. They lack an organizational structure. Many of the "socialist", "social-democratic" and "republican" parties have nothing in common with similar parties in the West. Most are Thatcherite and Reaganite in orientation, advocating the virtues of private property, the "hidden hand" of a market economy, anti-statism and privatization and the evils of state control and collectivism.

Perestroika and Socialist Pluralism

During the period of perestroika the relationship between the individual and society has changed radically. There has been a move from collective interest expressed through politics to one of market pluralism in which individuals and groups have had greater independence. In a collectivist society dissenting groups had a particular social status — they were identified not only by their political points of view, but by the marginalized status they were given by the political authorities. They constituted a social community. Socialist pluralism has undermined the social structure of dissent.

There has been a major change in the orientation of the leadership. Previously Marxism-Leninism has been associated with the traditional Russian communal value system and the autocratic traditions of state and Orthodox Church. Under perestroika, by an odd quirk of history, those who support the traditional values associated with Stalinism and the state socialist system of central management and control are marginalized. A major difference, too, is that they are not repressed, though their access to the mass media is restricted.

The dissident movement of the 1970s was an indicator that there were demands for greater individual rights. The adoption of many of their demands, however, should not be regarded as the result merely of the pressure of the dissidents. Important, also, have been its international aspects and the demands made on the Soviet leadership by the leaders of the Western powers, particularly Presidents Carter and Reagan. The underlying social tendency was the maturation of Soviet society. The greater social demands for rights that were articulated internally were responses to the ideological and economic stagnation of the Brezhnev era. The rise of Gorbachev and the reformers around him reflect the "within-system" dissent that had gathered momentum under Brezhnev.

With the abolition of the formal political hegemony of the CPSU and the retraction of Marxism-Leninism as arbiter of rights claims, the void was first filled by the President who was then in a unique position to interpret and enforce the USSR Constitution. The operation of parties is constrained legally by Article 7 of the Constitution as amended in March 1990: "The formation and operation of parties, organizations and movements having the aim of forcibly changing the Soviet constitutional system and the integrity of the socialist state, undermining its security or undermining social, national or religious strife are not permitted." As in all modern political systems, the dominant groups place or attempt to place limitations on the articulation of demands and on the ability of those opposed to the system. Successful democracies (those of contemporary Europe and the USA) are based on consensus in which loyal oppositions function within the parameters of capitalism.

In this respect, Gorbachev's policy failed: he believed, probably sincerely, that a loyal opposition would evolve based on a new form of consensus and democratic exchange (what I have called "organic solidarity"). The lack of economic growth and the decline in living standards gave him little political space in which to operate — the expected massive economic aid from the West did not arrive as his own economy ground to a halt in the early 1990s. While his policies were popular abroad, at home the decline in living standards and the rampant inflation and internal strife ensured a discontented population which was indifferent to or supported more radical changes or no changes in policy. Here he and his advisers failed to anticipate antagonistic opposition to his policies, and when it became visible, he was unwilling or unable to act. A retreat from the democratic aspects of perestroika would have led to claims that he was acting like his political predecessors as Head of State, and in the West he would have lacked credibility and would have been thought of as being unable to move to a market economy under democracy. Both the leaders of the failed coup of August 1991 and Eltsin have grasped this salient political fact. Eltsin has made it clear by his proscription of the Communist Party, the seizure of its property and the banning of its literature, that he will act to eliminate opposition. He recognizes that pluralism and civil society can only operate under stable conditions and that effective government can only occur in a society where all the dominant elites agree to play the rules of the game.

CONTINUITY, CHANGE AND INSTABILITY

In the first three chapters of this book we have reviewed different approaches taken toward the Soviet Union and the policies introduced under Gorbachev. The "grand sweep" of totalitarianism and traditional Marxism do not grasp the reality of the contemporary USSR and the reorganizations taking place therein. The utility of these theories is ideological in the sense that they sustain political claims of legitimacy or illegitimacy.

In the early stages of perestroika, the changes were reforms rather than revolution. The major institutional structures endured. The Communist Party of the Soviet Union had been weakened but remained hegemonic; it preserved a dominant role over political mobilization and organization. The CPSU had changed significantly in character. It jettisoned its direct control over government and its administrative role over the economy. It became more like one of the traditional Western social-democratic parties. The presidency strengthened the head of state. But he was still confronted with the dilemma of the tsars, noted above by Mill: how to enforce his power in a vast empire.

Until September 1991, the main features of planning and central control had been kept. The direction and levels of investment were decided by the Cabinet of Ministers and the President. A shift to market pricing of commodities, to an open exchange rate for the ruble were items for the agenda. Gorbachev's administrative reorganizations noted above did not break the power of the centrally controlled administrative system; rather they were skilfully reshuffling the cards. (See for instance the composition of his Cabinet of Ministers in the Appendix to chapter 2.)

Gorbachev's policy has led to new types of contradictions between the perpetuation of central planning and the creation of market forms, between political pluralism and the Communist Party's quest for political leadership, between democratic group rights and presidential power and control between center and republics. Political debate is increasingly focused around diverse interests.

The shift to a greater pluralism, to more autonomy for groups in society, is always fraught with dangers. In the West regional, religious, ethnic, and class consciousness always provide potential and often violent sources of cleavage, conflict, and confrontation. Under Stalin and his successors up to Gorbachev, such manifest social struggle was contained by a unitary ideology, by political manipulation, and, when all else failed, by force. In breaking this ideological and political mold, Gorbachev has undermined the ideological and political basis on which rule has been legitimated since 1917. The reform leadership has been confronted by pent-up passions and emotions that often do not have a rational basis; some groups (particularly in the national republics discussed below) challenge the very basis of the Soviet state. Marxism-Leninism and the formal monopoly of power of the CPSU have been toppled. The old order stemming from the ideals of the Bolsheviks was based on a form of mechanical solidarity having its roots in Russian culture and Party ideology and control. The reforms of Gorbachev have sought an organic solidarity, or a moral order which would give rise to a social and political consensus. This has been lacking and a consequence was a crisis of legitimacy.

When confronted with the contradictions inherent in the reform process, as Eltsin and Andreeva pointed out, Gorbachev vacillated. In the early 1990s, he was harshly criticized by the reform wing of Eltsin who alleged that he appeased the "hardliners". His Cabinet of Ministers was indeed drawn from the more traditional Party-backed forces, the centrally controlled economy had been weakened but market forces were only marginal. Investment and prices were still controlled centrally. His political constituency was the Communist Party: he had evolved as President with its support and was symbolically attached to it as its General Secretary. Dissatisfied reformers like Eltsin and other ex-communists put their faith in greater decentralization to the republics, in the extension of private property rights and in a greater role being given to the market. Its "hidden hand", they believed, would ensure stability, growth and cohesion. They called for his resignation and backed strikes in order to unseat him. Gorbachev's popularity at home plummeted to single percentage figures in the public opinion polls. His reputation was greater abroad: he had abandoned support to his client states and those in Eastern Europe had anti-communist governments; the collapse of Marxism-Leninism created an ideological vacuum internally, but in relations with the West this was a virtue, especially when linked to the promise of entry to the Soviet and East European markets by Western commerce.

The traditional political forces were also disgruntled. Gorbachev had undermined the accepted ways of doing things: central planning had been undermined by marketization, the Party had been emasculated in its established form, its symbols had been vilified, civil war had not been contained in the republics of the USSR and crime and speculation was rife. Gorbachev's own version of the Union Treaty (see below chapter 6) went too far and, they claimed, would lead to the break up of the Union. Economic indicators of well-being — gross national product, exports, employment and growth — were all negative. As in 1990, in the summer of 1991 famine was predicted for the winter. The country was falling apart and Gorbachev appeared complacent and incapable of action. Both sides agreed that Gorbachev's version of perestroika had failed.

The events of August 1991 and their aftermath have resolved politically these contradictions. The leaders of the State Committee for the State of Emergency represented the traditional forces of the government apparatus. Their policy would have continued with the processes of perestroika within a system of Party hegemony and a centrally controlled economy. The movement to marketization and privatization would have been halted. The industrial ministries would have been kept intact — though in the form of state corporations, rather like nationalized concerns such as the Coal Board in Britain. The conditions for the formation of a new union of states would have preserved the powers of the center. The state of emergency would certainly have repressed the forces of opposition, as witnessed by the immediate clampdown on the media.

The staging of the coup played into the hands of the reformist opposition. The coup leaders had disparaged constitutional methods. Gorbachev's political judgement was discredited: the coup was led by his own hand-picked team — "all the President's men". Though the Party did not lead the coup, many of its prominent members did, and others in the apparat sympathized with them: this gave Eltsin the opportunity to ban the Party as unconstitutional.

Eltsin and the reform leadership, aided by factions of the established elites, seized the initiative and control of the state. Theirs is a policy in which the leaders in the republics will increase their participation. Privatization and the extension of private property on a republican basis will be speeded up. The Union government will only exercise powers with the consent and agreement of the sovereign republic states.

Is Eltsin's rise to power a case of "people's power"? Though he had support against an unpopular administration, the events do not suggest a popular revolt precipitated by groups in civil society. Eltsin's call for a general strike went unanswered: even in Moscow ordinary life went on very much as normal during the days of the coup. There is no evidence of representatives of collectivities such as enterprises or institutions at the demonstrations: compare them, for instance, to the mass support given to Solidarity in Poland, or to the associations forming the Campaign for Nuclear Disarmament in the West. The anti-coup demonstrators were largely professionals and students. The call for support was answered by other anti-communist elites in the republics and cities such as Leningrad (now St Petersburg). The established elites were also divided: they lacked cohesion and the will to execute power, and important factions in the KGB, internal security forces and army sympathized with and supported Eltsin. Eltsin represented an alternative elite formation rather than the expression of "people's power".

It is unlikely that the post-coup political situations will consolidate a stable democracy within a framework of open political parties. While there were over 100 political parties in the Russian Republic in 1991, they were extremely weak: their membership is usually in two or three figures and they lack policy and organization. Western market systems are buttressed by classes based on property and the hegemony of a powerful state system of formal and informal controls developed during hundreds of years of capitalist development and nation building. In the West, political parties and associations such as trade unions have had a long period of gestation leading to the evolution of loyal oppositions prepared to work within the structure of law and informal "rules of the political game". Even here there can be violent confrontations between the state and opposition, such as in Northern Ireland, or large scale strikes, such as the air traffic controllers in the USA and miners in England. Russia and the other states of the Union have never had a capitalist class system and its attendant forms of civil society and control. A period of class and state formation are now on the political agenda. This will be a period of political instability and conflict.

What, then, are the sources of these changes? Totalitarianism and traditional Marxism-Leninism do not focus on social forces that initiate innovation within socialist systems. The political developments described throughout the book have been precipitated by movements in the social structure, by the maturation of Soviet society, and the changing world context of the late twentieth century. This evolution has brought new aspirations, conflicts, and contradictions that the reform leadership is seeking to resolve. These changes are multidimensional and will be the concern of the next part of this book.

READING TO CHAPTER 4

Nina Andreeva, "I Cannot Forego Principles"

Source: Sovetskaya Rossiya, 13 March 1988. Translated in BBC World Broadcasts, 15 April 1988.

I decided to write this letter after lengthy deliberation. I am a chemist and I lecture at Leningrad's Lensovet Technology Institute. Like many others, I also look after a student group. Students nowadays, following the period of social apathy and intellectual dependence, are gradually being charged with the energy of revolutionary changes. Naturally, discussions develop: About the ways of restructuring and its economic and ideological aspects. Glasnost', openness, the disappearance of zones where criticism is taboo, and the emotional heat in mass consciousness, especially among young people, often emerge in the raising of problems which are, to a greater or lesser extent, "prompted" either by Western radio voices or by those of our compatriots who are shaky in their concepts of the essence of socialism. And the variety of topics that are being discussed! A multiparty system, freedom of religious propaganda, emigration to live abroad, the right to broad discussion of sexual problems in the press, the need to decentralise the leadership of culture, abolition of compulsory military service ... There are particularly numerous arguments among students about the country's past.

What are the misgivings? Here is a simple example: You would think that plenty has been written and said about the Great Fatherland War and the heroism of those who fought in it. Recently, however, a student hostel in our Technology Institute organised a meeting with Hero of the Soviet Union Col (Reserve) V. F. Molozeyev. Among other things, he was asked a question about political repressions in the army. The veteran replied that he had never come across any repressions and that many of those who fought in the war with him from its beginning to its end became high-ranking military leaders ... Some were disappointed by the reply. Now that it has become topical, the subject of repressions has been blown up out of all proportion in some young people's imagination and overshadows any objective interpretation of the past. Examples like this are by no means isolated.

It is, of course, extremely gratifying that even "technicians" are keenly interested in theoretical problems of the social sciences. But I can neither accept nor agree with all too much of what has now appeared. Verbiage about "terrorism", "the people's political servility", "uninspired social vegetation", "our spiritual slavery", "universal fear", "dominance by boors in power" ... These are often the only yarns used to weave the history of our country during the period of the transition to socialism. It is, therefore, not surprising that nihilistic sentiments are intensifying among some students and there are instances of ideological confusion, loss of political bearings and even ideological omnivorousness. At times you even hear claims that the time has come to take communists to task for having allegedly "dehumanised" the country's life since 1917.

The February plenum of the Central Committee emphasised again the insistent need to ensure that "young people are taught a class-based vision of the world and understanding of the links between universal and class interests. Including understanding of the class essence of the changes occurring in our country." Such a vision of history and of the present is incompatible with the political anecdotes, base gossip and controversial fantasies which one often encounters today.

I have been reading and rereading sensational articles. For example, what can young people gain — disorientation apart — from revelations about "the counter-revolution in the USSR in the late 1920s and early 1930s", or about Stalin's "guilt" for the coming to power of fascism and Hitler in Germany? Or the public "reckoning" of the number of "Stalinists" in various generations and social groups?

We are Leningraders and therefore were particularly interested in watching recently the good documentary film about S. M. Kirov. But at times the text which accompanied the shots not only diverged from the film's documentary evidence but even made it appear somewhat ambiguous. For example, the film shots would be showing the outbursts of keenness, joie de vivre and spiritual enthusiasm of people building socialism, while the announcer's text would be about repressions, about lack of information ...

I am probably not the only one to have noticed that the calls by party leaders asking the "exposers" to pay attention also to the factual and real achievements at different stages of socialist building seems, as if by command, to bring forth more and more outbursts of "exposures". M. Shatrov's plays are a notable phenomenon in this — alas! — infertile field. On the day the 26th Party Congress opened, I went to see the play "Blue Horses on Red Grass". I recall young people's excitement at the scene where Lenin's secretary tries to empty a teapot over his head, confusing him with an unfinished clay sculpture. As a matter of fact, some young people had arrived with preprepared banners whose essence was to sling mud at our past and present ... In "The Brest Peace" the playwright and director make Lenin kneel before Trotsky. So much for the symbolic embodiment of the author's concept. It is further developed in the play "Onward! Onward! Onward!" A play is, of course, not a historical document. But even in a work of art truth is guaranteed by nothing but the author's stance. Especially in the case of political theatre.

Playwright Shatrov's stance has been analysed in detail and in a well-reasoned way in reviews by historians published by *Pravda* and *Sovetskaya Rossiya*. I would like to express my own opinion. In particular, it is impossible not to agree that Shatrov deviates substantially from the accepted principles of socialist realism. In covering a most crucial period in our country's history, he absolutises the subjective factor in social development and clearly ignores the objective laws of history as displayed in the activity of the classes and masses. The role played by the proletarian masses and the Bolshevik Pary is reduced to the "background" against which the actions of irresponsible politicos unfold.

The reviewers, on the basis of the Marxist-Leninist methodology of analysing specific historical processes, have convincingly shown that Shatrov distorts the history of socialism in our country. He objects to the state of the dictatorship of the proletariat without whose historical contribution we would have nothing to restructure today. The author goes on to accuse Stalin of the assassination of Trotsky and Kirov and of "isolating" Lenin while he was ill. But how can anyone possibly make biased accusations against historical figures without bothering to adduce any proof? ...

Unfortunately, the reviewers have failed to show that, despite all his pretensions as an author, the playwright is far from original. I got the impression that, in terms of the logic of his assessments and arguments, he rather closely follows the line of V. Suvarin's book published in Paris in 1935. In his play Shatrov makes his characters say things that were said by the adversaries of Leninism about the course of the revolution, Lenin's role in it and the relationships between Central Committee members at different stages of intra-party struggle ... This is the essence of Shatrov's "fresh reading" of Lenin. Let me add that A. Rybakov, author of "Children of the Arbat", frankly admitted that he had borrowed some incidents from emigre publications.

Without having read the play "Onward! Onward! Onward! (it had not been published yet), I had read rapturous reviews of it in some publications. What could have been the meaning of such haste? I learned later that the play was being hastily staged.

Soon after the February plenum, *Pravda* published a letter entitled "Coming Full Circle?" and signed by eight of our leading theatrical figures. They warn against what they see as possible delays in staging M. Shatrov's play. This conclusion is drawn on the basis of critical reviews of the play in the press. For some unknown reason, the writers of the letter exclude the writers of critical reviews from the category of those "who treasure the fatherland". How can this be reconciled with their desire for a "stormy and impassioned" discussion of our historical past, both distant and recent? It appears that they alone are entitled to their opinion.

In the numerous discussions now taking place on literally all questions of social sciences, as a higher education establishment lecturer I am primarily interested in the questions which have a direct effect on young people's ideological and political education, their moral health and their social optimism. Conversing with students and deliberating with them on controversial problems, I cannot help concluding that our country has accumulated quite a few anomalies and one-sided interpretations which clearly need to be corrected. I would like to dwell on some of them in particular.

Take for example the question of I.V. Stalin's position in our country's history. The whole obsession with critical attacks is linked with his name and, in my opinion, this obsession centres not so much on the historical individual itself as on the entire highly complex epoch of transition. An epoch linked with unprecedented feats by a whole generation of Soviet people who are today gradually withdrawing from active labour, political and social work. The industrialisation, collectivisation and cultural revolution which brought our country to the ranks of great world powers are being forcibly squeezed into the "personality cult" formula. All this is being questioned. Matters have gone so far that persistent demands for "repentance" are being made of "Stalinists" (and this category can be taken to include anyone you like) ... There is rapturous praise for novels and films which lynch the epoch of storms and onslaught, which is presented as a "tragedy of the peoples". It is true that such attempts to place historical nihilism on a pedestal do not always work. For example, a film showered with praise by critics can be extremely coolly received by the majority of audiences despite the unprecedented publicity.

Let me say right away that neither I nor any member of my family are in any way involved with Stalin, his retinue, his associates or his extollers. My father was a worker at Leningrad port, my mother was a fitter at the Kirov works. My elder brother also worked there. He, my father and my sister died in battles against the Hitlerites. One of my relatives was repressed and then rehabilitated after the 20th Party Congress. I share all Soviet people's anger and indignation about the mass repressions which occurred in the 1930s and 1940s and for which the party-state leadership of the time is to blame. But common sense resolutely protests against the monochrome depiction of contradictory events which now dominates in some press organs.

I support the party call to uphold the honour and dignity of the trailblazers of socialism. I think that these are the party-class positions from which we must assess the historical role of all leaders of the party and the country, including Stalin. In this case, matters cannot be reduced to their "court" aspect or to abstract moralising by people far removed both from those stormy times and from the people who had to live and work in those times. And to work in such a fashion as to still be an inspiring example for us today.

For me, as for many people, a decisive role in my assessment of Stalin is played by the candid testimony of contemporaries who clashed directly with him both on our side of the barricades and on the other side. It is the latter that are quite interesting. For instance, take Churchill who, back in 1919, boasted of his personal contribution to organising the military intervention by 14 foreign states against the young Soviet republic and, exactly 40 years later, was forced to use the following words to describe Stalin, one of his formidable political opponents:

"He was an outstanding personality who left his mark on our cruel time during his lifetime. Stalin was a man of exceptional energy, erudition and unbending willpower, harsh, tough and ruthless in both action and conversation and even I, brought up in the English Parliament, could not oppose him in any way ... A gigantic force resounded in his works. This force is so great in Stalin that he seemed unique among the leaders of all times and all peoples ... His effect on people is irresistible. Whenever he entered the Yalta conference hall, we all rose as if by command. And, strangely, we all stood to attention. Stalin possessed a profound, totally unflappable, logical and sensible wisdom. He was a past master at finding a way out of the most hopeless situation at a difficult time ... He was a man who used his enemies to destroy his enemy, forcing us — whom he openly called imperialists — to fight the imperialists ... He took over a Russia still using the wooden plough and left it equipped with atomic weapons." This assessment and admission by the loyal custodian of the British Empire cannot be attributed to either pretence or political timeserving.

The main elements of this description can also be seen in the memoirs of De Gaulle and the reminiscences and correspondence of other European and American politicians who had dealings with Stalin both as wartime ally and as class adversary.

Considerable serious food for thought on this question is provided by Soviet documents which are available to anyone wishing to consult them. Take the two-volume "Correspondence between the Chairman of the USSR Council of Ministers and the US Presidents and British Prime Ministers during the Great Fatherland War 1941–1945", published by the Political Literature publishing house back in 1957. There is no doubt that these documents evoke pride in our state and its position and role in a stormy and changing world. I recall the anthology of Stalin's reports, speeches and orders dating from the last war on which the heroic generation of the victors of fascism was raised. It could perfectly well be reissued to include documents which were secret at the time, like the dramatic order No 227, which some historians are indeed pressing for. Our young people are familiar with none of these documents. Particular importance for the cultivation of historical awareness attaches to the memoirs of military leaders Zhukov, Vasilevskiy, Golovanov and Shtemenko and the aircraft designer Yakovlev, who all knew the Supreme Commander personally.

There is no question that this period was extremely harsh. But it is also true that personal modesty bordering upon asceticism did not feel ashamed of itself and that potential Soviet millionaires were still afraid to peck away in the quiet of minor offices and trading centres. Furthermore, we were not so business-like and pragmatic, and prepared young people not for the finer points of consuming wealth accumulated by their parents but for Labour and Defence, without demolishing young people's spiritual world with masterpieces imported from "the other side" or home-grown imitations of mass culture. Imaginary relatives were in no hurry to invite their fellow-tribesmen to "the promised land", turning them into "refuseniks" of socialism.

Long and frank conversations with young interlocutors lead us to the conclusion that the attacks on the state of the dictatorship of the proletariat and our country's leaders at the time have not only political, ideological and moral causes but also a social substratum. There are quite a few people interested in expanding the bridgehead for these attacks, and they are to be found not just on the other side of our borders. Along with professional anti-communists in the West who picked the supposedly democratic slogan of "anti-Stalinism" a long time ago, the offspring of the classes overthrown by the October Revolution, by no means all of whom have managed to forget the material and social losses incurred by their forebears, are still alive and prospering. One must add to them the spiritual heirs of Dan and Martov and other adherents of Russian social democracy, the spiritual followers of Trotsky or Yagoda, and the offspring of NEP-men, Basmachis and Kulaks with grudges against socialism . . .

It is well known that any historical figure is shaped by specific socioeconomic and ideological and political conditions which have a determining effect on the subjective-objective selection of contenders called upon to solve diverse social problems. Having appeared on the proscenium of history, in order to "remain afloat" such a contender must satisfy the needs of the epoch and the leading social and political structures and must apply objective laws in his activity, inevitably leaving the "mark" of his personality on historical events. By way of an example, when all is said and done, hardly anyone today is disturbed by the personal qualities of Peter the Great, but everyone remembers that during his rule the country became a great European power. Time has condensed the result, which now provides the basis for an assessment of the Emperor Peter's historical personality. And the flowers which are invariably laid on his sarcophagus at the Peter and Paul Fortress cathedral are an expression of the respect and gratitude felt by our contemporaries who are removed from the autocracy.

I think that, no matter how controversial and complex a figure in Soviet history may be, his genuine role in the building and defence of socialism will sooner or later be given an objective and unambiguous assessment. Of course, unambiguous does not mean an assessment that is one-sided, that whitewashes or that eclectically sums up contradictory phenomena making it possible to produce subjectivism, albeit with slight reservations, "to forgive or not forgive", "to reject or retain" in history. Unambiguous means primarily a specifically historical assessment detached from short-term considerations which would demonstrate — according to historical results! — the dialectics of the correspondence between the individual's actions and the basic laws governing society's development. In our country these laws were also linked with the solution of the question "Who will defeat whom?" in its domestic and international aspects. If we are to adhere to the Marxist-Leninist methodology of historical analysis, then, in M. S. Gorbachev's words, we must primarily and vividly show how the millions of people lived, how they worked and what they believed in, as well as the coupling of victories and failures, discoveries and errors, the bright and the tragic, the revolutionary enthusiasm of the masses and the violations of socialist legality and even crimes at times.

I was puzzled recently by the revelation by one of my students that the class struggle is supposedly an obsolete term, just like the leading role of the proletariat. It would be fine if she were the only one to claim this. A furious argument was generated, for example, by a respected academician's recent assertion that present-day relations between states from the two different socio-economic systems apparently lack any class content. I assume that the academician did not deem it necessary to explain why it was that, for several decades, he wrote exactly the opposite — namely, that peaceful coexistence is nothing but a form of class struggle in the international arena. It seems that the philosopher has not rejected this view. No matter, people can change their minds. It does seem to me, however, that duty would nevertheless command a leading philosopher to explain at least to those who have studied and are studying his books: What is happening today, does the international working class no longer oppose world capital as embodied in its state and political organs?

It seems to me that many of the present debates centre on this question: Which class or stratum of society is the leading and mobilizing force of restructuring? This in particular was discussed in an interview with the writer A. Prokhanov published by our city newspaper 'Leningradskiy Rabochiy'. Prokhanov proceeds from the premise that the specific nature of the present state of social consciousness is typified by the presence of two ideological currents or, as he puts it, "alternative towers" which are trying, from different directions, to overcome the "socialism which has been built in battles" in our country. Though he exaggerates the significance and acuteness of the duel between these two "towers", the writer is nevertheless correct in emphasising that "they agree only on the slaughter of socialist values". But both of them, so their ideologists claim, are "for restructuring".

The first and most swollen ideological current which has already manifested itself in the course of restructuring claims to offer a model of some sort of Left-wing liberal intellectual socialism which allegedly expresses the most genuine humanism, "cleansed" of class accretions. Its champions counter proletarian collectivism with the "intrinsic value of the individual" — modernistic quests in the cultural sphere, God-seeking tendencies, technocratic idols, homilies to the "democratic" charms of contemporary capitalism and kowtowing to its real and supposed achievements. Its spokesmen claim that what we have built is supposedly not proper socialism, and that apparently "an alliance between political leadership and progressive intelligentsia has been formed for the first time in history" only today. While millions of people on our planet are dying from starvation, epidemics and military adventures by imperialism, they demand immediate formulation of a "legal code to protect animal rights", attribute an extraordinary and supernatural reason to nature and claim that intelligence is not a social but a biological quality genetically transmitted from parents to children. Can you explain to me what all this means?

It is the champions of "Left-wing liberal socialism" who shape the tendency towards falsifying the history of socialism. They try to make us believe that the country's past was nothing but mistakes and crimes, keeping silent about the greatest achievements of the past and the present. Claiming full possession of historical truth, they replace the socio-political criterion of society's development with scholastic ethical categories. I would very much like to know who and why needed to ensure that every prominent leader of the Party Central Committee and the Soviet government — once out of office — was compromised and discredited because of actual and alleged mistakes and errors committed when solving the most complex problems in the course of historical trailblazing? Where are the origins of this passion of ours to undermine the prestige and dignity of leaders of the world's first socialist country?

Another peculiarity of the views held by "Left-wing liberals" is an overt or covert cosmopolitan tendency, some kind of non-national "internationalism". I read somewhere about an incident after the revolution when a delegation of merchants and factory owners called on Trotsky at the Petrograd Soviet "as a Jew" to complain about oppression by the Red Guards, and he declared that he was "not a Jew but an internationalist", which really puzzled the petitioners.

In Trotsky's views, the idea of "national" connoted a certain inferiority and limitation compared with the "international". This is why he emphasised October's "national tradition", wrote about "the national element in Lenin", claimed that the Russian people "had inherited no cultural heritage at all", and so on. We are somehow embarrassed to say that it was indeed the Russian proletariat, whom the Trotskyites treated as "backward and uncultured", who accomplished — in Lenin's words — "three Russian revolutions" and that the Slav peoples stood in the vanguard of mankind's battle against fascism.

This, of course, is not to denigrate the historical contribution of other nations and ethnic groups. This, as it is said nowadays, is only to ensure the full historical truth ... When students ask me how come thousands of small villages in the non-black-soil zone and Siberia are deserted, I reply that this is part of the high price we had to pay for victory and the post-war restoration of the national economy, just like the irretrievable loss of large numbers of monuments of Russian national culture. I am also convinced: Any denigration of the importance of historical consciousness produces a pacifist erosion of defence and patriotic consciousness, as well as a desire to categorise the slightest expressions of Great Russian national pride as manifestation of great power chauvinism.

Here is something else that also worries me: The practice of "refusenikism" of socialism is nowadays linked with militant cosmopolitanism. Unfortunately, we remember it suddenly only when its neophytes plague us with their outrages in front of the Smolnyy or by the Kremlin walls. Moreover, we are gradually being trained to perceive the aforementioned phenomenon as some sort of almost innocent change of "place of residence" rather than as class and national betrayal by persons most of whom graduated from higher education establishments and completed their postgraduate studies thanks to our own nationwide funds. Generally speaking, some people are inclined to look upon "refusenikism" as some sort of manifestation of "democracy" and the "rights of man", whose talents were prevented from flourishing by "stagnant socialism". And if it so happens that people over there, in the "free world", fail to appreciate bubbling entrepreneurship and "genius" and the special services are not interested in the trading of conscience, one can always return ...

It is well known that, according to their specific historical role, K. Marx and F. Engels described entire nations at a given stage of their history as "counter-revolutionary" — and I emphasise, not classes, not strata but nations. Standing on the firm foundation of the class approach, they did not hesitate to use sharp terms to describe a number of nations, including Russians and Poles, and even the nationalities to which they themselves belonged. The founders of scientific-proletarian world outlook seem to remind us that, in the fraternal community of Soviet peoples, every nation and ethnic group must "cherish its honour from youth" and not allow itself to be provoked into nationalist and chauvinist sentiments. Each people's national pride and national dignity must be organically fused with the internationalism of the united socialist community.

While "neo-liberals" look toward the West, the other "alternative tower", to use Prokhanov's expression, the "conservationists and traditionalists", are striving "to overcome socialism by regression". In other words, by reverting to the social forms of pre-socialist Russia. The spokesman of this variety of "peasant socialism" are fascinated by this image. In their opinion, the moral values accumulated by peasant communes in the misty fog of the centuries were lost 100 years ago. The "traditionalists" certainly deserve credit for what they have done in the exposure of corruption, the fair solution of ecological problems, the struggle against alcoholism, the protection of historical monuments and the opposition to dominance by mass culture, which they correctly evaluate as consumerist mania ...

At the same time, the views of the ideologists of "peasant socialism" contain a lack of understanding of October's historical importance for the fate of the fatherland, a one-sided assessment of collectivisation as a "terrible atrocity against the peasantry", an uncritical perception of mystical religious Russian philosophy and the old tsarist concepts in our historical science, and an unwillingness to perceive the post-revolutionary stratification of the peasantry and the revolutionary role of the working class.

When it comes to the class struggle in the countryside, for example, excessive emphasis is often placed on "rural" commissars who "shot middle peasants in the back". There were, of course, all sorts of commissars at the height of the revolutionary conflagration in our vast country. But the mainstream of our life was nevertheless determined by commissars who were shot at. Commissars who had stars carved on their backs or were burned alive. The price the "attacking class" had to pay consisted not only of the lives of commissars, Checkists, rural Bolsheviks, members of the Committees of Poor Peasantry, or the "Twenty Thousand", but also those of the first tractor drivers, rural correspondents, girl teachers, rural Komsomol members and the lives of tens of thousands of other unknown fighters for socialism.

The education of young people is rendered even more complex by the fact that informal organisations and associations are being formed in the wake of the ideas of "neo-liberals" and "neo-Slavophiles". Sometimes the upper hand in their leadership is gained by extremist elements capable of provocations. A politicisation of these informal organisations on the basis of a by no means socialist pluralism has recently emerged. Leaders of these organisations often speak of "power-sharing" on the basis of a "parliamentary system", "free trade unions", "autonomous publishing houses" and so on. In my view, all this leads to the conclusion that the main and cardinal issue of the debates now taking place in the country is this question: Whether or not to recognise the leading role of the party and the working class in building socialism and therefore in restructuring. Of course, with all the ensuing theoretical and practical conclusions for politics, economics and ideology.

This key problem of social historical world outlook produces the question of the role of socialist ideology in the spiritual development of Soviet society. By the way, this question was emphasised by K. Kautskiy back towards the end of 1917 when, in one of his brochures devoted to October, he declared that socialism is distinguished by iron planning and discipline in the economy and by anarchy in ideology and spiritual life. This caused jubilation among Mensheviks, Socialist Revolutionaries and other petty bourgeois ideologists, but was firmly rebuffed by Lenin and his comrades-in-arms who consistently defended, as they said at the time, the "commanding heights" of scientific proletarian ideology.

Let us recall: When V. I. Lenin clashed with sociologist Pitirim Sorokin, who was popular at the time, over the latter's manipulations of statistics on divorce among residents of Petrograd and with Prof Vipper over his religious conservationist writings (which, incidentally, seem quite innocent compared with what is being printed now), he attributed the appearance of these publications to inexperience among mass media workers at the time and concluded that "the working class in Russia has managed to gain power but still has not learned how to use it". Otherwise, Vladimir Ilyich pointed out, the revolutionary proletariat would have "politely shown the door" out of the country to these professors and writers who "are no more suited" to educating the masses than "notorious libertines would be suited as mentors in education establishments for youngsters." As a matter of fact, many of the 164 who were exiled at the end of 1922 according to the list issued by the All-Russian Central Executive Committee returned home later and honestly served their people, including Prof Vipper.

It seems to me that the question of the role and position of socialist ideology is extremely acute today. The authors of timeserving articles in the guise of moral and spiritual "cleansing" erode the dividing lines and criteria of scientific ideology, manipulate glasnost and foster non-socialist pluralism, which objectively applies the brakes on restructuring in the public conscience. This has a particularly painful effect on young people which, I repeat, is clearly sensed by us lecturers in higher education establishments, schoolteachers and all who have to deal with young people's problems. As M. S. Gorbachev said at the February plenum of the CPSU Central Committee, "our actions in the spiritual sphere — and maybe primarily and precisely there — must be guided by our Marxist-Leninist principles. Principles, comrades, must not be compromised on any pretext whatever."

This is what we stand for now and this is what we shall continue to stand for. Principles were not given to us as a gift, we have fought for them at crucial turning points in the fatherland's history.

Selected Bibliography for Part One

Listed here are the principal sources used in the text. Russian language sources are excluded. Most, if not all, national statistics have been taken from Soviet government sources especially the handbook *Narodnoe khozyaystvo SSSR*, which is published yearly. Data on Party membership have been derived from the publication *Izvestiya TsK KPSS* (published monthly). Election results have been taken directly from reports in the Soviet press.

Useful articles may be found in the journals *Problems of Communism, Soviet Economy*, and *Soviet Studies*. The *Current Digest of the Soviet Press* (published weekly) is an invaluable source of original documents and should be consulted by students wishing to read the speeches of Soviet leaders. The journals *Soviet Government and Law* and *Soviet Economics*, published by M. E. Sharpe, Armonk, New York, contain good selections of Soviet articles in translation. Radio Liberty's *Report on the USSR* (published weekly) contains many topical reports of contemporary developments. Much lively Soviet literature is available in translation: *Moscow News* published weekly has many interesting articles written from a very committed pro-perestroika point of view. The journal *Russia and the World* (previously *Detente*) publishes Soviet articles and commentary on Soviet affairs.

Aage, H. 1987. "Consumption, Income Distribution and Incentives." *The Soviet Economy; A New Course?* Bruxelles: NATO, 47–70.

Aganbegyan, A. 1987. *The Challenge: Economics of Perestroika.* London: Hutchinson.

Bergson, Abram, and Herbert S. Levine, eds. 1983. *The Soviet Economy Towards the Year 2000.* London: Allen and Unwin.

Bialer, S. 1980. *Stalin's Successors: Leadership, Stability and Change in the Soviet Union.* Cambridge: Cambridge University Press.

———1986. *The Soviet Paradox: External Expansion, Internal Decline.* New York: Knopf.

Bloch, S. and P. Reddaway. 1978. *Psychiatric Terror: How Soviet Psychiatry Is Used to Suppress Dissent.* London: Future Publications.

Breslauer, G. 1982. *Khrushchev and Brezhnev as Leaders: Building Authority in Soviet Politics.* London and Boston: Unwin Hyman.

Brown, A. 1985. "Gorbachev: New Man in the Kremlin," *Problems of Communism.* (May–June): 1–23.

———1991. *The Gorbachev Factor in Soviet politics.* Oxford: Oxford University Press.

Brus, W. and H. H. Ticktin. 1981. "Is Market Socialism Possible or Necessary?" *Critique* 14: 13–39.

Bunce, V. and J. M. Echols III. 1980. "Soviet Politics in the Brezhnev Era: 'Pluralism' or 'Corporatism'?" *See* Kelley 1980.

Chiesa, G. 1990. "The 28th Congress of the CPSU." *Problems of Communism* vol. 39, no. 4 (July–August): 24–38.

Cushman, T. 1988. "Ritual and Conformity in Soviet Society," *The Journal of Communist Studies* 4, no. 2 (June) 162–80.

Ellman, M. 1989. *Socialist Planning.* Cambridge: Cambridge University Press. A detailed planning study useful for more detailed work on the economy.

Evans, A. J. 1977. "Developed Socialism in Soviet Ideology." *Soviet Studies* 29 (3): 409–28.

———1986. "The Decline of Developed Socialism?" *Soviet Studies* 38 (1): 1–23

Feher, F. and A. Arato, eds. 1989. *Gorbachev: the Debate.* Cambridge: Polity Press.

Friedrich C. J. and Z. Brzezinski. 1966. *Totalitarian Dictatorship and Autocracy.* New York: Praeger.

Gooding, J. 1990. "Gorbachev and Democracy." *Soviet Studies* vol. 42, no. 2 (April): 195–231.

Gorbachev, M. S. 1987. *Perestroika: New Thinking for Our Country and the World.* London: Collins.

Gustafson, T. and D. Mann. 1986. "Gorbachev at the Helm." *Problems of Communism.* (May–June): 1–9.

Hahn, J. 1988. "An Experiment in Competition: The 1987 Elections to the Local Soviets." *Slavic Review* 47 (5): 434–37.

Hammer, 11. 8. 1990. *The USSR: The Politics of Oligarchy.* Oxford and Boulder: Westview Press.

Hanson, P. 1989. "Inflation versus Reform." Radio Liberty *Report on the USSR* 1, no. 16 (21 April): 13–17.

Hewett, Ed. A. 1988. *Reforming the Soviet Economy: Equality versus Efficiency.* Washington D.C.: The Brookings Institute.

Hill, Ronald J. and J. A. Dellenbrant. 1989. *Gorbachev and Perestroika: Towards a New Socialism?* Aldershot: Gower. Overview of changes in Soviet society.

Hill, R. and P. Frank. 1987. *The Soviet Communist Party.* London: Unwin Hyman.

Hoffmann, E. P. and R. F. Laird, eds. 1984. *The Soviet Polity in the Modern Era.* New York: Aldine Publishing. This is a collection containing many seminal articles.

Hough, J. F. 1979. "The Brezhnev Era: the Man and the System." *Problems of Communism* (July): 1–17.

————1980. *Soviet Leadership in Transition*. Washington D.C.: The Brookings Institute.

————1988. *Russia and the West*. New York: Simon and Schuster.

————1990. "Gorbachev's Endgame." *World Policy Journal* no. 4: 639−72.

Jones, Anthony, and William Moskoff. 1989. *Perestroika and the Economy: New Thinking in Soviet Economics*. New York: Sharpe.

————1989. "Private Enterprise and Perestroika: The New Soviet Cooperatives." *Problems of Communism* 38, no. 5 (November/December).

Joyce, W., H. Ticktin, and Stephen White, eds. 1988. *Gorbachev and Gorbachevism*. Special number of the *Journal of Communist Studies* 4, no. 4 (December). (This is a useful collection of articles on the politics of perestroika, particularly the events around the Nineteenth Party Conference of June/July 1988.)

Kagarlitsky, B. 1990. *The Dialectic of Change*. London and New York: Verso.

Kelley, D. R. ed. 1980. *Soviet Politics in the Brezhnev Era*. New York: Praeger.

Kornai, J. 1980. *Economics of Shortage*. 2 vols. Amsterdam: North Holland Publishers. A major criticism of traditional forms of planning and exposition of the idea of a "shortage economy." See particularly vol. A, chapter 11.

Kux, E. 1984. "Contradictions in Soviet Socialism," *Problems of Communism* 33, no. 6 (November−December): 1−27.

Lane, D. 1985a. *Soviet Economy and Society*. New York: New York University Press.

————1985b. *State and Politics in the USSR*. New York: New York University Press.

————1987. *Soviet Labour and the Ethic of Communism*. London: Wheatsheaf; Boulder: Praeger. Role of labour in Soviet society.

Lane, D. ed. 1988. *Elites and Political Power in the USSR*. Aldershot: Gower. Analysis of elite politics suitable for upper-level students.

Lerner, Lawrence W., and Donald W. Treadgold, eds. 1988. *Gorbachev and the Soviet Future*. Boulder: Westview Press. Overview of Soviet developments by notable Western Soviet specialists.

Light, M. 1988. *The Soviet Theory of International Relations*. Brighton: Harvester. This is a good outline of current Soviet thinking on international relations.

Litvin, V. 1987. "Reforming Economic Management," *Problems of Communism* (July−August): 87−92.

McCauley, M., ed. 1987a. *The Soviet Union under Gorbachev*. London: Macmillan.

————1987b. *Khrushchev and Khrushchevism*. London: Macmillan.

Novc, A. 1986. *The Soviet Economic System*. 3d ed. Boston: Unwin Hyman.

————1989. *Stalinism and After: The Road to Gorbachev*. 3d ed. Boston: Unwin Hyman.

Problems of Communism 36, no. 4 (1987). Special section on perestroika contains useful articles by Hough (21−43) and Mann and Gustafson (1−20).

Sakwa, R. 1990. *Gorbachev and his Reforms, 1985−1990*. London: Philip Allan.

Shmelev, N. and V. Popov. 1990. *The Turning Point: Revitalising the Soviet Economy*. London: Taurus.

Teague, Elizabeth, 1989. "Fall of Representation of Party Apparatus in the CPSU Central Committee." Radio Liberty, *Report on the USSR 1*, no. 19 (12 May): 3−5.

Urban, M. E. 1990. *More Power to the Soviets: The Democratic Revolution in the USSR*. Aldershot and Vermont: Edward Elgar.

U. S. Congress. Joint Economic Committee. 1987. *Gorbachev's Economic Plans*. 2 vols. Washington D.C.: U. S. Government Printing Office. Wide-ranging review of Soviet economic thinking.

USSR Academy of Sciences. 1988. *Economic Strategy of the CPSU*. Soviet Economic Science Series, no. 6. Moscow: Social Sciences Today. (This is a convenient Soviet collection of articles.)

Walker, Martin. 1986. *The Waking Giant: The Soviet Union under Gorbachev*. London: Michael Joseph.

White, S. 1988. "Reforming the Electoral System." *See* Joyce, Ticktin, and White 1988.

———1990. "'Democratisation' in the USSR", *Soviet Studies* vol. 42, no. 2 (January): 3–24.

White, S. and A. Pravda, eds. 1988. *Ideology and Soviet Politics*. London: Macmillan.

Yanov, A. 1988. "Russian Nationalism as the Ideology of Counterreform." In *Russian Nationalism Today*, Radio Liberty, Special Edition. (December): 43–52.

Zaslavskaya, T. 1984. "The Novosibirsk Report." Reprinted in *Survey* 28 (1): 83–108.

———1990. *The Second Socialist Revolution*. London: Taurus. Exposition of the dynamics of the reform program by leading Soviet sociologist and reformer.

Part Two

SOCIAL CLASSES AND GROUPS

Chapter 5

THE CHANGING SOCIAL STRUCTURE

The developments that have occurred under the leadership of Gorbachev reflect major social changes in the USSR, resulting in a social structure that is qualitatively different from that ruled by Stalin and Khrushchev. Gorbachev should be considered not as changing society from the top, instead the changes taking place during his leadership should be viewed as a result of new social groups and interests that have developed in the past thirty years. The USSR is now a modern society comparable in many respects to the advanced nations of the West. The expectations of the population of both systems are alike and industrialism and urbanism have led to similar problems in capitalist and state socialist society.

By the term social structure we mean an array of positions or statuses, the conditions that shape them, and a network of relationships between people and groups. Statuses give rise to patterns of behavior, to norms and expectations; they are foci that give people a sense of social and individual identity. Statuses include occupations and social groups that may be divided into many categories, such as sex and age, urban and rural, ethnic and religious, white collar and blue collar, professional and peasant.

One of the important tasks of sociologists is to delineate the salient groups in the social structure. In the chapters that follow we shall consider the changing balance of urban and rural divisions, occupational and educational differences, age and gender differentiation, and the rise of ethnic and national consciousness.

CLASS STRUCTURE

Social class would figure prominently in any analysis of social relations in Western societies. While social scientists and laypersons use this term regularly, they do so with imprecision and ambiguity. Social class may refer generally to the social position one holds in society, to the status or social recognition that one is afforded. This may reflect a person's occupation, education, racial and social origin, level of wealth and income, quality of life, or attainment in culture. One might say that social class in Western societies is pluralistic by definition, because it is based on many criteria, and it is a multidimensional concept.

Sociologists refine the concept of class and distinguish between its distributive and relational aspects. Distributive aspects of class refer to the quantitative and qualitative attributes of various strata, that is, the level of income, the standard of living, and the more intangible style of life of the rich or the poor. Relational aspects have to do with interpersonal or interclass relations; essentially, the aspects of authority or power between class groups.

Sociologists also attempt to tease out underlying factors that determine class relations; this is a more controversial area of study. But one might generalize that ownership of wealth, type and level of occupation, political position, ethnic origin, and sex are among the most important determinants of social division or class in a distributive and relational sense.

The description and interpretation of classes in Soviet society is significantly influenced by the political assumptions the analyst makes. To do justice to the subject one must analyze social class from different theoretical points of view, and also take account of social change involving shifts between social classes. Two standpoints may be demarcated in the literature. First, Soviet society is composed of unequal social groups in a distributional sense, but in a relational or political dimension there is no major or antagonistic division between dominant and subordinate classes. In essence, this is the line adopted by those Soviet sociologists and proponents of the Soviet system who have emphasized its homogeneity and social harmony. A second approach argues that not only are there significant distributional forms of class inequality, but also in a relational sense there are conflicts between various elite groups and antagonisms between those in authority and the public.

THE TRADITIONAL SOVIET CONCEPTION OF CLASSES: CONSENSUS

In considering the Soviet understanding of classes in socialist society, we must distinguish between accounts that have been made at different times by various people. While in the early evolution of the USSR there was a widely accepted definition of classes that was articulated and enforced under Stalin, the position is more complicated today because of disagreement within Soviet society about where to draw class boundaries and about the nature of class relations. Under Gorbachev most Stalinist assumptions have been abandoned.

The advantage, and thus the appeal, of the Soviet definition of classes is its simplicity; it is the social parallel to the notion of a unitary political community discussed above. Class relations in a socialist society, it is contended, are fundamentally different from those under capitalism. The Marxist theory of class conflict under capitalism rests on private property. The Bolshevik Revolution put an end to the exploiting class: property was nationalized and brought under state ownership and control. The state represented the interests of workers and peasants; it was considered further that in a relational sense there was no class antagonism under Soviet socialism.

There was, however, inequality of a distributive kind, even formal class division, between manual workers and collective farmers. Collective farmers (*kolkhozniki*) have different market positions from workers: the former are in collective agricultural production, whereas the latter receive wages for their work. Juridically collective farmers as a group have always owned the seeds, produce, and (nowadays) the equipment of the collective farm, but they could not own and cannot sell the land, which has been nationalized. The cooperative farm exchanges its output for income from the government. Hence in the traditional Soviet view, cooperative production and the limited ownership relations (of tools and seeds) put the collective farmer politically at a lower level than the worker. There are other significant social and cultural differences that will be discussed below.

Moreover, Soviet writers have always pointed out that the occupational division of labor gives rise to social stratification of the labor force: a major divide exists between manual and nonmanual workers. The latter are sometimes referred to as the *intelligentsiya* and this term can be used to include all types of "workers by brain" from clerks to leading Party officials. Intelligentsiya is an ambiguous term, and Soviet sociologists now tend to restrict its use not to all unskilled and unqualified white-collar workers but to those strata with specialist qualifications, including engineers, technicians, as well as employees in the executive, political, artistic, scientific, and administrative roles, and self-employed professionals (artists).

In the traditional Soviet Marxist concept of stratification it is pertinent to note that these social strata (including the classes of worker and collective farm peasant) enjoy mutually cordial relationships, which may be characterized by distributional inequality in terms of lifestyle, income, and social honor but not by class conflict. Equality is conceived narrowly — the elimination of classes based on ownership relations. In Soviet parlance there are no antagonistic contradictions between social groups in the USSR.

Even traditional Soviet theorists conceded, however, that contradictions would persist in socialist society. The causes of such contradictions under socialism were held to be derived from underdevelopment or from forces outside the Soviet social formation. Examples of underdevelopment are contradictions between town and country in the form of unequal medical facilities and educational opportunities. Prejudices against women, national, and religious groups are *perezhitki*, or vestiges, from the previous social formation of the tsars. Various types of antisocial behavior such as crime, speculation, and political dissent might have their origin in the external capitalist formation.

THE EVOLUTION OF SOVIET CLASSES

The Growth of Urban Society

Statistics in themselves do not tell us about expectations or human relationships, but they do indicate the direction and magnitude of changes in social structure. A study of the urban and occupational composition of the population establishes that by the 1980s the USSR was an urban industrial society comparable in many respects to advanced Western states. Table 5.1 (Figure 5.1) shows the rise of population between 1917 and 1989 (from 163 million to 286.7 million); the urban population in 1989 comprised 66 percent of the population. By way of comparison, in the mid-1970s, North America was 72 percent urbanized, and North Europe had an urban population of 83 percent. (These are only rough approximations because the basis of definition of urban and rural varies between countries.)

Only in the early 1960s did the USSR become mainly urban — a condition reached in Britain before the mid-nineteenth century. One

Table 5.1

Urban and Rural Population Balance, 1917—89 (in percentages)

	Total population (millions)	Urban	Rural
1917	163.0	17.9	82.1
1940	194.1	32.5*	67.5
1959	208.8	47.9†	52.1
1970	241.7	56.3	43.7
1979	266.6	63.4	36.6
1989	286.7	66.0‡	34.0

Source: Narodnoe khozyaystvo (hereafter *Narkhoz*) SSSR v 1987g. (Moscow, 1988); *Pravda*, 29 April 1989.
* 63 million.
† 100 million.
‡ 217 million.

Figure 5.1 Total and Urban Population, 1917—89

Source: Based on data from *Narkhoz* SSSR v 1987g. (Moscow 1988); *Pravda*, 29 April 1989.

must also bear in mind the great regional diversity of the USSR, wherein the Western European republics are more highly urbanized, and the Central Asian republics are predominantly rural. In 1989, for example, the Russian republic had an urban population of 74 percent, Latvia 71 percent, and the Ukraine 67 percent, whereas Tajikistan had only 33 percent, Kirgiziya 38 percent, and Uzbekistan 41 percent. (We will return to these regional differences later in the chapter on nationalities.)

The movement of population from countryside to town has been accompanied by important changes in employment, both by economic sector and by occupation. From Table 5.2 and Figure 5.2 we may deduce that

Table 5.2
Employment by Economic Sector, 1940–87 (percentages)

	1940	1960	1987
Agriculture	54	39	19
Industry and Building	23	32	38
Services (including transport)	23	29	43

Source: Narkhoz, 1988.

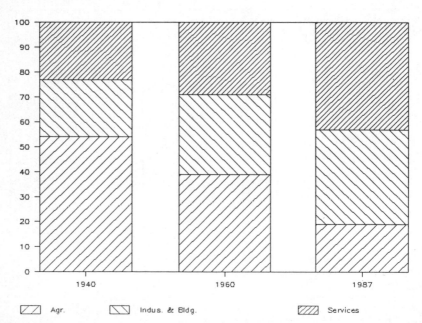

Figure 5.2 Employment by Economic Sector, 1940–87
Source: Based on data from *Narkhoz*, 1988.

employment in agriculture in 1987 was only 35 percent of that of 1940; and by 1987, the largest economic sector was services and transport (43 percent).

Table 5.3 and Figure 5.3 show changes in the population structure from the point of view of the Soviet definition of classes: manual, nonmanual, and collective farm. Figure 5.3 depicts the predominance of manual workers (82.1 million in 1987) and the large nonmanual group (36.4

Table 5.3
Occupational Class Background (in millions)

	1940	1960	1970	1980	1987
Nonmanual workers	10.0	15.8	25.3	33.7	36.5
Manual workers[a]	23.9 (37.99%)	46.2	64.9	78.8	82.1 (62.7%)
Collective farmers	29.0 (46%)	21.8	16.6	13.1	12.2 (9.3%)
Total	62.9	83.8	106.8	125.6	130.9

Source: Narkhoz, 1988.
a. Manual workers here include 9.7 million manual agricultural workers on state farms.

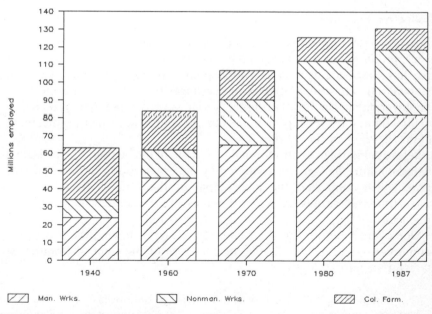

 Man. Wrks. Nonman. Wrks. Col. Farm.

Figure 5.3 Occupational Class Background
Source: Based on data from *Narkhoz,* 1988.

million) and allows us to make a number of fairly obvious but important observations that will be discussed further below.

By the 1980s there was a large educated, settled and nonmanual urban population. In terms of size the manual working class has replaced the peasant population of the interwar years. The social base of politics has changed. Under Stalin, the peasantry was a major social prop to the regime; under Brezhnev and Khrushchev this mantle fell to the unskilled manual worker. The professional nonmanual and skilled blue-collar work force are ascendant groups and they, it will be argued, are the social base on which Gorbachev's policies rest. This new social base makes demands to which the leadership responds. Such exchanges, moreover, have to be interpreted in the context of the presence of more traditional interests and groupings (the unskilled manual workers are still a very large group) and in the cultural legacy of previous epochs of Soviet history.

While the data in Figure 5.3 inform us about some very general patterns of development in the USSR, we need to study in more analytical terms the nature of social classes and stratification. Such study will indicate the socially relevant units and the ways that expectations and norms are created that give rise to group consciousness and patterns of behavior.

Collective Farmers

Under the laws of the Soviet system collective farmers as a group own the seeds, produce, and (nowadays) the equipment of the collective farm, but they have not been able to own and cannot sell the land, which has been nationalized. The cooperative farm exchanges its output for income from the government. In the traditional Soviet view, cooperative production and the limited ownership relations put the collective farmer politically at a lower level than the worker.

Before perestroika the traditional way of life of the peasant, the peasant's "attachment to the soil," was vitiated by the organization of the collective farm, which controlled the labor input of the farmer, fixed rates of remuneration, centrally determined quotas and the content of agricultural production.

Moreover, conditions in the villages have lagged behind the towns. As Gorbachev stated in March 1989 to a plenum of the Central Committee on agrarian reform:

> The peasant way of life has lost its attractiveness and prestige. People and particularly the young, are leaving the countryside. Migration of the population from the countryside for many years has surpassed its natural growth. Death

rates among the able-bodied people in the villages are 20 percent greater, and among children 50 percent higher than the towns.

With the passage of time the relevance of the collective farm peasantry as a major actor in Soviet society has declined. The sheer weight of economically active people has dwindled. In 1987 there were only 12.2 million collective farmers, which accounted for only 9.3 percent of the work force compared to 26 percent in 1960 and 46 percent in 1940 (see Figure 5.3).

The collective farmer has been and still is separated socially and economically, if not politically, from the urban manual worker and nonmanual employee, which may be illustrated by considering educational levels and the structures of family income and expenditures of collective farmers as compared with manual and nonmanual workers.

In the census of 1979 of every 1,000 manual urban workers, 351 had a secondary education; the corresponding figure for collective farmers was 220. The differences were somewhat greater for women — 350 and 201, respectively. When one considers higher (and incomplete higher) and secondary specialist education levels, differences are much more marked: 102 per 1,000 for urban manuals (both men and women) and 58 for collective farmers (both men and women) and for women 41 and 19 respectively.

Some of the differences in levels of education are accounted for by the age structure of the different social groups: collective farmers are older because the villages have suffered an exodus of younger, more educated people. Table 5.4 and Figure 5.4 show that although the comparison between collective farmers, manuals, and nonmanuals gives collective farmers substantially less education in 1939, by 1987 the gap between the educational levels of collective farmers and manual and nonmanual workers had been significantly decreased.

Ratios of real income between collective famers and manual and nonmanual workers have risen from 70:100 in 1960 to 80:100 in 1970 and 92:100 in 1986. Indeed, the income of *kolkhozniks* rose 29 percent during the Eleventh Five Year Plan (1981—85) compared to a planned increase of 20 percent. This represents a significant equalizing tendency in Soviet society. Table 5.5 compares in more detail the way that income and expenditure is distributed between manual workers and collective farmers. Note particularly the decline in the share of expenditure for food of collective farmers from 45.2 percent to 32.3 percent between 1965 and 1986. There has been considerable equalization of income between workers and collective farmers and the latter now have considerably more savings, reflecting both their increased incomes and the lack of commodities to buy.

Table 5.4
Post-Primary Education, 1939—87 (in thousands)

	1939	1959	1970	1987
Manual workers	87	401	590	861
Nonmanual workers	546	911	956	990
Collective farmers	18	226	393	763

Source: Narkhoz v 1987g. (1988); *Narkhoz za 70 let* (1987).

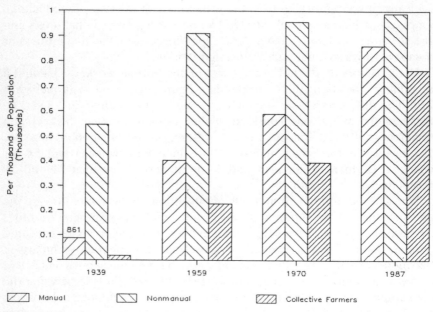

Figure 5.4 Post-Primary Education, 1939—87
Source: Based on data from *Narkhoz v 1979g.* (1978); *Narkhoz za 70 let* (1987).

Collective farmers have occupied the bottom rungs of the stratification order in the USSR, although the status of this group has improved in recent years. When the farms were founded, they were expected to provide social security (for example, sick pay, pensions) from their own resources; their members had no internal passports and could not legally leave the farm without permission of the collective farm meeting, its governing body. Now collective farmers are able to join the Agricultural Workers' Trade Union and have rights to social security provisions. Also,

Table 5.5
Income and Expenditure of Families of Industrial Workers and Collective Farmers

	Workers			Collective farmers		
	1940	1965	1986	1940	1965	1986
Income						
Wages of family members	70.3	73.1	69.4	5.8	7.4	8.9
Pensions, stipends, payments in kind	14.3	22.8	23.8	4.9	14.6	18.9
Private farming	9.0	1.7	0.7	48.3	36.5	23.1
Income from collective farm	—	—	—	39.7	39.6	45.5
Other sources (gifts from relatives, alimony, other income)	6.4	2.4	6.1	1.3	1.9	3.6
	100	100	100	100	100	100
Expenditure						
Food	53.0	37.9	27.9	67.3	45.2	32.3
Purchase of goods	16.0	20.8	25.2	18.5	22.5	28.6
Social, cultural and services[a]	17.4	24.3	23.2	4.8	14.0	14.5
Savings	4.6	2.8	8.1	6.3	8.0	11.3
Taxes	4.1	7.2	8.8	1.4	1.4	1.6
Other outgoings	4.9	7.0	7.0	1.7	8.9	11.7
	100	100	100	100	100	100

Source: Narkhoz v 1979g. (1980): 410–11; *Narkhoz za 70 let* (1987): 444–45.
a. Including education and government services.

like urban workers, collective farmers are issued internal passports giving them the right to travel.

Collective farmers also have considerable representation in the Communist Party. In 1989 11.4 percent of the Party's total membership was constituted of collective farmers, 45.4 percent were manual workers, and 43.2 percent were nonmanuals (see Figure 5.5).

The more conventional view of class relations saw nonantagonistic contradictions between the collective farm peasantry and the employed population. These contradictions were compounded of cultural differences and differences in production relations. Until Gorbachev's leadership prevailed, it was anticipated that collective property would wither away: industrialization and modernization would lead to the merging of the

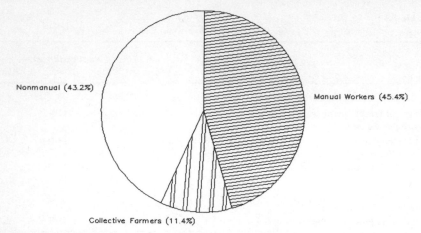

Figure 5.5 Party Membership

Source: Based on data from *Isvestiya Tsk. KPSS* 1 (2): 1989.

collective farm peasantry with the working class, and collective farms would be transformed into state farms.

This line of argument was developed by Kosolapov, the editor of the theoretical Communist Party journal *Kommunist* (until he was sacked by the new leadership in 1986.) Kosolapov opposed the development of private plots and the extension of private enterprise in the countryside. In its place he advocated the industrialization of agriculture (rather on the pattern of agribusiness in the West) and the integration of the collective farmer and collective farms into the state sector. Kosolapov regarded such developments as in keeping with the evolution of a collectivist and more homogeneous socialist society — a system quite distinct from the commodity production inherent in private plots and leasing arrangements.

Social contradictions between the collective farm peasantry and other social classes have certainly declined with the passage of time and the improvement in the real income of the collective farmer as well as the mechanization of agriculture. However, agricultural output has lagged behind plan: between 1981 and 1985 output was intended to rise by 13 percent, but only a 6 percent increase was achieved. At the same time, urbanization in the USSR has been extremely rapid: between 1950 and 1979 the urban population rose by 94.2 million; and between 1959 and 1989 it climbed from 100 million to 217.9 million. This rapid urbanization has raised considerably the expectations of the population for a quality food supply that has not been forthcoming. Agriculture was not able to meet the demands for food, and productivity did not improve.

The shortfalls in agricultural supply have led some economic commentators to demand further incentives and to encourage a privatized form of agricultural production for the market. Agrarian policy under Gorbachev has moved considerably away from the idea of merging collective farm property with that of state property and developing large industrial farms: Gorbachev's policy has encouraged the leasing of land from the collective farm and an increase in trade on the market. As he put it at the March 1989 plenum of the Central Committee on agrarian reform: "The essence of economic change in the countryside has to consist of granting farmers broad opportunities for displaying independence, enterprise and initiative."

Present plans advocate the development of family groups or teams working on contracts from the farm manager or chairperson. These groups have rights to lease the land and, after fulfilling their contract, to farm as they please, marketing their own produce for their own profit. Gorbachev has come down against formally dismantling the existing state and collective farms, but sees the leasing and the development of personal land holdings taking place in the context of the existing farms as a means of providing an infrastructure "satisfying many requirements of the lease-holder." From 1990, greater privatization of land has been advocated (see above, chapter 2). Moves have been made in this direction in many of the republics, including the RSFSR. Legislation for the USSR allows for different forms of property but, up to 1991, no significant strides had been taken to develop private land ownership and private farms.

Manual Workers

In the days of rapid industrialization under Stalin, when the newly arrived peasantry was extolled to work for the public good, their consumption needs were primitive: housing, public transport, and food were cheap, education and basic social services were free. The benefits assured to workers no doubt did not fulfill the objective needs of the population; but they were an improvement on life in the village.

Between 1940 and 1987 the percent of manual workers employed in the national economy has increased from 37.99 percent of the total of employed workers to 62.7 percent.

The manual working class is changing in character. In the days of rapid industrialization, unskilled labor was cheap and the urban working class was made up of raw, uneducated, peasant immigrants to the city. Training was done on the job and was rudimentary.

Since the 1960s education and skill levels have risen considerably. In 1939 only 87 per thousand employed manual workers had more than primary education; the figure rose to 401 in 1959, 590 in 1970, and 861 in 1987 (see Table 5.4). Since 1980 over a million technicians have graduated per year in specialist secondary institutions (1,279,000 in 1987); between 1960 and 1986 over twenty million craftspersons were trained at vocational schools (secondary vocational trade schools and vocational trade schools); in the 1980s their members were growing at the rate of over 250,000 per year. The quality of tuition has also undoubtedly improved.

The working class has high job security and the worker is cushioned by overfull employment and a labor shortage. As we noted in chapter 2, while there is frictional unemployment (workers changing jobs) at levels similar to those of Western capitalist states, mass unemployment has been unknown.

The Soviet regime has maintained very high levels of paid work for men and women. There has been a slow but constant rise in wages coupled with low price inflation: the index of real income for manual and nonmanual workers rose from 100 in 1970 to 155 in 1986; and it rose 17 percentage points between 1980 and 1987. The amount of money spent on food has declined and savings have increased (see Table 5.5).

While it is misleading to depict the working class, as does the Soviet Constitution, as the "leading force" in Soviet society, the working class in the USSR probably has had a greater influence in society than has the working class in capitalist society. At least symbolically the working class participates in the institutions of Soviet power. Its share of membership in the Communist Party rose from 40.1 percent in 1971 to 45.4 percent in 1989 (that is, a rise of from 5.759 million to 8.843 million). Studying the social background of people joining the Party brings out some important trends: the proportion of manual workers rose from 57 percent (1971−75) to 59.4 percent (1981−85), but has fallen since then to 56.4 percent (1986−88) and 51.9 percent in 1988 (see Figure 5.6). Approximately 10 percent of all manual workers (in appropriate age categories) are Party members. This has been the political ballast of the ruling groups around Khrushchev and Brezhnev. We noted above the ways that manual workers' participation increased in the Party under Brezhnev.

The levels of Party memberships of the manual workers illustrate that this class is well integrated into the structure of the Soviet political system. But as we shall see its position is changing, and recently the formal representation of workers in the organs of power has declined. Up to the time of Gorbachev the working class acted as an effective "veto group" on the political elite and those who sought to increase the extraction of surplus by increasing workers' productivity. By veto group we mean that the working class as a collectivity has the power to prevent any action by the government or the employers unless it is perceived to be in its interests.

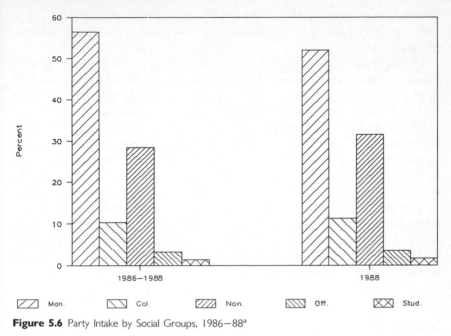

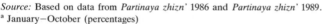

Figure 5.6 Party Intake by Social Groups, 1986–88[a]

Source: Based on data from *Partinaya zhizn'* 1986 and *Partinaya zhizn'* 1989.
[a] January–October (percentages)

In the 1980s the rising levels of education have led manual workers to desire satisfaction in work and gratification through the things that money can buy. Studies conducted in the USSR have shown that greater acquisitiveness and the rise of a consumer mentality among young workers, which has resulted from an increase in workers' disposable incomes, have been instrumental in changing workers' attitudes toward work.

The greater use of the market is a strategy that the leadership has adopted not only to meet consumer demands but also as a means of disciplining the work force in an attempt to raise productivity. These factors had led to greater instability among the industrial work force. We will discuss labor disturbances in the final section of this chapter.

Labor productivity has declined because standards of punctuality, workmanship, and labor discipline have been poor. Technological advance requires the relocation of personnel. Under capitalism, unemployment and the price system are levers of change; the working class has been weakly organized relative to management and capital. In the Soviet Union it is very difficult to legitimate the laying off of workers that is necessary when technology improves. The workers can use their political influence to prevent layoffs and the speeding up of the tempo of production, and thus they can "veto" the management's quest to increase levels of productivity.

The political leadership in its desire to "modernize," to catch up with the West, must extract greater surplus product and must increase levels of productivity. The use of administrative means to do this has not been successful in the past and overmanning has been a characteristic of Soviet industry. As Hillel Ticktin (1988) has put it when discussing the efforts to assert control, leadership cannot do so "without massive unrest from a work force which is potentially uncontrollable, working in giant establishments and living close to one another. The very idea of attacking the workers under such conditions is unthinkable without a new strategy of containment." The Soviet leadership has been aware that administrative attempts to discipline the working class have led to resistance in Poland, to the fall of the political elite, and the proclamation of marshall law. The massive miners' strikes of 1989 (discussed below) were a potent demonstration of workers' power.

Nonmanual Workers

While the collective farm peasantry is in numerical decline, at the other end of the scale the professional, technical, and executive personnel — the Soviet intelligentsia — represent a dynamic social element in Soviet society. The term *intelligentsiya* is an ambiguous one, its meaning ranging from independent political critics rooted in cultural traditions, to people who work with their brains. In the contemporary USSR the Soviet intelligentsia is considered a social group distinguished by higher and specialized secondary education that performs superior technical, executive, or administrative work roles.

The Soviet intelligentsia in recent years has grown enormously in size. Taking as an index people with higher education, in 1939 there were only 1.2 million people in the USSR with complete higher education (that is, 8 per 1,000 of the population over the age of 10; see Table 5.6 and Figure 5.7). By 1987 the number had risen to 20.8 million (90 per 1,000) and, in addition, there were another 3.5 million with incomplete higher education and 30.9 million with a secondary specialist background. Even between 1980 and 1986 the number of specialists employed in the economy rose by 4.5 million — reaching a total of 34.6 million. The elite of the intelligentsia, those with higher degrees, rose from just over a third of a million in 1960 to 1.5 million in 1987. Soviet authorities claim that they have a quarter of the world's trained scientists.

Table 5.6

Education Levels of the *Intelligentsiya* (in millions)

	1939	*1959*	*1984*	*1987*
Higher education				
full	1.2	8.3	18.5	20.8
incomplete	—	1.7	3.6	3.5
Secondary specialist	—	7.9	28.2	30.9
	1941	*1960*	*1984*	*1986*
Specialists employed in the economy	2.4	8.78	33.0	34.6

Source: Narkhoz v 1987g. (1988).

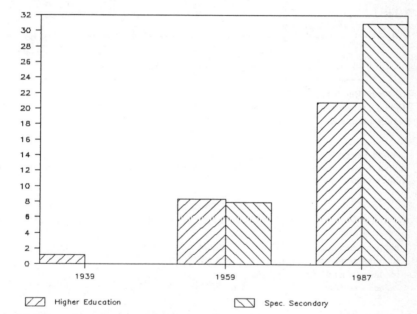

Figure 5.7 Education Levels of the *Intelligentsiya*

Source: Based on data from *Narkhoz* v. 1987g (1988).

This group has a higher level of expectations, a more sophisticated view of the world, and greater political awareness. The rise of this social stratum of urban nonmanual personnel has great significance for the political culture of the USSR: it is likely to aspire to greater political participation. We noted above that nonmanual workers constituted 43.2

percent of party members. If we take education to be an indication of class position, those with higher educational qualifications have become a growing and now a major constituency in the Party membership.

Table 5.7 shows the educational background of all Party members and the Party's leading cadres. Since the 1970s people with higher educational qualifications have accounted for a disproportionate share of Party membership: they constituted more than one third of all Party members in 1989 (see Figure 5.8). As one analyzes the background of people with authority in the Party, this proportion rises even more: some 70 percent of the members of the central committees of the Party had higher education. Furthermore, of full-time party secretaries in the localities (*raykom*, *gorkom* and *okruzhkom* committees), in 1957 only 28.1 percent had full

Table 5.7
Education of Party Cadres, 1957–89

	1957	%	1971	%	1981	%	1989	%
All Party Members								
Higher education	869,000	11.6	2,810,000	19.6	4,880,000	28.0	6,680,000	34.3
Incomplete higher	267,000	3.6	337,000	2.4	391,000	2.2	378,000	1.9

Leading Cadres
Members and candidates of City, District, (*raykom*) and Area (*okrug*) Committees and Auditing Commissions

	Elected prior to 26th Congress (1980–81)	%	Elected prior to 27th Congress (1985–86)	%
Higher education	218,069	54.8	230,926	56.7
Incomplete higher education	8,535	2.1	6,408	1.6
Higher academic degrees (*uchenoe zvanie*)	5,575	1.4	5,828	1.4

Members and candidates of Central Committee and Auditing Commissions of Central Committees of Union Republican Parties and Provinces (*obkom*) and Territories (*krai*) Committees

Higher education	21,974	69.9	22,118	69.4
Incomplete higher education	311	1.0	220	0.7
Higher degrees	2,193	7.0	2,295	7.2

Source: "KPSS v tsifrakh," *Partiynaya zhizn'*, no. 4 (1986): 23, 29, no. 21 (1987): 10; Iz. Ts K. no. 2 (1989):140.

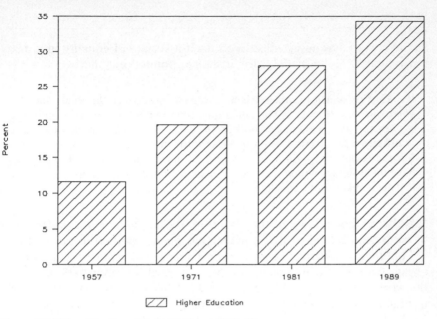

Figure 5.8 Higher Education of Party Members, 1957—89

Source: Based on data from "KPSS v tsifrakh," *Partiynaya zhizn'*, no. 4 (1986): 23, 29; *Partiynaya zhizn'*, no. 21 (1987): 10; *Iz. Ts K.* no. 2 (1989): 140.

higher education; by 1987 the proportion had risen to 99.9 percent. As for top secretaries at provincial and Central Committee level, the comparable proportions had risen from 86.8 to 99.9 percent.

We noted above in chapter 3 that the electoral system introduced under Gorbachev is leading to increased representation of the professional non-manuals in the representative institutions. As Gorbachev put it at the Nineteenth Party Conference, "We should not be afraid of the dispropor-tionate representation of various strata of the population."

This stratum has also played a dominant role as social critic in the USSR. A Western study of over two thousand Soviet Jewish immigrants to the United States found that the higher social groups were more likely to read *samizdat* (uncensored critical literature) and had a greater critical awareness than did blue-collar workers.

It is my contention that not only will this social stratum improve its relative position under perestroika, but that it is a major force in shaping the political policy of the political elite under the leadership of Gorbachev.

DISTRIBUTIONAL AND RELATIONAL INEQUALITIES

Soviet society has never considered itself a society of equality in a distributive sense. Stalin in 1932, for instance, pointed out that

> the kind of socialism under which everyone would get the same pay, an equal quantity of meat and an equal quantity of bread, would wear the same clothes and receive the same goods in the same quantities — such a socialism is unknown to Marxism ... Equalitarianism has nothing in common with Marxist socialism ... Only people who are unacquainted with Marxism can have the primitive notion that the Russian Bolsheviks want to pool all wealth and then share it out equally.

It is the relational sense of the abolition of class domination (in the sense of ownership relations) that equality has been espoused in the USSR.

The unequal distribution of earned income under Soviet socialism has always been legitimated on the basis of reward for labor performed: "to the worker according to his or her work." This is an attractive slogan, but in practice it is extremely difficult to measure the skill and complexity of work effort and the differential contribution of different kinds of labor to society. How does one evaluate the productive contribution of a soldier, doctor, dustman, dentist, storekeeper, political representative, or insurance agent? And how are people rewarded who are not in paid employment, such as mothers, children, the disabled, the sick and the old?

The state has been able to regulate effectively the allocation of resources between communal services (welfare, education, defense), investment and renewal, and personal consumption. Education and welfare have been provided for the population free of charge (though, as we noted earlier, various benefits such as pensions were denied to collective farmers, who were required to finance them through earnings from the farms). Housing and utilities (gas, electricity) have been priced cheaply. The principle was to provide, as far as possible, services according to people's needs. (Welfare expenditure is considered below in chapter 10.)

With the development of the system of planning, it was thought that a scientific approach to labor would enable planners to work out a rational set of wage differentials that would be just and would reward the worker for his or her effort. These would also replace the capitalist market system with its arbitrary levels of wages that developed as a result of the unequal bargaining position and employers who dominated the transactions to extract profit. This approach was lauded by socialists and egalitarians in the West as it was thought that it enabled a more rational and equitable distribution of income.

Contradictory principles reign with respect to rewards. On the one hand, the system assumes that a socialist society should be based on equality, or at least policy should lead towards the reduction of differentials: "everybody has the same kind of stomach, so all should have the same pay." On the other hand, the system is concerned with giving rewards according to the merit of the wage earner and the worker's contribution to the community.

There is also an ambivalence regarding how merit should be determined: some regard physical effort and material production as worthy of higher reward, whereas others emphasize the complexity of work and justify pay with respect to qualifications.

In the absence of a labor market in which bargaining can take place, administrative decision can lead to arbitrary and unjust payments. A polictical dimension becomes important in the distribution of rewards. In practice a number of ad hoc criteria were adopted for determining wage payments. The first criterion was the skill necessary to perform a job. Industry jobs were divided into scales ranging usually from one to five or six: unskilled work (floor sweepers) is graded in group one, and highly skilled manual work (electricians, plumbers) in group five or six. The differential between the top and bottom varies by industry but is around 2.5:1. Second, average wages also are differentiated by industry. The state planners give priority to certain industries which they seek to promote: heavy industry, such as mining, iron and steel, has been favored in this way — at the expense of light industry, such as textiles. Third, state planners consider the criteria of arduousness and danger involved in some jobs — furnacemen and miners receive higher wages and benefits (early retirement, longer holidays). Fourth, state planners consider the geographical location when setting differentials so that they can encourage workers to go to inhospitable regions, such as the frozen north or Siberia. Fifth, productivity is often rewarded through piecework rates, which may, of course, upset differentials established by skill. Sixth, positions that demand greater responsibility or authority determine amount of income — managers of large factories receive more than those of smaller ones — and the level of qualification also influences quantity of pay — employees with higher degrees, for instance, usually receive higher salaries.

These criteria have led to arbitrary wage payments for different kinds of labor employed in different industries and to significant differentials between categories of workers, men and women, for instance. They have also led to unintended and resented inequalities, which are sources of contradictions built into state socialism.

Despite the current policy of glasnost', Soviet published data have been inadequately detailed to pinpoint elite incomes, though there can be no doubt that considerable advantages accrue to people in authority positions — not least from access to special forms of resources, such as closed shops and the black market. We shall return to this aspect below. The highest paid groups are nonmanual workers with higher education. One study of Soviet immigrants to the United States, found that 60 percent of the top 10 percent of wage earners had a higher education (data for early 1980s). In this group, however, 20 percent of the respondents were skilled production workers, who constitute a kind of workers' aristocracy. In the lowest 10 percent of incomes, 30 percent were manual workers in the services sector and 25 percent were skilled nonmanual workers, for example nurses and clerks. Differences in the sexual composition of wage earners are also important, as we shall see later. Manual workers, moreover, have bettered their position vis-à-vis the technical intelligentsia and other nonmanual workers. Changes in differentials among the three main groups of workers — manual workers, managerial/technical workers, and office workers — are shown in Table 5.8. As we can see, the relative position of manual workers' wages has improved dramatically during the last fifty years or so: by 1986 they received on average 20 percent more than office workers (*sluzhashchie*), whose income was 50 percent greater in 1932; the difference between manual workers' and managerial/technical staff wages has fallen from 1 : 2.6 to 1:1.1 over the same period. Managerial/technical wages were 2.1 times greater in 1940, but only 1.1 times greater in 1986. The difference in office workers' wages fell even more, from 1.09 to only 0.79 times between two dates. The declining ratios are strikingly shown in Figure 5.9.

Comparisons with the West have highlighted these differences in wages. Hans Aage, a Danish economist, has calculated differentials between occupational groups in Britain and the USSR, taking the skilled worker's wage in each country as 100. Some of his results are shown in Table 5.9 (Figure 5.10).

In the USSR the highest salaries were held by senior academicians (members of the Academy of Sciences) whose earnings (393 percent

Table 5.8

Wage Ratios of Managerial/Technical, Office, and Manual Workers in Industry, 1932–86

	1932	1940	1960	1970	1985	1986
Manual workers	100	100	100	100	100	100
Managerial/Technical	263	210	148	136	110.1	110.4
Office workers	150	109	82	85	77.7	79.57

Source: Narkhoz v 1984g. (1985): 417; *Narkhoz za 70 let* (1987).

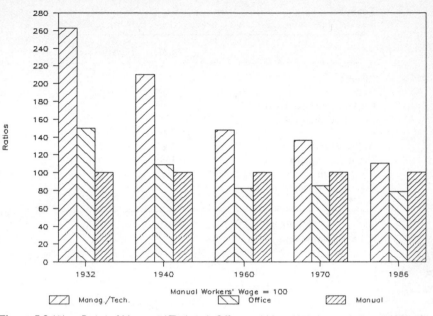

Figure 5.9 Wage Ratios of Managerial/Technical, Office, and Manual Workers in Industry, 1932–86

Source: Based on data from *Narkhoz v 1984g.* (1985):417; and *Narkhoz za 70 let* (1987).

higher than skilled workers' wages) expressed a greater differential than the largest in Britain (the 387 percent for an ambassador). Professionals universally did better in Britain than did their counterparts in the USSR: nurses, dentists, teachers, engineers, lawyers, economists, doctors, university teachers all having considerably higher salaries than skilled workers. On the other hand, in the USSR, of the manual workers only underground coal miners and drivers had higher differentials than in Britain. Unskilled manuals receive somewhat less in relation to unskilled workers than in Britain, although the ratios, as shown in Table 5.9, also show striking similarities in the wage ratios.

As to monetary comparisons, it is usually quite meaningless to translate rubles into dollars or other foreign currencies. The ruble is not a freely convertible currency, and the rate of exchange is fixed administratively. There are many different rates of exchange used in commercial transactions. Until November 1989, the official exchange for tourists was completely unrealistic at 6.2 rubles for $10.00, and dollars on the black market were sold for as much as 60 rubles to 70 rubles for $10.00. In November 1989, however, the rate of exchange was raised tenfold, and for tourist purposes $10.00 (£6.25) purchased 62.6 rubles. As the costs of living are quite

Table 5.9
Relative Wages in the USSR and United Kingdom in the Early 1980s[a]

	USSR	United Kingdom
Cleaner	43	74
Dentist	56	233
Unskilled manual worker	70	77
Female textile worker	72	70
Driver	100	85
Ambassador	208	387
Graduate engineer	108	148
Chief doctor	178	368
Coal miner (underground)	267	146
Academician	393	—

Source: Aage 1989: 19−20.
a. 100 = skilled worker.

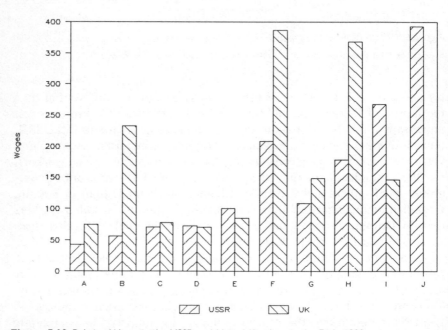

Figure 5.10 Relative Wages in the USSR and United Kingdom in the Early 1980s

Note: 100 = skilled worker.
Source: Based on data from Aage 1989: 19−20.
Key: A = Cleaner; B = Dentist; C = Unskilled Manual Worker; D = Female Textile Worker; E = Driver;
F = Ambassador; G = Graduate Engineer; H = Chief Doctor; I = Coal Miner; J = Academic

different in the USSR and the West, it is usually not appropriate to translate rubles into Western currency. In many cases in this book, comparisons should more appropriately be made with other ruble values.

The range of wage differentials in Soviet society, even if one makes some allowance for administrative privileges, is not great. A Soviet emigré, Konstantin Simis, has estimated that even if one takes account of illicit payments in kind, the highest real income in the USSR is about sixty times the average wage of that country. Differentials from cooperative enterprises in the late 1980s are unlikely to exceed twenty times the average wage, even in the most successful enterprises. A top soccer star playing for Kiev Dynamo (on a self-financing status) received 3,500 rubles per month, or 42,000 rubles per year. This is just over seventeen times greater than the average monthly Soviet wage of 202 rubles in 1987. But some speculators are estimated to receive 100,000 rubles per year.

Like other Politburo members Gorbachev was reported to have earned a modest 14,400 rubles per year — about six times the average wage. When questioned at the Supreme Soviet in June 1989, Ryzhkov revealed that ministers receive a monthly salary of 800 rubles, which with bonus might be increased to 1,200 rubles per month, or 14,400 rubles per year. Tax is payable at a standard rate of 13 percent. In addition, a minister is provided with a car. Ryzhkov, when questioned, revealed that other privileges had been removed (he mentioned access to special food stores); ministers also pay for their flats. Gorbachev interjected that good collective farm chairpersons could earn 1,200 to 1,700 rubles per month.

Consider the rich in the West: Jean Paul Getty is reliably said to have had an income 7,000 times greater than the average American's. In 1987 David Sainsbury, deputy chairman of a supermarket food chain, reportedly earned £14,846,816 in that year alone: this is 1,535 times the average wage of a full-time British worker (£9,672 — about $16,926) in that year. (These data are figured before tax; with the current maximum rate of tax at 40 percent, this represents an income of £8,907,600, or $15,588,300.) Margaret Thatcher's gross take-home pay as Prime Minister (1988–89) was £34,157, but she also has a stipend of £22,548 as a member of Parliament (a total of £56,705 before tax and ignoring expense allowances). The average wage in Great Britain for all women employed (with whom Mrs. Thatcher should be compared) was £7,701 in 1987, which gives Mrs. Thatcher a differential of 7.3; compared to male earners, the differential is 4.8. The relative wage differences are similar to those in the USSR. (Both the Prime Minister and Gorbachev have quarters in the capital: the former also has a country residence; whereas Gorbachev has only the use of a *dacha* (country cottage) — he has no private *dacha*.)

At the other end of the scale, poverty has not been eliminated in the

USSR, despite the wide range of government financed welfare services. Establishing levels of poverty is a complex matter that cannot be discussed here. Mervyn Matthews in his book *Poverty in the Soviet Union* has estimated that about two-fifths of the noncollective farm labor force earned "less than the sum needed to achieve a minimum level of subsistence proposed by Soviet scholars for small urban families" (1986:176). Soviet estimates are that around one-fifth of the population lives near the poverty level of 70 rubles ($126) per month. The Soviet newspaper *Trud* estimated in 1989 that 15 percent of the population was below a 75 ruble per month minimum threshold. This tallies with a much-quoted statement by Boris Eltsin that some 48 million people live below the poverty line. The four major groups that fall around the poverty level are, first, pensioners; the majority, who retired in the 1960s, live in poverty, receiving less than 50 rubles per month. In 1989 data were published showing that 40 percent of pensioners received less than 60 rubles per month. Second, young families with children often find it hard to make ends meet. Third, male low-wage earners with children, many of whom must work on the side. Finally, single mothers with no other family support. The rapid inflation and growing unemployment of the early 1990s have increased the numbers of those living in poverty.

Uravnilovka (Leveling of Incomes)

These scales of wage differentials have led to feelings of injustice by employees in the USSR, not only among professionals but also among poorly paid skilled nonmanual workers such as nurses, teachers, and clerks. This puts the system in an ironic position from the viewpoint of an equalitarian distribution of incomes. Whereas in the West injustice of wage distribution is usually associated with differentials that are too high, in the USSR (and other socialist countries) income differentials are said to be too narrow, not rewarding properly the skilled and highly motivated worker.

The social policy adopted prior to Gorbachev assumed that social strata were and ought to be sharing more equal incomes. A public consciousness that links egalitarianism to socialism has developed in the USSR: "*No one* in the country does more difficult and at the same time skilled work than a foundry worker and hence no one *should* receive a higher wage under socialism than he does." (A physicist, cited disapprovingly by G. S. Batygin in an article advocating the introduction of greater differentials, Batygin's italics.) Nevertheless, as Professor A. Zdravomyslov (1988), a contemporary specialist on social policy in the USSR, has put it:

A tendency to be overcome in social policy is that of "averaging" workers' requirements and interests. It is based on an oversimplified interpretation of structural changes in socialist society, on an "equalized" notion of socialism. Social structure studies tended to emphasize that the working class, collective farmers, and intellectuals, the main social groups, were in the process of drawing closer together. Such studies ignored conflicting tendencies and new differentiation in the relations between and inside the groups.

These "conflicting tendencies" included a gap between popular conceptions of the status or worth of occupations and the levels of remuneration in them. This led to certain occupational groups resorting to selling their services *na levo* (on the side), or to the corrupt use of administrative position to procure deficit goods and services, thus leaving other workers feeling disgruntled and losing motivation for work. The operation of the economic mechanism giving rise to overfull employment has led to payment for labor services when little or no labor has been performed.

Studies done in the USSR and the West have shown that despite the income differentials noted above, the status and prestige of occupational positions in the USSR are similar to those in the West. Numerous studies of the desirability of occupations have been conducted in the USSR and careful studies have been made in the West of the perceived status of jobs on the part of recent Soviet emigrants. These studies show that professional jobs are the ones with the most prestige. Physician, scientist and top political posts invariably head the list followed by university teachers and members of the creative intelligentsia, such as writers and artists. Unskilled manual and nonmanual workers such as cleaners, press operators, mail carriers, unskilled agricultural workers, clerks, and shop assistants fall at the bottom. Occupations also generate different kinds of social consciousness or ways of life that influence the way that people think and behave. For instance, professionals read more literature and go to the theater more often than manual workers whose preferences are for television or popular music. There appears, then, to be a scale of social prestige or hierarchy in the USSR that is similar to that of the West.

But income scales do not always reflect these rankings of prestige in the same way as they do in the West. (We noted some of the discrepancies above.) This in itself creates feelings of injustice by certain social groups. The lack of fit between popular evaluation of occupations and levels of pay has led to an increase in privately marketed services. Just as in capitalist countries where people work "on the side" thereby evading tax, so individuals in the USSR provide their services for payment. They are not constrained by what the government says the proper rate for the job is, but simply by what customers are prepared to pay. Hence doctors, dentists, carpenters, mechanics, and teachers can all provide services that they can sell for a market price — and at the same time avoid tax.

A study of immigrants to the United States in the mid-1980s has shown that physicians and dentists in the USSR earned only 1.21 rubles per hour in their regular public sector jobs (where the average income per hour was 1.08 rubles), but in taking private patients they earned 32.96 rubles; unqualified nonmanuals earn 0.77 rubles at their regular jobs and 4.2 times as much on the side. Unskilled manuals, however, increase their earnings from 0.96 rubles to 18.9 rubles by working on the side — hence increasing their differential (Vinokur and Ofer 1986). Poor wages and welfare in the service sector leads to the setting up of people in private trade and services: *shabashniki* (self-employed work groups) take on building work at wages from twice to eight times the regular rate for the job. Car owners (or chauffeurs of institutions' transport) ply their vehicles for hire.

Employees with access to deficit goods (ranging from meat to lipsticks) are able to sell them for a premium and gain "unearned income." This not only leads to the pilfering of materials from state enterprises (and thus fewer supplies in the shops for sale) but it also reverses the planners' priorities. Rather than rewarding the industrial heavy industry sector, an "aristocracy of labor" is created among those skilled and unskilled who can serve the retail consumer. Employees with skills that cannot be sold to consumers (atomic physicists, anthropologists, librarians, political scientists, unless they are famous and have newspaper columns) are captives of the public sector and have to be satisfied with the salaries offered there or (as many do) take up unskilled part-time work.

Another form of "unearned income" is derived from the operation of the labor market. In the past wages have been low and employers have secured relatively large wage funds. It is in their interest to procure as much labor as they can — this compensates for the time that workers are absent and allows for a reserve supply of labor that can be used in periods of intense activity. Most of the time, however, many workers receive pay for just being at work for much of the time. Employers also inflate their wage funds and regularly pay bonuses to all workers to retain them on the payroll, rather than differentiate between efficient and inefficient employees. Another form of "injustice" is held to be the large proportion of income in kind (a 42 percent addition to the average wage in 1986) in the form of social benefits (free education, health, subsidized accommodation, and utilities) that is distributed among all workers and employees regardless of the level of their work. This practice, it is held, is not in keeping with the maxim of "payment according to work," and reduces the motivation of workers.

Whereas money wages in the Soviet Union do not show great inequalities, privilege linked to position may provide compensations to the elite groups. Top dogs in all societies receive preferential treatment, higher incomes, a more pleasant lifestyle and more in general of what is in short supply. Under capitalism, the market ensures that money is the medium through which most goods and services can be obtained. As noted above, money does not have a similar function in a state that takes a more active role in directly and indirectly distributing resources. Rather than taking a room at the Ritz by paying for it, a high Soviet functionary would have access to hotels unknown to the general public.

Such privilege gives the elite access to special shops, restaurants, housing, hospitals, transport, and recreational facilities (holidays, tickets for major events). The network of communications of members of the elites gives them the Soviet know-how they need to place members of their families in desirable colleges and jobs. (This is not unlike the networks built up in British fee-paying top schools, at Oxbridge, or in the Ivy League.) Such privileged access to goods and services is dependent on position attained in Party or government service. Also leading members of the military, press, academia, culture, and government departments, as well as members of the Politburo, fall under this category.

Many Soviet citizens resent this kind of privileged position, as many people in Western states resent the privileges of the very rich. A survey by *Moscow News* of a sample of Moscow adults found that 84 percent thought access to commodities in restricted shops and restaurants was unjust, and 80 percent likewise objected to privileged access to tickets for theaters. Access to special hospitals and clinics for certain privileged groups was considered unjustified by 60 percent, and 44 percent objected to the private use of cars provided by the state. This cause was taken up at the Nineteenth Party Conference in 1988 by the leading populist politician, the then recently dismissed Party chief from Moscow, Boris Eltsin.

I know how many millions of rubles are transferred to the Central Committee from the Moscow City and Sverdlovsk Province Party organizations. But I don't know where that money is spent. I only see that, in addition to reasonable expenditures, luxurious private residences, dachas and sanatoriums ... are being built. This money should be used to provide material support to the primary Party organizations, including their leaders' pay. And then we are surprised that some major Party leaders have gotten mired in corruption, bribe-taking and report-padding and have lost their decency, moral purity, modesty and sense of Party comradeship ...

   In my opinion, it should be like this: If we, people in a socialist society, lack something, the shortage should be felt equally by everyone, without exception. Differing labor contributions to society should be regulated by differing pay. We must, at long last, eliminate the food "rations" for the, so to speak, "starving" officials on the Party appointment list, rule out elitism in society and rule out, both in essence and in form, the word "special" from our lexicon, since we have no special communists.

It should be noted, however, that the salaries of many political officials are relatively low. A provincial Party secretary, who had received a 50 percent cut in salary in taking up his Party post, countered the accusations of privilege by Party and government officials. He explained his position as follows:

> By average salary, Party officials are in twenty-sixth place at 216 rubles per month [the average salary for the whole of people employed in the national economy in 1986 was 195.6 roubles]. Like people at any institution, we have our snack bars and cafeterias, of course. More than once I have seen a comrade invited to a talk eagerly await the chance to get to our buffet or cafeteria. His disappointment is sometimes amusing: it turns out that there are no "special" delicacies or goodies, and the prices are standard. . . .
>
> It is noteworthy that the privileges enjoyed by other categories of employees are almost never mentioned. One day I found myself in Novosibirsk's Akademgorodok for the first time . . . [It was pointed out to me], "Academician A. lives there. He has many rooms, two cars and a salary of over 2,000 rubles [per month]."
>
> It is only right, in our current open society that people learn the real incomes of writers, artists, composers, Academicians, gold miners and some members of cooperatives. (S. Karnaukhov, *Pravda*, 1 August 1988)

The kinds of inequalities above are distributional rather than relational ones. As our discussion has illustrated, one cannot make a sharp distinction between the two kinds of inequality. The division of labor gives rise to unequal life opportunities. Bureaucratic positions give their holders rights over the allocation of resources that they may misuse, and control over people that they may use unjustly. Distributional inequality may involve speculation, corruption, and unearned income. Furthermore, positions of authority determined by the division of labor may give rise to privilege in the distribution of commodities.

Relational Inequality

People in senior administrative positions in the state and Party bureaucracy may form a stratum with a different relational interest to other groups. This was suggested by the leading Soviet sociologist Zaslavskaya who has suggested that entrenched bureaucratic forces might be the basis for conflict in Soviet society and possible opposition to the policy of perestroika. This approach shifts attention from differences among social groups (collective farmers, manual workers, and intellectuals) to divisions within them. Such divisions lead to tensions and conflict that have their roots in socialist society. This critique is based on the notion that administrative position gives rise to self-interest and privilege, which create incompatibilities of interests within a socialist state.

The reformist scenario is illustrated in Figure 5.11. The division of labor gives rise to distributional and power variations, both legitimate and illegitimate. The solution to these problems is greater reliance on the market. The objective of the present economic strategy is to encourage initiative, to put production on a profit and loss basis and to set up brigades in which the workers themselves will (subject to some restraints) fix the number of workers and their levels of remuneration. Proposed reforms will reduce administrative positions and the privilege that goes with them, while more activity will be market oriented rather than administratively linked. It is likely that social transfers (pensions, housing) will be more closely related to work record or ability to pay than in the past. The sociologist Rutkevich has argued that some previously provided free services should be brought into the field of paid services: cultural and athletic facilities and polyclinics (see chapter 10) are among them.

Ironically, whereas socialism in the West is associated with policies advocating greater equality of income and wealth, in the Soviet Union social justice is about widening income differentials to overcome administrative privilege and "unearned income" received from speculation. The economic policy adopted at the Nineteenth Party Conference in 1988 explicitly aimed to "extirpate wage-levelling in all forms," which will undoubtedly mean greater differentials in the sphere of wage rates in the national economy. It will also, however, increase the wages of some lowly paid groups. The policy will undermine attempts to allocate differentials

---

Inequality

Division of Labor   Occupation ➤ Life chances ➤ Control of allocation
                                                           of resources and people

Distributional Dimension   Division of labor (legitimate)
                            Speculation (illegitimate advantage)

Relational Dimension   Incompatibilities, exploitation derived
                            from control of the productive forces
                            and people, control of allocative process

---

Figure 5.11 Soviet Reformers' View of Class Inequality under Socialism

rationally, that is, on the basis of skill and qualifications. Differentials of earnings will grow: the efficient will be better rewarded. As Rutkevich put it in an authoritative article on Socialist Justice (1986):

> The existence of both inequality in distribution according to work, as well as inequality in the degree of realization not of the right to work in general but of a type of work corresponding to a person's already-developed and revealed abilities, must be considered as just from the standpoint of society and its long-term interests. . . . An increased differential in wages is inevitable when profit and loss accounting is introduced.

Differentials will not be based on trade and qualification, as determined by administrative definition, but instead on the ability of the work unit and its factory to organize production. This in turn will depend on the level and regularity of supplies of inputs — as well as the efficient organization of labor. The outcome may well be higher productivity. The present leadership's policy of reducing administrative privileges will lead to higher salaries for government and Party executives and concurrently to the decline in privileged outlets such as closed canteens and retail outlets. But the greater use of market forces themselves will lead to different kinds of contradictions and inequalities.

The earnings of private enterprise in the form of cooperatives has fueled popular indignation about new forms of "unearned incomes." At a rally of Moscow workers under the banner of the Moscow United Front of Workers, held in the Fall of 1989, it was alleged by one speaker that 100,000 millionaires had surfaced in the USSR. As we noted in our discussion of Nina Andreeva's views (chapter 4), opposition to the inequality promoted by market forces and cooperatives is an important aspect of a working-class critique of perestroika. These new contradictions were manifested in 1989 in a novel form of relational conflict for Soviet society: massive manual worker protest.

Manifest Social Conflict: The Miners' Strike of 1989

Until the summer of 1989, strikes in the Soviet Union had been localized affairs with workers protesting against conditions and pay. Trade unions and management concerted their actions to get the strikes back to work. The unions in promoting "social harmony" fulfilled a management role.

In July 1989, an industry-wide strike occurred in mining, embracing over 300,000 miners in Western Siberia and the Ukraine. During its duration, workers committees took control not only of the organization of the strike but also maintained public order and commanded existing coal stocks. In total some half a million workers took part in the strikes.

The stoppages shook the Soviet government. In July at a meeting of the USSR Supreme Soviet Gorbachev said that the miners' strike was the "worst ordeal to befall our country in all the four years of restructuring." The strike took the political leadership and the population by surprise not only because of its national and apparently coordinated character but also because it came from a group of workers who enjoyed preferential treatment and were generally thought to be a ballast of support for the Communist Party.

There were three main demands on the part of the strikers: better conditions and pay, a share in profits, and greater autonomy for individual mines. Interviews with strikers carried out after the strike in the Donets revealed the following causes of discontent as perceived by the miners: 86 percent said "shortages of basic supplies," 79 percent, low wages; 62 percent, brevity of vacations; 56 percent, inadequacy of pensions; 40 percent, high prices of supplies; 33 percent, poor working conditions; 32 percent, "lack of social justice"; and 25 percent, poor medical services (survey reported in David Marples [1989]). The survey reported that 91 percent of the miners felt that the unions were incapable of leading a strike, and 60 percent thought that the unions were acting as agents of management rather than defending workers' interests.

In an attempt to make the men go back to work, the government reacted by conceding most of the demands made by the strikers. The regional strike committee, USSR Council of Ministers and the AUCCTU (the trade union organization) agreed on the following measures in the Ukraine and similar proposals were accepted elsewhere. Enterprises and mines and pits were to be given complete economic and legal independence in accordance with the Law on the State Enterprise. Industrial enterprises were to be granted the right to sell above contract output at contract prices within the country and other countries. (Sales with abroad were only to take place with the USSR government's permission.) In the reform of wholesale prices, increases were anticipated for coal. Working conditions and pay for unsocial hours were to be improved. Additional payments were promised for long service, death grant, and leave entitlement. Better pensions and payments for industrial injury were also assured.

While the thrust of these demands was mainly economic, the strike movement had important political implications. The "official" trade unions were publicly shown to be inadequate and lacking in grass-root support. Calls for independent trade unions had not only been voiced but the strike committees had thrown up new leaders outside the existing trade union and Party organizations. Leaders of the strike committees had formed a coordinating committee to organize the workers' activity and to negotiate with the management and the various government bodies responsible for the coal industry. (For a short but lucid account, see Teague 1989.)

A more immediate result of the strikes of the summer of 1989 has been the formation of workers' unions outside of the official bureaucracy. These would seem to be the logical result of the pluralist policies advocated by the political leadership. In the short run at least, these bodies appear to be developing along the economic lines of British and American trade unions rather than copying the more political and confrontational role of Poland's Solidarity.

Underlying the workers' unrest have been the economic effects of perestroika that have been detrimental to many in paid employment. The wage relativities we noted earlier, whereby the miners have been highly ranked, have been undermined by the more market orientation of perestroika. The inability of official channels to provide goods in the shops has led the workers to turn to the black market or to cooperatives. This has fulled speculation and the high incomes of traders in the coops. Shortages of commodities have led to purchases from abroad and it is indicative that the miners called for a share of profits earned in foreign currency.

Other demands of a more political kind have been articulated. At the Supreme Soviet discussion on 24 July, Deputy Lushnikov (from Vorkuta) reported that in his area calls had also been made to transfer more power to the Soviets, for land to be transferred to the peasants and factories to the workers. The article in the Constitution defining the leading role of the Party should be abolished, and he claimed that there were demands for direct and secret elections of many leading national and regional officials. Another deputy, Alekseev, pointed out that political reform was also necessary to meet people's needs, and he supported the view that property should be transferred to the economic jurisdiction of work collectives and that new channels outside of the unions to represent workers should be developed.

As in neighboring Poland during the rise of Solidarity, other independent political groups with a wider political platform attempted to influence the workers' activity. Groups such as the Democratic Union and the Ukrainian Helsinki Union distributed their literature to the strikers and proposed political assistance to the miners.

Legalization of Strikes

Trade union activity, particularly strike action, in all societies is regulated by law. Until 1989 the assumption in the Soviet Union was that a conflict of interest between management and labor was caused by maladministration and could be resolved through management and the trade unions taking the correct action. Under perestroika, conflicts are conceived to be derived from sectional interests that are endemic in society. Under these circumstances, legislation has been enacted to govern the relations between labor and management.

In October 1989, a law was enacted by the USSR Supreme Soviet that gave workers the right to strike. Such rights are limited: they do not allow strikes for political motives and withdrawal of labor in key economic sectors is banned. The latter includes the transport, fuel, energy, and defense industries. Strikes can only take place after negotiations have failed; and the parties are required to take initially three days to resolve the dispute; this is followed by a five-day period during which a "conciliation commission" attempts to reach agreement. To be legitimate a strike must be backed by a majority vote of the work force. Intimidation of nonstrikers is forbidden and no pay is to be forthcoming for the period of strikes. The more pluralistic forms of workers' activity are recognized by the provision that trade unions, work councils, and "other organs" supported by the work collective may conduct strikes. The legality of strikes is decided by the courts.

THE RISE OF AN INDEPENDENT WORKERS' MOVEMENT

Linked to the strikes of miners and other unrest by the working class, a Russian United Workers' Front has been formed. This is an organization based on fronts of Russians, which have been formed in the major industrial regions: there are strong branches in Leningrad and Moscow. At its first congress held in Sverdlovsk in September 1989, 110 delegates attended from 29 towns of the Russian Federation, and representatives from the "international" movements in the Baltic and Central Asian parts of the country also came. These organizations are composed not only of manual workers but also the intelligentsia. Much of the organization is provided by disaffected activists in the official trade union movement and other officials who have lost their prestige and often their positions under the thrust of perestroika.

The first objective of the Russian United Workers' Front is to "ensure the unity of Soviet society." It opposes the regional nationalist movements (to be considered in the next chapter) and tendencies towards regionalisation, which are regarded as divisive. It has also campaigned against price rises, the introduction of the profit motive, and the growing power of the market. It supports price freezes on essential goods and resists many in the cooperative movement whom it considers to be speculative in character. The movement is critical of the progressive "left" liberals who are active in the reform movement. (Nina Andreeva and her husband have been reported to be members of the Leningrad United Workers' Front.) In order to increase the representation of manual workers in the Soviet elective bodies, the Russian United Workers' Front has also called for constituencies for elections to the Soviets to be organized on a "production" basis (that is, at the place of work). This, it is believed, will ensure a greater representation for workers. (For a brief account of this movement, see Tolz 1989.) The movement has organized mass meetings attended by tens of thousands of persons in Leningrad and Moscow.

This movement must be regarded as a serious threat to the government's market strategy under perestroika. As noted above, the manual working class has been a major support for previous Soviet governments. The policy of strengthening market relations and using them to increase productivity will shift differentials away from manual workers and this stratum will become more differentiated. The fear of unemployment, the burden of price inflation, and resentment against the "cooperatives" will be felt greatest by this stratum.

CONCLUSION: PERESTROIKA AND THE SOCIAL STRUCTURE

Coinciding with the rise of the Gorbachev generation, the Soviet political culture has seen the development of a large number of individuals and groups that have a positive conception of their own interests and constitute a force that is critical of the government's actions. Soviet society has changed from one with a massive peasantry under Stalin to a society that is dependent on the participation of the intelligentsia and the rising productivity of the skilled manual working class.

A contented working class has been the basis of the political stability of the Soviet system, and until the advent of Andropov it was cultivated by all Soviet leaders. The cost of stability has been absenteeism, poor labor discipline, and poor quality production, in short, low labor productivity. The falling levels of economic growth and the nonfulfillment of plans have led to widespread consumer dissatisfaction despite an improvement in living standards. Suppressed inflation (commodities being priced below market value) has entailed severe shortages, and has led to a black market and corrupt practices by people who have access to goods. The contradiction here is in the relation between goods and money: the quality and quantity of goods need to be improved and increased, and money has to be earned as a reward for productivity.

In the wake of modernization, the population has come to expect a rising standard of living and a better quality of life. Partly due to the influence of the West as a consequence of better communication, but also because the leadership has realized that people will have no incentive to work harder unless they have goods to buy, the idea of a consumer society has gained ground. "Moral" incentives and commitment to work as a collective duty are not regarded by the present leadership as being effective.

"Social justice" in the USSR calls for greater rather than lower income differentials, as in the West. Current policy seeks a recalibration of the differentials between various groups and the ways that they are calculated, favoring the creation of higher differentials linked to greater productivity. Such a policy will reduce administrative privilege and the activity of the "second economy"; it will give money more real value and reduce the gap between public perceptions of the worth of occupations and their financial rewards.

The development of private enterprise through cooperatives in the service sector (particularly restaurants, motor and building repairs) will improve service but will undoubtedly lead to greater income differentials, which in turn become recognized as new inequalities. On the other hand, administratively based privilege will decline as more activity is brought within the scope of the market. But the range of incomes in the USSR is still very much less than in the Western capitalist countries. Most Western writers acknowledge that the range of earned incomes in the USSR has been much more equal than in advanced capitalist ones, especially if the level of modernization is taken into account (at earlier phases of industrialization, inequality tends to be greater). The high labor utilization rate has tended to reduce the level of poverty compared to capitalist countries.

The policy of glasnost' (openness or public criticism) recognizes the surge of individual and group demands. If one assumes that the political leadership is dependent on the loyal support and creativity of the intelligentsia, it seems likely that as this stratum grows in size and maturity their opinions particularly with respect to their professional competence will increasingly be taken into account. To compete technologically with the West, a competent, creative, and contented intelligentsia is required. Concurrently, the thrust for reform has come from the professional classes.

Undoubtedly Gorbachev has shifted the political fulcrum away from the manual working class and the traditional Party and state bureaucracy toward an alliance with the more technologically inclined and modernizing forces among the political elite and the intelligentsia. The restive working class — facing inadequate material supplies, inflationary pressure, possible layoffs, and the rise of new forms of social injustice through the growing wealth of the emergent cooperative movement — is a group to whom the displaced traditional forces of trade union official and Party functionary as well as committed socialist may appeal.

Furthermore, the intelligentsia is not composed of a single unitary social stratum unequivocally in support of the new political leadership of Gorbachev. The political leadership is confronted by different groups of intellectuals from the arts, sciences, and economy: the army, police, and the Party also have their intellectual cadres. The intelligentsia, therefore, should not be considered a homogeneous group, but rather a conglomeration of different constituencies with various ways of thinking, acting, and presenting inputs to, and even vetoes on, the political leadership. There is a changing balance of forces that has to be taken into account when political policy is being considered.

The social basis of the system of political power requires a new ideological shell. The notion of a homogeneous class-based society with narrowing differentials and a growing community of interests has been replaced by a society with a plurality of conflicting interests founded on greater monetary differentials motivated by self-interest. The old slogan "unity of Party and the people" has been replaced by a plurality of socialist interests. Politics was the mechanism for "developed socialism" under Brezhnev, the market and law is the intended mechanism to reconcile the conflicting interests of competing groups under Gorbachev. In this context, the rise of an autonomous trade union movement and other groupings along occupational and professional lines may be expected. The period of transition from the traditional socialist ideology to a new one will be one of internal upheaval. While those with marketable skills (qualified workers, professionals and business people) will become richer, the burden of unemployment, inflation and decline in welfare subsidies will be borne by those on fixed income and in weak market position (pensioners, one parent families, and public sector employees). Many women will find that their work will shift from paid employment to domestic labor and housekeeping. Increasing marketization and privatization under a Eltsin-type administration will lead to the rise of a wealthy property-owning class. A period of protracted social conflict between the government and the emerging groupings in civil society has set the scene for Soviet politics under perestroika.

Chapter 6 ─────────────────────────────
NATIONALITIES AND ETHNIC RELATIONS

I pointed out earlier that by the social structure of a society we mean an array of statuses, the conditions that shape them, and a network of relationships between people and groups. While social class, as discussed in chapter 5 in terms of occupation, education, and "style of life" is a recognized way of marking off the social layers of society, ethnic origin and nationality are often perceived as a basis of social evaluation, consensus, discrimination, and identity.

The defining characteristics of a nation are its common culture, history, values, and political aspirations. Nations may provide a basis of social identity and, by the same token, discrimination and social division. A *nation* is usually located in a settled territory, it may (or may not) constitute a sovereign state (or nation-state). Soviet writers accept this approach, though following Stalin's definition of a nation they also add that a nation has a common language and insist that it must have a common territory. An *ethnic* group usually denotes a less inclusive social entity distinguished by language, religious affiliation, and skin pigmentation.

A nation-state, such as the United States, may be constituted of many different ethnic groups. A distinction may be made between a common shared national culture and the relational aspects of such groupings, which may define them as entities of collective advantage or disadvantage. A further distinction may be made between shared sentiments of national identity and nationalism. The former is a subjective consciousness of an individual about his or her personal national identity, the latter includes a political dimension — an ideology that legitimates the national (or ethnic) group as a political actor in addition to a social entity.

The Soviet Union is a multinational society. All its citizens are members of a supranational Soviet people (*Sovetski narod*). In the dominant ideology of the USSR, its defining characteristics are a common citizenship of the Soviet state (the USSR); subscription to a unifying ideology (Marxism-Leninism); a common political goal (communism); shared beliefs in patriotism to the Soviet motherland; and a common language (Russian).

The USSR is composed of twenty-two major ethnic groups made up of more than one million people each (see Table 6.1). The USSR has one of the most diverse and heterogeneous ethnic populations in the world; according to Soviet ethnic specialists there are 120 peoples and 140 distinct ethnic identities. (These are smaller subgroupings of peoples identified by ethnographers that have either split off from a major nation or are separate nations, groups, or tribal entities.) Figure 6.1 illustrates vividly that Russians are by far the largest nationality, and the Ukrainians still greatly exceed the rapidly growing Muslim Central Asian nationalities.

Table 6.1 National Composition of USSR Population (in millions)

	1970 census	1979 census	%	1989 census	%
Total population	241.71	262.08	100.00	285.60	100.00
Russians[a]	129.01	137.39	52.38	145.07	50.78
Ukrainians	40.75	42.34	16.15	44.13	15.45
White Russians (Belorussians)	9.05	9.46	3.61	10.03	3.51
Uzbeks	9.19	12.45	4.75	16.68	5.84
Tatars	5.93	6.31	2.41	6.64	2.32
Kazakhs	5.29	6.55	2.50	8.13	2.85
Azerbaydzhanis	4.38	5.47	2.08	6.79	2.38
Armenians	3.55	4.15	1.58	4.62	1.62
Georgians	3.24	3.57	1.36	3.98	1.39
Lithuanians	2.66	2.85	1.08	3.06	1.07
Jews	2.15	1.81	0.69	1.44	0.50
Moldavians	2.69	9.96	3.80	3.35	1.17
Germans	1.84	1.93	0.73	2.03	0.71
Chuvases	1.69	1.75	0.66	1.83	0.64
Latvians	1.43	1.43	0.54	1.45	0.51
Tadzhiks	2.13	2.89	1.10	4.21	1.48
Poles	1.16	1.15	0.43	1.12	0.39
Mordvinians	1.26	1.19	0.45	1.15	0.40
Turkmen	1.52	2.03	0.77	2.71	0.95
Bashkirs	1.24	1.37	0.52	1.44	0.50
Estonians	1.00	1.02	0.38	1.02	0.36
Kirgiz	1.45	1.90	0.72	2.53	0.89
Other nationalities	9.10	3.11	1.17	12.19	4.26

Source: Censuses of population
a. Defined by nationality, rank ordered by the 1958 census.

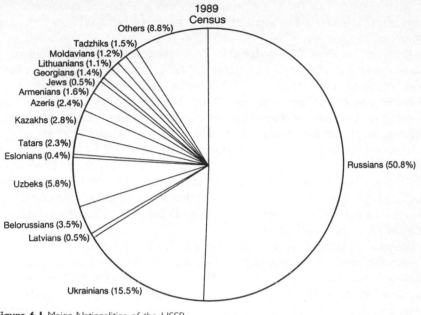

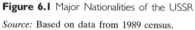

Figure 6.1 Major Nationalities of the USSR

Source: Based on data from 1989 census.

Discrepancies in percentages between Figure 6.1 and Table 6.1 are due to rounding.

We noted in an earlier chapter that the dominant ideology from Stalin to Brezhnev was one of consensus, collectivity, and social harmony. In terms of national relations, the political and economic foundations of the USSR — the unitary Communist Party of the Soviet Union and the state-owned means of production — are held to give rise to a community of interests between the various nationalities making up the USSR. The social relationships between nationalities and ethnic groups were held to be similar to those between classes; there were considered to be contradictions but not of an antagonistic kind.

Until the advent of the Gorbachev leadership, harmony was emphasized. Ideologically, policy was said to reduce the advantages enjoyed by the historical development of some nations, such as the Russians, and to eliminate ethnicity as a form of collective advantage. Here we are considering ideology; in practice we shall see below that other factors are more important. Socialist pluralism has led to the recognition of much greater differences not only in the distribution of resources but also in relations between national groups.

Soviet policy had three major components: a policy of cultural development (*raztsvet* or blossoming), "drawing together" (*sblizhenie*), and "merging" (*sliyanie*).

Raztsvet involves the recognition of vernacular languages, folkways, customs, and traditions. The federal political structure (discussed below) was intended to facilitate this. This policy reflected the recognition of national and ethnic consciousness, but policy was structured in a political context of Communist Party hegemony and socialist values. Stalin put this succinctly in the phrase: "National in form, socialist in content."

Cultural national traditions as opposed to class and political ones are and were not seen to be antagonistic to socialist values. A process of *sblizhenie*, it was considered, would take place, in which the different national groups would be drawn together in a socialist community in which characteristics of political modernization would have a significant impact on traditional values.

Sliyanie (merging) is a much stronger concept; it invloves the creation of a common international unity and the replacement of previous national and ethnic consciousness. This was a long-term goal that would come about with the consolidation of communism on a world scale.

In practice, however, the merging and drawing together of the various ethnic groups has not materialized. National consciousness has been an endemic and ineradicable feature of Soviet society. The deideologizing effect of perestroika has been to undermine Marxism-Leninism in its integrative national aspects and glasnost' has exposed the punitive effects of Soviet policy on many nations. The major components of Soviet cultural policy, described above, have been completely undermined, and conflict rather than consensus has been endemic in inter-ethnic relations. This has led to the rise of separatist movements and demands for independence from the USSR in the early 1990s.

THE NATIONAL AND ETHNIC COMPLEXION OF THE POPULATION

Generalizing about nationalities in the Soviet Union leads to compounding groups that are not comparable in size, historical and cultural development, political identification, or linguistic ability. One might distinguish among three major groupings.

The Slavs, which include Great Russians, Ukrainians, and Belorussians and numbered 199.2 million in 1989, are the largest grouping. These nationalities speak languages with a strong affinity to Russian, and are sometimes called "Russians," although they are distinct nationalities. Belorussians are literally "White Russians" in English translation. They originate in the Western European areas of the country, although many of these ethnic groups have emigrated and settled to the East — particularly in Siberia and Kazakhstan. All historically have been Christian by religion: the Russians have had allegiance to the Orthodox Church; the Ukrainians and Belorussians have also been Orthodox, but many have subscribed to Catholicism.

Balts, which include Estonians, Latvians, and Lithuanians, and numbered 5.5 million in 1989, inhabit the area to the Northwest of the USSR adjacent to Poland in the west and the Scandinavian countries across the Baltic coast. They too have had a Christian tradition: the Lithuanians are largely Catholic, and the Estonians and Latvians, Lutheran. Their vernacular languages are of a different origin to Russian and are written in Latin rather than Cyrillic script. These states were annexed to Russia in the eighteenth century, but were given independence after the First World War. In 1940 following the Rippentrop-Molotov Pact, they were incorporated into the USSR as constituent republics. The legality of this incorporation is contested by many in the Baltic republics; and Western states such as the United States and Great Britain have not recognized these states as component parts of the USSR.

The Muslims constitute the third group. These are constituted of the Uzbeks, Kazakhs, Azeris (Azerbaydzhanis), Kirgiz, and Tadzhiks, a group numbering 34.2 million in 1989. They are located in the Central Asian parts of the country (except for the Azeris, who hail from the Caucasus). Apart from the Tadzhiks, who speak a language akin to Persian, their languages are from the Turkic group.

In addition, there are two large groups of Caucasian people with a Christian heritage (Armenians and Georgians), numerous peoples of the East (Buryats, Komi, Udmurts, Yakuts), and significant minorities of other people of European stock (Jews, Germans, Moldavians, and Poles).

This heterogeneous constellation reflects the movement of peoples to the Russian areas of the country before the October Revolution (Germans, Jews); the expansion of Imperial Russia to the East to annex Siberia, Kazakhstan, and Uzbekistan; and the reincorporation of the Baltic provinces, parts of prewar Poland and Moldavia into the USSR after the Second World War.

THE ADMINISTRATIVE SETTING

Soviet policy has always recognized the sense of identity given by nationality and the leadership has promoted a culture "national in form and socialist in content." The administrative form took the shape of a federal state based on national ethnic groups. The idea here was to construct various politico-administrative units that would respect the ethnic character of the USSR as it then was. To take account of the size and level of development of the ethnic groups, four different tiers of administrative unit below the government of the USSR have been devised (see Table 6.2). At the top (below the Federal or All-Union government of the USSR, discussed in Chapter 3) are fifteen union republics (see Figure 6.2). These include the major nationalities that give each republic its title. These are (with the percentage of nationalities in the population corresponding to the name of the titular republic in 1979): Russian (RSFSR), 83 percent; Ukrainian, 74 percent; Belorussian, 79 percent; Uzbek, 69 percent; Kazakh, 36 percent; Georgian, 69 percent; Azeri, 78 percent; Lithuanian, 80 percent; Moldavian, 64 percent; Latvian,

Table 6.2
Union of Soviet Socialist Republics: Tiers of Government

			Distinctive characteristic
1. *All-Union government* (1)* (USSR)			The supreme political body: declares war, defines plan. Right to citizenship of USSR.
2. *Union-Republican governments* (15)			
Russian RSFSR	(83%)†	Ukrainian (74%)	Have rights to secede from USSR.
Belorussian	(79%)	Uzbek (69%)	Have rights to republican
Kazakhstan	(36%)	Georgian (69%)	citizenship.
Azerbaydzhan	(78%)	Lithuanian (80%)	
Moldavian	(64%)	Latvian (54%)	
Kirgiziyan	(48%)	Tadzhik (59%)	
Armenian	(90%)	Turkmen (68%)	
Estonian	(65%)		
3. *Autonomous republics* (20)			Have constitutions. Territory cannot be altered without consent, but union republic can suspend laws. Can ensure conformity of economic plans.
4. *Autonomous regions* (8)			No constitutions. Conduct business in national language.
5. *Autonomous areas* (10)			Laws dependent on union republics.

* Numbers in parentheses indicate number of administrative units.
† Percentages refer to proportion of nationality of titular republic in the republics.

Figure 6.2 Map: The Union of Soviet Socialist Republics

54 percent; Kirgiz, 48 percent; Tadzhik, 59 percent; Armenian, 90 percent; Turkmen, 68 percent; and Estonian, 65 percent (see Figure 6.3).

Formally, such republics have had their own constitutions, national plan, and budget; all (including the RSFSR since 1990) have had separate Communist parties. Each republic has the sanctity of its borders and the guarantee of republican citizenship for its permanent inhabitants; there is also a constitutional right to secede from the USSR. The All-Union government (and the USSR President) can suspend the laws of the republics and can intervene to ensure that their activities are in conformity with the economic plan and constitution of the USSR.

In the third tier are twenty autonomous republics that are subordinate to their parent union republic. These include the Bashkir autonomous republic (one of sixteen in the RSFSR) and Abkhaz autonomous republic (one of two in the Georgian republic). They have been formed to take

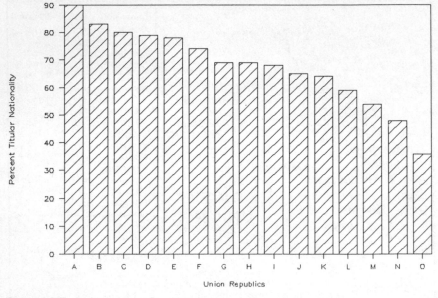

Figure 6.3 Titular Nationality in Republics

Source: Based on data from Soviet Census, 1979.
Key: A = Armenia; B = Russia; C = Lithuania; D = Belorussia; E = Azerbaydzhan; F = Ukraine; G =
Georgia; H = Uzbekhistan; I = Turkmeniya; J = Estonia; K = Moldavia; L = Tadzhikistan; M = Latvia;
N = Kirgiziya; O = Kazakhstan

account of ethnic groups located in a given republic: the objective is to
recognize their social identity and to give some elements of self-government. These units have constitutions and their territories cannot be altered
without their consent. Union republics can suspend the laws of the
autonomous republics and can intervene to ensure that their activities are
in conformity with the economic plan of the republic.

In the fourth and fifth echelons, come the eight autonomous regions
and ten autonomous areas. These lower levels include the smaller ethnic
groupings such as the Khakass autonomous region and the Taimyrski
autonomous area (both in the RSFSR) and groupings of national minorities, such as the Armenians in the Nagorno–Karabakh autonomous
area in Azerbaydzhan. These are units of administration that conduct
business in their own vernacular languages but do not have Supreme
Soviets and constitutions. Their laws are subject to ratification by the
Union Republic in which they are located.

The objective of the administrative division is to aggregate national
sentiments and to give ethnic groups a sense of identity. Important ex-

ceptions are the Jewish, German, and Polish nationalities, which have no single territory and therefore are not members of a distinct political unit. (There is a Jewish autonomous area in the RSFSR, but it contains only 10,000 Jews out of a Soviet Jewish population of 1.44 million.) It must also be remembered that the various national geographically based administrative units are not of a homogeneous national composition and through population movement and growth contain other significant ethnic groupings. We noted above, for instance, that in Kazakhstan, Kazakhs in 1979 accounted for 36 percent of the population, in addition Russians constituted 41 percent and Germans 6 percent.

This administrative system has strengthened the social and political consciousness of the republican titular nationalities (that is, Uzbeks in Uzbekistan) within their territorial areas. The power of local units has also been circumscribed, at least in theory, by the centralization of the economy and the Communist Party of the Soviet Union and by the doctrine of democratic centralism, which asserts the accountability of lower bodies to higher ones. The CPSU effectively prevented republican parties from being autonomous political units — at least until the advent of Gorbachev and perestroika. From the beginning of perestroika, the decline of the traditional forms of political cohesion has been accompanied by a heightened sense of national consciousness and the rise of national political parties which have demanded sovereignty and independence for their republics.

COMPARATIVE LEVELS OF DEVELOPMENT IN THE REPUBLICS

There are considerable differences in the levels of development of the various republics and their class structures. The level of urbanization is shown in Table 6.3. The Russian, Baltic and Armenian republics are all over two-thirds urban, whereas the Central Asian republics and Moldavia are largely rural and agricultural. The Soviet Union's rural population declined by some ten million between 1959 and 1989, while the total population increased by 78 million. In Central Asia (including Kazakhstan), however, between 1959 and 1978 the rural population rose from 14 million to 25 million — a rise of 75 percent. This increase is due to the higher birth rate of the indigenous population in rural areas.

The occupational and educational levels of these populations vary considerably. The share of nonmanual workers in the employed population in 1979 was 29 percent in the USSR as a whole: 30.7 percent in the RSFSR, 26.2 percent in the Ukraine, 26.8 percent in Belorussia, 24.2 percent in Uzbekistan, 29.8 percent in Kazakhstan, 30.4 percent

Table 6.3
Union Republics by Degree of Urbanization, 1970 and
1987 (in percentages)

	1970	1987	Change
USSR	56	66	+10
RSFSR	62	74	+12
Ukraine	55	67	+12
Belorussia	43	64	+21
Uzbekistan	37	42	+ 5
Kazakhstan	50	58	+ 8
Georgia	48	55	+ 7
Azerbaydzhan	50	54	+ 4
Lithuania	50	67	+16
Moldavia	32	47	+15
Latvia	62	71	+ 9
Kirgiziya	37	40	+ 3
Tadzhikistan	37	33	− 4
Armenia	59	68	+ 9
Turkmeniya	48	48	0
Estonia	65	72	+ 7

Source: *Narkhoz za 70 let* (1987): 378.

in Georgia, 25.8 percent in Azerbaydzhan, 28.1 percent in Lithuania, 21.4 percent in Moldavia, 31.1 percent in Latvia, 25.2 percent in Kirgiziya, 21.2 percent in Tadzhikistan, 30.3 percent in Armenia, 23.2 percent in Turkmeniya, 32.1 percent in Estonia. (These data of course compound different nationality groups in each republic.)

Economic development, however, has had an equalizing effect on the social composition of ethnic groups. Table 6.4 (see also Figure 6.4) illustrates that all nationalities have experienced a decline in the numbers of collective farmers. With the exception of Moldavians (where manual workers increased by 69 percent between 1970 and 1979) and Tadzhiks, the working class has increased only slightly. The proportion of nonmanual workers has risen, with the exception of the Tadzhiks. Urbanization has risen for all ethnic groups, but large differences remain between the European nationalities (Russians and Latvians) and the Muslim peoples (Kazakhs and Tadzhiks).

The effects of modernization (in the form of nonmanual, skilled manual, and postsecondary education) are correlated to a falling family size. In the 1979 census the Central Asian nationalities had very large families — Uzbeks had an average 6.2 children under eighteen, Tadzhiks, 6.5 — where-

Table 6.4
Social Composition of Selected Ethnic Groups (in percentages)

	Manual workers	Nonmanual workers	Collective farmers	Urban
1970				
Russians	63	25	12	68
Latvians	54	23	23	53
Armenians	60	25	15	65
Kazakhs	65	22	13	27
Tadzhiks	37	15	48	26
Moldavians	32	7	61	20
Average USSR	57	23	20	56
1979				
Russians	63	31	6	74
Latvians	58	28	14	58
Armenians	62	31	7	70
Kazakhs	64	28	8	32
Tadzhiks	55	15	30	28
Moldavians	54	15	31	27
Average USSR	60	25	15	62

Source: Y. V. Arutyunyan. 1982. *Sotsialisticheskie Issledovaniya*, no. 4 (1982): 23.

as the Russians had only 3.16 and the Latvians 3.0. These demographic changes have important political consequences.

Statistics give us a broad picture of the composition of Soviet nationalities. What is of interest are the relationships between national groups. We shall discuss them in terms of distributional and political inequality, and the ways that the policy of perestroika has influenced relations between national groups.

Republican Economic Inequalities

Given the dispersion of ethnic groups over the USSR and the lack of adequate survey data, it is not possible to make accurate estimates of income differentials on an ethnic basis. Some inferences may be made, however, by considering the uneven development of various republics. It must be emphasized again that data about republics do not necessarily refer to ethnic groups.

The legacy of history must be taken into account when appraising regional national differentials. Before 1917 industrial development had

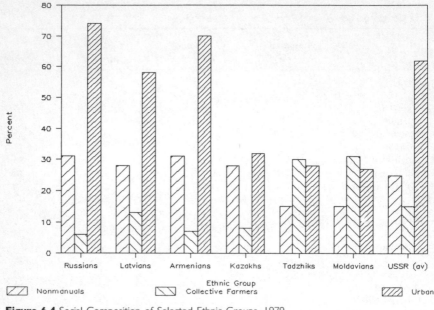

Figure 6.4 Social Composition of Selected Ethnic Groups, 1979

Source: Based on data from Y. V. Arutyunyan. 1982. *Sotsialisticheskie Issledovaniya*, no. 4 (1982): 23.

hardly begun in Soviet Central Asia. It is to their credit that the Bolsheviks attempted to equalize standards between the regions. Between 1913 and 1935 in Turkmenia industrial output of large-scale industry increased eightfold, in Kazakhstan it rose 8.5 times, and in Kirgiziya 8.3 times, whereas the corresponding figure for the USSR was 5.7. Such growth rates, however, were not difficult to achieve from a very low base and economic development has not consistently favored the underdeveloped non-Russian areas. The comparative advantage of developing heavy industry in areas of existing industry has led to greater economic growth of the Russian territories of the Urals, Volga, and Siberia; the Ukraine has also benefitted. Kazakhstan has been the subject of most industrial development, but the territory has witnessed a massive increase of Russian settlers to operate the new industrial enterprises.

The rate of urbanization may be used as an index of industrialization and here we see the lagging of some of the Soviet Central Asia republics. In Turkmenia and Tadzhikistan, the proportion of the rural indigenous population remained the same or even increased between 1970 and 1987 (see Table 6.3). Industrialization has been at too low a level to compensate for the large growth in the rural (native) population in most of the Muslim republics.

Despite this unevenness, there has been on the whole a remarkable equalization in the delivery of services during the years of Soviet power. Charles K. Wilber (1969) has shown that from being on a par with (or below) countries like India, Iran, and Pakistan in 1926, by the early 1960s the Central Asian Republics were similar to countries like Italy so far as economic development and cultural and welfare facilities were concerned. As he puts it, "Central Asia has been transformed from a stagnant, illiterate, disease-ridden, semi-feudal society into a modern progress-orientated society."

However, important differences among ethnic groups remain. Average wage payments vary considerably between republics and are likely to be to the disadvantage of the non-European peoples. Table 6.5 ranks the republics from top to bottom by average income per head for manual and nonmanual workers (average earnings per head in 1986 are shown in the first column). The highest-earning republics are all in the European parts of the USSR (Estonia, the Russian republic, Latvia, and Lithuania); at the other end are Azerbaydzhan, Moldavia, Tadzhikistan, Uzbekistan, and Kirgiziya. The percentage growth in real income per head from 1970

Table 6.5
Earned Income of Manual and Nonmanual Workers

	Growth in per capita income, 1970–86 (%)	Average per capita income for 1986 (rubles)
USSR	167	195.6
Estonia	159	221
RSFSR	173	207.8
Latvia	153	201.4
Lithuania	157	194.7
Turkmeniya	156	193.1
Kazakhstan	165	192.7
Armenia	164	184.5
Belorussia	178	180.5
Ukraine	165	179
Georgia	189	170.6
Kirgiziya	163	166.4
Uzbekistan	164	165.9
Tadzhikistan	151	162
Moldavia	181	161.8
Azerbaydzhan	165	161.7

Source: Narkhoz za 70 let (1987). Calculations added.

to 1986 using 1970 as the base year and relating to the total population appears in the second column. (This figure includes nonmoney income, such as medical and social services.) These data exclude earnings in collective farms or from private agricultural production; if these were included Georgia would increase its relative share.

The above-average figures for the RSFSR and the Baltic republics in the first column reflect the location of high-paying heavy and "high-tech" industries in those areas. Kazakhstan is only 2.9 rubles below average due to the location of heavy industry there. The Baltic republics also have much higher rates of pay for collective farmers — remarkably so in Estonia, where they earned 283.5 rubles from the social sector in 1986 compared to the average collective farmer's wage of 163 in that year.

The second column of Figure 6.5 shows the growth of real income per head from 1970 to 1986 (the data are expressed as the percentage rise between 1970 and 1986); these figures relate to the total population. These figures indicate the extent to which the more backward areas are

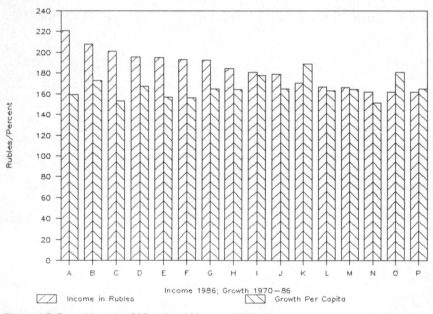

Figure 6.5 Earned Income of Manual and Nonmanual Workers

Source: Based on data from *Narkhoz za 70 let* (1987). Calculations added.
Key: A = Estonia; B = Russia; C = Latvia; D = USSR; E = Lithuania; F = Turkmeniya; G = Kazakhstan; H = Armenia; I = Belorussia; J = Ukraine; K = Georgia; L = Kirgiziya; M = Uzbekhistan; N = Tadzhikistan; O = Moldavia; P = Azerbaydzhan

(or are not) reducing the gap. In the European republics, the RSFSR showed a 6 percent rise above the USSR average; the Ukraine was 2 percent below; Belorussia, 11 percent above; Lithuania, 10 percent below; Latvia, 14 percent below; and Estonia, 8 percent below. The Central Asian republics all had a below-average percentage increase: Uzbekistan, −3 percent; Kazakhstan, −2 percent; Kirgiziya, −4 percent; Tadzhikistan, −16 percent; and Turkmeniya, −11 percent. The southern-tier republics of Georgia and Azerbaydzhan had above-average rises of 22 percent and 2 percent, though Armenia had a reduction of 3 percent. Overall these figures show a tendency for the RSFSR to increase its relative lead, Belorussia, Georgia, Moldavia, and Azerbaydzhan caught up somewhat. At the other end of the scale, the gap with the RSFSR widened for Tadzhikistan and Turkmeniya. Republics with above-average wage earners coming closer to the mean were Estonia and Latvia.

The tables show that the richer republics are the Russian (RSFSR), Estonia, and Latvia; the poorest in terms of income are Tadzhikistan, Kirgiziya, Moldavia, Azerbaydzhan, and Uzbekistan.

Distributional Inequality: Education

In modern industrial societies, education is a crucial determinant of a person's life chances. In socialist societies education has added significance for defining social position and giving access to social mobility for the formal inheritance of wealth and the economic and social status that goes with it was abolished in the revolution.

The legacy of backwardness for many non-Russian groups was particularly great with respect to education. Before the revolution of 1917 in Russia only 24 percent of the population over nine years of age was literate. In the Central Asian provinces the proportion ranged from 2.3 percent (Tadzhikistan) to 8.1 percent (Kazakhstan). Compulsory schooling and mass campaigns against illiteracy led to its eradication by the eve of the Second World War: by 1939 adult literacy rates ranged from 78 percent to 84 percent in the Central Asian republics. By the 1960s literacy in one language was universal. This has represented an immense equalization of opportunities between ethnic groups in the USSR.

Other inequalities remain, however. Jones and Grupp (1984) have measured interethnic differences and their relative decline. Some of their findings on ethnic educational enrollment are shown in Table 6.6 and Figure 6.6. The calculations are expressed, for a particular republic, as a ratio to that of Russian participation. A score of one hundred represents equality with Russians; over one hundred, greater participation and below,

Table 6.6
Index of Ethnic Educational Enrollment for 1980

	Special Secondary	*Higher Education*
Estonian	98	122
Georgian	71	119
Lithuanian	114	117
Latvian	94	109
Russian	100	100
Kazakh	78	92
Armenian	71	89
Kirgizian	58	86
Ukrainian	95	86
Belorussian	90	84
Uzbek	53	69
Tadjik	40	65
Moldavian	62	52

Source: Jones and Grupp 1984: 163.

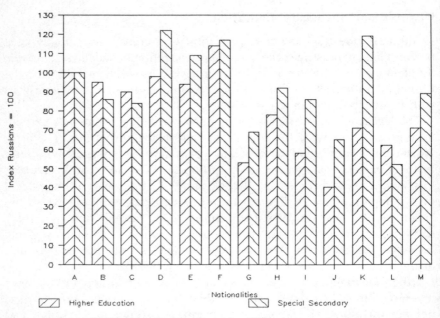

Figure 6.6 Index of Ethnic Educational Enrollment for 1980

Source: Based on data from Jones and Grupp, 1983
Key: A = Russians; B = Ukrainians; C = Belorussians; D = Estonians; E = Latvians; F = Lithuanians; G = Uzbeks; H = Kazakhs; I = Kirgiz; J = Tadzhiks; K = Georgians; L = Moldavians; M = Armenians

lesser. These figures show the constant superiority of the Baltic nations, Russians, and Georgians.

The Muslim nations have fared less well in higher education. The increase in population and the rising number of young people of university age has not been accompanied by an increase in higher educational institutions. This shortfall provides a structural basis for unequal opportunity of Uzbeks, Azeris, and some other nationalities.

These quantitative data need qualification, however. It is generally agreed that the quality of education is lower in newly developed areas than in older ones, and in rural compared to urban areas. The prestigious higher educational institutions are located primarily in the European areas of the country and are attended by European nationalities. One might safely conclude that educational levels are higher in the European urban areas and that with some notable exceptions (such as the Georgians) educational opportunities are greater there. At the same time, however, there has been a considerable overall improvement in educational opportunity and a widening of educational openings for the non-Russian nationalities in general and the non-European ones in particular.

Language

Language is an important index of national identity. Russian is the lingua franca of the USSR. Until 1989 Russian was the only official language throughout the USSR. Outside the Russian republic (RSFSR), local languages are used in the educational system as the medium of instruction, Russian is the second compulsory language in non-Russian schools. In addition, Russian-language schools are available in non-Russian republics. Since 1989, many union republics have adopted legislation making the vernacular language of the republic the "official" language for the conducting of government business within the republic.

The 1979 census identified those who considered the language of their nationality to be their native (*rodnoy*) language and those who thought Russian to be so. Of the nationalities having a republican base, the following proportions considered Russian to be their native language: Russians, 99.5 percent; Ukrainians, 17 percent; Belorussians, 25 percent; Armenians, 8.4 percent; Moldavians, 6 percent; Georgians, 1.7 percent; Azeris, 1.8 percent; Kazakhs, 2 percent; Uzbeks, 0.6 percent; Tadzhiks, 0.8 percent; Lithuanians, 1.7 percent; Kirgiz, 0.5 percent; Latvians, 4.8 percent; and Estonians, 4.6 percent.

Other nationalities, however, had higher levels of linguistic identification with Russian: Germans, 42.6 percent; Jews, 83.3 percent; Poles, 26.2

percent; Udmurts, 23.4 percent; Koreans, 44.4 percent; Komi, 23.7 percent; the "nations of the North", 28.7 percent; Karely, 44.1 percent; Finns, 50.3 percent; Vepsi, 61 percent; Karaimy, 81.2 percent; Khalkha-Mongolians, 91.3 percent. The dispersed European nationalities (Poles, Germans) and the small indigenous ethnic groups are the ones that have been most assimilated. Russian is considered the second language by 23.4 percent of the population of the USSR. Of the nationalities of the titular republics from 74.2 percent (Belorussians) to 98.7 percent (Turkmens) consider their "native" language to be the same as their nationality.

In the non-Russian republics, the vernacular language has not been made compulsory for immigrants and in many factories Russian is the language of communication, consequently Slavic immigrants often have a poor knowledge of the vernacular language. This has proved to be a cause of friction and has led to the demand by some national republics for laws strengthening the local languages.

We may sum up here the salient facts we have noted above to give some idea of what these figures signify for the lives of the various nationality groups, bearing in mind, of course, that stratification occurs within these groups. The most privileged groups in terms of income, nonmanual occupation, urban residence, and education are the European nationalities: Russians, Estonians, and Latvians followed by the Georgians. The Baltic republics of Estonia and Latvia have a particularly high standard of living and these republics have a mixed population including a large presence of Russians. At the other end of the scale are the Central Asian republics. Here also there has been European immigration, which has resulted in a large European ethnic presence in the cities. The Central Asian republics (with the exception of Kazakhstan, which has a large Russian population) are rural, have lower per capita incomes, and inferior levels of education. Ethnic groups that have had a national republic have maintained their own vernacular languages; those without (Jews, Germans, and Poles) have fared less well in this respect.

NATIONAL IDENTITY AND CONSCIOUSNESS

Occupational and educational developments linked to urbanization would lead one to believe that a convergence is taking place in the lifestyles of the nations of the USSR. This does not mean, of course, that conditions or aspirations are the same, merely that an equalization is taking place. Self-identity and national consciousness, moreover, have to be analyzed as distinct social categories that may develop quite independently of living standards and conditions. All evidence shows that the trends to modernization noted above have not seriously diminished national consciousness. Intermarriage has not led to the assimilation or absorption of minority cultures by the dominant ones. Muslim and European nationalities do not intermarry very much. When they do, usually Slavic women marry Muslim men. In Central Asia, intermarriage is between the indigenous nationalities — Uzbeks, Kazakhs, and Karakalpaks.

Until the advent of the political leadership of M. S. Gorbachev, discussion and study of interethnic relations in the USSR was muted, though research conducted in the early and late 1970s in the areas of the Russian republic, Uzbekistan, Georgia, Moldavia, and Estonia found that "national exclusiveness" existed among ethnic groups. Soviet researchers found that among the older rural ethnic populations prejudice about other nationalities was of a traditional type and was acute among people who had not had many interethnic contacts. This was considered a contradiction caused by a vestige (*perezhitok*) from the pre-Soviet epoch. More serious was interethnic prejudice precipitated by processes within Soviet society. It was found that in Moldavia and Uzbekistan, for example, young people of the indigenous nationality who failed to gain admission to higher educational institutions expressed their resentment in a form of antagonism projected against other nationalities.

A revealing study of interethnic relations and consciousness of Soviet immigrants to the United States has been made by Rasma Karklins. On the basis of interviews in the 1980s mainly with Jewish immigrants, it was found that consciousness of nationality and resentment of other nationalities varied by region. With respect to the privileges enjoyed by national groups, it was widely believed that Russians (particularly in their own republic) and nationals of the titular union republics (that is, Georgians in Georgia) were favored over other nationalities and ethnic groups. Rather than a homogeneous system of domination by Russians, privileges pertain to dominant national groups within a republic. The national groups who felt most subject to national discrimination were the minorities in republics — this included Russians in republics with a predominantly indigenous population, for example, Armenia, Azerbaydzhan, or Uzbekistan.

Karklins points out that the Soviet policy of proportional ethnic representation and access promoted ethnic identity. Other data may also be cited to show, for example, that though the Russians make up 19 percent on average of the 14 republics outside of the RSFSR, they account for only about 12.5 percent of the deputies elected in the local Soviets (data for 1988). The federal structure of the USSR before perestroika had the significant effect of strengthening national and ethnic consciousness. Those groups that have lost out are dispersed nationalities having no territory, such as the Jews, Poles, and Germans. As we have shown above, the vernacular language capacity of these nationalities has declined.

In a study based on interviews with emigré Soviet Germans Karklins found that the intensity and direction of national consciousness varied by republic. The greatest intensity of preference for the local nationality within the republic is in Central Asia, the Caucasus, Moldavia, Lithuania, and Estonia. In Belorussia and Latvia (republics with 12 percent and 32 percent Russian populations), Russians were seen as holding equal or superior positions. In the Baltic and Central Asian republics where cultural identity was strong, respondents thought that interethnic relations were getting worse. The power of the local nationality was thought to be increasing in Kazakhstan and Central Asia, whereas in the Baltic provinces the local peoples were less buoyant and it was felt that Russians were coming out on top and thus creating a sense of resentment among the locals. In Kazakhstan, Kazakhs had secured considerable power in the Party and government apparatus at the expense of the Russians; and in the Baltic, resentment was publicly expressed against the non-Baltic nationalities in 1988–89.

Soviet national policy has had the effect of heightening the awareness of the dominant republican nationalities. Underlying the rise of consciousness is the increase in educational levels; the knowledgeable professional classes provide much of the intellectual leadership for the national movements. At the level of the individual, job dissatisfaction and educational failure give rise to feelings of ethnic resentment. The effects of urbanization and rising educational standards have led to a homogenization in lifestyles: wage labor (rather than home working), the television with its standardized and Western oriented output, and the widespread availability and aspiration for consumer durables. But in the formation of a personal identity, the merging (*sliyanie*) of cultures into a generic Soviet culture has not occurred. Rather there has been a revival and reaffirmation of traditional foci of identity. The greater striving for status and success and the intense competitiveness of modern life bring nationalities into contact in a contentious rather than in a supportive role. This has lead to animosity and tension; national origins can be a scapegoat for individual failure. Such social tension can be manifested in political form: nationalism is the major component of Soviet domestic politics in the late 1980s and early 1990s.

Ethnicity as a Form of Advantage and Discrimination

Ethnicity is not only a form of self- and group-identity based on language, skin pigmentation and culture; it may also have political implications.

National or ethnic status may determine on a collective basis access to resources (political power, education, occupation, income). Societies may be divided into dominant ethnic groups that perpetuate their advantage to the exclusion of others. As noted above, research carried out in the Soviet Union and in the West indicates that feelings of a shared culture and history give rise to the pursuit of collective ethnic group advantage. Sociologists call this a form of "social closure," meaning that a particular social group passes on to its members privilege and advantage. Language, religion, and skin pigmentation are ciphers that can be used to identify social groups and to allocate privilege, power, and prestige. Hence ethnicity may be the basis of a political movement rather than a cultural form of identification.

Brzezinski and Huntington coined the acronym SRAPPS (Slavic-Stock Russian-born Apparatchiks) to define a stratum of ethnic origin that has political, economic, and social advantage. It is from this group that the various elites that rule the USSR are drawn. A caveat is necessary here: one must be careful to distinguish between the social origins or composition of a controlling group and its policy. A group with a given social background (say Russian or Jewish) may not necessarily act to the exclusive advantage of that group. There may be other group or institutional loyalties (such as to profession, region, or religion) or there may be ideological determinants (such as a belief in socialism or free competition) that shape social preferences and the outcomes of decisions. In addition, even a nationally homogeneous political elite may be subject to external pressures from other nationalities, institutions, and groups. Nevertheless, study of access by ethnic groups to positions of authority indicates the extent of openness of elite positions and, when coupled with political outcomes, may shed some light on the distribution of power in a society. At least we may learn whether ethnicity is the basis for the exclusion of a given ethnic (or social) group.

The All-Union institutions of political power include the most powerful in the USSR. As noted in chapter 3, the range of powers of political leaders is much wider than that covered by chief politicians in the West — either by the president and officials of the U.S. federal government and its agencies or by the ministers and civil servants of Western European states. In the USSR the executive arm of government includes ministries and committees concerned not only with foreign affairs, security, social and welfare services, but also with the organization and functioning of the economy. Rather than private or corporate firms as in the West, in the USSR government the "All-Union" ministries and committees perform entrepreneurial activities over the whole range of economic affairs: money, banking, and industrial production.

Until the advent of perestroika the formal division in Western capitalist societies between the economic elites (the top executives and owners of corporations and banks) and the political ones (leaders of government and political parties) did not exist in the USSR. There was a fusion between politics and economics, with the latter being formally dependent on the former. The Communist Party was the social organization that mobilized and controlled the ministerial apparatuses. Through its allocation of personnel, it sought to guide and coordinate the government bureaucracy. The extent to which it did so is a matter of dispute. Here it is important only to emphasize the administrative forms of power in the USSR and their implications for the national republics.

The major institutional forms have been described above (see Figure 3.6). The Politburo was the supreme body and was composed of the top officials from government and Party bodies, that is, from the apparatus of the Party and the leading government executives.

The ethnic composition of the Politburo (including its secretariat) is shown in Table 6.7. The growing predominance of Russians, the overall inclusion of Slavs, and the small and random representation of other nationalities are clear. Under Brezhnev, non-Russian nationalities were represented in the top All-Union (federal) political leadership: the first secretaries of the Uzbek, Belorussian (White Russian), Azerbaydzhan, and Georgian Communist Parties were candidate members of the Politburo. In May 1988, only 16 percent of the first secretaries were of non-Russian nationality, compared to 32 percent in 1988 and 44 percent in 1972.

Table 6.7
Ethnic Composition of Politburo-Presidium and CPSU Secretariat 1973, 1980, and July 1988 (percent)

	1973	1980	1988	1988 (number)
Russians	56	68	84	21
Ukrainians	16	7	8	2
Belorussians	12	7	4	1
Latvians	4	3.5	0	0
Uzbeks	4	3.5	0	0
Kazakhs	4	3.5	0	0
Azeris	0	3.5	0	0
Armenians	6	0	0	0
Georgians	0	3.5	4	1
Jews	4	0	0	0

Table 6.8 shows data collected on the ethnic background of one hundred leading officials in office in February 1981 and March 1986. These include all members and secretaries of the Central Committee of the CPSU, the chiefs of departments of the Central Committee, the first deputy chiefs of key departments of the Central Committee not included above, leading officials in the army and defense, mass media and research institutes, the first secretaries of the central committees of the republican and district (*oblast'*) committees of the Communist Party, members of the Presidium of the Council of Ministries, and heads of selected ministries and state committees. This table includes a fair sprinkling of minority nationalities, most of whom were secretaries of the republican parties. Overall, however,

Table 6.8
Ethnic Backgrounds of the Top 100 Officials in 1981 and 1986, and Members of the Council of Ministers in 1988

| | Top 100 Officials | | Council of Ministers | |
| | 1981 | 1986 | 1988 | |
			number (percent)	
Russian	69	73	82	69
Ukrainian	13	7	16	13
Belorussian	3	5	5	4
Estonian	0	0	1	1
Latvian	3	1	1	1
Lithuanian	0	0	1	1
Bashkir	2	0	0	0
Mordovian	0	1	0	0
Uzbek	1	1	0	0
Tadzhik	0	0	1	1
Tatar	1	0	0	0
Turkmen	0	0	1	1
Kazakh	1	1	1	1
Kirgiz	0	0	1	1
Azeri	1	2	2	2
Armenian	1	1	1	1
Georgian	1	2	2	2
Greek	0	0	1	1
Jewish	1	0	0	0
Moldavian	1	0	1	1
Adygeez	0	0	1	1
Unknown	2	6	1	1
	100	100	118	102[a]

Source: Data from *A Biographic Dictionary of 100 Leading Soviet Officials*, compiled by A. G. Rahr (Munich: Radio Liberty Research, 1986) and biographies.
a. Exceeds 100 due to rounding.

we again witness a predominance of the Slavic (and particularly Russian) nationalities in top positions.

On the right hand side of Table 6.8 are collected data on all members of the Council of Ministers of the USSR in office in November 1988. Of a total membership of 146 (which includes heads of organs, as well as ministers) three posts were vacant, and twenty-five members had occupations that were unknown. Of the 118 members with known nationality, a similar pattern to that discovered above was found: 69 percent were Russian, 13 percent Ukrainian, 4 percent Belorussian, and there was only a sprinkling of other nationalities. These data help explain the widely held view in the republics of the USSR that the All-Union government and its operations are dominated by Russians and a "Moscow interest".

Republican Elites

In the republics there is much evidence that there is "reverse discrimination," meaning that non-Russians enjoy preference over Russians in certain posts; these include the first party secretaries. Members of the republican politburos are mostly of the titular nationality, as are most ministerial and government positions in general (including the important chairpersons of republican Councils of Ministers), jobs in public relations, and certain posts in local industry and trade. It is sometimes suggested that in Central Asia the indigenous population is, as Rywkin has put it, "often given preference [in the job market] over Europeans, unless the latter are the only ones having indispensable skills" (Rywkin 1979: 9). Rywkin has proved to be correct. In December 1986 a clampdown by Moscow on local Kazakh officials led to two days of rioting in Kazakhstan. Local native leaders were dismissed and the first secretary of the Party was replaced by a Russian. It was later stated at the Kazakh Party Plenum in December 1986 that ties of "personal friendship between Kunaev [the Kazakh Party boss] and Brezhnev played its part in the incorrect and clearly exaggerated assessments of the situation in the republic. This was favoritism at the highest level."

Bialer (1980: 214) in a study of "native cadres" in the national republics of 1976 found that in the Party Central Committee bureau and Presidium of Council of Ministers of all national republics, 252 or 75.8 percent of the members were of indigenous cadres, in Uzbekistan the figure was 76 percent, in Latvia 74 percent, and in Georgia 94 percent. Russians, however, occupied a number of key posts — they are invariably second party secretaries, heads of the state security organs (KGB) and communications — and Russians are usually chiefs of factories under All-Union (that is, Moscow-based) ministries. The commander of military forces in a republic is also usually Russian.

At lower levels of the Party structure, there has been a massive influx of non-Russians into the Party since the mid-1970s (see Table 6.9 and Figure 6.7). One has to bear in mind when interpreting these statistics that the Central Asian republics have a large population under adult age that is not eligible for Party membership and skews the percentages above.

Table 6.9 shows Party membership between 1973 and 1989 and increases in Party membership by selected nationalities for 1973–83 and 1973–86. The growth for Russians was less than the average rise in the two periods. In the Central Asian republics, however, membership by the non-Russian nationalities increased remarkably: in the 1973–83 period, the range was from 43.7 percent to 55.5 percent and between 1973 and 1986 from 58.9 percent to 72.7 percent. This enlargement, of course, reflects the aging of the growing non-Russian population stock. It should be noted, moreover, that the density of these groups in the Party is very low, which is shown by the data for 1989: (see Figure 6.7) the largest non-Slavic group, the Uzbeks, constituted only 2.3 percent of party membership in 1983, and 2.5 percent in 1989. One might conclude that, even before perestroika, the politically active people in the republican governments were recruited from the indigenous nationalities. With the greater autonomy given by Gorbachev's policy, the republican parties (particularly when it suited their own interests) identified with their own republics rather than with the USSR.

PERESTROIKA AND THE NATIONAL PROBLEM

In the early days of perestroika, the organizational principles of democratization and glasnost' associated with it were not linked very much to relations between nationalities. The leadership was mainly concerned with changes in the economy and the means to effect them. The greater pluralism, glasnost', and promises of decentralization, however, had important repercussions in the national republics. In 1988 and 1989 the leadership was confronted with serious outbursts of unrest by the nations of the Baltic and by bitter interracial conflict in the Caucasus. People's Fronts based on nationality appeared in all of the constituent republics of the USSR.

Democratization, glasnost', and pluralism have had a significant impact on the various national groups making up the USSR. Democratization has encouraged people to participate, glasnost' has allowed them to

Table 6.9

Party Membership by Nationality, 1973–89

	Number in Party (millions)					Percentage increase		
	1973	1983	1986	1989	1989 (%)		1973–83	1973–86
Total:	14.08	18.01	19.00	19.487	100	Average rise:	22.2	28.3
Russians	9.02	10.81	11.24	11.428	58.6		19.8	24.6
Uzbeks	0.292	0.428	0.465	0.491	2.5		47.0	59.2
Azeris	0.212	0.304	0.337	0.366	1.8		43.7	58.9
Turkmen	0.044	0.0687	0.076	0.081	0.4		55.5	72.7
Latvians	0.062	0.0742	0.078	0.080	0.4		20.2	25.8
Lithuanians	0.096	0.134	0.147	0.156	0.8		39.7	53.1

Source: Data from Izvestiya TsK. KPSS nos. 1 and 2, 1989.

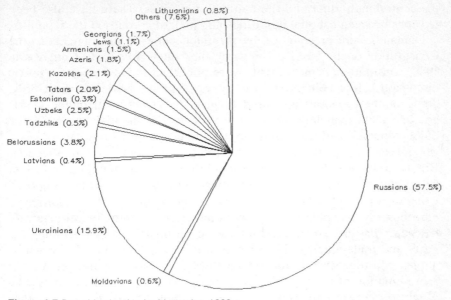

Lithuanians (0.8%)
Others (7.6%)
Georgians (1.7%)
Jews (1.1%)
Armenians (1.5%)
Azeris (1.8%)
Kazakhs (2.1%)
Tatars (2.0%)
Estonians (0.3%)
Uzbeks (2.5%)
Tadzhiks (0.5%)
Belorussians (3.8%)
Latvians (0.4%)
Russians (57.5%)
Ukrainians (15.9%)
Moldavians (0.6%)

Figure 6.7 Party Membership by Nationality, 1989

Source: Based on data *Izvestiya Ts.K. KPSS*, nos. 1 and 2, 1989.

articulate their feelings, and pluralism has legitimated the rights of groups to form on the basis of a consciousness of self-interest. The idea of *khozraschet* (economic self-balancing) has been applied to republican units as a basis for greater regional economic and political independence.

The effects of these policies have been manifested in many ways: People's Fronts have advocated the cause of ethnic groups, and mass meetings and demonstrations have occurred in support of national and regional rights. Many of the activists in these movements are also Party members, though previous dissidents figure prominently among the leaders. The line taken by the political leadership (noted above in chapter 3) is that a greater division should be made between state and civil society and that the Party should not attempt to interfere in all activities. The People's Fronts, therefore, have a legitimate right to independent existence. Such independence before 1990 should be seen in the context of the Party's leading role in society — a condition not accepted by some of the leaders of the Fronts, and subsequently abolished.

In some of the republics the legislators (the Soviets) have demanded concessions from the center in favor of their constituents. Overall there has been a heightening of national consciousness and tension between the central authorities and the national minorities. There have also been tensions between national minorities and majority groups in the republics.

Demands were precipitated by the publication of amendments to the Constitution of the USSR. Following the Nineteenth Party Congress in 1988, constitutional amendments were published in November for public discussion before being voted on by the Supreme Soviet of the USSR. Some of the proposals appeared to give the government of the USSR greater rights than hitherto to intervene in the internal affairs of the union republics and to declare void republican legislation. There was a general feeling on the part of the indigenous population in the non-Russian republics that the proposals did not give the republics sufficient autonomy. A second issue was the election of members of the proposed Congress of People's Deputies. As we noted in chapter 3, in addition to elections on a population and regional basis, a third constituency of delegates was elected from All-Union social organizations (including the Party and trade unions). The objection here was that the social organizations' constituency (elected on an All-Union basis) would reduce the representation of the republics, and particularly they might increase the weight of delegates sponsored by the Communist Party in Moscow, thus watering down the pluralistic elements rising to the surface in the republics under perestroika.

To illustrate the greater assertiveness of the national groups in the late 1980s, two examples will be given here: the conflict over Nagorno-Karabakh and the rise of the nationalist movement in the Baltic. Finally, we will note the rise of Russian ethnic consciousness.

The Case of Nagorno-Karabakh

In February 1988 the Soviet of the Autonomous *oblast* of Nagorno-Karabakh, having a 76 percent Armenian population, but situated within the borders of the Republic of Azerbaydzhan voted to join the Armenian republic. The vote was taken by the Armenian deputies (110); the Azeris were absent. The matter was discussed the next day by the Politburo, which rejected the demands to incorporate Nagorno-Karabakh into Armenia, though it was recognized that the rights of Armenians in Karabakh had been infringed. The Azerbaydzhan and Armenian Communist Parties were called upon to normalize the situation. There followed a long period of demonstrations of sympathy in the streets of the capital of Armenia, Erevan. These protests were attended by crowds of up to 100,000 people. Politburo member Dolgikh and Party Secretary Luk'yanov appealed to the Armenian population to support the Politburo's position.

But demonstrations continued in Armenia and clashes between Armenians and Azeris occurred in Nagorno-Karabakh. Gorbachev further asked for calm, but trouble spread to Baku, where Azerbaydzhani youths attacked Armenians. Violence escalated and pogroms occurred before troops were brought in. Deaths were estimated in the hundreds.

In March and July 1988 the Supreme Soviet of the USSR discussed the matter and concluded that the boundaries could not be changed as this constitutionally required the agreement of the republic (Azerbaydzhan) to which Karabakh was subordinate. The argument advanced by Gorbachev at the Supreme Soviet when the matter was discussed there in July 1988 was that many minority national groups lived in other republics: there were as many Azeris in Armenia as there were Armenians in Azerbaydzhan, and there were many analogous cases in other republics. Gorbachev called for both republics to overcome shortcomings in their own affairs — particularly "neglect in the ideological sphere" (chauvinism, lack of internationalism), violations of socialist morality, manifested in favoritism, bribetaking, and the growth of a second economy.

Social and cultural development in Karabakh was recommended in the short run to assuage the Armenians and the Party chiefs of both Armenia and Azerbaydzhan were called to improve their leadership. As a long-term policy, the Presidium of the Supreme Soviet decided to set up a commission of the Council of Nationalities to study the problems that had been raised by Karabakh's wish to join Armenia. Further proposals would be considered by the Presidium.

The underlying causes of the tension in Karabakh were not resolved. In the Autumn of 1988 further disturbances occurred in Karabakh and pogroms took place against the Armenians in Baku, Stepanakert, and Kirovabad. A curfew and martial law were proclaimed. Clashes took place between Azeris and Armenians. Both Azeris and Armenians in mixed areas fled their homes to join their countryfolk. Tens of thousands of refugees crossed the borders. In Baku there was a strike and mass meetings and demonstrations in the public square. The consciousness of the Azeris was heightened: posters of Ayatollah Khomeini appeared in the streets of Baku to symbolize the links of Azeris with Muslims and Persians abroad. Troops attempted to keep order; many woundings and deaths took place. In November the mayhem spread to Georgia.

In December 1988 Armenian activists organized in the "Karabakh Committee" continued the pressure for secession despite Moscow's censure. This led to a clampdown and to the arrest of some 150 campaigners for violating racial equality laws. In January 1989 the powers of the Nagorno-Karabakh Soviet were suspended and a special administrative committee was formed in its place, which would be directly responsible to Moscow. Karabakh would remain formally in Azerbaydzhan and links would be expanded with Armenia. In February all the leaders of the Militant Karabakh Committee were arrested. It was reported that eighty-seven civilians and four members of the internal troops had been killed during inter-nationality affrays.

In the summer of 1989, violent conflict continued. Azerbaydzhan blockaded Armenia, and Karabakh faced serious supply shortages with food and medicine being airlifted by military transports. In Nagorno-Karabakh, twenty thousand Soviet troops have tried unsuccessfully to keep order. The All-Union commission sent to administer Karabakh reported that it could not maintain law and order.

The reform movement here released forces that had built up over a long period of time. Historically at the foundation of the Republic of Armenia in 1920, Nagorno-Karabakh was part of the republic. In 1921 at the request of the Azerbaydzhan Party leadership, Stalin asked the Caucasian Bureau of the Party to reconsider the matter and Nagorno-Karabakh became a component of the Azerbaydzhan republic. This move was opposed both by the Armenian population of Karabakh (then 95 percent of the total) and Armenia. This then reinforced traditional animosities between the Christian Armenians and the Muslim Azeris. The government of the Azerbaydzhan republic was also accused by the Armenians of neglecting the welfare of the population of Karabakh.

A positive result of *demokratizatsiya* has been the articulation of griev-ances. But the Karabakh affair shows that the leadership is not easily going to be pushed very far by public protest. The limits of perestroika are determined by the political leadership: Gorbachev condemned the popular activity in Karabakh as the work of anti-perestroika forces. (Despite the fact that Armenian demonstrators proclaimed independence on the basis of glasnost' and perestroika.) The reform movement was not intended, he contended, to legitimate continuous demonstrations and strikes. Perestroika was being used according to Gorbachev for anti-democratic purposes.

In 1990, civil war broke out in the area and order was restored only with the intervention of massive military force and was followed by open protest and demands for independence from the Azeri National Front. Independence was declared in 1991.

The Case of the Baltic Republics

The other major area of manifest ethnic discontent is the Baltic republics. National consciousness by the indigenous peoples of the Baltic states is great. They show an attachment to the pre-Soviet forms of identification: language, the traditional flag, anthem, and dress. Glasnost' has paved the way for the rise of many popular movements in favor of greater independence of the republics of Estonia, Latvia, and Lithuania. Here we consider the example of Estonia.

Nineteen-eighty-eight and 1989 saw the eruption of nationalist sentiment on a mass scale. Mass public meetings took place in the Baltic states and nationalist organizations sent protests to the leadership in Moscow objecting to possible restrictions on the sovereignty of the republics. In Lithuania, for example, 1.5 million signatures were collected protesting against proposed changes in the USSR Constitution. Differences in opposition to the proposed amendments became apparent: whereas in the Soviet Union as a whole criticism of the amendments was focused on individual items, in Lithuania, Estonia, and Latvia the entire proposals were rejected. It is against this background that one may study the developments on the Baltic coast in 1988–89.

February 1988 marked the seventieth anniversary of "bourgeois" Estonia (it was given independent status in the war settlement of 1918) and many people demonstrated against not only the problems that had accumulated during the period of stagnation but also against Soviet power. This set off a stream of demonstrations and the growth of nationalist associations in the Baltic provinces. In June, for example, the Movement for the Independence of Latvia was formed. In August it commemorated the anniversary of the 1920 agreement guaranteeing the independence of Latvia: placards pronounced, "No occupation," "The Independence of Latvia is Lenin's National Policy."

The popular movement in the three Baltic Republics has involved the formation of People's Fronts and the reinstitution of popular symbols identified with the provinces' presocialist past (the adoption of previous coats of arms and national flags, for example).

People's Fronts with mass participation developed in the three republics in 1988. Demands were made not only for cultural autonomy but also for financial autonomy of the republics and control over enterprises presently controlled from Moscow.

Claims have also been made for greater autonomy in foreign affairs and for the creation of republican ministries of foreign affairs. Many such demands have challenged the legitimacy of the Soviet government over these republics that were incorporated into the USSR as a result of the Molotov-Rippentrop Pact of 1939. This pact included the Baltic states in the USSR without their agreement and forms much of the opposition to the Soviet government, which spills over into anti-Russian and anti-Communist sentiments in general. At the Congress of People's Deputies of the USSR held in 1989, a commission was set up to investigate the circumstances of the Pact.

Coupling an enhanced economic independence with the illegitimacy of the Molotov-Rippentrop Pact has presented the Soviet government with a serious threat to its sovereignty over the Baltic states. Economic independence would provide the material basis for material links with other states (particularly those in the Baltic) and political secession would be legitimated if the Molotov-Rippentrop Pact was found to be illegal.

The People's Fronts

The "People's Fronts" formed in all the Baltic states provided a comprehensive political platform of reform. This idea is not a new one. People's Fronts have been formed in the Eastern European socialist countries to bring together various groups in an association of national unity. The Estonian People's Front proclaimed its existence in the pages of *Sovetskaya Estonia* on 7 June 1988. Its provisional program published on that day advocated "socialist democracy and pluralism, the political and economic sovereignty of the union republics, the cultural autonomy of all nationalities, and the protection of the civil rights of the working people" (Article 4). This and later versions of its program did not recognize the political leadership of the Communist Party and "Leadership functions in the People's Front cannot be combined with full-time work in high-level posts in the Party, the Young Communist League or the trade union or state apparatus" (Article 9).

In Latvia in October 1988 the People's Front called its own congress attended by over one thousand delegates; it claims a membership of 130,000 people. It campaigns actively for greater independence for Latvia and the preservation of Latvian culture and language. Its program, published in October 1988, was similar in many respects to that of the Estonians. It called for strengthening the elected system of government, a division between party and state, a move from a centralized state to a "union of sovereign states, and for ensuring the republic's sovereignty proclaimed in the Latvian Constitution." It did not recognize the right of any political organization to a monopoly in administering the state. The program associated democracy with a "pluralism of opinions, interests, and organizational forms." It called for the "formation of territorial armed forces, in which Latvian citizens could do compulsory military service," and supported the "entire Baltic and Scandinavian region being declared a zone free from nuclear weapons." Latvian was "demanded" as the state language of the Latvian SSR; it was to be used as "the business language of the Latvian SSR state bodies and establishments." The Front called for the economic independence of Latvia to be based on its right "independently to administer its property and to have control over land and property in the Latvian state." It called for its own currency and the right to determine its own exchange rates. The Front had many clauses supporting an environmental policy for protecting natural resources.

The Fronts saw themselves as representing a revolution "from below" open to groups, not individuals. They sought to unite and coordinate the activities of societies, clubs, labor, youth and women's collectives, and all associations. They considered themselves open to people of all nationalities but in practice the Fronts named after the Baltic republics have become associated with people of Baltic ethnic origin. In the autumn of 1988 the Charters of the Fronts were published. (See reading below for the Estonian.)

Among the aims of the Estonian People's Front were the creation of "conditions for a transfer from nominal people's power to the real and absolute power of the Estonian people" (Article 2.3), pressing for the "recognition of the union republic as a sovereign state" (Article 2.4). Other objectives included the strengthening of the people's health and "genetic stock" (Article 2.7), and greater economic rights for Estonia, particularly against the supremacy of All-Union bodies (Article 5.5). The leading role of the Party was not mentioned: "The Communist Party participates in the People's Front movement via the Communists who belong to support groups and to bodies of the Estonian People's Front. The People's Front does not have any subordination to any organizations or institutions" (Article 36).

By the beginning of October 1988 over 1,500 support groups had registered as participants in the Estonian People's Front alone. Important among these associations are the Greens (an environmental group) and the Society for the Preservation of the National Heritage. The Estonian Green Movement has become an important public grouping. Its chairperson, Juhan Aare, considered its main role to act as a "people's control committee, monitoring the ecological situation and exposing institutions guilty of pollution." The Greens sought the right to nominate their own candidates for election to the USSR Congress of People's Deputies. (According to the Soviet weekly *New Times* some 300 "ecologically oriented" deputies, 15 percent of the total, in all were elected.) The Greens have organized demonstrations and pickets in support of its policies.

Mainly to combat the growing influence of the national Fronts in the Baltic republics, the local communist party organizations increasingly claimed independence from the Communist Party of the Soviet Union. In December 1989, the Supreme Soviet of the Lithuanian Republic voted to abolish the clause in its own Constitution on the leading role of the CPSU and it sought to institute its own multi-party system. In January 1990, the Lithuanian Party Congress declared independence for Lithuania and declared itself separate from the CPSU. The Estonian CP in November adopted the general thrust of the Front's position. However, the Estonian Party split along ethnic lines, one Party accepting the leadership of the CPSU and the other not. In February 1991, the CPSU, remarkably, recognized two Estonian Communist Parties.

In 1990 and 1991, the Baltic provinces, with Lithuania at the head, all clashed with the All-Union government, the latter asserting that independence could only be achieved through a legal process conducted by the USSR. Lithuania, however, went ahead with its own referendum on independence (overwhelmingly supported) and indicated its intention of coining its own currency and issuing its own passports.

The "Inter" Movement

Some reservations have been expressed in Estonia about the activity and composition of the Front. Letters had been written to the local newspaper from a Russian speaking collective (the *Dvigatel* factory) expressing concern about the lack of a stated policy against chauvinism. It was later reported that the mainly Russian work force here was strongly opposed to the Front. And a war veterans association also expressed the view that the Front was dominated by the Estonian intelligentsia. These caveats, however, should not obscure the ground swell of support for increased republican rights. Criticism was raised that the Estonians disregarded any rights for the Russian language on the republic's territory.

The nonindigenous people (mostly Russians) formed an "Interethnic movement" (sometimes called in English, "International" or "Inter"). This movement too has parallels in other republics in the Baltic and elsewhere. The "Inter" movement was composed of predominantly Russian manual and nonmanual industrial workers. The Estonian leaders of the Front were largely professional nonmanuals. There is an important political difference between the two movements: only a quarter of the board of the People's Front were party members, but of the comparable body of the Inter movement 70 percent were Party members.

Estonians for their part complained about chauvinism on the part of Russians. A *Molodaya Rossiya* (*Young Russia*) youth group reportedly has been carrying out acts of hooliganism and the desecration of Estonian monuments. Other Russian groups reportedly have been associating Estonians with collaboration with the Nazis. Politburo Member and CPSU secretary Chebrikov during his visit to Tallin in November 1988 reported that "the situation in the Republic [is] characterized by growing political tension ... especially alarming is the division on nationality lines." The

People's Front and the Inter movement were developing as opposing movements along national lines.

Important differences between the two movements surfaced over the position of the Estonian language and citizenship. In January 1989 the Estonian Supreme Soviet declared Estonian the state language. Article 8 decreed that "The business language of establishments of state power and state administration of the Estonian republic is Estonian. Sessions and working meetings of bodies of state power and state administration of the Estonian republic are chaired and their minutes recorded in Estonian." The language of business would also be Estonian.

The Russian (and the sizeable Ukrainian) population feared that the establishment of Estonian as the official language would be detrimental to their interests and viewed with concern a proposition that Estonian citizenship would be limited to those with Estonian language and residence qualifications. At the congress of the Inter movement in March 1989, its charter advocated the rights of the inhabitants of Estonia regardless of nationality.

The thrust of the formal political position of the People's Front was against Stalinism and conservatism and in favor of perestroika. Its slogans are: socialist democracy and pluralism, political and economic sovereignty, cultural autonomy of all nationalities, and the protection of the civil rights and interests of the working people. The Front did not claim to be a Party but a "civic initiative." Of particular importance to the Front were the possibilities in the reform program for strengthening the Soviets and involving people in the management of the economy. Initially, restructuring within the context of a political system led by the CPSU was accepted. The "leading role" of the Party was not explicitly mentioned and this had led to criticism from some Party leaders. (See Article 37 of Estonian People's Front.)

Some of the leading Communists in Estonia saw a danger that anti-Communist groups and others hostile to the Russian presence could use the Front to voice their own interests. Such associations, which became public in 1988, included the Estonian Party of National Independence, the Estonian Democratic Movement 1988 and several "independent youth movements." The Independence party which was formed in August had two hundred members, and unequivocally advocated Estonia's secession from the Soviet Union. In Lithuania full independence involving leaving the USSR was advocated by the Lithuanian Freedom League (sometimes called the Lithuanian League for Liberty). This association was formed in the late seventies and existed illegally until the period of perestroika when it campaigned openly but was not afforded recognition as an official social organization.

Surveys of public opinion in Estonia conducted by the Finnish newspaper *Ilta Sanomat* in April 1989 found that some 80 percent of Estonians and 43 percent of non-Estonians would abolish one party rule. The Communist Party was only favored by 7 percent of the voters of Estonian nationality when they were asked for whom they would vote if given a choice in a multiparty system. Of non-Estonian nationalities, however, 32 percent would have voted for the Communist Party. Only 2.4 percent of Estonians saw its future as a constituent republic in the USSR (though 54 percent of non-Estonians gave first choice to this option). (This data reported by Ilves 1989.)

Economic Self-management

A major dispute has raged between the Baltic republics and the All-Union (federal) government over the extent of "economic sovereignty."

Greater economic independence for the union-republics is also advocated by the government of the USSR. As we noted in chapter 2, the Supreme Soviet of the USSR in June 1989, handed the activities of the union-republican ministries to the republics. The proposals for self-management included devolving to the republics food and consumer goods and services, building, conservation, and local trade. This means that some industries of an All-Union status would be transferred to the republics. Local government services (education, culture, and tourism) are also thought to be the proper concern of the localities. These proposals would give the Baltic republics control over about 60 percent of the industrial output of their republics. More local taxes would accrue to the republics and profits from All-Union enterprises would be taxed with the republics retaining a share. The proposed changes would also take place firmly within the system of planning of the USSR government.

The Baltic states, however, seek a much more radical reform. The Estonian republic published its proposals in April 1989. The preamble to the proposals define the Estonian republic as a

sovereign Soviet socialist state, whence stems the priority of the Estonian people's rights with regard to the environment, production conditions and natural resources. ... The Estonian SSR's independent economic policy is implemented in the form of republican financial autonomy, under which the republic's spending is covered by its own income and the economic processes taking place on the Estonian SSR's territory are independently administered by the republic's bodies of state power and administration.

The Estonian government has sought control over banking and currency, including the introduction of an Estonian currency (and the possibility for its convertibility). Ownership relations of a mixed form have been advocated; these include state and cooperative ownership, but also ownership by individuals and other foreign states, including joint ownership. These provisions would allow the Estonian government to invite foreign capital to Estonia and to trade freely with the West. The objective here is to take advantage of Estonia's place within the international division of labor.

Russian Nationalism

The position of the numerically predominant Russian nationality has changed as a result of the greater assertiveness of the other national groups and the greater plurality associated with perestroika. As we have noted above, Russians could not be considered to be equal in status with the other ethnic groups in the USSR. The Russians have not only formed the largest group, but they have dominated culturally and politically in the Soviet Union. This is part of the legacy of the tsars but also a consequence of the strategic position of the country's capital and the greater level of development of the Russian people.

Russians have been regarded as "first among equals" or as the "elder brother" to the other nationalities. This has led to an affinity between things Soviet and Russian. The leaders of the Russians have regarded themselves as providing an international dimension to the USSR; its language is Russian and, as noted above, Russians have dominated the leading political and economic positions of the USSR. But unlike other nationalities, the Russians have not had their "own" republican capital, nor have they had their "own" Communist Party or Academy of Sciences. Many of their institutions have been submerged into a Soviet identity.

Under perestroika a revival of Russian nationalism has taken place. Many grassroots movements, such as the associations *Pamyat'* (Memory), *Otechestvo* (Fatherland), The United Council of Russia, the United Workers Front, and the All-Russian Cultural Foundation have arisen to establish and defend peculiarly Russian concerns. Commitment to the preservation of Russian culture is linked to the renaissance of the Russian Orthodox Church. These groups include a wide range of political currents that cannot be considered here. (See futher: *Russian Nationalism Today* 1988.)

Some of these groups tend to be traditionalist, support the greatness of Russia's past, and exalt the achievements of Stalin. The United Council of Russia has been said to be based on: "the sacred notions of Native Land, Fatherland, People." (For a brief description see D. Smith 1989.)

They are critical of non-Russian nationalities whom they regard as being responsible for the decline of the Soviet Union. They identify with Russian Orthodoxy and have played an important role in preserving ancient Russian monuments. Some of these groups have revived interest in the tsars and prerevolutionary flags and symbols. The United Front of Workers of Russia is concerned with protecting the interests of Russian workers in the national republics who are likely to be penalized as a result of the greater assertiveness of the indigenous people in the national republics.

In October 1989, the United People's Front of the RSFSR was founded at a meeting in Yaroslavl by 120 delegates from forty-one towns. These included a very wide range of political and cultural organizations, including those mentioned above.

The large land area of the Russian republic and the immense spread of the Russian people make the Russian nationalist movement less cohesive than the other People's Fronts but they have been a potent force for articulating the interest of the Russian republic and for gaining greater recognition of its needs.

A major development has come with the formation of the republic's own Communist Party in 1990 and with the election of Eltsin as President of the RSFSR and a leadership team strongly in favor of fortifying the RSFSR government and minimizing the power of the USSR and its president, Gorbachev.

In 1991, political division, as illustrated above in the Baltic states, was repeated all over the Soviet Union. With the relinquishment of the Party's monopoly of political organization in 1990, the People's Fronts developed into parties and they became even more assertive of national interests. Many republics have changed their names and in the process have dropped the "socialist" and/or "soviet" appellation. (See appendix to this chapter for other details.) In 1990–91 they demanded control of All-Union assets in their territories.

FROM GLASNOST' TO DISINTEGRATION

In the past the leaders of the Soviet state have attempted to create a supranational identity in the form of a Soviet identity. This has not succeeded in superceding the traditional forms of ethnic and national identification. National consciousness in the USSR has proved to be stronger than class allegiance, and for some national groups attachment to the USSR as a political unity has been put in question. To a considerable extent, the political leadership of perestroika has been hoisted on its own petard. By destroying Marxist class imagery and class interpretation of history, it has left an ideological vacuum that has been filled by a revived and amplified traditional national consciousness.

The rise of such consciousness has two intertwined underlying causes. First the modernization effect has led to greater aspirations on the part of the previously backward peoples: a national identity furthers their own exclusive rights to resources. Second, in times of change and uncertainty people turn to traditional emotional and psychological forms of identity; these involve the definition of their own group in terms of others on the basis of religion and history. The larger mass of educated people seek to preserve their own language and culture.

Perestroika has allowed for the development of nationalist cultures along the lines of "social closure." "Socialist pluralism" has worked against the unity of the nations of the USSR. Ideas of social justice have been used by certain ethnic groups to legitimate their own claims to resources when a past or contemporary grievance may be advanced. Democratization and glasnost' have led to a destabilization of the unitary system of government, not only from the periphery of the USSR but also from the government of the Russian Republic headed by Eltsin.

Politics in the peripheral areas has developed on national lines. This has important implications for the hegemony of the Communist Party. The rise of parties on an ethnic basis has become a destabilizing influence and this is one of the main reasons why a pluralism of political parties, even of Communist ones, was fiercely resisted by the central political leadership.

Nevertheless, within the parameters of democratization and glasnost', it has proved impossible to prevent the official "plurality of opinions" from becoming a plurality of groups, and where nationalist views are strong the People's Fronts have evolved on a local basis as effective political parties.

Major developments occurred in 1990 and 1991. First, there was the declaration of independence and sovereignty in the republics (including the RSFSR) and other national units. This involved a radicalization of proposals by the republican governments and a process of confrontation with President Gorbachev in Moscow. Second, Gorbachev responded by drawing up a union treaty which would preserve the USSR as a federation. Third, following the rise of Eltsin as leader after the coup of 1991 the USSR was replaced by a union of sovereign states which greatly strengthened the republics choosing to join it.

Demands for Constitutional Change

By 1 January 1991, politics had polarized between the republican and the All-Union government. National consciousness had heightened and was articulated by the Soviets in the localities. The assertion of local rights, as illustrated above in the case of the Nagorno-Karabakh Autonomous *oblast*, became commonplace. A major demand made by the republics and other units of government was control over assets which were the prerogative of the All-Union government.

During the course of 1990, fifteen Union Republics declared themselves to be sovereign and five Supreme Soviets (Lithuania, Estonia, Latvia, Georgia and Armenia) had declared their intent to become independent states — either immediately, as in the case of Lithuania, or after a transitional period. The Supreme Soviet of Moldavia endorsed a confederation effectively giving it political independence from the USSR. (For list of dates of declarations of sovereignty or independence see appendix 1 below.) Also, federal units below the republican level have made declarations of sovereignty. These include eleven autonomous republics, three autonomous *oblasts*, and four autonomous *okrugs*. Many republics adopted new names. A common theme of the declarations of sovereignty is that republican laws take priority over All-Union laws and that the republics have ownership of assets and natural resources in their territories. These two declarations are in conflict with the laws of the USSR and bring the republics into direct conflict with the USSR. The autonomous formations (autonomous republics and so on) have elevated their status to a higher level, thereby challenging the republic in which they are located. National minorities, fearful of repression by the dominant nations in republics, have demanded their own independent political units (as in the case of the Poles in Lithuania, and the Russian minority in Moldavia). Other minorities such as the South Ossetian Autonomous *Oblast* (self-defined as South Ossetian Union Democratic Republic) broke with their own superior republic (in this case Georgia) and pledged their allegiance as part of the USSR. Threatened national minorities in republics looked to the USSR government for support. There arose a constitutional problem over the allocation of powers between the All-Union government, the Union republics and autonomous territories.

These declarations were more than formal statements. The republics refused to concede the right of the USSR to budget appropriations in 1991. Many refused to fulfil the Union economic plan and did not deliver supplies to other units — often arguing that the payment was insufficient and below world prices, a somewhat perverse interpretation of *khozraschet*. Soviets also refused to sanction the call-up of conscripts to the armed forces and insisted that service should be performed in their own republics. The Baltic states advocated the creation of their own currencies and independent armed forces and called upon the West for recognition. Iceland was the first to respond to Lithuania's declaration early in 1991.

Gorbachev's response has been to declare a referendum on the Union. In April 1990, a law on the procedure for secession from the USSR was published. This clarified Article 72 of the Constitution of the USSR, which said: "Each Union Republic shall retain the right to secede from the USSR." This law specified the conditions in which such secession may take place. It required that a referendum be held and at least two-thirds of the USSR citizens permanently resident on the republic's territory must approve of such a move. It further envisaged a transitionary period of five years for secession to take effect. Gorbachev called for a referendum on the Union to take place in March 1991. All citizens were asked to vote yes or no for the following: "Do you think that the Union of Soviet Socialist Republics should be preserved as a renewed federation of equal sovereign republics in which the rights and freedoms of a person of any nationality should be fully guaranteed?"

The votes were recorded by each republic separately and used to determine the right of republics to exercise the prerogative to secede from the Union.

The governments of six Union Republics (Lithuania, Estonia, Latvia, Moldavia, Armenia and Georgia) boycotted the referendum. The three Baltic republics had conducted their own elections which resulted in massive majorities for independence (in Latvia, for instance, it was claimed that 93:1 percent of eligible voters participated of whom 85.7 voted for independence, 13.3 against and 1 percent spoiled their papers); similarly, in Estonia some 85 percent of the electorate voted of whom 70 opted for independence (considerable minorities in Russian speaking areas voted against independence). These elections were declared invalid by the USSR government.

The official referendum, which took place on 17 March 1991, was preceded by rallies of opponents and supporters of the motion. The all-union mass media strongly supported Gorbachev's position and gave little coverage to opposition. Eltsin relied on the radio station Radio Russia. The military, the Russian Communist Party, religious leaders and numerous political groups (such as "Soyuz" and "Unity") publicly supported the officially prescribed "renewal" of the union. Most of the "democratic" groups opposed it: the Belorussian National Front, the Democratic Party. Eltsin was equivocal: he opposed the referendum and advocated a union based on agreement from below. (His own major concern was a second question added to the RSFSR referendum: "Do you consider it necessary to create the post of Russian President, directly elected".)

The results are as follows: the total electoral roll of the USSR is 192 million, of these 184.2 million are in the nine republics taking part in the election. In total, 147.5 million people voted in the nine republics. The total voting "yes" (in the nine republics) was 112.1 millions. As a proportion of the electorate the result may be calculated in three ways: voting "yes" as a proportion (a) of the voters in the USSR — 58.4 percent (b) of those in the nine participating republics — 60.9 percent (c) of those voting — 76 percent. The three calculations and the voting in individual republics are shown in Table 6.10.

The results indicate overwhelming support for the union in the poorer central Asian areas. (The very high proportions voting in Turkmenistan and Uzbekistan may indicate excessive zeal by local activists in counting

Table 6.10
Voting on Referendum on the Union 17 March 1991

USSR				NINE VOTING REPUBLICS	
Total Electoral Roll	Voting "Yes"	Total Electoral Roll	Voting "Yes"	Total Voting	Voting "Yes"
millions	%	millions	%	millions	%
192	58.4	184.2	60.9	147.5	76

	Turnout (%)	"Yes" (%)	Percent of eligible Voters voting "Yes" (%)
REPUBLIC			
RSFSR (Russia)	75.4	71	52.8
Ukraine	83.0	70	58.1
Belorussia	83.0	83.0	68.9
Uzbekistan	95.0	93.7	89.0
Kazakhstan	89.0	94.0	83.6
Kirghizia	92.9	94.5	87.7
Tadjikistan	94.0	96.0	90.2
Turkmenia	97.7	98.0	95.7
Azerbaydjan	75.0	93.0	69.7

Of the total voting: 32.2 million voted "no" and 2.7 returned invalid ballot papers.

Voting in Republics boycotting the Referendum:

Lithuania　600,000
Latvia　　　500,000
Estonia　　250,000
Armenia　　　5,000
Georgia　　　50,000 (All from South Ossetia)

[Data cited here were available on 22 March, some results were still to be counted. These figures may be adjusted upwards by a few percentage points.]

the votes.) In the European areas the vote was much more divided with the major cities of Leningrad and Moscow only registering "Yes" for just over 50 percent of those voting. The total voting positively for the Union represented some 58 percent of the electorate (76 percent of those voting).

In the vote for an elected President conducted in the RSFSR, some 70 percent of those voting said "Yes". Of the total eligible votes the figure fell to around 52 percent.

Overall the figures are favourable to the Gorbachev leadership though are somewhat marred by the number of non-voters. Opposition to the Union is also considerable: politically, 30 per cent of those voting represents a considerable minority and to these of course must be added those in the six republics who did not participate in the referendum. The plebiscite did not give the political leadership a resounding majority to legitimate the use of force against opposition.

The Proposed Union Treaty

Gorbachev's other main strategy was to draw up a new Union Treaty. The proposed treaty whose wording was significantly "deideologized" has the following components: human rights rather than Marxism-Leninism is to be an ideological basis of the relations between republics. References to socialism have been dropped; in the first version of the draft treaty published in November it was proposed that the federal state be called the Union of Sovereign Soviet Republics, in the draft published in March 1991, this was amended and the traditional Union of Soviet Socialist Republics was retained. However, the draft agreed on 23 July 1991 reverted to the earlier appellation of Union of Soviet Sovereign Republics. Each republic party to the treaty was considered to be a "sovereign, federal, democratic state, formed as a result of the association of equal republics and exercising state power within the limits of its powers, which are voluntarily vested in it by the parties to the treaty". The powers of the Union government were defined as the protection of the sovereignty and territorial integrity of the union and its members, the provision of state security, pursuit of the union's foreign policy, the ratification of the union budget, monetary control, air traffic and All-Union communications and information, adoption of the Union constitution and amendments to it, leadership of federal law enforcement.

Under joint competence came the protection of the union's constitutional system, determination of the union's military policy, determination of the Union's state security strategy, foreign policy, socio-

economic development of the Union, policy on fuel and energy resources, social policy and employment, fundamental scientific research.

The laws of a republic take precedence on its territory on all questions except those which are assigned to the Union's jurisdiction, and disputes between the republics and the Union are resolved through a Constitutional Court (Article 11). The states have the right to develop all forms of property. They have their own budgets and taxes and can determine their own administrative state structure.

One other portentous proposal made in the first (November) draft union treaty was that the Council of Nationalities of the USSR Supreme Soviet would be "formed from delegations of the supreme representative organs of power of the republics and the organs of power of the national— territorial formations according to agreed norms". This provision, however, was dropped in the second (March 1991) version of the treaty where it was proposed that "the upper chamber of the USSR Supreme Soviet is formed from an equal number of representatives elected in the republics directly belonging to the union". In the July variant, however, the issue was fudged and "The procedure for electing representatives and their quotas are defined in a special agreement between the republics and the USSR electoral law" (Article 13). (For full details see articles 5 and 6 of the Treaty, Reading 3 below.)

At the beginning of 1991, six republics (Lithuania, Latvia, Estonia, Georgia, Armenia and Moldavia) declared that they would not sign a union treaty. Many of the republics favored a confederation of states rather than a federal system. Gorbachev's policy was to go ahead with signing the Treaty with as many states as possible and then negotiate an agreement with the others.

The Draft Treaty of July severely weakened the powers of the All-Union government and the compromise reached by Gorbachev displeased many of the more traditionally inclined statesmen. The impending signing of the Treaty precipitated the coup of 19 August. Its failure led to the Treaty not being signed, but also strengthened the resolve of the republics for even greater powers than those agreed in the Draft Treaty of July. During the state of emergency and immediately afterwards, Eltsin (as President of the Russian Republic) had effectively taken over the duties of President of the USSR. The "demonstration effect" of asserting the rights of the Russian Republic led to others doing the same and other republics declared their independence.

At the meeting of the Congress of People's Deputies in September 1991, a transitional policy for the Union and republics was worked out. This was based on agreement reached between Gorbachev and representatives from the following republics: Russia, Ukraine, Belorussia,

Uzbekistan, Kazakhstan, Azerbaydzhan, Kirhgizia, Tadjikistan, Armenia and Turkmenia. The republics of Estonia, Lithuania, Latvia, Georgia and Moldavia were absent: all had declared independence, but only that of the three Baltic states had been recognized (though Romania has recognized the independence of Moldavia). A system of government was set up which much strengthened the powers and position of the republics (see above chapter 3.) A Union of Sovereign States was born.

READINGS TO CHAPTER 6

Declarations of Sovereignty or Independence

UNION REPUBLIC DECLARATIONS OF SOVEREIGNTY OR INDEPENDENCE

18 November 1988	Declaration of Supreme Council of Estonian SSR "On Sovereignty of Estonian SSR"
18 May 1989	Declaration of Supreme Council of Lithuanian SSR "On State Sovereignty of Lithuania"
28 July 1989	Declaration of Supreme Council of Latvian SSR "On State Sovereignty of Latvia"
23 September 1989	Constitutional Law of Azerbayjan SSR "On Sovereignty of Azerbayjan Soviet Socialist Republic"
18 November 1989	Georgian Supreme Soviet adopted amendments to Georgian constitution giving republic right to veto All-Union laws and declaring natural resources republican property
9 March 1990	Decree of Supreme Soviet of Georgian SSR "On Guarantees of Defense of State Sovereignty of Georgia"
11 March 1990	Act of Supreme Council of Lithuanian Republic "On Restoration of Independent Lithuanian State"
30 March 1990	Decree of Supreme Council of Estonian SSR "On State Status of Estonia"
4 May 1990	Declaration of Supreme Council of Latvian SSR "On Restoration of Independence of Latvian Republic"
11 June 1990	Declaration "On State Sovereignty of Russian Soviet Federated Socialist Republic"
20 June 1990	"Declaration on Sovereignty" adopted by Supreme Soviet of Uzbek SSR
23 June 1990	Declaration "On Sovereignty of Soviet Socialist Republic of Moldova" (Moldavia)
16 July 1990	Declaration "On State Sovereignty of Ukraine"

27 July 1990	Declaration of Supreme Soviet of Belorussian SSR "On State Sovereignty of Belorussian Soviet Socialist Republic"
22 August 1990	Declaration "On State Sovereignty of Turkmen Soviet Socialist Republic"
23 August 1990	Declaration "On Independence of Armenia"
25 August 1990	Declaration "On State Sovereignty of Tajik Soviet Socialist Republic"
25 October 1990	Declaration on "State Sovereignty of Kazakh Soviet Socialist Republic"
31 October 1990	Kirgiz Supreme Soviet approved first reading of declaration on state sovereignty

ASSR Declarations of Sovereignty

10 August 1990	Karelian declaration of sovereignty
25 August 1990	Abkhaz declaration of sovereignty — Union republican status. Subsequently annulled by Georgian Supreme Soviet and revoked by meeting of just over half of the deputies of the Abkhaz Supreme Soviet that proclaimed itself a session of the Supreme Soviet
30 August 1990	Komi declaration of sovereignty
30 August 1990	Tatar declaration of sovereignty
19 September 1990	Udmurt declaration of sovereignty
27 September 1990	Yakut declaration of sovereignty
8 October 1990	Buryat declaration of sovereignty
11 October 1990	Bashkir declaration of sovereignty
18 October 1990	Kalmyk declaration of sovereignty
(18 October 1990)	(Discussion of Moldovian declaration of sovereignty postponed)
22 October 1990	Mari declaration of sovereignty
24 October 1990	Chuvash declaration of sovereignty

Autonomous Oblast Declarations of Sovereignty

20 September 1990	South Ossetian declaration "On Sovereignty and Status of South Ossetia" proclaiming autonomous (*samostoyatel'naya*) South Ossetian Union Democratic Republic. Only Ossetian deputies present. Annulled on 21 September by Presidium of Georgian Supreme Soviet
7 October 1990	Adigei declaration of sovereignty
25 October 1990	Gorno-Altai declaration of sovereignty

Autonomous Okrug Declarations of Sovereignty

29 September 1990	Chukchi declaration of sovereignty
9 October 1990	Koryak declaration of sovereignty

| 11 October 1990 | Komi-Permyak declaration of sovereignty |
| 18 October 1990 | Yamalo-Nenets declaration of sovereignty |

New Names Adopted by Republics and Autonomous Territories

Union Republics

Armenia	Republic of Armenia — Hayastan
Estonia	Estonian Republic — Estonia
Latvia	Latvian Republic — Latvia
Moldavia	Lithuanian Republic — Lithuania
	Soviet Socialist Republic of Moldova

Autonomous Republics

Bashkir	Bashkir Soviet Socialist Republic — Bashkortostan
Buryat	Buryat Soviet Socialist Republic
Chuvash	Chuvash Soviet Socialist Republic — Republic of Chavash'en
Kalmyk	Kalmyk Soviet Socialist Republic
Komi	Komi Soviet Socialist Republic
Mari	Mari Soviet Socialist Republic — Republic of Mariiel (or Mari-el)
Tatar	Tatar Soviet Socialist Republic — Tatarstan
Udmurt	Udmurt Republic
Yakut	Yakut-Sakha Soviet Socialist Republic

Autonomous Oblasts

| Adigei | (New title not known, but has declared itself an autonomous republic) |
| Gorno-Altai | Gomo-Altai Autonomous Soviet Socialist Republic |

Autonomous Okrugs

Chukchi	Chukchi Soviet Autonomous Republic
Koryak	Koryak Autonomous Soviet Republic
Komi-Permyak	Komi-Permyak Autonomous Oblast
Yamalo-Nenets	Yamalo-Nenets Republic

Source: A. Sheehy. "Fact Sheet on Declarations of Sovereignty." *Report on the USSR* vol.2, no. 45, 9 November 1990: 24–25.

The Charter of The Estonian People's Front
(Adopted at the Congress of the People's Front, 2 October 1988)

I   The Essence and Aims of the People's Front
  1. The Estonian People's Front (EPF) is a nationwide movement based on the
     initiative of Estonian SSR citizens in support of the process of renewal and its
     implementation in all walks of state and public life in the Estonian Soviet
     Socialist Republic.
     The EPF acts in the name of progress, humanism, peace and disarmament,
     taking the interests and rights of all the people of Estonia as its basis.
  2. The EPF's main aim is to raise the consciousness, political culture and civic
     activity of the people and to create a democratic mechanism in order to assist
     in the creation of a society based on real people's power and a balanced
     economy, in which all human rights are guaranteed.
     On this basis the EPF has set itself the following aims:
     2.1   with the assistance of the masses of people, who have joined together to
           support the CPSU's policy of restructuring, to stop any attempt to retard
           the process of democratization and development of openness in the
           Estonian SSR; to be a social guarantor of the renewal of society;
     2.2   to cooperate in the transformation of the ESSR into a state ruled by
           law, where law protects people, and where free development of the
           individual is the precondition for a free development of the society;
     2.3   to create the conditions for a transfer from nominal people's power to
           the real and absolute power of the Estonian people; to achieve separation
           of powers — legislative, executive and jurisdicial;
     2.4   to press for the recognition of the union republic as a sovereign state;
     2.5   to give citizens the opportunity for political self-realization, regardless of
           their nationality, or social status, religious or other convictions, sex or
           race;
     2.6   to make the Popular Front a true mouthpiece of the will of the Estonian
           People, while recognizing the right of the people to self-determination;
     2.7   to insist on the ending of the state of crisis which exists in the national
           economy, ecology, culture and education; to improve management in
           the social sphere and industrial management, to better conditions and
           safety at work, to raise people's standards of living and their welfare, to
           improve people's health and genetic stock; to protect the welfare of
           children and to strengthen harmony in the family as well as respect for
           moral values.
  3. The EPF bases its activity on the following principles: democracy and socialist
     pluralism, people's right to self-determination, respect for the individual and
     protection of human rights, friendship of the peoples and cultural autonomy
     of the national groups living in Estonia, legality and rule-of-law, social

justice, glasnost' and a recognized status of the party, collective decision-making and joint leadership.

4. The EPF takes upon itself tasks within the limits of its aims. The most important of those are developed and defined in the programs of the movement, including the policy of regional people's fronts and the action plans of support groups.

5. The EPF pursues its aims in the following ways:

    5.1 it organizes its activity in accordance with the Constitution and with the aim of observing its statutes; it aims at ensuring that citizens, various social and public groups, enterprises, official bodies and establishments should exercise their constitutional rights;

    5.2 it demands the explanation and classification of the Estonian SSR Constitution and other important legislative acts to the people; it demands amendment, improvement or repeal of out-dated and undemocratic legislative acts;

    5.3 it supports initiatives which deepen and speed up the restructuring process in society, which unite the masses and assist in resolving the problems of Estonia;

    5.4 it demands that the course of restructuring in Estonia should obtain legal, economic and political guarantees and that radical reforms should be implemented in the economy, education, culture, health care and other spheres;

    5.5 it initiates and supports the drafting of proposed laws and any other measures which would provide the soviets of people's deputies with real authority and the Estonian SSR Supreme Soviet and the government with the right to defend Estonia against the dictate and supremacy of the ministries and official bodies at Union level;

    5.6 it initiates and participates in the process of developing the concept of people's self-government, so that people are able to actively participate in the decision-making at various levels of state and social life;

    5.7 its aim is that in the organs of power and in the state apparatus, there should be citizens who represent and express the will of the people; it participates in election campaigns, putting up its own candidates or supporting candidates, nominated by others;

    5.8 it fights against corruption, the abuse of power, the administrative-command system;

    5.9 it makes proposals in respect of distribution (redistribution) of the national income in the Estonian SSR and in respect of changes in the structure of the national economy and management of the Estonian SSR, according to the needs of the society;

    5.10 it regularly organizes public opinion polls and makes the results available to the public; it makes proposals for organizing nationwide discussions and referenda and helps to carry them out;

    5.11 it prefers the method of persuasion, but where necessary will also use measures of public pressure (demonstration, open meetings and public appeals, votes of no confidence, pickets, and so on);

5.12 it associates with various associations and movements, work collectives and individuals, and other Soviet Government bodies;

5.13 it develops contacts with citizens' movements, public associations and individuals operating from other Soviet Republics and foreign states;

5.14 it monitors the observance of human rights pacts adopted at the UN and ratified by the USSR, of the European cooperation agreements and other international agreements in the Estonian SSR and supports the right of the union republic to participate in the disarmament process and in the organization of defense of the state.

II Participation in the Popular Front Movement

6. The People's Front movement is open to all citizens of the Estonian SSR. Participation in the EPF movement is one of the forms of exercising one's constitutional rights and freedom, it demonstrates the sense of responsibility for the process of perestroika and the fate of Estonia.

7. Citizens either join People's Front's support groups or participate in the events organized by the People's Front (discussions, actions and other) as they see fit. There is no definitive list of members, no membership cards or subscriptions.

8. Generally, the People's Front does not have collective members but within the framework of cooperation with societies, creative, professional unions and clubs, councils of war veterans and labor veterans, the Peace Committee, women's, Green and youth movements, various committees, religious congregations and organizations, informal groups and various public formations functioning in the Estonian SSR the elected bodies of the EPF may also invite representatives of the above to participate in their work.

III Structure and Organs of the People's Front

9. The EPF system consists of support groups, Regional People's Fronts, and their organs, Organs at Republic levels (People's Congress, the Council of Plenipotentiaries, the Governing Body; the Policy Committee, the Review Committee) as well as various groups attached to the People's Front.

(A) Support Groups as the Basic Link of the Movement

10. A support group is an informal association of citizens, who actively support the perestroika policy. Apart from their shared interests they are united by a high level of civic awareness and determination to act, positive stance on the ethical values of the individual and the norms of social behavior.

Support groups can be set up in work collectives, residentially, within creative associations and various societies, religious congregations, creative unions, schools and elsewhere.

11. The participants themselves determine the structure of a support group, its ways of functioning, its plan of action (program), links, procedures and order of meeting.

     The events of a support group are, as a rule, open to other citizens. Everybody present at the people's meetings has the right to express their opinion and make proposals. Those who are members of the support group have the right to vote.

12. A support group adheres to the Constitution of the Estonian SSR, any other legislation, the given Main Document and other resolutions adopted by the EPF bodies. It carries out the implementation of the People's Front's policy and participates in any People's Front's regional or Estonia-wide events as it sees fit.

13. As a general rule, a support group operates on a voluntary basis. It elects its representatives (Plenipotentiaries). A plenipotentiary is an attorney in fact, who is authorised to run matters. In the event of trust being forfeited they are to be reelected before term.

14. A support group participates directly in the shaping (electing) of the EPF regional and republic bodies. Everybody present at a people's meeting has the right to nominate candidates.

     A support group has the right to recall its representatives from the Councils of Regional People's Fronts, as well as initiate the recall of persons elected from the same area to the EPF's leadership organs.

15. A support group develops its cooperation with the Councils of the working collectives, and social bodies, as well as with the local organs of self-government and other various support groups, active in the area.

    (B) Regional People's Fronts and the Councils of Plenipotentiaries

16. The Regional People's Front is defined as a support group, exercising its activity in a region or a town within Estonian SSR. At the same time the Regional People's Front can incorporate separate independent units in the form of People's Fronts of agricultural councils, settlements, regional towns and town districts. Also possible are People's Front Unions which do not correspond to the existing administrative political division of the Estonian SSR.

17. A Regional People's Front determines itself its own program of work, actions and links.

18. An important sphere of the RPF is its active participation in the formation of the organs of power at all levels, strengthening links between the Soviets and the people, and promotion of responsibility of the deputies. It also works for attracting other social groups and civic movements to take part in the work of the Council (Soviets) as well as ensuring that the work of the Organs of Power and Executive bodies is widely publicized.

19. A Regional People's Front protects the citizen's rights. It makes certain that the local population has the opportunity to hold peaceful meetings (discussions,

debates, meetings), to organize demonstrations and other public events and to celebrate nationally important dates and holidays.

20. The leading body (the steering organ) of a Regional People's Front is the council (possibly councils at various levels — in village Soviets, in settlements, towns, urban rayons and elsewhere). It is elected by the support groups of the region for a term of two years. The council has the rights of a juridical entity. Other voluntary associations can be represented in the Council of Plenipotentiaries by their own EPF support groups. The Council is entitled to invite to its work the representatives of various organizations and associations as well as individuals, as it sees fit.

21. The mechanism of decision-making in the Council of Plenipotentiaries is specified in the Articles of Incorporation. The Resolutions of the Council are of a consultative nature; any dictate or interference in the internal affairs of the support groups or other organizations are to be avoided.

22. The council makes proposals to various bodies and organizations, writes letters and addresses the public at large in other ways. When carrying out actions, it assists in ensuring the safeguarding of public order.

23. The council elects its Board and review body.

    The Board solves current problems, is in charge of the financial means of the Regional People's Front, employs and dismisses administrative staff. At the same time it exercises its work on the principle of equality.

(C)   The People's Congress

24. The Congress of the People's Front is the supreme body of the Estonian People's Front movement. The Congress convenes every two years, an announcement being made at least 3 months in advance. In exceptional cases a Congress may be convened when demanded by no less than 3 regional Councils or by at least a third of all the support groups registered at the Council of Plenipotentiaries.

25. The composition of the People's Congress is nominated by the support groups and the Councils of Plenipotentiaries in accordance with the norms of representation. Invited to take part in the work of the Congress are representatives of public organizations and movements who support the People's Front. At the Congress they will have the right to speak and a passive right to vote.

    Sessions of the Congress of the People's Front are open to citizens.

26. Citizens, support groups, Regional People's Fronts, other voluntary associations of citizens, as well as the CP of Estonia Central Committee, Estonian SSR Supreme Soviet and its Presidium and the Estonian SSR government may present questions to be included on the agenda of the Congress of the People's Front.

27. The Congress of the People's Front has the power to adopt resolutions at a session if at least three-quarters of the delegates are present. When adopting resolutions, a two-thirds majority vote is required.

28. The Congress of the People's Front:

28.1 it determines which matters will be discussed, checks delegates' credentials and establishes the procedure and order for adopting resolutions as well as against working organs;

28.2 it ratifies the structure of the working bodies; adopts the policy and the Charter of the People's Front, and if needed brings alterations into the Charter;

28.3 it takes part in the raising of the reviews in respect of fulfillment of the program and also current reports of the republic organs of the EPF and reports on the work of the associations attached to the EPF. It adopts resolutions, statements/announcements, appeals, etc;

28.4 it confers and adopts resolutions on the matters of cooperation within the movement itself as well as with other integral bodies within the political structure of the ESSR, also with the People's Front of other union republics and democratic associations abroad;

28.5 it brings proposals on the legislative acts — whether in force or in the state of being drafted;

28.6 it confers the steps towards granting cultural autonomy to the national minorities of the Estonian Republic;

28.7 it elects the organ which is to function in between the sessions of the People's Congress — the Council of Plenipotentiaries, also the administrative Board of the EPF; the Policy Committee as well as the Review Commission;

28.8 it ratifies the EPF budget and the report on its adherence; it decides on the salaries' funds of the EPF administrative Board, it takes decisions on the grants, of the PEF symbols and on other matters.

29. The organs elected by the People's Congress of the PFE cannot be staffed by the paid office workes of the Party, Komsomol, trade union or state apparatus of the same level or at higher levels.

30. The Council of the People's Plenipotentiaries
    30.1 it convenes the People's Congress;
    30.2 it considers the principal matters of the PFE movement, various questions of joint actions, topical problems of the life in Estonia in general;
    30.3 it ensures the implementation of the EPF program and the People's Congress resolutions; it considers the financial aspect of the program in the Republic;
    30.4 it takes part in the election campaign during the period of the elections to the bodies of power in Estonia; it draws up the election platform of the PFE; it works on organizational measures aimed at sending its representatives to the commissions connected with elections and for nominating candidates for deputies from the EPF;
    30.5 it elects the editor (editors) for the EPF publishing organ.

31. Sessions of the people's council are held at least once a quarter. The people's council has decision-making power if three-quarters of its members are present at the session. A two-thirds majority vote is required for adopting a resolution.

32. The Advisory Board: members of the Advisory Board (Administrative) of the

EPF have equal rights, they are answerable to the People's Congress, during the term of their service they carry out the function of the chairman on a rotating basis.

32.1 within the limits of its brief, it organizes the EPF activities and leads these activities;

32.2 it convenes the sessions of the Council of People's Plenipotentiaries;

32.3 it maintains working contacts with the Regional People's Fronts, support groups, social organizations, and governing bodies of the Est. SSR; it represents the People's Front;

32.4 it organizes the EPF's finances; it has the power to hire or dismiss people within its salary budget; it coordinates the different functions of the EPF;

32.5 it forms a consultative organ — the Council.

(D) Public Commissions, Advisory Boards and Other Bodies Attached to the People's Front

33. Various public commissions, groups of experts, advisory boards and other formations operate at all levels of the People's Front movement.

34. The Council of EPF's Plenipotentiaries creates various working teams (relating to the matters of foreign affairs, social justice, election campaigns, protection of the environment, religion, etc.) and determines the ways they are created and the sphere of their activities. Suggestions of the Regional People's Fronts and public circles are to be taken into account in the decision-making.

35. The PF Councils of Plenipotentiaries can set up cooperatives and small enterprises, commissions, clubs etc., as they see fit. The clubs attached to the support groups are to be registered with the appropriate organ of the Region PF.

IV The Relationship and Cooperation of the EPF with the Government Bodies, Public Organizations and Other Voluntary Associations and Movements

36. The Communist Party and other public organizations participate in the People's Front movement via the Communists who belong to support groups and to EPF bodies. The PF does not have any subordination to any of the organizations or institutions.

37. Supporting the initiatives of the masses to create a mechanism of democracy and also to open up opportunities for citizens to participate in governing state and public affairs, the People's Front takes care to develop relations with the soviets of people's deputies and their bodies — first and foremost, with people's deputies at all levels.

38. The EPF creates links with public organizations and movements (including informal associations). It discusses with them topical problems of Estonian SSR state and public life; it aims at participating in the election of bodies of authority with its agreed platform and for holding joint events and so on.

39. The EPF holds a dialogue with religious organizations (associations) and considers freedom of religion as a traditional citizen's right in Estonia and supports the participation of believers in the discussion and resolution of the questions affecting the life of the people.
40. While creating and developing links with sections of the Estonian SSR political system, the EPF considers that these links must be based upon acknowledgement of respective rights, mutual respect and good will.

V Bodies of the People's Fronts as Juridical Entities/Property and Monetary Means/Auditing Bodies

41. Rayon and town councils of the EPF and the people's council elected at the Congress of the People's Front function within the rights of a juridical entity.
42. The Councils of Plenipotentiaries have their own budget, balance, a current bank account and a seal with its emblem.
43. PFE obtains its finances from its publications, distribution of its printed organs, various donations from individuals, organizations, associations etc., as well as from other sources.
44. The funds created cover the maintenance (salaries) of the staff workers, material incentives for activists of the People's Front movement, the establishment of grants and so on.
    Council boards of Regional People's Fronts and the EPF board are in charge of the finances.
45. The EPF auditing body is subordinate only to the Congress of the People's Front. It monitors the lawfulness of obtaining financial and other material means and the correctness of their use, checks the EPF budget and balance and resolves other matters. Members of the auditing body having a consultative vote, take part in the sessions of the people's council.
46. PFE uses financial means and its acquired property in accordance with the existing legislation. In case of the breach or abuses of law the guilty will be held responsible in accordance with the existing legislation.

VI Final Clause

57. The EPF, being a public movement, is legally regulated by the Estonian SSR Constitution and other legislation, and is a part of the Estonian SSR political system. The winding up of the activity of the People's Front is resolved by Congress.

Text of "Treaty on the Union of Sovereign States (Agreed 23rd July 1991)" (*Sovetskaya Rossiya* 15 Aug 1991)

The states signing the present treaty,
    proceeding from the declarations of state sovereignty proclaimed by them

and recognizing the right of nations to self-determination;

mindful of the closely related historical destinies of their peoples and fulfilling their will for the preservation and renewal of the union expressed in the referendum of 17th March 1991;

seeking to live in friendship and accord, ensuring co-operation based on equal rights;

wishing to create the conditions for all-around development of each individual, and reliable guarantees of his rights and freedoms;

concerned for the material well-being and spiritual development of the peoples, the mutual enrichment of national cultures, and the safeguarding of their common security;

learning the lessons of the past and taking into account the changes in the life of the country and throughout the world,

have decided to build their relations within the union on new principles, and have agreed on the following.

I Basic Principles

FIRST. Each republic party to the treaty is a sovereign state. The Union of Soviet Sovereign Republics (USSR) is a sovereign, federal, democratic state, formed as a result of the association of equal republics and exercising state power within the limits of its powers, which are voluntarily vested in it by the parties to the treaty.

SECOND. The states forming the union retain the right autonomously to resolve all questions of their development, guaranteeing equal political rights and opportunities for socio-economic and cultural development to all the peoples living on their territory. The parties to the treaty will proceed on the basis of the combination of panhuman and national values, and will resolutely oppose racism, chauvinism, nationalism and all attempts to restrict the people's rights.

THIRD. The states forming the union regard as a most important principle the priority of human rights in accordance with the UN Universal Declaration of Human Rights and other generally recognized norms of international law. All citizens are guaranteed the opportunity to study and use their native language, unhampered access to information, freedom of religion, and other political, socio-economic and personal rights and freedoms.

FOURTH. The states forming the union see the formation of a civil society as a most important condition of the freedom and well-being of the people, and of each individual. They will seek the satisfaction of people's needs on the basis of a free choice of forms of ownership and methods of economic management, the development of the unionwide market, and the realization of the principles of social justice and protection.

FIFTH. The states forming the union possess the full plenitude of political power, and autonomously determine their own national-state and administrative-territorial structure, and the system of bodies of power and administration. They may delegate some of their powers to other states party to the treaty of which they form part.

The parties to the treaty recognize as a common fundamental principle democracy based on people's representation and the direct expression of the peoples' will, and seek to create a law-governed state, which will act as guarantor against any trends toward totalitarianism and tyranny.

SIXTH. The states forming the union consider one of the most important tasks to be the preservation and development of national traditions and state support for education, health care, science and culture. They will promote the intensive exchange and mutual enrichment of humanist spiritual values and achievements of the peoples of the union and the entire world.

SEVENTH. The Union of Soviet Sovereign Republics acts in international relations in the capacity of a sovereign state and an entity in international law, as successor to the Union of Soviet Socialist Republics. Its main aims in the international arena are lasting peace, disarmament, the elimination of nuclear weapons and other weapons of mass destruction, and co-operation among states and solidarity among peoples in resolving mankind's global problems.

The states forming the union are full members of the international community. They are entitled to establish direct diplomatic and consular links, and trade relations with foreign states, to exchange plenipotentiary representative missions with them, to conclude international treaties, and to participate in the activity of international organizations, without detriment to the interests of each of the union states and their common interests, and without violating the union's international commitments.

II Structure of the Union

ARTICLE 1. Membership of the Union
    States' membership of the union is voluntary.
    The states forming the union join it either directly or as members of other states. This does not infringe their rights or relieve them of their obligations under the treaty. They all enjoy equal rights and undertake equal obligations.
    Relations between states when one of them is a member of the other are regulated by treaties between them, by the constitution of the state of which the other is a member, and by the USSR constitution. In the RSFSR — by a federal or other treaty and the USSR constitution.
    The union is open to be joined by other democratic states recognizing the treaty.
    The states forming the union retain the right freely to secede from it under a procedure prescribed by the parties to the treaty and enshrined in the union's constitution and laws.

ARTICLE 2. Citizenship of the Union
    A citizen of a state that has joined the union is simultaneously a citizen of the union.
    Citizens of the USSR enjoy equal rights, freedoms and obligations enshrined in the union's constitution, laws and international treaties.

ARTICLE 3. Territory of the Union
    The territory of the union comprises the territories of all states forming it.
    The parties to the treaty recognize the borders existing between them at the

time of signing the treaty.

Borders between states forming the union can be altered only by agreement between them, which does not violate the interests of other parties to the treaty.

ARTICLE 4. Relations Between the States Forming the Union

Relations between the states forming the union are regulated by the present treaty, by the USSR constitution, and by treaties and agreements which do not run contrary to them.

The parties to the treaty build their relations as members of the union on the basis of equality, respect for sovereignty and territorial integrity, non-interference in internal affairs, solution of disputes by peaceful means, co-operation, mutual assistance, and conscientious performance of obligations under the union treaty and interrepublic agreements.

The states forming the union pledge: not to resort to force or the threat of force in relations between themselves; not to encroach on one another's territorial integrity; not to conclude agreements running contrary to the union's goals or aimed against the states forming it.

The use of USSR Ministry of Defence troops is not allowed inside the country, apart from their participation in the performance of immediate national economic tasks in exceptional circumstances, in the elimination of the consequences of natural calamities and ecological disasters, and in cases provided for under the legislation on state of emergency regulations.

ARTICLE 5. Jurisdiction of the USSR

The parties to the treaty vest the following powers in the USSR:

— Protection of the sovereignty and territorial integrity of the union and its members; declaration of war and conclusion of peace; defence provisions and leadership of the armed forces and the union's border, special (government communications, engineering and technical, and other), Internal and Railway Troops; organization of the development [Russian: razrabotka] and production of armaments and military equipment.

— Provision of the union's state security; determining the regime and safeguarding the union's state border, economic zone, and maritime and air space; leadership and co-ordination of the activity of republics' security bodies.

— Pursuit of the union's foreign policy and co-ordination of republics' foreign political activity; representation of the union in relations with foreign states and international organizations; conclusion of the union's international treaties.

— Pursuit of the union's foreign economic activity and co-ordination of the republics' foreign economic activity; representation of the union in international economic and financial organizations, and conclusion of the union's foreign economic agreements.

— Ratification and implementation of the union budget, implementation of money emission; custody of the union's gold reserves, and its diamond and foreign currency funds; leadership of space research; management of air traffic and the all-union systems of communications and information, geodesy and cartography, metrology, standardization and meteorology; management of the nuclear power industry.

— Adoption of the union constitution and the introduction of amendments and additions to it; adoption of laws within the framework of the union's powers and prescription of fundamentals of legislation on questions agreed with the republics; supreme constitutional supervision.

— Leadership of the activity of federal law enforcement bodies and co-ordination of the activity of union and republic law enforcement bodies in the struggle against crime.

ARTICLE 6. Sphere of Joint Competence of the Union and Republics

The bodies of state power and administration of the union and the republics exercise jointly the following powers:

— Protection of the union's constitutional system, based on the present treaty and the USSR constitution; guaranteeing the rights and freedoms of USSR citizens.

— Determination of the union's military policy, implementation of measures to organize and guarantee defence; prescription of unified procedures for call-up for and performance of military service; prescription of the border zone regime; solution of questions concerning the activity of troops and the placement of military installations on republics' territory; organization of the national economy's mobilization preparation [Russian: mobilizatsionnaya podgotovka]; management of defence complex enterprises.

— Determination of the union's state security strategy and guaranteeing the republics' state security; alterations to the union's state border, subject to consent by the relevant party to the treaty; protection of state secrets; determination of the list of strategic resources and articles not allowed to be exported beyond the union's borders, prescription of general principles and normatives in the sphere of ecological safety; prescription of procedures for the acquisition, custody and utilization of fissionable and radioactive materials.

— The determination of the USSR foreign policy course and the monitoring of its conduct; the defence of the rights and interests of citizens of the USSR, and the rights and interests of the republics in international relations; the establishment of the foundation of foreign economic activity; the conclusion of agreements on international loans and credits, and the regulation of the union's foreign state debt; a single customs service; the protection and rational use of the natural resources of the economic zone and continental shelf of the union.

— The determination of strategy for the socio-economic development of the union and the creation of conditions for the formation of a unionwide market; the pursuit of a single financial, credit, monetary, tax, insurance and prices policy based on a common currency; the creation and use of the gold reserve, and the diamond and currency reserves of the union; the drafting and implementation of unionwide programmes; the monitoring of the implementation of the union budget and the co-ordinated emission of money; the creation of unionwide funds for regional development and elimination of the consequences of natural calamities and disasters; the creation of strategic reserves; the introduction of uniform unionwide statistics.

— The development of a unified policy and balance in the sphere of fuel and energy resources, the management of the country's power system and main gas and oil pipeline, unionwide railway, and air and sea transport; the establishment of the fundamentals for the utilization of natural resources and environmental protection, veterinary science, animal diseases and the quarantining of plants; and the co-ordination of action in the sphere of the management of water resources and resources of interrepublic significance.

— The determination of the fundamentals of social policy on questions of employment, migration, working conditions, pay and occupational safety, social security and insurance, public education, health care, physical culture and sports; the establishment of the bases for pension provision and the maintenance of other social guarantees, including when citizens move from one republic to another; the establishment of a uniform procedure for the indexation of incomes and the guaranteed minimum necessary for subsistence.

— The organization of fundamental scientific research, and the provision of incentives for scientific and technical progress, and the establishment of common principles and criteria for the training and certification of scientific and teaching cadres; the determination of a common procedure for the use of medicinal substances and methods; promotion of the development and mutual enrichment of national cultures; the preservation of the traditional habitat of small peoples; the creation of conditions for their economic and cultural development.

— Monitoring of observance of the constitution and the laws of the union, decrees of the president and decisions made within the framework of union competence; the creation of a unionwide criminal record and information system; the organization of the struggle against crimes committed on the territory of several republics; the determination of a unified system for the organization of corrective establishments.

ARTICLE 7. The procedure for the exercise of the powers of state bodies of the union and the joint powers of state bodies of the union and the republics

Questions falling within joint competence are resolved by the bodies of power and administration of the union and the states which form it by agreement [Russian: soglasovaniye], special agreements [Russian: soglasheniya], and the adoption of the fundamentals of legislation of the union and the republics, and corresponding republic laws. Questions falling within the competence of union bodies are decided by them directly.

Powers not directly assigned under articles 5 and 6 to the exclusive jurisdiction of union bodies of power and administration, or to the sphere of joint competence of bodies of the union and the republics remain under the jurisdiction of the republics and are exercised by them autonomously, or on the basis of bilateral and multilateral agreements between them. After the signing of the treaty a corresponding change takes place in the powers of the bodies of administration of the union and the republics.

The parties to the treaty proceed on the basis that as the all-union market develops, so the sphere of direct state management of the economy is reduced. The necessary redistribution or change in the volume of powers of the bodies of administration will be carried out with the consent of the states forming the union.

Disputes over questions of the exercise of the powers of union bodies, or the realization of rights and fulfilment of duties in the sphere of the joint powers of the bodies of the union and the republics are resolved through conciliation procedures. In the event that a consensus is not reached, disputes are submitted for examination by the union Constitutional Court.

The states forming the union participate in the exercise of the powers of union bodies through the joint formation of the said bodies, and also through special procedures for co-ordinating and implementing decisions.

Each republic may, by concluding an agreement with the union, additionally delegate to it the exercise of particular powers belonging to it, while the union, with the consent of all the republics, may transfer to one or several of the republics the exercise within their territory of particular powers belonging to it.

ARTICLE 8. Ownership

The union and the states forming it ensure the free development and protection of all forms of ownership, and create the conditions for the functioning of enterprises and economic organizations within the framework of the single unionwide market.

The land, mineral resources, water, other natural resources, and the plant and animal world are the property of the republics, and the inalienable assets of their peoples. The procedure for tenure, enjoyment and disposal of them (the right of ownership) is established by the republics' legislation. The right of ownership with regard to resources located on the territory of several republics is established by union legislation.

The states forming the union assign to the union state-owned facilities necessary for the exercise of the powers vested in union bodies of power and administration.

Property which is under union ownership is used in the common interests of the states forming the union, including the interests of the accelerated development of the more backward regions.

The states forming the union are entitled to their share of the gold reserve, and the diamond and foreign currency reserves of the union that are in existence at the time of the conclusion of the present treaty. Their participation in the future accumulation and utilization of the treasuries is defined by separate agreements.

ARTICLE 9. Union Taxes and Levies

In order to finance union budget expenditure linked with the implementation of the powers transferred to the union, unified union taxes and levies are set at fixed percentage rates determined by agreement with the republics on the basis of the items of expenditure submitted by the union. Monitoring of union budget expenditure is carried out by the parties to the treaty.

Unionwide programmes are funded by proportional contributions from the interested republics and the union budget. The volume and purpose of unionwide programmes are regulated by agreements between the union and the republics, taking into account their indicators of socio-economic development.

ARTICLE 10. The Union Constitution

The union constitution is based on this treaty and may not contravene it.

ARTICLE 11. Laws

The laws of the union, and the constitutions and laws of the states forming it, may not contravene the provisions of this treaty.

Laws of the union on questions within its competence take precedence and are mandatory for execution on the territory of the republics.

The laws of a republic take precedence on its territory on all questions except those which are assigned to the union's jurisdiction.

A republic is entitled to suspend the operation on its territory of a union law and challenge it if it violates the present treaty or contravenes the constitution or laws of the republic, adopted within the limits of its powers.

The union is entitled to challenge and suspend the operation of a republic's law if it violates the present treaty or contravenes the constitution or the laws of the union adopted within the limits of its powers.

Disputes are passed to the union Constitutional Court, which adopts a definitive decision within a month.

III   Bodies of the Union

ARTICLE 12. The Formation of Union Bodies

Union bodies of power and administration are formed on the basis of the free will of the peoples, and the representation of the states forming the union. They function strictly in accordance with the provisions of the present treaty and the union constitution.

ARTICLE 13. The USSR Supreme Soviet

The legislative power of the union is exercised by the USSR Supreme Soviet, which consists of two chambers: the Soviet of the Republics and the Soviet of the Union.

The Soviet of the Republics comprises representatives of the republics delegated by their supreme bodies of power. Republic and national-territorial formations retain no fewer deputies' seats in the Soviet of the Republics than they had in the USSR Supreme Soviet of Nationalities at the time the treaty was signed.

All deputies to this chamber from a republic that directly belongs to the union have a single common vote when deciding matters. The procedure for electing representatives and their quotas are defined in a special agreement between the republics and by USSR electoral law.

The Soviet of the Union is elected by the population of the whole country from electoral districts with an equal number of voters. Representation of all republics party to the treaty in the Soviet of the Union is guaranteed.

The chambers of the union Supreme Soviet jointly make changes to the USSR constitution; admit new states to the USSR; determine the fundamental principles of union domestic and foreign policy; approve the union budget and the report on its implementation; declare war and conclude peace; and approve changes to union borders.

The Soviet of the Republics adopts laws on the organization and procedure for the work of union bodies; examines questions of relations between the republics; ratifies the USSR's international treaties; and gives consent to the appointment of the USSR Cabinet of Ministers.

The Soviet of the Union examines questions of safeguarding the rights and freedoms of citizens of the USSR, and adopts laws on all questions except those under the jurisdiction of the Soviet of the Republics. Laws adopted by the Soviet of the Union enter into force after being approved by the Soviet of the Republics.

ARTICLE 14. The President of the Union of Soviet Sovereign Republics

The union president is the head of the union state, exercising supreme executive and administrative power.

The union president acts as guarantor of the observance of the union treaty and of the union constitution and laws; he is commander-in-chief of the union armed forces; he represents the union in relations with foreign countries and monitors the fulfilment of the union's international commitments.

The president is elected by union citizens on the basis of universal, equal and direct suffrage by secret ballot for a term of five years, and for no more than two successive terms. The candidate who receives more than half of the votes cast in the union as a whole and in the majority of states forming the union is deemed elected.

ARTICLE 15. The Vice-President of the USSR

The USSR vice-president is elected at the same time as the USSR president. The union vice-president exercises individual functions of the USSR president as empowered by him, and deputizes for the USSR president in the event of his absence or inability to perform his duties.

ARTICLE 16. The USSR Cabinet of Ministers

The union Cabinet of Ministers is the union body of executive power, is subordinate to the USSR president and is responsible to the Supreme Soviet.

The Cabinet of Ministers is formed by the union president in agreement with the union Supreme Soviet, Soviet of the Republics.

The heads of the republic governments take part in the work of the union Cabinet of Ministers with the right to vote.

ARTICLE 17. The USSR Constitutional Court

The USSR Constitutional Court is formed on an equal basis by the USSR president and each of the chambers of the USSR Supreme Soviet.

The union Constitutional Court examines questions of the compliance of legislative acts of the union and the republics, decrees of the union president and republic presidents, and normative acts of the union Cabinet of Ministers with the union treaty and union constitution, and also resolves disputes between the union and the republics and among republics.

ARTICLE 18. Union (Federal) Courts

The union (federal) courts are the USSR Supreme Court, the union Supreme Court of Arbitration, and courts in the union armed forces.

The union Supreme Court and the union Supreme Court of Arbitration exercise judicial power within the limits of the union's powers. The chairmen of republics' supreme judicial and arbitration bodies are ex-officio members of the union Supreme Court and the union Supreme Court of Arbitration respectively.

ARTICLE 19. The USSR Procurator's Office

Oversight of the implementation of union legislative acts is exercised by the union procurator general and the procurator generals (procurators) of the republics, and procurators subordinate to them.

The union procurator general is appointed by and accountable to the union Supreme Soviet.

The procurator generals (procurators) of republics are appointed by their supreme legislative bodies and are ex-officio members of the union Procurator's Office collegium. In their work of overseeing the implementation of union laws they are accountable both to the supreme legislative bodies of their own states and to the union procurator general.

IV Concluding Provisions

ARTICLE 20. The Language of Interethnic Intercourse in the USSR

Republics autonomously determine their own state language (languages). Parties to the treaty recognize Russian as the language of interethnic intercourse in the USSR.

ARTICLE 21. The Capital of the Union

The capital of the USSR is the city of Moscow.

ARTICLE 22. The Union's State Symbols

The USSR has a state emblem, flag and anthem.

ARTICLE 23. The Treaty's Entry Into Force

THE PRESENT TREATY IS APPROVED BY THE SUPREME BODIES OF STATE POWER OF THE STATES FORMING THE UNION AND COMES INTO FORCE THE MOMENT IT IS SIGNED BY THEIR AUTHORIZED DELEGATIONS.

For the states which have signed the treaty, from that date the 1922 Treaty on the Formation of the USSR is deemed to lose effect.

Most favoured status operates for states which have signed the treaty on its coming into force.

Relations between the Union of Soviet Sovereign Republics and republics belonging to the Union of Soviet Socialist Republics, but which have not signed the present treaty are regulated on the basis of USSR legislation and mutual obligations and agreements.

ARTICLE 24. Responsibility Under the Treaty

The union and the states forming it bear mutual responsibility for fulfillment of adopted obligations and make good losses incurred through violations of the present treaty.

ARTICLE 25. The Procedure for Amendments and Additions to the Treaty

The present treaty or its separate provisions may be rescinded, amended or augmented only with the consent of all states forming the union.

If the need arises, appendixes to the treaty may be adopted by agreement between the states which have signed it.

ARTICLE 26. Continuity of the Union's Supreme Bodies

For the purposes of continuity in exercising state power and administration, the supreme legislative, executive and judicial bodies of the Union of Soviet Socialist Republics retain their powers right up until the formation of the supreme state bodies of the Union of Soviet Sovereign Republics in accordance with the present treaty and the new USSR constitution.

Source: BBC World Broadcasts, SU/1152 C1 16 Aug 1991.

Chapter 7

REPRODUCING SOCIETY

Gender, Family, and Generations

At the beginning of this part I pointed out that "social structure" refers to an array of positions and statuses, the conditions that shape them, and a network of relationships between people. Statuses are what give people a sense of identity, they also are categories that are significant bases of social and political division. Traditional social science has emphasized social identification and cleavage in terms of class and ethnicity. Gender roles and generation (age group) are also important determinants of people's consciousness, evaluation, and status and may also be the basis on which resources are distributed and discrimination is made.

GENDER ROLES AND THE FAMILY

Sex is a biological and physiological characteristic of human beings. Gender roles are the social and cultural behavior and expectations that are associated with each sex. The relationship between sex and gender roles is a matter of dispute and one finds in the Soviet Union as well as in the West two major approaches to the problem.

On the one hand, gender roles adopted by males and females are sometimes considered to derive from their biological and sexual characteristics. Women are often referred to as caring and emotional, whereas men are considered selfish and aggressive. By nature, it is contended, women's roles are tending the sick and children, whereas men are born to work and to rule. This kind of biological determinism legitimates ascribed collective disadvantage to women and various forms of privilege to men.

People with a more sociological perspective take the stance that gender roles are socially determined and have no origin in biology. They regard such forms of discrimination as illegitimate. The subordination of women, it is held, is an expression of power relationships in society at large. Women's inferior position is circumscribed by the economic and political forms of closure exerted by men and expressed through the modern family. Gender role divisions, then, are inextricably bound up with the form taken by the family — with the provisions for the upbringing of children and with the position of women in the economy.

Women's Role in the Family

In industrial society the family is an institution typically made up of cohabiting adults and the children to whom they act as parents. There are of course variations in family structure: increasingly, one-parent families are formed following the death, separation, or choice of one of the spouses. Procreation also may be independent of marriage. Marriage defines the socially conventional and acceptable forms of sexual intercourse and reproduction. In short, the family ensures the reproduction of the human race. With the evolution of capitalism and socialism the family unit has increasingly combined in itself marriage, procreation, and the upbringing of children. In the USSR as well as in the West, the family structure is monogamous (individuals have one spouse at a time), although increasingly one family is dissolved to found another (this is called serial marriage).

The family, however, also takes on other functions. It legitimates the rights of offspring reared within it to the property, possessions, and name of the unit. It performs a socialization function: it inculcates ideas of right conduct in children and thereby it helps to reproduce a system of values and beliefs. The cultural and material background of families varies by social group, and the family is an agency of placement in the occupational and class structure and thereby an instrument for the perpetuation of inequality.

Gender relationships are defined within the family structure. Women bear children. This biological fact has led to a social division of labor wherein women have the responsibility for the upbringing of children and the maintenance of the home. Men have taken on the roles of breadwinner and political leader. Employment has given men control over income and effective ownership of assets (land and capital). The family name is usually taken from the male side. In the USSR and the West the family is patrilineal — families take the male name and property is typically owned by the father and passed on to the son.

The differentiation of gender roles within the family under capitalism and, as we will see, under socialism, is indisputable. But the causes, consequences, and legitimacy are matters of contention. Some sociologists view such role specialization involving male superiority and female subordination not as biologically determined but as a social mechanism to reduce rivalry between the sexes and to regulate sexual relations. Such structured relationships ensure social harmony, effective production relations, and human reproduction. The social evaluation of women is based on their physical beauty, sexual desirability, and charm. According to this line of thought, relations of inequality and asymmetry are legitimated through the process of human evolution.

Many contemporary reformers — not only those in the feminist movement — regard the sexual division of labor as unjust and illegitimate. Women are oppressed by men ideologically, economically, and physically. Women are subjected to physical abuse, forced sex, and violence. The family, rather than being a "haven of emotionality," as Talcott Parsons once described it, is an institution that imprisons women.

Marxist explanations of gender roles are most pertinent to policy in the USSR because the leaders of the Soviet state have sought to abolish the major forms of exploitation. For most Marxists an authoritative account of their position on gender inequalities is found in the writing of Engels, for whom the essence of gender inequality stems from class relationships. According to this view monogamy allows for the transfer of property from father to son and strengthens the motive for capital accumulation. The family perpetuates the socialization of class values, maintains a rudimentary division of labor, and ensures the reproduction of the work force at a low cost. From this point of view the family under capitalism is an agency of exploitation.

As we have noted in earlier chapters, Soviet Marxists have tended to attribute all forms of oppression to one common cause: class relations. But the abolition of capitalist relations also entails the withering away of male/female forms of domination and subjugation. For Engels and Lenin a new type of socialist family based on the reciprocity of spouse relationships, mutual love, and equality arises after the abolition of the bourgeoisie. Children would be reared in the family but society would increasingly take a greater responsibility for child care. Monogamy would regulate sexual relations but on the basis of choice of the partners.

A more radical line was taken in the USSR by the feminist writer Kollontai, a compatriot of Lenin who wrote after the October Revolution. She argued that with the abolition of private property the need for the family as a social institution also would disappear and sexual relations would not need to be regulated by monogamy. The crucial subordination of women to the care of children would be broken by the collective rearing of children and abortion would be universally available. Women would then have real equality with men, and the political and economic division of labor would cease. But her views were not taken seriously by the Soviet government and were never adopted as policy.

The postrevolutionary government in Russia sought to abolish women's inequality by abolishing private ownership of the means of production, which it believed would provide conditions for women's rights, particularly in the family. The provision of paid work and an occupation was a major component in the Soviet policy for liberating women: "To ensure the complete liberation of women and a true equality with men, there must be a social economy and women must participate in common productive labor" (V. I. Lenin).

Achievement, however, has fallen short of the aspiration of Lenin. This is because other elements of gender relations, noted above by feminists, have been ignored.

Forms of Sexual Inequality

As with class and ethnic relations, in the USSR today one may find considerable differences between the sexes in the distribution of income, status, political power, and life chances, although the effects of the October Revolution, Party control, and economic planning on the status of women should not be dismissed as inconsequential. The legal and economic position of women compared to that before the revolution has been transformed. A real attempt has been made to emancipate women. They have the same legal rights as men; discrimination on the basis of sex is forbidden. This has affected women's rights to property, inheritance, children of a marriage, and divorce. Through the opportunity for work, access to education, control over abortion, and widespread social services women in the USSR, probably to a greater extent than in Western capitalist countries at similar levels of development, have acquired independence from, but not equality with, men. In 1920 abortion was made legal and widely available, it was made a criminal offence in 1936, but since 1955 abortion is legally and freely provided by the health service. Divorce is easy to procure. Illegitimacy has no legal stigma but the status still carries social disapproval.

Paid employment and opportunities are defined in the Constitution as being "equal to those of men" (Article 35). Work and labor, however, have to be seen in the context of the constitutional provision "of conditions enabling women to combine labor and motherhood" (Article 35). Hence work that may affect motherhood, for example, heavy work, underground labor, and night work, is forbidden.

In education, women's share of places in institutions of higher education rose between 1928 and 1935 from 28 percent to 38 percent. Table 7.1 shows that by 1940–41 women accounted for more than half of the students in higher education and almost a third in secondary specialist education (56 percent and 42 percent respectively in 1986–87). In Western countries the proportion of women in higher education now is around 40 percent: 46 percent in the United States, 41 percent in the United Kingdom.

A similar trend may be perceived in paid employment. In 1928, women made up only 28 percent of workers in the economy; by 1940 the figure had reached 38.9 percent; and by 1987 it had risen to 51 percent. These figures indicate a very high labor participation rate for women; by the 1980s it was certainly the highest rate of employment in the world, standing at about 86 percent of women in the appropriate age groups. In the United States and Britain the proportion is about 60 percent.

Furthermore, women employees in the USSR are employed full time and can look forward to a permanent position and (though with limitations) to a career, whereas more than a third of women in Britain and about a quarter in the United States are employed part-time. By 1986 in the USSR women constituted 60 percent of all professional employees (*spetsialisty*) ; in trades schools women accounted for about a quarter of the pupils.

Table 7.1
Women in Higher and Specialist Secondary Education, 1940–87 (percent of students)

	1940–41		1970–71		1986–87	
	Higher Education	Specialized Secondary	Higher Education	Specialized Secondary	Higher Education	Specialized Secondary
Industry, building, transport, and communication	40	32	38	40	44	42
Agriculture	46	37	30	37	37	34
Economics and law	64	60	60	83	70	84
Health, physical education, and sport	74	83	56	87	63	90
Education, culture, and cinematography	66	60	66	81	74	87
Totals:						
Higher Education	58	—	49	—	56	—
Specialist Secondary	—	32	—	40	—	42

Source: Narkhoz za 70 let (1987): 556.

A study of Soviet immigrants to the United States conducted in the early 1980s found that women had been particularly satisfied with their work positions.

While the statistics on women not only in higher education but also in professional and skilled jobs illustrate the opening of opportunities, further examination of occupational trends shows significant inequalities with men. Women's education and employment are skewed to certain sectors. Examination of Table 7.1, for instance, shows that in 1986−87 over seventy percent of the students in economics, law, health, physical education, teacher training, and culture (*iskusstvo*) were female. This tendency is reflected in the occupational distribution of women, as shown in Table 7.2 and illustrated in Figure 7.1.

Table 7.2 shows the sectors where women are employed. Here we observe growing feminization between 1940 and 1987 in all sectors and most particularly in retail trades (shop assistants), education (teachers), health (doctors, nurses), culture and administration. (Though the proportion of women physicians fell from 76 percent in 1960 to 66 percent in 1987.) In all these sectors (except science in 1940) women's participation was greater than the increase in their share in the work force.

These sectors of the economy, moreover, are all associated with low wages and had worsening relative wage rates associated with feminization: in 1986 in the retail and public catering sectors the average wage was 78 percent of the average wage for all employed manuals and nonmanuals; for the health, physical education, and social security sectors it was 79.6 percent; in education the average wage was identical to the national average wage in 1940, but by 1986 it had fallen to 79.6 percent. In industries

Table 7.2
Feminized Sectors of Employment: Percentage of Women in Labor Force

	1940	1970	1986
Retail, wholesale, catering, sales, and purchasing	44.5	75.3	75.4
Health, physical education, and social security	75.8	84.8	81.4
Education	57.8*	72.7	75.5
Culture and art	—	60.3	67.6
Science	42.5	47.0	51.4
Administration, banks, and insurance	34.9	63.2	72.0
Proportion of women in total work force	38.9	50.8	50.8

Source: Based on *Narkhoz za 70 let* (1987): 412, 416.
*Including culture and art.

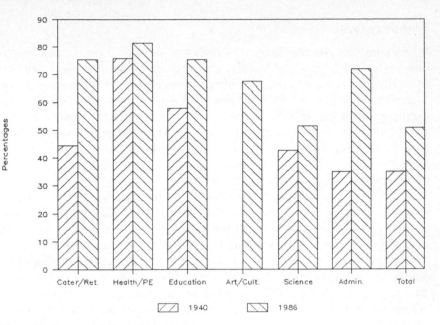

Figure 7.1 Feminized Sectors of Employment

Source: Based on data from *Narkhoz za 70 let* (1987): 412, 416.

paying much higher than the average wage, such as building and transport, women constitute less than a third of the work force.

Overall, women's average earnings arc about a third less than those of men. A Soviet sociologist, Rimashevskaya (1988), reports in an empirical study conducted in Taganrog that whereas a third of women earned less than 100 rubles per month, only 2 percent of men did; the modal average of women's wages was in the 100–140 bracket, the average for men was 180–240.

There is an obvious labelling of jobs based on ideas of gender roles, with women being thought particularly appropriate for the "caring" professions, such as medicine and teaching, cleaning, retail trades, and clerical work. The level of skilled jobs achieved by women is lower than that of the men. Studies conducted in the USSR have found that of male workers, 19 percent were in the top skill grade, and 9 percent were in the bottom skill grades; the comparable figures for women were 5 percent and 11 percent respectively.

Authority Roles

If one considers the distribution of men and women in positions of authority, one finds considerable evidence of discrimination against women. In medicine women constitute 69 percent of the physicians, but the number of female chief doctors falls to 53 percent (data for 1980); in the teaching profession, in 1982 women made up 72 percent of the profession; their share of the heads of eight-year schools was 40 percent and for middle schools 36 percent. Only some 9 percent of directors of enterprises are female, as are 12 percent of *mastery* (foremen); and less than 2 percent of collective farm chairpersons are women.

In public recognition for labor service between 1925 and 1986, 20,200 men were honored with the award of Hero of Socialist Labor, as were 5,200 women (20.5 percent of all awards). Of all orders and medals for work awarded in that period, women had 2,537,800 (19.9 percent of the total).

Of deputies elected to the Soviets in 1984, 32.8 percent of the Supreme Soviet were female, for the union republics (1985 elections) women made up 36.2 percent, and for local government (1987) 49.4 percent. As we noted in chapter 3 above, to the elections of All-Union Congress of People's Deputies in March 1989, only 15.8 percent of nominated candidates were women and of the total number of deputies elected women's share was 17.1 percent.

In 1981 women made up 26 percent of Party members (24.2 percent in 1976). In the Party Congress in 1981 they constituted 26.6 percent of the delegates, but only 3 percent of the voting members of the Central Committee. In 1988 29.3 percent of the Party members were female, though only 7 percent of leading (*obkom* and *raikom*) party secretaries and a third of party branch secretaries are female. The political elite is almost exclusively male. Of the top one hundred leading Soviet officials in 1988 only one, Aleksandra Biryukova, was a woman. Gorbachev has promoted her to the position of Secretary of the Central Committee of the CPSU and in 1988 she was elected a candidate member of the Politburo. Until her election, not one top official of the Central Committee apparatus nor any member of the Council of Ministers was female. She lost her place in 1990 and Galina Semenova was elected a full member and a secretary of the central committee. Gulchakhra Turgunova was also elected secretary but not a full member of the politburo.

Women also have less representation among the various elites. Postgraduate women students, for instance, made up only 28 percent of the postgraduate students (candidate of sciences) in 1982 and they constituted 14 percent of the doctors of science. In 1980 women accounted for approximately 10 percent of the academic elite (academicians, corresponding members of the Academy, and professors). Women tend to be occupied less in jobs requiring a directional role over men and more in tasks that require specialized knowledge. In 1986 58 percent of engineers were female, as were 86 percent of engineer economists, planners, and statisticians, 89 percent of bookkeepers, and 91 percent of librarians. (*Narkhoz za 70 let*, 1987: 416). While women constitute 60 percent of specialists, relatively few are in management and higher administration; and only one in twelve chief engineers and other industrial chiefs are selected from the large constituency of women (data for 1986).

There can be no doubt that for all the real advances made in women's employment and education, their present array of positions in the division of labor gives rise to average lower levels of skills and wages and subordinate positions of authority. Much of the inequality of women's position is caused by the dual burden of mother/housewife and paid employee. The traditional family responsibilities have not been transferred to men and this has militated against women's political and occupational upward mobility. Therefore, attention must be focussed on the reproductive functions of women.

Reproductive Role Issues

Whereas radical feminists and many Marxists regarded socialism as a necessary condition for the abolition of women's subordination within the family, the experience of the Soviet Union has shown no significant change in women's roles as a result of socialism.

Women bear the brunt of domestic chores such as shopping, housework, and cleaning. Numerous surveys conducted in the Soviet Union show that women spend more than 28 hours per week in such activities whereas men spend 10 hours (data for manual and nonmanual workers, 1985). On a working day men have an average 4.03 hours free time compared to women's 2.24 hours, on holidays and weekends men have 9.14 hours compared to women's 6.32 hours (data for manual and nonmanual workers). The amount of free time available to women is much less and they have less time to pursue avenues (courses, and so forth) for promotion.

The arrival of a child in a family has a negative effect for women's ability to advance in their chosen career, though it does not for men. Policy is geared to lightening women's burdens by extending the services and hours of restaurants and cafeterias and increasing the provision of household appliances. Cafeterias and restaurants, however, are inadequate both in the quantity and quality of service. The study of Rimashevskaya, mentioned earlier, found that psychological strain has led to an increase in smoking by women (40 percent of smokers in the USSR are women) and they had more illness and worse health than men.

The burden women carry of an occupation, care of the home, and the rearing of children has led them increasingly to reject childbearing. Non-working women have larger families than employed ones. As women receive education they aspire to the status and lifestyle given by an occupation. In the 1979 census, for example, it was found that per thousand women aged fifteen and over, there were 1,963 children, for women with higher education the figure was 1,279, with secondary specialists 1,365, incomplete secondary 1,648, elementary 2,718 and less than elementary 3,433. Level of education is also correlated with urban living and more younger than older women have higher education.

Current policy is far from that espoused by Kollontai. The family remains the mainstay of the system of reproduction. As the 1977 Constitution has put it:

> The family is under the protection of the state. Marriage is entered into with free consent of the woman and the man; spouses are completely equal in their matrimonial relations. The State aids the family by providing and developing an extensive network for child-care institutions, organizing and improving the community services and public catering, and by providing allowances and benefits for families with many children, and by paying benefits on the birth of a child. (Article 53)

Women have the biologically determined role of bearing children and their socially defined role is rearing children. As the decree on "Measures to Increase State Assistance to Families with Children" (1981) put it, measures are devised to create "more favorable conditions *for women* that will enable them to combine work in social production with the rearing of children" [Italics added].

There is, then, a dissonance (or internal contradiction) between the goal of female liberation in society, which involves equal rights to occupation and a career, and the socially defined role of women, which entails responsibility for child rearing. This is the double bind that creates conditions that effectively limit women's equality.

Women are at a disadvantage when it comes to sexual intercourse because it may lead to an unwanted responsibility for child rearing. Moreover, a separation of sexual fulfillment through intercourse from the act of procreation and the consequent care of her offspring by use of birth control may lead to a weakening of the reproductive facility of a society. A decline in population as a result of a fall in the birth rate would have significant effects on the military and economic strength of a country. All governments place human reproduction before sexual gratification: marriage as an institution limits the numbers of legitimate sexual partners, and restrictions on abortion and contraception also limit women's sexual freedom. Feminist politics place great store in giving women rights over their bodies and control over procreation. To what extent have conditions in the USSR given women such control?

For those women who choose not to bear children the chief methods of birth control in the USSR are abortion, coitus interruptus, and condoms. Less frequently used are other barrier methods, pessaries, IUD, and (rarely) the pill. Abortion is available by request up to twelve weeks of pregnancy. In the late 1970s the ratio of abortions to live births was between 2.5 and 3 to 1. This is the registered rate, anecdotal evidence suggests that it is higher than this due to the prevalence of illegal abortions (taken by married women wishing to conceal a pregnancy, and by some Asian women not wanting another child). Another index of the prevalence of abortion is provided by a survey of Soviet immigrants to the United States conducted in the early 1980s in which it was found that one third of the women interviewed had no abortion, one third had one or two abortions, and one third had three or more (Anderson 1987: 213). By way of comparison, in Britain in the mid-eighties the abortion rate per 1,000 women (aged 15−44) was 12.8, 27.4 in the USA and 181 in the USSR.

The high rate of abortion is injurious to women's health and is believed to be one of the causes of a high infant mortality rate. (This is dealt with in chapter 10.)

The Family in Crisis? Birth Rate and Divorce

Accompanying the processes of industrialization and modernization, the birth rate of societies tends to rise in concert with the lowering of the age of marriage and when couples form families at a relatively younger age. With the subsequent aging of the population and its urbanization, birth rates tend to fall as people restrict the size of their family. This happens in all modern industrial societies, as is shown in Table 7.3.

The data in Table 7.3 are inadequate for a detailed analysis of demographic changes, but they indicate te trends. In the USSR the birth rate fell in the 1970s and recovered in the 1980s. Both marriage and divorce has increased, following a pattern similar to that of the United States and Great Britain. In analyzing the table one must bear in mind that the indexes are expressed as a proportion of the total population, which may influence the rates.

Table 7.3
Crude Birth, Marriage, and Divorce Rates in the USSR (per thousand of the total population)

		1940	*1970*	*1986*
Birth Rate	USSR	31.3	17.4	20.0
	United States	—	18.4	15.5
	Great Britain	—	16.3	13.3
Marriage	USSR	6.3	9.7	9.8
	United States	—	10.6	10.0
	Great Britain	—	8.5	6.9
Divorce	USSR	1.1	2.6	3.4
	United States	—	3.5	5.0*
	Great Britain	—	1.2	3.0

Source: Naselenie SSSR, 1987.
* 1985.

The size of families in the USSR has fallen: in 1965 35 percent of all births were to mothers who had 3 or more children; in 1986 the corresponding figure was 26 percent. The average number of births per woman has fallen consistently since 1938 when it was 4.4 (3.4 in urban areas, 5.0 rural); in 1975 it was 2.4 (1.9 urban, 3.5 rural); in 1986 it reached 2.5 (2.0 urban and 3.6 rural). But the crude indicators above have to be disaggregated to distinguish different national regions and social groups. The size of families is much higher in the countryside than in the town, and lower in the European areas than the non-European ones. The average size of families by republic, and average family size for urban and rural areas are shown in Table 7.4 and the descending order of family size is illustrated in Figure 7.2. Examination of Table 7.4 shows the higher rural family size, and the larger families of the non-European nationalities (for example, Uzbeks, 6.2, Kazakhs 5.5); these of course are largely rural peasants. In the European rural areas of the country, family size is much lower: 3.4 in the Russian republic, 3.3 in Lithuania, 3.1 in Latvia and Estonia. In the Baltic republics the decline in the birth rate poses the possibility of less than replenishment of the Baltic peoples and explains the reference to the improvement in the "genetic stock" of the population in the programs of the People's Fronts in those republics (see, for instance, paragraph 2.7 in the Estonian People's Charter appended to chapter 6).

This decline in family size is not due to a failure of the family as a social institution. The number of people living in family groups in the

Table 7.4

Average Size of Family by Republic in Urban and Rural Areas, 1979

	Urban	Rural	Average for Republic
Russian Republic	3.2	3.4	3.2
Ukraine	3.2	3.3	3.4
Belorussia	3.3	3.3	3.3
Uzbekistan	4.6	6.2	6.2
Kazakhstan	3.7	4.7	5.5
Georgia	3.9	4.2	4.0
Azerbaydzhan	4.5	5.8	5.5
Lithuania	3.3	3.3	3.3
Moldavia	3.2	3.6	3.5
Latvia	3.1	3.1	3.0
Kirgizia	3.8	5.3	5.7
Tadzhikistan	4.5	6.6	6.6
Armenia	4.5	5.2	4.7
Turkmenia	4.6	6.5	6.3
Estonia	3.1	3.1	3.1
USSR (all families)	3.3	3.8	3.5

Source: Derived from 1979 Census.

Soviet Union has risen from 83.6 percent of the urban population in 1939 to 87.2 percent in 1979 when the rural figure stood at 92.3 percent. Women are marrying earlier and more women are getting married. Of the generation born in 1931–35, 51.6 percent were married by the age of twenty-three, of the cohort born in 1952–54, 68.5 percent were married by age twenty-three.

Legal provisions have influenced the divorce rate in the USSR: it was more difficult to get a divorce in the years of Stalin's administration and thus the divorce rate for those years underestimated family breakup. Similarly the trend for couples to cohabit without a legal marriage will tend to underestimate the real separation rate. The number of divorces per thousand married couples in the USSR has risen from 5.3 in 1958–59 to 14.1 in 1984–85. This reflects a genuine rise in rates of family breakups, caused by the higher level of urbanization, the greater proportion of the female population at work, and the growing dissatisfaction with marriage on the part of married women. Also, registered divorce has increased from 1.3 per thousand of the population in 1960 to 3.4 per thousand in 1986. By the end of the 1970s, however, only between 2 to 3 percent of the total number of marriages broke up per year. Looked at from this

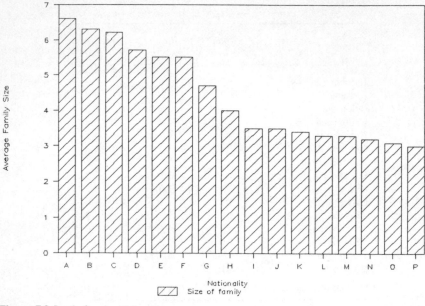

Figure 7.2 Family Size by Nationality

Source: Based on data from Soviet Census, 1979.
Key: A = Tadzhiks; B = Turks; C = Uzbeks; D = Kirgiz; E = Kazakhs; F = Azeris; G = Armenians; H = Georgians; I = Moldavians; J = USSR (all families); K = Ukrainians; L = Belorussians; M = Lithuanians; N = Russians; O = Estonians; P = Latvians.

point of view, these rates of family breakup are not a serious indictment of family life and put into perspective the over pessimistic interpretation of family disintegration often met in the literature.

In this context an increasing number of women choose to bring up children alone. In 1979 there were 7.8 million single parent families (out of a total of 66.3 million families) and most of these families were headed by women. The number of children born to single mothers was 9.84 percent of the total number of births in 1986: it was 9.48 percent in 1965, a dramatic reduction from the early 1950s when the rate was 17.48 percent. The figures for the 1950s, following the war, reflect the depleted families caused by the death of a husband during the war: the shortage of men after the war led many women to have children outside of marriage.

These rates hide great variations between republics: in 1986 in Estonia the proportion was 21.96 percent, only 3.85 percent in Turkmenia, and 12.4 percent in the Russian republic. The varying rates are explained not only by demographic variables, but also by social attitudes — the Baltic people have a much more tolerant attitude toward illegitimacy compared to an unsympathetic and even hostile outlook in the Muslim Central Asian republics.

Though no exact statistics have been published, it is widely asserted in the USSR that the children of these fatherless families create social problems: they have high rates of crime and many of the girls take to prostitution. From the women's point of view, care of such children creates strain and prolonged absence from the work force seriously imperils pension and other welfare benefits.

The Family and Perestroika

How then will the leadership resolve the problem of the need for women's emancipation with the requirements of society for population replacement? The present leadership's policy is to strengthen the family. Recognition of the strain on women brought on by their roles of homemaker, mother, and worker has led Gorbachev to see women as having a more feminine role. As he has put it in his book *Perestroika*,

> we failed to pay attention to women's specific rights and needs arising from their role as mother and home-maker, and their indispensable educational function as regards children. Engaged in scientific research, working on construction sites, in production and in the services, and involved in creative activities, women no longer have enough time to perform their everyday duties at home — housework, the upbringing of children and the creation of a good family atmosphere. We have discovered that many of our problems in children's and young people's behavior, in our morals, culture and in production — are partially caused by the weakening of family ties and slack attitude to family responsibilities. That is why we are now holding heated debates ... about the question of what we should do to make it possible for women to return to their purely womanly mission. (117)

At the Twenty-Seventh Party Congress (1986), Gorbachev further pointed out: "A precondition for the solution of any problems of the family is the creation of working and living conditions for women that would make it possible to combine successfully motherhood with active participation in labor and public activity." The leadership also has called for a reduction in women's employment in dangerous jobs and jobs with health hazards. The reforms of the present leadership have to be interpreted in this context.

Due to the inordinate amount of time women spend in coping with shortages and standing in queues, the retail market requires a thorough-going reform, which has been one of the Gorbachev leadership's priorities. Consumer goods of more convenience to women are starting to appear: a joint enterprise for the manufacture of Tampax tampons has been set up; no doubt babies' disposable diapers will soon arrive.

Current policy, however, also espouses greater equality for women. Gorbachev has called for the promotion of more women to adminis-trative positions and he has supported the further development of the *zhensovet*, or women's councils. In his address to the party's Nineteenth Conference in July 1988, he said:

> A mass women's organization [the women's councils] has been created, or more accurately revived. ... We must work to change the situation sub-stantively, to open a wide road for women to executive agencies, from top to bottom, and to see to it that questions directly affecting the interests of women are not resolved without their participation and decisive opinions.

There is something of a contradiction here, for a return to women's "purely womanly mission" would make the conditions of women's greater participation in authority and work roles more difficult. Obviously, Gorbachev and some sections of the leadership would like to enhance the position of women, but the priority will most certainly be given to women's reproductive role.

Policy is pronatalist — to encourage births and the rearing of children by women. In the Twelfth Five Year Plan (1985–89) women who have had at least one year at work (or have been in full-time study) are to receive paid maternity leave for eighteen months (50 rubles per month in the Far East, Siberia, and the North, and 35 rubles elsewhere). Since 1981 the birth of a first child qualified for a grant of 50 rubles and 100 rubles for the second and third. It is intended to develop part-time and home working, to encourage women to work and look after children. Additional holiday entitlement is available to women who have two or more children under twelve years of age; these women also have priority for leave in the summer or at holiday time and the right to two extra weeks unpaid leave and fourteen days paid leave per annum to look after a sick child.

While such support for mothers with children is helpful, it is not com-parable to earned income — it is less than the minimum wage of 70 rubles per month in the late 1980s. Domestic work and the raising of children have less status than an occupation. Strengthening the family will undoubtedly lead to a widening gap between the social attainment of women and that of men. There are no proposals for paternity leave.

The extra leave entitlement may make women's labor less reliable to employers who will be forced under the cost-cutting policy of perestroika to secure a stable and more selective labor force. Women will be encouraged to see their work as complementary to that of their husband — rather than as a career.

The conflict in roles may be observed in the actions of different leading Soviet ladies. Raisa Gorbachev plays a complementary role: she is an adjunct to her husband's presidential role and in this respect she differs little, except in age and education, from Barbara Bush. She is representative of Soviet femininity.

Gorbachev, however, has also called for placing women in higher authority positions (January Plenum 1987). Yet the more pluralistic and democratic system of elections has reduced the participation of women in the Congress of People's Deputies (as noted above in chapter 3). This pattern is likely to recur with respect to other elective posts.

Other politically active women take a more critical view of gender inequality. Tereshkova (the first female Soviet astronaut) at an All-Union conference of women in 1987 argued for less occupational role specialization, citing the levels of inequality in access to authority roles and the sexual stereotyping of occupations. She pointed to the differential socialization of boys and girls at school and encouraged girls to be more interested in technology. Rimashevskaya, a leading Soviet sociologist (cited previously) has also argued that the achievement of social equality for women should not be directed towards decreasing women's employment, but toward improving living conditions and changing the social division of labor. This may reflect a more demanding attitude on the part of women for more interesting work. A study of work attitudes done in Leningrad in the late 1970s reported that women's claims for "interesting work" were similar to men's.

Women's rights activists are not as common as in the West. Writers such as Tatyana Mamonova (see her essays in Russian Women's Studies [1989]) regard the system of gender relations in the Soviet Union as patriarchy. And as a candidate in the elections for the Congress of People's Deputies put it in 1989, "For many years our society has been ruled almost exclusively by elderly and middle-aged men. ... Under *muzhekratiya* [rule by men] there can be no democracy" (Elvira Novikova). Such, however, are very much minority views in the USSR. Women's rights and feminist consciousness, as understood in the West, are not a public issue.

The growing consumerism and market orientation has lifted previous restrictions on *nekulturny* (vulgar) and demeaning behavior by women. Beauty contests with contestants replete in bikinis are now an accepted part of Soviet life: the first Soviet beauty queen contest occurred in

1987; in 1988—89 an All-Union competition for the title of "Miss Photo — USSR" was held. These competitions are arranged by the new (private enterprise) cooperatives. Prostitution and marketing of sex seems to be more acceptable. Female nudity is permissible: a female Soviet skating champion at the European championships even made the front page of the British mass tabloid press for the daringness of her see-through costume.

The policy of glasnost' has led to public discussion of many previously taboo subjects such as AIDS, venereal diseases, and prostitution. The high infant mortality rate, like prostitution and ill health of children and women, have become matters of public concern.

Conclusion

In ensuring the reproduction of the population, the family in modern industrial society has taken on a patriarchal form. This has entailed a division of social labor and the inequality of women. The traditional line of argument adopted in the USSR has been that the abolition of classes and the provision of employment will provide the basis of female emancipation. Constitutional provisions guarantee women equality with men, and women have secured a high labor participation rate, many opportunities in education, and the right to abortion. Nevertheless, many injustices remain with respect to access to jobs, levels of income, rights to authority positions, and exploitation within the household and family unit. Apart from the sphere of labor, the position of women in society is not qualitatively different in the USSR than that of welfare state societies such as Britain.

The reform movement of Gorbachev has espoused a contradictory position as far as women are concerned: policy seeks to reduce women's multiple roles and at the same time it calls for the enhancement of their roles in politics and work. But the main thrust of the policy is strengthening women's position in the family. Greater individualization, a more consumer-oriented lifestyle, and better opportunities for leisure and career are afforded by a small family and this seems to be a trend in all advanced societies.

The emphasis on glasnost' has made public discussion of many topics affecting women, infant mortality, health, and employment being among the more important. Market forces will reduce the level of employment and it is likely that women's advancement through employment will be curtailed. While part-time work may be acceptable to harassed mothers, it will diminish women's equality of opportunity with men. The poverty of single mothers will remain. The strengthening of the family will have negative consequences for women: the longer women are at home, the lower will be their insurance contributions and hence their entitlement to pensions and sickness benefits will be diminished.

Improvements in retail trade and food supply should make housework and shopping easier, giving women more time for leisure. Rights to birth control are unlikely to be infringed and abortion will be replaced by the pill as the major form of family planning.

In the political sphere, the abolition of social quotas of deputies will reduce even more the representation of women in government. The higher one ascends the ladder, the fewer women are incumbents of authority roles. Overall, as in other areas, perestroika will give rise to more freedom and less equality. The costs of a transition to a market economy will be disproportionately borne by women: their unemployment is likely to increase and social benefits will be cut.

GENERATIONS

Societies are in a process of constant renewal in the sense that children are born and grow up and older people pass away: there is a continuous cycle of birth, aging, and death. This process give rise to social stratification by age groups or generations. As the renewal of human beings is continuous, it is not possible to make rigorous cut-off points to define sociologically a generational group. Age groups, like class and national groups, however, possess certain characteristics in terms of common interest, experience, and behavior, which give rise to shared expectations, and forms of social solidarity that separate groups of people on the basis of age.

Generational Change

One might distinguish between two types of age-based cleavage: life-cycle differences and generational change. Life-cycle differences involve statuses that are linked to age. People progress from infant to schoolchild to student to adult: different types and levels of behavior, authority, and possessions are associated with each age group. Students typically have no independent income and are maintained by their parents. It is only with adulthood that full legal and social rights are achieved. The significance of a life-cycle difference is that with the aging of a given cohort, its status changes in a fairly regular progression. The younger generation replaces an older one and its behavior accommodates to a new set of rules and expectations. In a life-cycle analysis, age groups are in flux: there may be a permanent tension between generations, which reflects inequalities of status and lifestyles, that may be inherited by subsequent age groups.

The second form of age-based cleavage is a generational change, which will be the foundation for exploring changes in consciousness in the Soviet Union. A change in generational age group brings new attitudes, behavior, and expectations. A younger group adopts a form of social distinction and identity engendered by growing up in a particular socio-political environment. At a formative stage of social and personal development, an age group may adopt a set of orientations, attitudes, or behaviors that are distinct from the set of attributes of other generations.

Unlike in the case of the life-cycle process, in a generational shift proper, attitudes and conduct developed in the formative years are not modified with age but continue into adult life. The new adult generation will have sets of behaviors different from the aging cohorts whom they replace. Generational changes may originate from a variety of causes. A generation might have experienced higher education, for instance, and this would have led to higher levels of skill and expectations in adult years. A generation might have grown up in a period of political turmoil or war, which would have had a greater impact on consciousness than on the former generation. For instance, military service in Vietnam, the Falklands, or Afghanistan leaves participants with attitudes that will remain with them for the rest of their lives.

To the extent that individuals of generational cohorts share sentiments in common and identify as a group, they form a subculture. Contemporary Soviet society should be conceived of as being made up of many such subcultures, and the generational attributes of those subcultures, I shall argue, are some of the most important causes of change in the contemporary USSR. They are independent of the boundaries of class, occupation, and nation and represent different forms of social mobilization. If they are in contradiction with the form of social structure legitimated by the dominant ideology, they constitute a counterculture.

How then does one demarcate shifts of a generational type? As we noted above, the constant passage of time and the steady stream of births make it impossible to mark off distinct generational boundaries. We may, however, make approximations concerning people who in their youth were exposed to different experiences in Soviet history. We may distinguish between five political generations:

• The revolutionary generation, born between 1900 and 1917 (under seventeen years of age in 1917) that grew up after 1917;

- The Second World War generation born between 1919 and 1930, at the beginning of the Second World War (1941) they were between eleven and twenty-two years of age;
- The postwar generation born between 1930 and 1940, between five and fifteen years of age in 1945;
- The post-Stalin generation born after 1941, the oldest were twelve years old at his death in 1953;
- The post-Khrushchev generation born after 1956, the oldest were seven years old at the downfall of Khrushchev in 1964.

These generations are illustrated in Figure 7.3.

To examine the changing attitudes of the younger generation in Soviet history is beyond our scope. One might, however, make some generalizations in terms of major attitudes that are likely to be linked with the rise of political generations. Three groups may be distinguished. First, a compliant generation which accepts the values of the ruling party and state, and is in support of the regime. Second, a privatized generation is subject to the output of government, but attempts to distance itself from politics; it is concerned more with individual advancement and benefits; and it is not compliant but is resigned to the regime. Third, a nonconformist generation disagrees openly with some major value of the regime and actively asserts its interest against it; and it is critical of the system of political and economic power.

Those born after 1917 and before 1930 spent most of their youth and adult years under Stalin. This was a period of intergenerational conflict. Studies of Soviet refugees conducted in the United States after the Second World War found that the younger generation was more supportive of the regime than the older generation that had known life before the revolution. The post-1917 generation had been "mobilized" by the Stalinist regime and had experienced social advance through education and jobs. The intergenerational conflict that arose in the 1930s is described by Inkeles and Bauer.

> We can understand why conflicts over religion and political belief permeated the reports on family life given by those from peasant and worker backgrounds. From the parents' point of view it seemed that their children were being torn away from them and won over to or at least significantly influenced to be irreligious and to support the Communist regime. The children, in turn, often felt their parents to be backward or ignorant, and thus were alienated from them. This was especially evident when the children were advancing themselves and thus coming ever more under the influence of values which ran counter to those of the parents. (1959: 216)

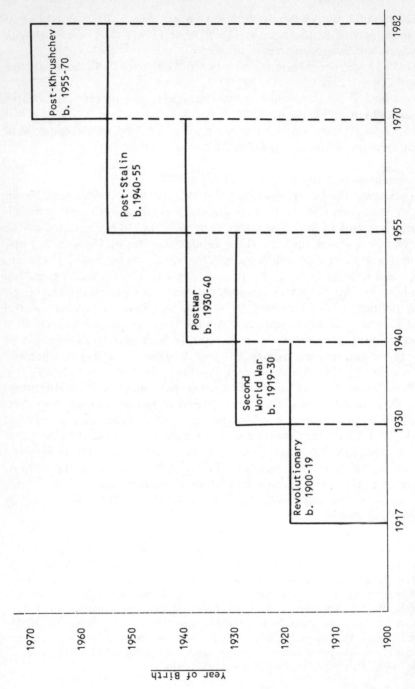

Figure 7.3 Political Generations

Since the death of Stalin in 1953, the post-Stalin generation (born between 1940 and 1956) has become more privatized. This generation has sought greater individual advancement, better housing, and a higher standard of living following the deprivation of the Second World War. A study of the second wave of Soviet immigrants to the United States (arriving in the 1970s) found that the older groups had greater support for the regime. In the 1970s and 1980s, nonconformity to regime norms and processes was greatest among the younger generation. The older generation (among whom figure a high proportion of manual and less well educated workers) were the most satisfied with the period of Brezhnev's rule. This group had experienced political stability, secure employment, and a steady rise in their standard of living. Unlike the adult revolutionary and Second World War generations that shared strong collective sentiments, the postwar generation was more concerned with individual advancement.

A Nonconformist Generation

The younger generation maturing after the fall of Khrushchev has been found to be far less compliant. This group contains a high proportion of second-generation urban dwellers who are better educated than their fathers and mothers. They have higher expectations for career development and an improvement in the standard of living. The consumer standards and way of life in the West are a major focus of this generation's concerns. A study of Soviet emigrants to the United States conducted in 1983 found that the younger the respondent, the less the satisfaction with health care, housing, jobs, and the standard of living (see Millar and Clayton 1989).

The post-Khrushchev generation is not only less compliant to established norms but is more actively nonconformist. It is assertive of its own individuality and seeks to express a consciousness foreign in many ways to that of the older generation.

The essence of the shift in outlook is from a consciousness of collective interest and an acceptance of a paternalistic regulated statist regime to a consciousness of self-interest, individual striving, and success. The paternalism of the statist regime and administered services takes second place to individualism, a consumer mentality, and a greater concern with money as a means of securing individual achievement. Table 7.5 shows the values of school pupils at a trade school and a high school (between fifteen and seventeen years of age approximately). All the questions posed referred (except the loaded final question) to individual rather than

Table 7.5
Moscow School Pupils' Values and Ambitions

	Trade School	Secondary School
Having close friends	97.7	95.9
Love	90.8	94.8
Interesting job	88.5	92.2
Being fashionable	77.7	90.6
Having a family	61.1	90.0
Study	53.8	57.8
Rock music	47.7	56.9
Money	38.2	60.2
Brand name items	37.7	69.9
Career	37.5	54.5
Sex	31.9	45.9
Emulating the West	16.9	33.7

Source: Interviews reported in *Literaturnaya gazeta*, 2 September 1987.
Selected items cited. Reported in *Soviet Sociology* 4 (26), 1988.

collectivist values. Friendship, love, and a profession all scored very highly. More "consumerist" values also had some high scores: "being fashionable" (77–90 percent), brand name items (38–70 percent), and money (38–60 percent). The article also pointed out that a significant number of secondary school pupils bought goods privately at speculative prices — in Erevan a third of the students did so (31 percent Moscow, 25 percent Leningrad, and 16 percent in Ashkhabad). Radios, stereos and clothing were the major items traded.

These changes in attitude are encapsulated by the Soviet sociologist Vladimir Yadov:

> For more than twenty years now we have been observing changes in the attitudes of young Leningrad workers to work. These changes are very significant. Public opinion in the 1960s condemned the striving for money and material comforts. It was considered vulgar even when the question was only a matter of recompense for labour. ... Today young people ... are more rationalistic. They fully expect material recompense, and there are few who are confused about this.

As the economy has developed enormously during the forty years of peace since the end of the Second World War, individual satisfaction for the Soviet citizen has taken the place of collective effort. Consumerism has become a motivating principle for life and it is not surprising that Soviet people have looked to the consumer societies of the West for artifacts. This trend is particularly important for the younger generation of the 1980s.

Also a change has taken place in the level of maturation. In earlier generations the period between physical maturity and an adult role was short. Since the 1950s there has been a considerable extension of full-time education, which has been coupled with a rising standard of living and a greater availability of money. This has given rise to a youth culture and has been accompanied by earlier physical maturity — a direct consequence of better nutrition. Social acceptance of the need for youth to indulge individual gratification through sexual intercourse has increased. Support for this view is given by a Soviet sociologist, Golod, who found that the age of initiation for sexual intercourse had fallen between the middle of the 1950s and the 1970s. The most frequent age of initiation into intercourse was 16—18 years for males (a figure rising in a twenty-year period from 22 percent to 40 percent) and 19—21 years for females (40 percent to 54 percent). Studies conducted by Golod among young people in the USSR show that those born and raised in large towns approved of premarital sexual relations. Educational level also is correlated with the acceptance of sexual relations outside of marriage. One study found that sexual relations between partners in love was considered legitimate by 88 percent of male and 95 percent of female students; for manual male workers the figure fell to 69 percent (82 percent for female); for clerical workers with a complete secondary education the figure was 86 percent for men (91 percent for women); it rose to 97 percent for men and 100 percent for women with higher education. Prostitution (sex for money) is certainly rising — Golod estimates that from 3 to 5 percent of youths have sex with prostitutes (for mature men the figure is much higher). A survey of the prostitutes themselves conducted in the Georgian Republic in the mid-1980s and reported by A. A. Gabiani and M. A. Manuil'ski, in the Soviet sociological journal, *Sotsiologicheskie issledovaniya* (no. 6, 1987), found that nearly three-quarters of the ladies questioned needed the money for clothes and cosmetics.

The longer prework period associated with extended education has strengthened peer culture and the increased paid labor participation of women in the economy has weakened the traditional binding effect of the family. All these factors have combined to strengthen bonds between members of the younger generation and to create a youth subculture with values and ways of behavior that are different from their parents'. This development has made it difficult for the formally organized official organization the Komsomol (discussed below) to maintain its leadership of Soviet youth. Although glasnost' has allowed for the expression of this youth subculture it has not caused a youth subculture to come about.

The nonconformist youth culture has taken many forms. Among the many *neformalnye* or "informal groups" (sometimes referred to as *samodeyatel'nye initsiativy*, independent initiatives) that have arisen are those devoted to rock and heavy metal music, drug addiction, Slav neofascism, Hare Krishna, Christianity, Islam, socialist fundamentalism, and assertive nationalism. The history of these groups may be traced back to the late 1950s. The Soviet writer Sundiev, for example, notes in *Sotsiologicheskie issledovaniya* in 1987 the rise of informal youth musical groups in the late 1950s (a group that coincides with what I have called the postwar generation). In the 1960s (the post-Stalin generation), Hippies, "Flower-children," and rock music made their appearance. In the 1970s and 1980s Sundiev points out that requirements in the Komsomol were ritualistic and formalistic and young people (the post-Khrushchev generation) increasingly turned to nontraditional ideas and types of activity.

In 1988 it has been estimated that 50 percent of the young people belonged to around thirty thousand informal groups (*Pravda*, 5 February 1988). In addition to the groups mentioned above are the various National Fronts, ecological and "Green" movements, and overtly nationalistic groups, such as *pamyat* among the Russian youth. The Komsomol, however, is still the largest youth organization although it is under pressure to change.

The Komsomol (Young Communist League)

The Young Communist League, the Komsomol, is the official organization to which nearly all young people between the ages of fourteen and twenty-eight years belong. The Komsomol is a professionally run organization directly linked to the Communist Party. It is not, however, a narrow political youth organization, such as the youth wings of Western parties: it includes activities associated with the Girl and Boy Scout movement — and much more. It owns, for example, three publishing houses and prints over 230 newspapers and magazines. It has premises for its clubs, and runs holiday camps, theaters, and sports activities; it has a vast travel bureau that caters not only to Soviet but also to foreign young people.

For youth in the early years of Soviet power (and perhaps for many conformist youth today), joining the Komosomol was a proud milestone in one's life because the organization symbolizes the collective consciousness that characterized the early Soviet regime. Induction is celebrated collectively in a joining ceremony usually held annually before some public monument. In semimilitary fashion, following a parade, rather like the Boys' Brigade of the British Commonwealth countries, the new member receives his or her membership card. A Soviet Jewish emigré recalls his feelings as follows: "I joined the Komsomol for purely ideological reasons when I was fourteen or fifteen years old and when I truly believed in the cause of the party and in the general cause of Soviet power" (cited by A. L. Unger 1981: 109).

The present younger generation is critical of the organization and activity of the Komsomol. There has been a high level of direction over the membership by the officials who fear change and want to replicate formal and old-fashioned activities. Soviet surveys and statements by leaders reveal that many members are disenchanted with the Komsomol. In 1987, for instance, Gorbachev criticized the privileged out-of-touch leaders of the Komsomol. According to an estimate by Jim Riordan, an authoritative Western writer, only about a "fifth or less of present members" would stay in the league if it were a genuinely voluntary body (1989).

At present, Komsomol membership can ensure success in many leisure activities, and a reference from the Secretary is often necessary for admission to college or for some jobs. For politically ambitious people, the Komsomol is an essential avenue to a Party career. This, of course, has led to accusations that "careerists" use the Komsomol to further their own advantage while they neglect the rank and file members. As Gorbachev remarked at the Komsomol's twentieth Congress in 1987, sometimes one "gets the impression that young people are walking on one side of the street, and Komsomol activists on the other. At times they even seem to be going in opposite directions." A lack of morale characterizes the official youth organization and in February 1988 it was reported that since 1985 membership had dropped by four million to a still not inconsiderable total of 38 million.

Informal Youth Groups

Disappointment with the Komsomol pushes Soviet youth in the direction of "informal" youth groups. A survey conducted in Moscow in March 1987 reported by Vera Tolz found that 52 percent of young engineering/technical members, 65.1 percent of young manual workers, 71.4 percent of students, 71.7 percent of tenth-grade high school pupils, and 89.4 percent of students at vocational-technical schools were members of "informal groups." In 1988 *Pravda* (1 February 1988) estimated that there was a total of thirty thousand such groups in the USSR. In June 1988 an article in *Kommunist* calculated that 7−8 percent of the urban population over the age of fourteen belonged to these organizations.

Informal groups are spontaneous circles of like-minded acquaintances and they span a very wide range of activities. While "informal groups" include older people, many of the activities are dominated by the younger generation and sets them off from their elders. It is these groups which will be our concern here.

Such associations have a counterculture: this entails an active opposition or rejection of a dominant value, process, or institution and its replacement by an alternative. The informal spontaneous youth groups that have blossomed in the major urban areas of the USSR under Gorbachev are manifestations of a nonconformist and individualistic orientation.

Such groups range from circles of friends following a football team, *fanaty*, to performers and devotees of rock and heavy metal music. They also include fascists, skinheads, punks, *Afghantsy* (veterans from Afghanistan), and *lyubery* (working class "hard cases" from the Moscow district of Lyubery). (The Green movement is very important and has much support among youth, and the "Democratic Union" also with large youth membership will be discussed below in Chapter 9, as part of the discussion of civil society.)

Pop music and rock groups (age group sixteen to twenty-two years) are probably the most numerous; they have been estimated at around one hundred thousand groups in 1985. Dating from the 1980s such groups copy Western styles embellished with their own originality. They are hampered in finding places to play, especially when the Komsomol organization is unsympathetic, because it can effectively control the opportunities for people to play publicly. "Groupies" (band followers) meet informally: in Leningrad, for instance, the youthful (fourteen to seventeen years old) followers of the Russian pop groups called *Sekrety* and *Alisovtsy* meet in the Rumyantsevski public gardens or at the Kazan Cathedral. They have adopted their own peculiar ways of dressing.

Sports fans (fourteen to twenty years old) follow all the well-known teams: the followers of Moscow Spartak are particularly notorious for creating trouble. Such groups develop a sense of identification with a local team which can lead to baiting and violence between fans. While not on the same scale as the mayhem caused by English or Italian supporters, often nasty incidents take place including attacks on the vehicles of opposing fans.

"Break dancers" (fourteen to twenty-five years old) were a mass phenomenon in the mid-1980s, and official breakdance competitions began in 1986. Punks and skinheads may be observed in Soviet cities doing much the same as they do in the West.

Pop music fans, football fans, and punks aspire to Western lifestyles. They adopt Western artists and groups and copy or buy Western attire on the black market. These groups are apolitical in a formal sense and most concerned with consumerism and leisure pursuits. They form counter-cultures in the sense that they reject the officially sponsored types of leisure and the commitment it entails: theirs is a protest against the authorities' control of culture. This is illustrated by the following lyrics from a Soviet rock song collected by Paul Easton ("The Rock Music Community," Riordan 1989: 64); it plays on the word "closed," which does not do justice to the Russian word *zakryt'*. (It has the sense here of an intransitive exclusion of people from things that make life worth living and creates a kind of alienation of a person from the world.)

I'm a closed citizen, lads and lasses,
I've a closed family.
Now I'm going to the closed shop
To buy some closed wine.
At home I'll crack it open
With my closed wife
And polish off my closed booze.
I'll hit the sack feeling queer.

The Soviet rock and pop scene is free from censorship. In Estonia a pop concert joint venture with Helsinki Radio One (ensuring hard currency earnings) in 1988 featured British Public Image Limited vocalist and former Sex Pistol star John Lydon, ironically then banned from performing on his home territory at the London Hammersmith Odeon.

Other informal youth groups are explicitly anti-Western and traditional in orientation. The *lyubery* are a notorious gang who emphasize martial arts and physical strength (a Soviet version of Kung Fu). They are particularly opposed to the extravagant style of hippies and punks, whom they physically attack (often with police connivance, it is asserted). The *fashisty*, literally fascists, are opposed to not only the Western decadence epitomized by pop and punks, but also the Communist values of the Soviet regime. The groups that have arisen in Moscow and Leningrad adopt Nazi symbols — the swastika, the salute — gather to celebrate Hitler's birthday, and some groups desecrate Jewish cemeteries. Some *fashisty* are not ideological fascists, but adopt fascist and Nazi symbols as a sign of opposition to the existing order, as emblems of rejection of things Soviet. Like many Nazis in Europe they see fascism (national socialism) as providing a means to a new society: the image is not unlike the goal of communism. The following was shown on a 1988 Soviet television film about Soviet young fascists:

Interviewer: Doesn't it seem like blasphemy to you that you are adopting the philosophy against which the country fought and which cost it quite a lot of blood?

Young man: We are still told that the country fought against this philosophy. Fascism can very quickly and effectively give what people need: first, wealth, second, living conditions, of course, which neither socialism or capitalism can offer ... fascism can build a really perfect society of perfect people very quickly.

The system (*sistema*) group (fourteen to thirty years old) is more concerned with spiritual renewal and shows some interest in religious ideas and mysticism. Pacifist groups (*pasifisty*) are more overtly political, arguing against militaristic tendencies and the political systems that promote them. Many reports have been made on Soviet television about the forcible procurement of conscientious objectors by the army. The *doveriya* (trust) group has been formed in support of such people. Such groups oppose more consciously some essential feature of the regime and organize their lives around an alternative.

To complete the political circle, a "Federation of Socialist Clubs" of young people has arisen out of the various "clubs for social initiatives" formed in the late 1980s. These groups support a renewed form of socialism and extol the virtues of perestroika and are a Soviet "New Left" similar in outlook and style to European groups of that name of the 1960s. Unofficial meetings between groups have been called in support of Gorbachev's policy and in opposition to adherents of Stalinism. The groups are beginning to form links one with another: on the seventieth anniversary of the Komsomol (1988) 170 political clubs, including the Federation of Socialist Public Clubs, the Democratic Faction, and supporters of the Moscow People's Front, debated in Moscow. At the Komsomol Conference itself, members of these groups made demands for greater independence from the Communist Party and for a more democratic leadership — elected from below, rather than allocated from the top.

The fighting by Soviet troops in the Afghanistan civil war was mainly carried out by young conscripts, of whom 13,833 died and 30,000 were wounded. In the period of Soviet intervention (1980–89) between fifteen and twenty thousand Soviet conscripts per year were sent to battle (some 140,000 men) — much fewer than the number of Americans in Vietnam — there were some half million American troops per year in Vietnam between 1965 and 1969. (The two operations are not strictly comparable: American discipline and morale were much lower, and the war more strongly opposed than was the Soviet presence in Afghanistan

— note the remarks cited at the Congress of People's Deputies, chapter 3.)

The Afghanistan experience marks off a segment of Soviet youth from the rest. Soviet forces were sent to Afghanistan to "fufill their internationalist and patriotic duty" to socialism. On return to the Soviet Union, many of these conscripts found life not to their liking. The reportage of the war did not portray the issues and the horror the Soviet troops encountered. The casualties in Afghanistan were suppressed. Soviet ex-servicemen were treated with indifference and insufficient respect by institutions and people responsible for their resettlement.

While most of the *afghantsy* found a niche in civilian life, many have formed associations to battle with the authorities for their rights. Campaigns have been instigated to secure services for the disabled. The *afghantsy* have opposed privilege and corruption — particularly the practice of not sending the sons of the upper status groups to war.

The more militant *afghantsy* are opposed to the Western values of consumerism adopted by other "nonconformist" Soviet youth. After they have fought for the good of the cause, they oppose the cynicism and corruption of Soviet life. They have tended to react against the influence of the West in the Soviet Union and seek a return to more traditional patriotic values. This group indicates a tendency towards a more assertive nationalism. Soviet television, for example, after covering the destruction of a criminal's grave — because it was placed near one of their deceased comrades — reported the following: the Afghan circumstances "somehow brought us together and gave us a kind of combat comradeship. But this comradeship doesn't always take the form of good actions aimed at things which are necessary and noble, nor is it always on the right side of the law." The *afghantsy* have not the significance of the American Vietnam vets, as the number of soldiers involved was much smaller.

Conclusion

It has been argued that there has been a generational shift away from a collectivist, compliant consciousness to one of self-interest, individual striving, and success. Glasnost' and demokratiya have led to the flowering of numerous "informal" groups of young people. The official youth organization, Komsomol, does not meet the aspirations of many youths and is in decline. This, again, reflects a difference in generational attitudes — a greater aspiration for individual expression rather than collective activity. Individualistic "pluralism" has replaced socialist collectivism.

The range of informal young people's groups illustrates the pluralism that has developed in the USSR. Individualism is expressed through various forms of consumerism and self-gratification as well as opposition to such consumerism. The previous forms of social solidarity — through *kollektivnost'* — have lost their binding effect. It is improbable that the Komsomol will be able to encompass such informal groups of youth.

The policy of perestroika involves the recognition and freedom of the individual. Pluralism is likely to lead to informal groups becoming increasingly independent of the Komsomol. Under Gorbachev the market is replacing administrative control — the market in the social sphere is reflected in the kind of pluralist associations described above. But the advent of *afghantsy*, *fashisty*, and *pasifisty* illustrates that the market in the sense of consumer fetishism is insufficient to hold society together.

Young people are searching for a different set of ideological values. There are analogies here with Christian revivalism and the antiabortion movements in the West (although there is no sign of the latter in the contemporary USSR). Pluralism and consumerism may be insufficiently powerful to fill the gap left by the collapse of traditional Soviet ideology. Into this vacuum may step a right-wing form of authoritarianism drawing on Stalinism, or — and most likely — an assertive Russian nationalism. The latter is likely to be fuelled by the nationalist movements in the non-Russian republics.

Selected Bibliography for Part Two

For journal and newspaper coverage and sources of statistical data see notes at the beginning of Reading for Part One. In addition *Soviet Sociology: A Journal of Translations* (M. E. Sharpe, Armonk, New York) contains very useful translations of Soviet sociological work.

Aage, Hans. 1989. "Wages, Education and Prestige for Various Occupations." Berkeley-Duke occasional papers on the Second Economy in the USSR. Durham, N.C.: Duke University, Department of Economics.

Anderson, B. A. 1987. "The Life Course of Women Born 1905–1960." *See* Millar 1987.

Bahry, D. 1987. *Outside Moscow: Power, Politics, and Budgetary Policy in the Soviet Republics*. New York: Columbia University Press.

Batygin, G. S. "'Virtue' against Interests." Translation. 1988. *Soviet Sociology* 27 (1): 37–57. Originally published in 1987 in *Sotsiologicheskie issledovaniya* 3: 24–36.

Bennigsen, A. and M. Broxup. 1983. *The Islamic Threat to the Soviet State*. London: Croom Helm.

Bennigsen, A. and S. E. Wimbush. 1986. *Muslims of the Soviet Empire*. New York: St. Martin's Press.

———1990. *The Islamic Threat to the Soviet State*. London: Routledge.

Bialer, S. 1980. *Stalin's Successors: Leadership, Stability and Change in the Soviet Union*. Cambridge and New York: Cambridge University Press.

Bialer, S., ed. 1989. *Politics, Society, and Nationality Inside Gorbachev's Russia*. Boulder: Westview Press. A good collection of articles on the Soviet Union written by prominent Western specialists.

Browning, G. K. 1987. *Women and Politics in the USSR: Consciousness Raising and Soviet Women's Groups*. Brighton: Wheatsheaf; New York: St. Martin's Press. Focuses on political inequalities from a socialist and feminist perspective.

Buckley, M. 1989. *Women and Ideology in the Soviet Union*. London: Harvester, Wheatsheaf.

Carrere d'Encausse, H. 1979. *Decline of an Empire: The Soviet Republics in Revolt*. New York: Newsweek Books.

Clem, R. S. 1988. "The Ethnic Factor in Contemporary Soviet Society." *See* Sacks and Pankhurst 1988.

Connor, Walker. 1984. *The National Question in Marxist-Leninist Theory and Strategy*. Princeton, N. J.: Princeton University Press.

Conquest, Robert. 1986. *The Last Empire*. Stanford: Hoover Institution Press.

Eberstadt, N. 1988. *The Poverty of Communism*. New Brunswick: Transaction Books.

Field, M. G. 1987. "The Contemporary Soviet Family: Problems, Issues, Perspectives." In *Soviet Society under Gorbachev: Current Trends and the Prospects for Reform*, ed. M. Friedberg and H. Isham. Armonk, N. Y.: M. E. Sharpe 3–29.

Golod, S. I. 1988. "Prostitutsiya v kontekste izmeniya polovy morali." *Sotsiologicheskie issledovaniya*, no. 2: 65–70.

Goble, Paul. 1989. "Ethnic Politics in the USSR." *Problems of Communism* 38, no. 4 (July–August): 1–14.

Gruzdeva, E. B. and E. S. Chertikhina. 1987. "The Occupational Status and Wages of Women in the USSR." *Soviet Sociology* 26 (3): 67–82.

Hoffmann, E. P. and R. F. Laird, eds. 1984. *The Soviet Polity in the Modern Era*. New York: Aldine Publishing. This collection contains many seminal articles.

Holland, B., ed. 1985. *Soviet Sisterhood*. Bloomington: Indiana University Press.

Ilves, T. 1989. "Estonian Poll on Independence, Political Parties." Radio Liberty, *Report on the USSR* 1, no. 22 (June): 14–16.

Inkeles, A. and R. A. Bauer. 1959. *The Soviet Citizen*. Cambridge, Mass.: Harvard University Press.

Jones, A., W. A. Connor and D. E. Powell (eds) 1991. *Soviet Social Problems*. London and Boulder: Westview.

Jones, E. and F. W. Grupp. 1984. "Modernization and Ethnic Equalization in the USSR." *Soviet Studies* 36 (2): 159–84.

———1987. *Modernization, Value Change and Fertility in the Soviet Union*. Cambridge and New York: Cambridge University Press. A scholarly and detailed study; useful to the specialist.

Kagarlitsky, B. 1987. "The Intelligentsia and the Changes." *New Left Review* 164 (July–August): 5–26.

Karklins, R. 1981. "Nationality Power in Soviet Republics: Attitudes and Perceptions." *Studies in Comparative Communism* 14, no. 1 (Spring): 70–93. This study is based on Soviet German emigrés.

———1986. *Ethnic Relations in the USSR*. London and Boston: Allen and Unwin.

———1987. "Nationality Policy and Ethnic Relations in the USSR." *See* Millar 1987.

Lapidus, G. W. 1978. *Women in Soviet Society*. Berkeley: University of California Press. A thorough comprehensive and scholarly study.

———1984. "Ethnonationalism and Political Stability: The Soviet Case." *World Politics* 36, no. 4 (July): 555–80.

Lubin, Nancy. 1984. *Labor and Nationality in Soviet Central Asia*. Princeton, N.J.: Princeton University Press.

Lyubery, 1987. (A collection of articles) *Current Digest of the Soviet Press* 39, no. 10 (8 April).

Mamonova, Tatyana. 1989. *Russian Women's Studies: Essays on Sexism in Soviet Culture*.

Oxford and New York: Pergamon Press. Short essays illustrating the Soviet feminist dissident viewpoint.

Marples, David. 1989. "Why the Donbass Miners Went on Strike." Radio Liberty, *Report on the USSR* 1, no. 36 (8 September): 30–32.

Matthews, M. 1986. *Poverty in the Soviet Union*. Cambridge and New York: Cambridge University Press.

McAuley, A. 1981. *Women's Work and Wages in the Soviet Union*. London: Allen and Unwin.

Millar, J. R., ed. 1987. *Politics, Work and Daily Life in the USSR: A Survey of Former Soviet Citizens*. Cambridge and New York: Cambridge University Press. Survey of Soviet immigrants to the United States (mainly Jewish).

Millar, J. R. and E. Clayton. 1989. "Quality of Life: Subjective Measures of Satisfaction." *See* Millar 1989.

Muckle, James. 1988. *A Guide to the Soviet Curriculum*. London: Croom Helm.

Rimashevskaya, N. 1988. "Current Problems of the Status of Women." *Soviet Sociology* 27 (1): 58–71. Useful study of Soviet sociologist's approach to women in the USSR.

Riordan, J. 1988. "Soviet Youth: Pioneers of Change." *Soviet Studies* 15, no. 4 (October): 556–72.

Riordan, Jim. ed. 1989. *Soviet Youth Culture*. London: Macmillan. This book contains some contributions on "The Rock Music Community" by Paul Easton, and two articles by Riordan: one on "Teenage Gangs, *Afgantsy* and *Neofascists*," the other, "The Komsomol."

Russian Nationalism Today. Radio Liberty. Special Bulletin (19 December). Contains articles by two American specialists, John B. Dunlop and Darrell P. Hammer, and Soviet emigrés Andrey Sinyavsky and Alexander Yanov.

Ryan, M. 1990. *Contemporary Soviet Society: A Statistical Handbook*. Aldershot and Vermont: Edward Elgar. Useful source book of Soviet statistics under perestroika. Includes basic population data, education, crime, women and life expectancy.

Rytkevich, M. N. 1986. "Sotsialisticheskaya spravedlivost." *Sotsiologicheskie issledovniya* 3: 13–23. This was translated in 1987: "Socialist Justice." *Soviet Sociology* 27, no. 3 (Winter): 52–66.

Rywkin, M. 1979. "Central Asia and Soviet Manpower." *Problems of Communism* 28, no. 1.

———1989. *Soviet Russia Today*. New York: M.E. Sharpe.

Sacks, M. P. 1982. *Work and Equality in Soviet Society: The Division of Labor by Age, Gender and Nationality*. New York: Praeger.

———1988. "Women, Work and Family in the Soviet Union." *See* Sacks and Pankhurst 1988.

Sacks, M. P., and J. G. Pankhurst, eds. 1988. *Understanding Soviet Society*. Boston and London: Unwin Hyman.

Shchekochikhin, Iiuri. 1988. "Before the Mirror." *Soviet Sociology* 26, no. 4 (Spring): 16.

Shlapentokh, V. 1990. *Soviet Intellectuals and Political Power*. London: Taurus.

Simis, K. 1982. *Secrets of a Corrupt Society*. London: Dent.

Smith, D. 1989. "Formation of New Russian Nationalist Group Announced." Radio Liberty, *Report on the USSR* 1, no. 27 (7 July): 5–7.

Smith, Graham (ed.) 1990. *The Nationalities Question in the Soviet Union*. London and New York: Longman. Individual chapters on 20 Soviet nationalities, written by eminent specialist.

Szporluk, Roman. 1989. "Dilemmas of Russian Nationalism." *Problems of Communism* 38, no. 4 (July–August): 15–35.

Teague, E. 1989. "Embryos of People's Power." Radio Liberty, *Report on the USSR* 1 (32): 1–4.

Tedstrom, J. 1989. "USSR Draft Program on Republican Economic Self-Management: An

Analysis." Radio Liberty, *Report on the USSR* 1, no. 16 (21 April): 1–8.

Ticktin, Hillel. 1988. "The Contradictions of Gorbachev." *Journal of Soviet Studies* 4, no. 4 (December): 83–99.

Tolz, Vera. 1988. "Informal Groups in the USSR." *Washington Quarterly* (Spring): 137–144.

———1989. "The United Front of Workers of Russia: Further Consolidation of Antireform Forces." Radio Free Europe and Radio Liberty, *Report on the USSR* 1, no. 39 (29 September): 11–13.

Trehub, A. 1989. "The Congress of People's Deputies on Poverty." Radio Liberty, *Report on the USSR* 1, no. 24 (16 June): 5–9.

Unger, A. L. 1981. "Political Participation in the USSR: YCL and CPSU." *Soviet Studies* 33, no. 1 (January): 109.

USSR Academy of Science. 1988. *Social Policy of the CPSU*. Moscow: Nauka. Contains useful collection of Soviet articles particularly by A. G. Zdravomyslov, and T. Zaslavskaya.

Vinokur, A. and G. Ofer. "Inequality of Earnings, Household Income and Wealth in the Soviet Union in the 1970s." *See* Millar 1987.

Walker, Martin. 1986. *The Waking Giant: The Soviet Union Under Gorbachev*. London: Michael Joseph. Especially Chapter 11, "The Women's Lot."

Wilber, C. K. 1976. *The Soviet Model and Underdeveloped Countries*. Chapel Hill: University of North Carolina Press.

Yadov, V. 1988. Discussion cited in I. Shchekochikhin, "Before the Mirror," *Soviet Sociology* 26, no. 4 (Spring): 16.

Yanowitch, M. 1986. *The Social Structure of the USSR*. Armonk, N.Y.: M. E. Sharpe. A useful collection of Soviet articles on social stratification.

Yanowitch, M., ed. 1989. *A Voice of Reform: Essays by Tat'iana I. Zaslavskaia*. Armonk, N.Y.: M. E. Sharpe. Translated essays by one of the leading sociologists of the reform movement. Contains the important "Novosibirsk Report."

Zdravomyslov, A. G. 1988. "Social Policy in Socialist Countries: Common and Specific Features." In *The Social Policy of the CPSU*. Moscow: Nauka, 76–93.

Part Three ——————————————————

SOCIAL CONTROL

Chapter 8

FORMING THE SOVIET PERSON

Education, Socialist Ritual, and Tradition

At the beginning of part 2, I pointed out that a society may be thought of in terms of a social structure: positions, statuses, networks of relationships, and patterns of behavior between groups of people. Furthermore we discussed the kinds of groups that give human beings social and individual identity: "class groups" of workers and collective farmers; occupational segmentation of professionals, white-collar and unskilled workers; ethnic and national groups; and divisions by gender and age. In this and the following chapters we will consider the ways that social control is exercised in Soviet society: Do the various groups and processes cohere to form a whole? How do the dominant institutions and people manage tension and adapt to the physical environment to ensure the reproduction and growth of human life? How are deviance and conflict between the various social strata contained?

In the chapters that follow this one we shall examine the mass media, which plays a dominant part in creating values and beliefs, and the role of resistance to the dominant institutions. Finally, we will study the ways that consensus is achieved through the provision of social and collective services — the provisions of the Soviet welfare state. As in earlier chapters, the ways in which the policies and outlook of the Soviet leadership are responding to and attempting to adapt to the changing social structure is a common theme.

In this chapter we consider first the process of education: the explicit attempt to mold the younger generation through the provision of systematic instruction in schools. As the eminent sociologist Emile Durkheim put it, education is the "methodical socialization of the young generation." Secondly, we will consider the informal ways in which socialization takes place through exploring how the rituals and traditions of cultural management unite and divide people.

At first sight, it may appear a trifle curious that education, rituals, and traditions are grouped under the rubric of socialization. The three processes have like ways of ensuring compliance in society and maintaining cohesion and integration. Education is a mechanism that principally uses persuasion to ensure the compliance of the population to the dominant values of society. Rituals and traditions appeal to emotions, to people's sentiments and passions, and are manipulative in character.

VALUES AND NORMS

All societies have systems of values and norms, which are notions of what constitutes appropriate social behavior. They involve expectations about conduct in the multiplicity of social situations in which people find themselves. For instance, at the personal level we all have ideas about punctuality and about the proper authority of parents, policemen, and priests. At the level of the state, we all have views about the legitimacy of democracy or private ownership and about the rightness of sending American or British troops to quell "forest fires" when they break out in Third World countries. The process of socialization is concerned with the ways that children and adults learn about and are inculcated with the ideas of social behavior and right conduct (social justice) — how they learn about a society's culture.

Communities are often defined by their different patterns of values and beliefs or their unique cultures. Travellers often perceive what they consider to be oddities in the behavior of foreigners, which they put down to the fact that they have had a different form of upbringing. Even within societies, various social groups may be seen to have different patterns of values and behavior. Western societies pride themselves on being "pluralist," containing many partial societies and independent groups; notably the existence of religious denominations, ethnic, professional, and linguistic groupings. In addition, however, sociologists and political scientists often assert that there are common values and beliefs that unite all people in a nation. Despite the ethnic, regional, and religious differences within the United States, Great Britain, or the USSR, it is generally held that these countries are distinctive in certain ways and the people within these societies share a common value system. Just what these value systems are and how far they cohere is a matter of opinion.

As noted in the first chapter, the USSR is labelled in the West a "Communist" society inhabited by "Communists." In return, Soviet writers and social scientists used to define the Western states as "capitalist," and the leading ones, particularly the United States, as "imperialist." According to those who view Soviet society as totalitarian, the state inculcates a common pattern of "Communist" values through the schools and mass media. The existence of autonomous groupings in society is prevented by the omnipotent state. Until the time of Gorbachev this ideological position was not disputed by Soviet writers and statesmen who emphasized the political unity and solidarity of Soviet socialism, its *kollektivnost'*.

These black-and-white pictures have never been true. The indoctrination of political Marxist-Leninist values has always taken place in conjunction with traditional, nationalist, religious, and patriotic beliefs. While the state may attempt to inculcate a unitary pattern of political sentiments, it may not be successful; individuals and groups may be resistant to the effects of propaganda. Attitudes to the West have also been more differentiated — the perspectives we have already studied in our discussion of nationality and ethnic consciousness in the Soviet Union are witness to this fact.

THE EDUCATIONAL SYSTEM

The educational system in all societies has a crucial role to play in the process of socialization. Under state socialism it is a major institution that the political rulers may utilize as a means of effecting social change or indoctrination. In the USSR, however, education is not only concerned with the formation of the "Communist person": it plays an important role in teaching those skills required by the economy. Furthermore, higher education is often encumbered with a research role, with not only reproducing knowledge but creating new knowledge. In recognition of the division of labor, education not only prepares pupils for life but allocates them to different occupations and the social statuses that go with work. Education also promotes the cultural and technical achievements of a society: it acquaints pupils with language, literature, science, and art.

These various functions of educational institutions help to explain why schools and colleges often perform inadequately as instruments of the political order. Integration in society ("toeing the Party line") may be at variance with the innovative frame of mind required in science and business. Teachers and educators themselves have considerable discretion in the emphasis they may put on political or creative demands. The needs of the economy, in turn, may be spurned by the educational community, which may be more concerned with the creative roles of personality development through art, language, and science than with vocational training. Hence one cannot regard educational institutions as instruments of the apparatus or political elite, but as sites in which conflicting demands are mediated by educators. Governments can and do influence the content and process of the educational system, which is one of the chief instruments in all societies for imparting values and norms.

Primary and Secondary Education

One of the successes of Soviet education has been the mass inculcation of elementary knowledge of language and basic math skills. Before the revolution literacy was low: according to the 1897 census only 24 percent of the total population over nine years of age was literate. The younger age cohorts enjoyed better educational opportunities and by 1914 the tsarist order had succeeded in creating ten million places in primary and secondary schools. In Central Asia under 10 percent of the population was literate, though in the Baltic provinces of Lithuania, Latvia, and Estonia rates ranged from 65 to 79 percent of the total population. Some progress with higher educational institutions had been made by 1914: there were 105 colleges, including eight universities; enrollment totalled 127,400 students.

During the period of industrialization, the educational system was rapidly expanded. In 1930 four years of compulsory primary education was instituted in the countryside and seven years of secondary education in the towns. This development succeeded in inculcating basic ideas of order, numeracy, and literacy, and by 1939 it was claimed that 81 percent of the population over nine years of age could read.

Today there is a universal state system of education and there is no private school sector. Schools are coeducational. With the exception of some special schools, education is comprehensive and pupils pursue a common syllabus. The schools "with a special profile" are elitist: they number about 1.2 percent of secondary schools and specialize in languages, sciences, and technical subjects. In addition there are segregated schools for physically disabled and retarded children, many of which are residential. There is no movement for the integration of the latter groups into ordinary schools.

The education system attempts to maintain uniform standards throughout the USSR; syllabuses are drawn up centrally though modified by the Union Republics. Variations in syllabus reflect regional differences, most importantly education is in the vernacular language in the Republics — though Russian-language schools are also available. Teaching methods are prescribed. The main emphasis has been on factual mastery and rote learning. Until the 1980s there was little project or individually based problem solving teaching. "Moral education" was guided by the values of Marxism-Leninism spiced with patriotic sentiments: discipline, socialist labor, and loyalty to the Soviet state and the Communist Party are explicit objectives of socialization.

Until the 1970s Soviet education was regarded as successful. The flight of Yuri Gagarin (the first man in space) was widely considered to be a success of the Soviet educational system. The number of people with higher educational qualifications increased from 65 per thousand employees in 1970, to 125 in 1987 (*Narkhoz za 70 let* (1987): 524). The pupil teacher ratio is low — only 17 pupils per teacher in 1980, falling to 14.6 in 1986 (*Narkhoz za 70 let* (1987): 528). Soviet science, it was claimed, had caught up with and even outstripped the United States in space research; its nuclear capacity was an indication of technological advance.

Nevertheless, in the 1970s concern was expressed at the inadequacies of the system. Other indicators showed that education was not receiving sufficient investment: in 1970 educational spending accounted for 11 percent of the Soviet budget, by 1986 it had dropped to 8 percent. Politburo member Ligachev, in 1988, deplored the low level of capital investment in education, the inadequate buildings, and the lack of computers and relevant educational facilities.

The major shortcomings of the educational system were the lack of vocational preparation of pupils for the world of work, and the mismatch between the aspirations of pupils and the supply of jobs. School graduates and their parents preferred nonmanual professional and research jobs over those on the shopfloor. Furthermore, whilst the supply of graduates from the educational system was supposed to be geared to the needs of industry, some fifty percent of the graduates from higher education performed jobs not needing their educational qualifications. Education, it was argued, was separated from life.

Reform of the Schools
In the 1980s, education became more differentiated and closely linked to the needs of a more sophisticated and specialized economy. In 1984 an educational reform was enacted. It emphasized vocational-technical education and a greater concern for a more analytical understanding by pupils. A key phrase in the draft guidelines of the 1984 act declared that "all main indicators of the system of education and training of manpower must be strictly determined by the requirements of the national economic complex."

The 1984 act increased the length of schooling by one year: there are now eleven grades and children begin school at the age of six. The first nine years of education are common to all pupils because the objective is to provide a general and common education for all with regional variations and adaptation for children with special needs.

The 1984 reform has led to greater differentiation and a greater vocational emphasis after the ninth grade. The general schools, which prepare pupils for higher education, are targeted for only 30 percent of the student cohort, the remainder will enter vocational schools. In the final two years (tenth and eleventh grades) vocational students will continue their education in language, mathematics, physical education, and science, but in addition they will have considerable production training and become skilled in a trade. Students attending a secondary trade school (SPTU) will reach a standard in their general studies sufficient to qualify for entry to a university or institute.

The 1984 reform will probably lead to a more highly stratified educational and social system. Even before the 1980s the educational system did not afford equal opportunity. Figure 8.1 compares the social composition of the population of the USSR with the percentage of first year students of higher education in day departments. Whereas manual workers accounted for 60 percent of the population, the full-time students entering higher education in 1979 from that background only came to 47.3 percent; the

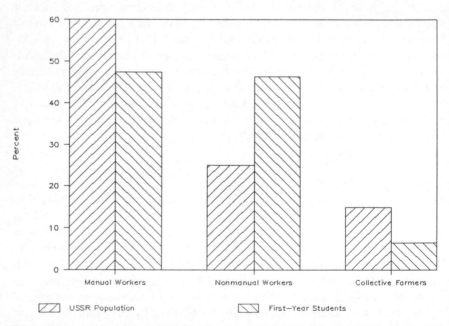

Figure 8.1 Social Composition of First-Year Students of Higher Education (Day Departments), 1979
Source: Based on data from Rutkevich et al., *Sovetskaya sotsiologiya*, 1982.

respective proportions for nonmanual workers were 25 percent and 46.2 percent and for collective farmers 15 percent and 6.5 percent.

When one considers the recruitment of students by educational institutions one again sees important social differences in the composition of the student body. Figure 8.2 shows the four types of higher educational institution — university humanities faculty, technical institutes, agricultural institutes, and medical institutes — and attending students by occupation of father in four groups — manual workers, unqualified nonmanuals, specialists (professionals), and collective farmers. Although they represent only 25 percent of the population, the children of professional background predominated in the medical institutes, technical institutes, and the humanities faculty of the universities. Collective farmers' children were well represented in the agricultural institutes, and manual workers' offspring did best in the technical institutes. There is, as in Western countries, a definite correlation between parental background and educational achievement, measured in terms of access to higher educational institutions.

The reforms will strengthen this tendency. The universities and higher educational institutes (having the status of institutions of technology in

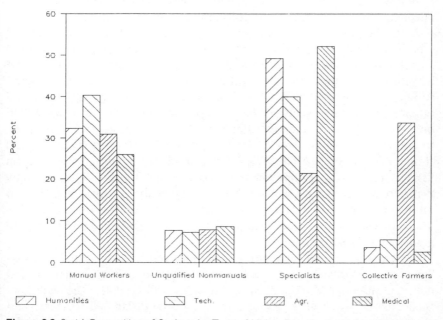

Figure 8.2 Social Composition of Students by Type of Higher Education Institution, 1977–78

Source: Based on data from Rutkevich et al., *Sovetskaya sotsiologiya*, 1982.

the United States or polytechnics in Britain) will continue to attract pupils wanting professional and executive positions in industry and government. Social selection will be in favor of the children of the intelligentsia, who will be able to compete educationally more successfully than children with lower social backgrounds. The smaller number of students admitted to the general secondary schools will necessitate greater educational selection earlier on in the educational life of the pupils.

While the state has a monopoly over the provision of schools, some extra schooling can be provided privately through tutoring. Coaching for entrants to universities is widespread with from 50 percent of university applicants in the provinces to 90 percent in Moscow receiving such instruction. Such teaching compensates for inadequacies in the teaching in secondary schools, which, in turn, creates further inequalities in educational opportunity as social class of parents determines whether school pupils receive such help. The tendency towards greater educational inequality will continue.

Although no major movement towards privatization is planned, possible sources of finance are production done in schools, or payment for pupils' labor by industrial enterprises. Another variant of industrial "sponsorship" would be contractual relations between educational institutions and industry whereby schools that "deliver" trained labor receive per capita payment. This is sometimes debated in the Soviet press but is not yet policy.

As to the content of education, the post-1984 program in the general school is heavily weighted towards science. The number of periods over an eleven-year school course are the following: (Russian) language and literature 81, mathematics 60.5, other science subjects 40.5, physical education 22, vocational and labor training 28, foreign language 14, and other humanities subjects 57 (state and law and social studies totalled only 3.57). (Figures refer to total periods per week over eleven years: to find the average per week, per year, divide by eleven.) (Data derived from Muckle 1988: 19.) The 1984 reform has mildly supported an extension in the number of "options" in the secondary school; but there are only two periods per week set aside for options in the seventh, eighth, and ninth grades; three in the tenth; and four in the last year. Computer studies are compulsory in the tenth grade (one session per week) and in the final grade (two classes per week).

The emphasis in the curriculum is on industrial/scientific skills, whereas "political" indoctrination is a relatively small part of the curriculum and the inculcation of Marxist-Leninist ideology will decline. The values of "collectivism" defined as "a concrete, all-proletarian, all-socialist, and all-communist fusion of millions of wills into a single will" have in the past been emphasized by Western and Soviet commentators. This quotation is taken from a book on Marxist ethics published in 1976. (For further discussion see Zajda 1980: 118−19.) But the reforms of the 1980s have played down such sentiments, which are now replaced by a more individualist and self-seeking orientation.

The formal authoritarian methods of teaching favored in the pre-1980 period have been widely condemned by educational reformers in the USSR. The syllabuses introduced in 1984 aim to reduce the amount of information to be memorized and put a greater emphasis on pupils' own activity and interest-centered learning, thinking, and independent initiative. As Ligachev put it in 1988 when commenting on the reform, the goal "consists in giving schools the right to be creative, to choose the methods of instruction and of organizing the instructional and upbringing process and to work out innovative ideas of upbringing. ... [We should] devote our main attention to the development of pupils' individual abilities."

These attitudes are influenced by and in turn impact on the political culture of the USSR. The educational reform is designed to link education more closely with the economy and to create a more pluralistic and individualistic society. In the 1960s Western observers of the Soviet scene were impressed by the consensus and good public behavior of children. As Bronfenbrenner put it in 1971 after doing a comparative study of Soviet and American and European children "Soviet children, in the process of growing up, are confronted with fewer divergent views both within and outside the family and, in consequence, conform more completely to a homogeneous set of standards" (1971: 81). In the 1980s the scene changed. The greater heterogeneity, pluralism, and assertiveness of youth noted above in chapter 7 is a reflection of the influence of divergent and conflicting claims. Eltsin in a speech to the Executive Committee of the Moscow Soviet in 1986 criticized the deficiencies in the methods of upbringing of school children and complained about the incidence of narcotics and crime, as well as the inadequacy in military patriotic upbringing. These shortcomings are not just a failure of the teachers, but, as argued in chapter 7, they have come about as a result of a generational change and are a source of tension in the educational system.

Higher Education

Higher education in the Soviet Union replicates the functions of the secondary schools: it inculcates values; forms adult personalities; allocates statuses, jobs, and professions; trains personnel for the economy; and pursues the discovery of new knowledge. In doing so, it reproduces the system of social relations. Higher education is not simply a "transmission belt" for the Communist Party's political elite to indoctrinate the intelligentsia, rather it is a site of contradictions or tensions between the achievement of these objectives.

Until the 1980s the main thrust of the system of higher education was to inculcate values in the student community appropriate for "nation building" and to train skilled specialists for the economy. Higher education was expansionist and mass based. In the latter respect Soviet higher education is more like that of the United States than European states, the emphasis being on educating large numbers rather than on producing a high quality educational elite. In 1987–88 there were 898 higher educational establishments, including 69 universities. (Between 1965 and 1985, 138 new higher institutions of education (*vuzy*) were founded.) In the 1987–88 school year, for example, there were over five million students in various forms of higher education (181 per ten thousand of the population), in Britain in 1979–80 the comparative figure was 0.58 million (105 per ten thousand). Of Western capitalist countries only the United States and Canada had higher levels of participation: the United States had 6.1 million students in 1983–84 (263 per ten thousand of the population).

Degree courses are largely vocational in nature. In 1986 students pursuing degrees related to industry, building, transport, communications, and agriculture were some 54 percent of the total; economics, law, health, physical education, art, and cinematography 14.4 percent; and the remaining students were in the humanities — destined mainly to become school teachers. Unlike in the United States and Canada, there are no liberal arts courses intended to give a general education suitable for citizenship or a wide range of jobs in business, administration, and public services.

A second feature of Soviet higher education that is different from the West is the large number of part-time and correspondence course students: in 1986 of first year entrants to higher education, only 59 percent were full time; 12 percent were in evening classes, and 29 percent were studying by correspondence. Due to high levels of dropouts by part-timers these levels are not maintained in subsequent years.

Courses in higher education last from four to five and a half years: medicine, five and a half; law, history, and journalism, four and a half; engineering, five. Courses include other subjects (about 10 to 16 percent of a student's contact hour time) — including a foreign language and physical education. In their final year students usually prepare a dissertation. There is an emphasis on didactic methods: there are many lectures, and comprehension and memorizing factual knowledge are stressed. As in the schools, individual project linked work and analysis has not been much favored.

In the 1987–88 school year, of the student body of five million,

35 percent were doing correspondence courses and another 11 percent studied in evening schools. Costs of higher education are low: the direct costs of education for a full-time student in the 1970s were 920 rubles, for an evening student 268 rubles and by correspondence only 107 rubles. This reflects the relatively low pay of teaching staff, and low outlays on buildings, libraries, and materials. Fees are paid by the state, not the students. Students receive grants from the government that are linked to parental income and that are sufficient to cover modestly the needs of students.

As in the secondary school system, there are no private institutions or schools funded or sponsored by charitable trusts. All higher education is carried out by agencies of the government or Party. It would be mistaken, however, to think of higher education as being homogeneous and controlled by a unitary state agency. The USSR has never been "a single bureaucracy, writ large," as some commentators have asserted. Various institutions and ministries organize and effectively control their own educational institutions. Research is carried out by the USSR and fourteen republican academies (the RSFSR does not have one), which include academies of various professions (agriculture, medicine, art, and pedagogy). Most teaching is carried out under the auspices of the State Committee for Education, which in 1988 replaced two previous ministries. (The previous Ministry of Higher and Specialized Secondary Education controlling 351 institutions organized higher education.) In addition, ministries in industry, health, social services, and culture all run separate higher educational institutions, for example, the ministry of agriculture organizes ninety-nine institutions and civil aviation five. Such institutions pursue teaching and research in their respective fields of expertise. Finally, the Communist Party has its own system of academies and schools concerned with training specialists in the social sciences, policy-related research, and the education of cadres. Such courses range from part-time evening courses to research at the postdoctoral level.

Reform of Higher Education
Soviet higher education has accomplished much in terms of raising the general standards of the masses. It was particularly appropriate for the demands of rapid industrialization, and it has also succeeded in training an elite in science and mathematics comparable to the best in the West. In the 1980s, however, the slowdown of the economy was partly attributed to an inappropriate and inadequate system of higher education. As with the school provision noted above, the proportion of the state budget allocated to higher education declined from 1.47 percent in 1965 to 0.97 percent in 1986.

The USSR was particularly backward in electronics, computer science, and high technology in general. While the number of trained specialists with qualifications increased, their qualifications and the training of pupils were held to be inappropriate for the needs of an advanced economy. A reform of higher education ("Basic Directions for the Restructuring of Higher and Specialized Secondary Education") was enacted in 1987.

We may itemize the major difficulties that it attempted to confront as follows:

1. A decline in attractiveness of higher education on the part of intending pupils and staff. This was due to a decline in wage differentials between "specialists" (professionals) and other types of work, particularly manual work;
2. The "wastage" of graduates who failed to pursue jobs related to their training courses. For the 1975–80 period, one study showed that only 57.2 percent of graduates of teachers' colleges took teaching jobs and only half of graduates in industry used their specialist qualification directly in their work;
3. Inefficiency on the part of teachers, insufficient awareness of new knowledge, and absence of innovative research;
4. Lack of linkage and coordination between higher education and the needs of industry. This was due to the large number of independent education establishments (as noted above) and inadequate penetration of new disciplines (such as management education) in industry. It is gratifying to read that the USSR needs sixty to seventy thousand sociologists, but disappointing that in 1989 they were only turning out 100 per year;
5. Because of low standards many students with inadequate knowledge were "pushed through"; evening and part-time students were universally considered to be at much lower levels than day students;
6. Inappropriate teaching methods; courses were overspecialized and lacked intellectual flexibility to meet the requirements of technical change; an excessive emphasis on lectures and rote learning conjoined with "formalism" and mechanistic examining; in short, the absence of independent thinking and creative problem-solving.

Degree programs are to be evaluated to bring them closer to life. More independent study and seminar work is projected to replace lectures. Computer technology and knowledge of foreign languages are to be developed. Economic principles — the ideas of cost consciousness and efficiency — as well as management methods are to be introduced more widely into the curriculum. Educational institutions are to be drawn into market relations. In the social sciences and humanities a more open frame of mind and Western techniques and theories are to be encouraged.

Salaries of staff in higher education are to be raised but linked to the evaluation of lecturers' work. More emphasis is to be put on "raising the qualifications" of professionals in employment and in-service training. Higher educational institutions are to benefit from higher levels of investment and refurbishment.

Many of the above inadequacies also confront educational systems in the West. Educational institutions find it easier to replicate existing knowledge rather than act as agents of inquiry. The absence of a direct market link to reject irrelevant knowledge or incompetent provision in institutes of higher education has attracted the attention particularly of right-wing reformers in the West in the 1980s.

The "Basic Directions for Restructuring ..." indicate the kinds of reforms that the political leadership under Gorbachev would like to introduce. The major objective is to bring the educational system into line with the requirements of *uskorenie* (acceleration); linkage with the economy (efficiency) and its needs are uppermost. "Deepening the integration of higher education and production is not just one aspect of the restructuring; it is the basis for understanding all aspects of it."

Greater emphasis is to be put on research contracts and the ability of research institutions in higher education to "sell" their research to industry, which means that in applied fields, institutes will increasingly have to find their own sources of funding or be dissolved. It is proposed that joint units on the lines of Western "science parks" be created. These are to be called "instructional-scientific-production complexes." Such units combine industrial production and research with educational institutions.

"Contracts" are advocated between industry and educational institutions. (These are similar to schemes introduced in Britain in the late 1980s.) Faculties or departments contract to provide industrial enterprises with qualified students who on graduation will join the factory. These schemes involve general theoretical training during the first few years at the higher educational institute followed by more specific on-the-job training and work at the enterprise. Such links enable research projects to be completed at the enterprise and allow for the exchange of staff; enterprises are to help in the financial provision of the training; in return, they receive qualified and motivated staff.

In order to strengthen the link between education and industry, certain institutions have geared student recruitment to "contracts" received from industry. The Moscow Plekhanov Institute, for instance, starting in 1988−89 takes students for whom a future employer is ensured − and the students have to accept the employer before admission (see Cooper

1988: 220). It is envisaged that the financing of the student will eventually be provided by the student's employers, which will make the Institute "self-financing." Such schemes, however, have been criticized on the grounds that they commercialize education, and many industrial enterprises are not particularly interested in them and are unwilling to commit resources to them.

Education and Perestroika

Study of the educational system draws attention to the conditions that gave rise to perestroika and to some of the contradictions in Gorbachev's policy.

The educational system was formed in the period of rapid industrialization of the USSR. According to a commentator at the Congress of Workers in Public Education in December 1988, "For sixty years, all we did was fulfill and execute directives." The system of education succeeded in creating a literate population and a stratum of professionals and workers with adequate levels of knowledge and skill. It made rudimentary education available for all and sought to inculcate norms of loyalty and solidarity to the new Soviet power. Teaching methods encouraged the absorption of knowledge and passive learning techniques were employed. By the 1980s such goals and methods were obsolete.

The objective of *uskorenie* (acceleration) requires a different type of Soviet person and the educational system needs to repond to this agenda. Reforms propose that the educational process be based less on "command" and more on "cooperation." This involves a more negotiated style of management in the schools, with head teachers taking note of the wishes of staff, pupils, and parents. The aim here is to create a more participatory rather than an authoritarian subculture in the schools.

A closer integration of education with the requirements of the economy is the first priority of the government. This has led to a greater emphasis on vocational education and firmer links between industry and education. Greater store is also placed on quality and greater differentiation of the educational system is likely. Computerization is a major goal. The status of higher education will be raised by rewarding graduates with greater income differentials.

Glasnost' is a lever to be used against inertia and vested interests, particularly in the industrial educational institutes, but also against sloppiness in teaching, research, and study elsewhere. But educational systems are resistant to change: because their purpose is to replicate knowledge, the creation of new knowledge sits uneasily with traditional practices. Many Soviet leaders have pointed to the opposition to the new policies from educators. Eltsin complained in 1986 about the lack of glasnost' in the educational system and the absence of a sense of the need for reform on the part of teachers. Gorbachev objected in 1987 that "the work of the USSR Ministry of Education and all its organs is at a standstill." Ligachev in February 1988 pointed out that reform has "been limited to insignificant shifts" and complained about the "listlessness of organizational work to advance the projected transformations. ... Management of the schools by the Ministry of Education and the USSR State Committee for Vocational and Technical Education is carried out primarily by bureaucratic methods and in a conservative spirit." Communist Party Secretary Zimyanin in 1988 said:

> The main thing called for in the reform — substantial changes in the organization and content of the teaching and educational activities of the general and vocational schools, changes in the effort to enhance the level of students' knowledge, changes in the style and methods of a substantial portion of teaching collectives and teachers — has yet to take place.

Government policy now requires greater initiative and independent thought on the part of citizens. People are to become self-motivating and self-interested. A greater independence in thought is thus required in the educational sphere. Soviet education is likely to become more "pluralistic," and less the agent of overt political socialization. It will support the twin objectives of marketization and democratization, which are integral to the reform movement.

But educational systems themselves are not inert bodies. Schools, colleges, teachers, and students have their own conception of their interests. Teachers who have been accustomed to central control and authoritarian methods will resist change. As a school head put it at the All-Union Congress of Workers in Public Education in 1988, "As long as society needs the state, it will need coercion. And as long as the school remains a state institution ..., we cannot rule out elements of coercion."

Education is not only an instrument of the economy, and the policy of "self-financing" may destroy its humanitarian and altruistic aims. Paradoxically, perestroika in strengthening pluralism may also fortify the independence of the educational sector, which may resist innovation and greater "cooperation" with the economy.

RITUAL AND CEREMONY

The educational system in a fairly explicit way "prepares pupils for life" and in so doing inculcates beliefs, values, and patterns of behavior. They, in turn, secure ideologically the compliance of the population to the established order and the division of power between elites and masses. There are other informal and implicit social processes that link the masses symbolically to society and that identify citizens with the state. We noted in our discussion of the nationalities that national flags and emblems are foci of social identity for the peoples of the Baltic states. Rituals, traditions, and ceremonies condition the patterns of relationships that make up the social structure: they are important influences on the ways that people behave, giving meaning to life and contributing to a consciousness of personal and group solidarity.

In modern societies cultural management is a ubiquitous form of political manipulation, particularly in states where the political authorities take responsibility for transforming the society according to some ideology or set of goals and where old symbols have to be destroyed. As Trotsky put it in *Literature and Revolution*, revolution meant "the people's final break with the Asiatic, with the seventeenth century, with Holy Russia, with icons and cockroaches."

The political leadership, in developing and newly freed colonial societies, as well as in socialist ones, has to take seriously the creation of symbolic forms that help identify and link the citizens to the "new society." Rituals are created where there is ambiguity about the behavior that defines social situations. Revolutions create their own forms of ritual and ceremony: one cultural tradition is replaced by another. The English puritans smashed the ornate glass of the established church; in its place they whitewashed the walls. After the French Revolution, a cult of martyrs was introduced in place of Christian rituals; under Robespierre a state religion of patriotism was introduced. Mass festivals were held in which participants praised the leaders while effigies of opponents, particularly religious ones, were burned; mass patriotic oaths were dedicated to liberty, equality, and fraternity.

In the Soviet Union, as one Soviet writer puts it: "The basic social significance of Soviet rituals and holidays is the affirmation and reproduction in the consciousness, feeling and conduct of members of our society, standards of the socialist way of life" (cited by Lane 1981: 23). Unlike the group stratification and individual consciousness we have noted above, Soviet rituals and traditions have sought to engender a collective consciousness and identification with Soviet society.

In practice, however, prerevolutionary cultural practices, traditions, and rituals are not easily superceded and they have a way of reasserting themselves often in a different form and becoming part of the "official" political culture. Certain types of ritual and ceremony become concealed. In the USSR the observation of church holidays has been forbidden, but collective farmers have never opened the collective farm market at such times. The Orthodox Church is one area where rituals "alien" to socialism have always been legally performed. In other churches, rituals and ceremonies such as baptism have been illegally carried out.

In Soviet Central Asia, the *kalym* or bride price — a gift given by the groom (or his family) to the bride — continues as part of the traditional marriage contract in arranged marriages. Although the gift should be the property of the bride, it is often taken by the parents as a "bride price." This practice is a criminal offense according to the Constitutions of the Central Asian republics, but is widespread. It has led to self-immolation among women in Uzbekistan — 270 women attempted suicide by this method in the period 1986—87. Such actions on the part of women may reflect the conflict between the Western value of individual choice in marriage and the traditional practice of arranged marriages.

The strict moral code of traditional Islam is in conflict with the more easygoing morality of Russians and Soviet Communism. Letters have been published in *Komsomol'skaya Pravda* from an Uzbek young woman claiming that "an inability to produce a bloodstained 'white sheet' as proof of virginity ... had driven many girls to suicide" (cited by Bohr 1988).

In the Islamic republics Islamic symbols associated with burial continue. New cemeteries contain monuments decorated with crescents and Arabic inscriptions. Mazars entomb members of family clans. In Kazakhstan funeral rites are still conducted by mullahs. According to the Secretary of the Tadzhikistan Young Communist League,

> Religious vestiges and a feudal-bey attitude toward women are being over-
> come at a slow pace. Instances of the payment of bride money, albeit now
> in hidden forms, are still frequent. YCL committees know about these in-
> stances but generally ignore them. Instances of the self-immolation of young
> women — the ugliest manifestation of religious fanaticism, the patriarchal
> system and strict obedience to the head of the family — continue to occur.
> The struggle to eradicate Moslem and Christian ceremonies and holidays
> still lacks aggressiveness. (Twenty-fourth Congress of the Tadzhikistan
> Communist League, February, 1989)

In pluralist capitalist societies the ceremonies of churches, particularly the Catholic Church, are a good example of the type of managed form of ritual and ceremony that was initiated by the political leadership of the USSR after the revolution. Much ritual and ceremony in the West, however, is spontaneous. Associations conduct their own symbolic enactments. Mass pop festivals, the American Super Bowl, the British Football Association Cup Final, popular extravaganzas such as the Miss World Contest, as well as the more formalized religious ceremonies such as the

Billy Graham Television Services are spontaneous in the sense that they are created by private groups and associations. State or politically managed rituals are relatively minor: these include the public celebrations of Independence Day and the ubiquitous cult of the American flag. In Britain, sponsored political ritual is widely regarded as an anachronism. The opening of Parliament, the Trooping of the Color and Remembrance Day Parades hardly compare with the state ritual and ceremony of Revolutionary France. The symbolism of the Queen and members of the royal family does not function as a politically integrating force, although their portraits are frequently displayed as symbols of loyalty in British government offices.

In both the United States and Britain, political rituals and ceremonies are pluralistic and spontaneous. Political parties have their own symbols ranging from the candidate-sponsored bumper stickers of American election campaigns to the socialist songs of the British Labour Party. The Campaign for Nuclear Disarmament's symbol has been adopted by peace movements throughout the world and gives immediate identification to all peaceniks, as do emblems condemning abortion. Party conferences and election campaigns are public ceremonies but are controlled by the parties themselves. Moreover, mass rallies and demonstrations are invariably antigovernment and deployed with particular effect by antiwar and antinuclear campaigners: the banners, slogans, chants, effigy and flag burnings are all spontaneous. They should not be considered simply as manifestations of negative sentiments about the political and social system, but are also a form of democratic participation that strengthens belief in a pluralistic democratic society. Ironically perhaps, the greater the freedom to demonstrate openly against the state, the less potent becomes the cause of protest.

In Soviet and state socialist societies, forms of ritual and ceremony have been created by the political authorities with the conscious intention of establishing solidarity between the people and the state. Under perestroika, a movement away from this form of political management has occurred in keeping with a more differentiated and pluralist society. Before discussing current changes, we shall consider the way that ritual and ceremony have developed in the USSR.

Soviet authors in the 1960s and 1970s believed that there were three ideological components guiding state sponsored ritual in the USSR: the tradition of the revolution (and Civil War), the patriotic tradition (particularly, the defense of the USSR against fascism), and the labor tradition (the value of work). (See Lane 1984: 207–17.)

The Revolutionary Tradition

The revolutionary tradition was the "holy of holies," placing the Communist Party and its leaders from Lenin to Brezhnev as central objects of ritual and ceremony. Public places abounded with pictures and slogans of the political leaders. "Hail the CPSU," "The Unity of Party and Nation is Indestructible," festooned public buildings and public transport. Pictures of political leaders were not only prominently displayed on public holidays, but also were a regular part of the billboard architecture: the words Lenin and CPSU on public billboards in the Soviet Union were as ubiquitous as the words Coca Cola in the United States. (There is no equivalent political person in the advanced Western states; there are no posters dedicated to Abraham Lincoln, for example. In Britain at the height of its empire, Queen Victoria may have had a similar symbolic role.)

Organizations, streets, libraries, universities, and towns were named after political leaders, particularly Lenin: Leningrad, Leninabad, Lenin Library, and so on. Some leaders have disgraced themselves and then places become unnamed: in December 1988 the Central Committee resolved that the names of Brezhnev and Chernenko given to places would be withdrawn. (This has happened previously to Stalin; the historic battle ground of Stalingrad, has been renamed Volgograd.) Literally millions of copies of the works of Lenin and the speeches of Brezhnev were published. Many books, speeches, presentations, and concerts even began with homilies to Lenin, the Party, and other political leaders. Truly, "Lenin is always with us" as one of the popular slogans put it.

The anniversary of the revolution is commemorated in November with a public holiday, and with parades in which the Party is given pride of place. People are reminded of the achievements of the USSR, the implacable opposition to imperialism, and the poverty of capitalism. The effects of perestroika may also be seen here. In the celebrations in November 1988 the general traditional slogans did not appear, instead slogans emphasized aspects of perestroika: typical banner headings were "Perestroika," "Let us reinforce the powers of the Soviets with the Party's authority," "All power to the Soviets." There were also banners devoted to the themes of cost accounting, the lease-contract system, the development of the cooperative movement, and the economic roles of the Soviets. The military continued to have a presence in the October parade, but its place was downgraded: there was no display of strategic missiles. More emphasis was placed on people's groups. In the Baltic republics there were major changes in the celebration. In Lithuania a city meeting that included the participation of informal groups was held instead of a demonstration.

In Estonia the Greens were prominent, and in the Baltic republics the new national coats of arms and republican flags were prominently shown.

The Patriotic Tradition

The "patriotic tradition" emphasizes the solidarity of the Soviet nation and the people of the USSR. Its political content is manifested against enemies: the intervention against the new Soviet republic in the Civil War. Even greater salience is given to the "Great Patriotic War" (1941–45) against fascism. Fascism might be likened to the devil in Christian thought: the war embodied all that is evil in capitalism and all that is good about socialism because socialism triumphed. Victory Day (May 9) is the epitome of patriotic symbolism. On this public holiday the television and radio are dominated by patriotic themes, especially the history and legacy of the war with Germany, and every town, village, and collective farm has its parade. Pride of place is given to the military, veterans, and partisans. As in Britain on Armistice Day and the United States on the Fourth of July other organizations (youth groups such as the pioneers and factory workers) send detachments to march in the parade.

Patriotic ceremonies and rituals, however, are not solely socialistic in character. Traditional sentiments and values overlie the Marxist-Leninist content of the ritual: appeal is made to traditional enmity between Russia and its Germanic neighbors; even the church has a place in Soviet patriotic symbolism. Soviet patriotism has deep roots and has successfully adapted traditional Russian sentiments. The following poem in a dissident writers' satirical book on the Soviet Union sums up this feeling:

> Why have you stayed, and not fled with the rest?
> I shrugged and shook my head, I felt depressed.
> I long have fought for this my motherland,
> For her I've lain and shivered in the frost,
> For her I've starved when no food came to hand,
> Here I grew up. I'm hers at any cost.
> I weep, but not a maudlin drunkard's tears;
> They're tender recollections I can't hide
> Of all the love I've given her down the years.
> My only love, my own grey land, my bride.
> Bereft of wife and babes one can survive;
> To leave one's land though I can't endure.
> Better by far be buried here alive
> And feed her — be it only as manure.
> (Alexander Zinoviev, 1981. *The Yawning Heights*, 811.)

Labor Rituals

Ritual connected with and glorifying labor is derived from both the Marxist-Leninist concern with the working class as the leading force in Communist society and the need to develop a work ethic during the process of rapid industrialization. This ritual is effected through the deployment of banners and slogans that are intended to raise consciousness: "Glory to Labor" is one of the most popular slogans. Ceremonies are conducted that seek to create solidarity. The "initiation into the working class" is a ceremony epitomizing the Soviet glorification of labor. It seeks to bind workers to the collective and the collective to the society.

An initiation ceremony at the Leningrad Kirov works has been described as follows:

> The ritual starts with some veterans of labor lighting a giant torch from the blazing flame of the factory's open furnace. Before bringing it to the ceremony proper in the factory's palace of culture, they carry it around the whole town during the evening hours as a symbol of Leningrad's remarkable labor and revolutionary traditions. The factory palace of culture is festively decorated with slogans on the walls, such as "Hail to the New Generation of Workers," "Be Worthy of the Traditions of the Fathers," "Labor Lays the Way to the Stars." ... On a raised platform, against the background of the Red Flag, sit the factory's veteran workers and leading people from the town's Party, Komsomol and trades union organizations. In the audience are parents and friends. After an initial fanfare by bugle players, the chandeliers "blaze up," the doors open and the new workers enter to the tune of a solemn march and the clapping of hands. After the young workers have sat down various heroes of labor and the Revolution relate their experiences on a cinema screen. Then the drums start up and the guard of honor brings the torch into the hall. A representative of the initiates goes up to the torch and gives the labor oath:
> We swear to follow always and in every way the traditions of the Petrograd proletarians.
> We swear.
> We swear to carry forward with honor the baton of our fathers.
> We swear.
> After this oath the ceremony continues with further speeches, congratulations, music and film. (Lane 1981: 110–11)

Further rituals are linked to the life cycle of the workers: there is a ceremony at the time of the first wage packet, the first labor rating, the acceptance into a Brigade of Communist Labor, retirement, the honoring of a worker's dynasty (three or more generations employed in a given factory).

As with the patriotic and revolutionary traditions, statutory holidays are linked with certain occupational groupings. There is the Day of the Miners, the Day of the Shop Assistant, and so on — a total of eighteen such holidays. There are occasions when the occupations gather to celebrate their occupation, to honor outstanding workers — "the best in the profession" — and to distribute other prizes and awards. Sports events and other spectacles are organized. Rituals also glorify work. *Subbotniks* are collective unpaid work activities carried out on holidays (originally on Saturday, *subbota*, hence *subbotnik*, one who works on a Saturday). Such collective activities nowadays are more symbolic than real work activities, although much useful collective manual work is performed by them: tidying up public places, gardens, and housing blocks' collective spaces are among the jobs performed.

These three traditions are interdependent. They share and reinforce a consciousness of collectivity or *kollektivnost'*. Revolution, patriotism, and labor may be regarded as three ideological norms that have legitimated the Soviet political order. On many public occasions, for example, the places of honor will be given to three "heroes" — an old Bolshevik (the revolutionary tradition), a war hero (patriotic tradition), and a hero of labor (labor tradition). Parades will have detachments of the Party that often display pictures of political leaders (Lenin, or members of the Politburo), military ranks (accompanied by weaponry) and workers (arranged by labor collectives), symbolizing the three traditions and the social unity and collectivism of the people.

Socialist Civic Ceremonies

We noted above that prerevolutionary culture exerts its own influence. To combat the ingrained traditions of generations, especially those linked to the church, civic ceremonies have been invented to displace them. In the days immediately after the revolution, militant atheists celebrated anti-Easter and anti-Christmas campaigns. These observances have been discontinued and a range of Soviet rituals have been invented to mark the life cycle. There is a civic ceremony to mark the registration of a newborn child, a wedding ceremony, and funeral rites. Holidays to celebrate the calendar — the first day of spring, the longest day of the year, harvest festival, winter carnival — continue the prerevolutionary tradition of celebrations.

While public ceremony symbolizes the political themes noted above, many other remaining rituals may be traced to prerevolutionary times.

Christmas is not celebrated as a public holiday, though at the New Year celebration Grandfather Frost makes an appearance much as does Father Christmas or Saint Nicholas in the West. Private family celebrations include personal themes more in the tradition of prerevolutionary and Western ceremonies. These include the presentation of flowers, the exchange of greetings cards, feasts with liberal lacings of vodka, singing and dancing. Street revelry takes place much in the same way as people gather in Trafalgar and Times Squares. At home, presents are given, especially at the New Year, which appeals most to children. Just as the Queen gives her Christmas Day broadcast message to her subjects in the Commonwealth, so too the Soviet leaders address the nation — reflecting on achievements and plans for the future. In prerevolutionary times and in the West today, Christmas is celebrated by groups singing carols door-to-door. In modern Russia, groups circulate collectives (orphanages, hospitals) and gifts are dispensed. Old traditions continue in the form of dress: costumes of the bear, fox, or Grandfather Frost are worn.

In the days after the revolution, religious ceremonies were not replaced and the assumption of the political leadership was that they would die a natural death. Marriage was marked by official legal registration (rather like joining a public library). To counter church ceremonies and to meet people's demands for a ceremony to mark the event, a more elaborate Soviet event has been introduced. It is hoped by the Soviet authorities that a solemn ceremony and the seriousness of marriage vows will engender attitudes that will strengthen the family and help maintain its cohesion.

The marriage ceremony takes place in a purposely built "Palace of Happiness" in a Palace of Culture or some other public building (such as that of the local Soviet). This secular ceremony stresses the obligation of the couple to Soviet norms.

The ceremony is not much different from that of a registry office marriage in Europe or a Justice of the Peace in the United States. The couple arrive in decorated cars, the male dressed in a dark suit and the bride in a bridal costume. Music (the Wedding March) and flowers accompany the guests. An official from the local Soviet, dressed usually with a red sash, presides, often in an ornate room specially used for this kind of ceremony. Speeches are made and the register is signed, often to the accompaniment of a flashing camera.

After this ceremony the couple often pay their respects to the war dead at a monument or eternal flame, or they may visit a grave of one of their own family. The wedding party returns to celebrate at a hotel, restaurant, or at home. There is much merriment, drinking, and feasting.

Perestroika and Socialist Ritual

The forces that have led to "rethinking" in other parts of Soviet society also have the same effects in the area of socialist rituals and ceremonies. Such developments have lagged behind other changes and are
often latent rather than manifest, but the implications are clear. "Socialist ritual" is fading away, being replaced by a more individualized or
traditional ceremony or by no ceremony at all.

The organizing principles of the revolution, patriotism, and labor were
the foundations on which the collectivist and homogeneous Soviet public
consciousness was constructed. The political rituals and ceremonies that
have been developed in the USSR have sought to reflect, consolidate,
and create a unitary worldview and a collectivist social consciousness. Many
of these assumptions are no longer shared by the reform leadership.

As we pointed out earlier, unlike previous Soviet leaders, Gorbachev
has made little if any reference to the revolutionary character of the
Soviet past, because reform has been essentially internal: it involved
consolidation of the revolution and the resolution of problems of socialist
construction in the USSR. Thus Gorbachev has sought to present the
image of a dynamic and modern leader bringing the Soviet Union into
line with the advanced societies of the West. Marxism-Leninism as the
symbol of revolution no longer holds the central part in contemporary
ideology it did under Stalin, Khrushchev, and Brezhnev.

The person previously identified as the "Great Leader of the Soviet
people," Joseph Stalin, has been publicly condemned. Leonid Brezhnev
has also been vilified, and his leadership is considered one of "stagnation"
incompatible with the needs of contemporary Soviet society.

In January 1987 at an important Plenum of the Party Central Committee,
Gorbachev condemned the managed forms of ritual and ceremony that
arose during Brezhnev's leadership. "Serious shortcomings in ideological
and political education were in many cases disguised with ostentatious
activities and campaigns and celebrations of numerous jubilees. The
world of day-to-day realities and that of make-believe well-being, were
increasingly diverging."

The leaders who exemplified the revolutionary activity of the working
class and the leading role of the Party are no longer idealized symbols of
the state. Such ideological reverses have had disorienting effects on the
populace and undermine the collective and traditional socialist symbolism.

Present policy is to diminish the extent of the role of the Party in its
controlling position in society. Policy involves greater participation and
less "management and control." The market is increasingly favored as
a mechanism of coordination. Collectivism as an organizing principle is

being replaced by individualism. This has important implications not only for the more ritualistic elements of labor ritual but also for the cultivated attitude to work under socialism. All these tendencies undermine the political content of the ritual and ceremonial enactments noted above.

Patriotism as a basis for socialist ritual will fare much better than the other two traditions we have discussed because it is much more firmly rooted in the Russian (or other national) consciousness than revolution and labor. It appeals to the instinct of self-preservation. Russian history has learned many lessons from foreign invasions. While Gorbachev in his early years as leader emphasized the "undying" fears of Soviet soldiers, and the military took its usual symbolic place in parades, this type of patriotic stance is changing.

The system of communication is more open, the cruder anti-imperialism and anti-Americanism is being replaced by a benign image of the West. Soviet patriotism, moreover, is confronted with the stronger assertion of nationalism in many of the constituent republics. This has led to a decline in the symbolism of Soviet ritual that has developed throughout the USSR and the rise of a stronger national identity and patriotism on a republican basis. Forms of identification are taking on a more traditional character as nationalities seek symbols of identity with the past. Ancient names are being given back to places and those of revolutionary leaders are jettisoned; Leningrad has been renamed St. Petersburg. Old monuments (particularly churches) are being restored and opened where appropriate. Other public forms of celebration, such as the chiming of church bells, are also indications of a greater cultural pluralism.

As an intrinsic value of Soviet communism, the idea that labor is self-realization is rapidly being abandoned and replaced by a recognition that work is a necessity for earning money. The moral incentives that provided a stimulus to work will be replaced by money and the carrot of what money will buy. The work brigade as a financial mechanism for the payment of its members replaces the *kollektiv* as a social and political unit that creates a consciousness of the collective value of labor under communism.

New mercenary tendencies are epitomized by a 1989 Soviet joke:

Entrepreneur of a new cooperative venture: Have you heard the latest joke about our cooperatives?
Respondent: No. What is it?
Entrepreneur: Give me five rubles and I'll tell you.

Our knowledge of capitalist societies informs us that rituals and ceremonies are part of industrial society. They have significance during periods of stress, catastrophe,and upheaval. In the USSR the managed rituals and ceremonies have not been universally observed and have had more effect on the young and uneducated: the intelligentsia have been skeptical. In the future in the Soviet Union, the managed ritual of the past will be replaced by a greater plurality and spontaneity, by a revival of prerevolutionary, religious ritual on a wider scale. The rise of a "pop" culture with its attendant rituals and idols — blue jeans, heavy metal, and automobiles — are symbols of an individualistic consumer culture. Rather than being unitary in form, rituals will parallel the more pluralistic group structures discussed above.

Public demonstrations in Moscow following Eltsin's triumph in August 1991 indicate that psychological stress was reduced by attacks on the symbols of Soviet power and the revolution: the destruction of Dzerzhinski's statue outside the KGB headquarters, the closure of the Lenin museum and moves to remove Lenin's body from Red Square to the newly renamed city of St Petersburg (previously Leningrad). These actions signal the end of the era brought in by the 1917 Revolution.

The development of national consciousness with popular demonstrations, nationalist slogans, flags, and the invocation of nonsocialist images and personalities will diminish the appeal of the "managed" political culture we have known in the past. This process is further evidence of the social trends we have noted earlier: the greater critical awareness and individuality of the population. These changes reflect the maturation of the Soviet Union from a postrevolutionary and developing society to a modern pluralistic industrial state. Cultural management can only be effective where political control presents a unitary and homogeneous front to the people and when its form strikes a resonance with them. These conditions no longer hold. The rituals and ceremonies that commenced under Stalin will be disbanded but the secular ones, those linked to the life and calendric cycles and public holidays, will survive.

Chapter 9 ———————————————————

GLASNOST'
The Mass Media

The totalitarian perspective considered Soviet society as composed of isolated individuals unable to articulate their interests in the face of an omnipresent state. Earlier, we noted the way that thought control has been likened to the malevolent utopia of George Orwell's *1984*. This work showed the way that manipulation of communication by a state monopoly ensured the isolation and exploitation of the individual. Such social regulation may be exercised in modern societies through control of information, suppression of facts and opinions, through their biased selection and manipulation, thus exposing the population to a constant stream of "politically approved" messages and prohibiting other views and opinions.

What is the factual basis of such claims? How far have they been modified under perestroika and glasnost'? We noted in chapter 3 in our discussion of the elections to the government organs (the Soviets) and their relations with the Communist Party that democratization involves greater pluralism and a recognition of the diversity of interests in socialist society. It involves accountability of officials for their actions, a narrower and legally bounded range of activities for the state on the one hand and a "dramatically increased independence of enterprises and associations" (Gorbachev 1987: 33), on the other. But democratization also involves a recognition of greater autonomy of individuals and groups and the development of civil society, which is accompanied by greater freedom of association and the press and what Gorbachev referred to as a "socialist pluralism of opinions" in his speech to the Nineteenth Party Conference in June 1988.

It also affects the position of the individual and personal rights. During the same address he elaborated on this concept:

315

The ultimate goal of the reform of the political system and the main criterion of how successfully we implement it are the all-round enrichment of human rights. ... The exercise of [political freedoms] is a real guarantee that any problem of public interest will be comprehensively discussed, that all the "pros" and "cons" will be weighed, and that this will help us find the most correct solutions, taking into account all the diverse opinions and real possibilities. In short, comrades, what we are talking about is a new role for public opinion in the country.

In this chapter we shall consider the ways that the media operate in the USSR and examine whether the state (as suggested by the theory of totalitarianism) has a stranglehold on the communication that manipulates the people or whether glasnost' has in practice led to the evolution of a "free press."

MEDIA AND COMMUNICATION

In simple societies and in primary groups (such as the family) in industrial society communication between people is direct and reciprocated: people talk and respond to each other. In a modern society, however, communication becomes increasingly indirect. Recipients of messages do not have the opportunity to respond in an interactive way — to "answer back," as it were. Modern forms of media, such as the press, radio, television, books, and videos, become a major source of information, education, and leisure, but they also have a major effect on people's consciousness and outlook and are a major source of political integration and control. Just how much effect is a matter of controversy — not only in the contemporary USSR but also in Western societies.

The study of communication in modern society has five different aspects:

1. mode: the kind of media (newspaper, television, radio, video);
2. initiators: the people or institutions that disseminate communications (broadcasting and newspaper companies, video firms);
3. audience: those who absorb communication (television viewers, newspaper readers);
4. message: the content of the communication (the essence of a play, a presidential address, newspaper report of a catastrophe);
5. effect: modification of recipient's attitude, behavior, or state of being.

For communication to have taken place, there must have been some effect. The audience must have experienced something as a result of exposure to the message: a learning experience, a sense of well-being, pleasure, a stronger (or weaker) attitude to or belief in something linked to the content of the communication.

The development of mass media has given the controllers or initiators of messages considerable power to influence the public. Even in Western liberal "open" societies concern has been expressed about the potential if not the actual determination of people's perceptions through exposure to the media.

In the West, powerful commercial and political pressures make for a homogeneity in the mass media, especially television, and the mass media provide a politically sanitized view of the world. Commercial interests establish limits to mass communication: anarchists, communists, and fascists do not have an equal chance to influence the population. Commercial stations are not interested in propagating views advocating the demise of capitalism.

Concern over the effects of the media is usually expressed when the message is monopolized by a group of initiators, when people are not exposed to other points of view on the content of the communication, and particularly when certain common messages build up over a long period of time.

The effect of mass communication has been likened to that of a hypodermic needle: the recipient is "injected" with a message that has a drug-like effect, leading even to dependency on the medium. (For further discussion see Mickiewicz 1988: chapter 5.) Recent thinking on the subject, however, has rejected the more extreme versions of the hypodermic needle viewpoint and gives more attention to the ways that recipients react towards the messages. For example, their experience may lead them to respond in quite different ways from those intended by the initiators of the communication: A documentary condemning pornography may, by the display of explicit sexual acts, give rise to erotic sensations and arouse interest in pornography; or a religious or political program may have the effect of "switching off" the members of an audience. A subject's scientific knowledge, predisposition, or life experience may counteract the content of the television sermon or political presentation and lead him or her to reject not just the particular message of a given program but the legitimacy of its originator.

THE ORGANIZATION OF THE SOVIET MEDIA

By any comparison, Soviet media operations are vast and comprehensive. In 1986 over eighty-three thousand books and brochures, 5,275 journals and current periodicals, and 18,515 newspapers were published. Print runs are enormous: over 2.234 billion books and brochures, 18.4 billion copies of journals and 45.2 billion newspapers were printed in one year. In 1988 *Trud*, the paper of the trade unions, had a print run of 18.7 billion. Editions of *Pravda*, the Party newspaper, ran to 10.7 billion copies per issue, *Komsomolskaya Pravda* (the paper of the Young Communist League) printed 14.6 billion. With similar printing volumes, sometimes popular papers, such as *Literaturnaya gazeta* and the satirical weekly, *Ogonek* sell out.

Readership is further encouraged by the public display of papers in reading cases in the main streets. There are over 134,000 "mass libraries" open to the public with a stock of over 2.136 billion books and journals. These numbers are eclipsed by cinema attendances: in 1986 there were 153,000 cinemas with 3.882 billion attendances, although this represents a decline from 1970, the peak attendance year, when 4.652 billion people went to the pictures.

Whereas television is currently the most popular and influential mode of mass media in the USSR, until recently the radio, newspapers, and books played a more important role than they do in the West. Loudspeakers in public places and in transport, such as trains, have regularly broadcast news and items of information (as well as providing a background of popular music). The cinema has played a major role in entertainment and in the dissemination of propaganda. Voluntary societies (such as *Znamiya*, or Knowledge) and Party organizations have organized mass public lectures and information campaigns. This emphasis on oral and visual mass media reflects the low level of literacy of the past.

In the 1980s modernization of communication has occurred and television has become the major medium. In the late 1980s there were over ninety-five million television sets in the USSR. The advent of communication satellites made television broadcasts available in nearly all the land mass giving around 95 percent of the population access to television. Video cassette recorders are little used. In the late 1980s there were less than a million recorders, most of which had been imported illegally as Soviet production was only seventy thousand per year in 1988. Production, however, is planned to rise to two million VCRs per year by 1995.

Nearly all media programs are made in the Soviet Union. Before the advent of the current leadership, very little programming had been imported from the West, and those Western programs that were aired were carefully selected to show the worst aspects of exploitation, hooliganism, and crime. There are no privately owned companies in the field of communications and media as there are in the West. As the profit motive is absent as a motivating force for the initiators of messages in the USSR, the cultivation of a mass public for private profit by the owners of the media has not occurred.

Restrictions have been placed on the activity of the cooperatives (private trade), which include publishing, film and video production, rental of media equipment, and the copying of programs. This effectively keeps all mass media under direct state control. In commenting on these prohibitions, the Vice Chairman of the USSR Council of Ministers' Bureau for Social Development said that this practice was justifiable to protect society from "mass-consumption publishing in the worst sense of the term: from pornography, from the propaganda of ideas that are alien to socialism or harmful to our society and system" (*Izvestiya*, 2 January 1989). Cooperatives in publishing can, however, create media productions in collaboration with controlled "patron enterprises." These legal provisions represent important limitations on the development of an independent means of communication.

Rather than the profit motive operating through satisfying "what the consumer wants," in Soviet society the media functions through state control linked to the dominant ideology of the Communist Party. The state, however, is not a homogeneous body, and in practice various institutions have been set up with the responsibility of organizing the mass media. These bodies have had to act in keeping with the values propagated by the Communist Party. There has always been tension between many of these bodies and the controlling Party institutions. In practice, "the values" (of Marxism-Leninism) have always been sufficiently vague to allow for different interpretations by various "initiators." Under Gorbachev the autonomy of many institutions has been strengthened and the controlling influence of the Party has been greatly reduced.

The Content of Communications

As the Soviet Union developed under Stalin, three main constraints operated to determine the content of the mass media. First, ideologically the message had to reflect socialist values. Second, controls were exerted through key committees and censors (known as *glavlit*) to gauge the ideological and political correctness of newspapers, radio, books, journals, and television. Third, the originators of messages having mass currency were restricted to organs having the approval of the dominant political power.

Socialist realism was the doctrine coined under Stalin to promote socialist and Soviet values. It sought to present societies in the spirit of revolutionary development, to educate and influence people in the "spirit of socialism." Writers were to be, in Stalin's words, "engineers of the soul." *Partiynost*

(Party spirit) was to penetrate all communication and its nature was determined by the Party authorities. This policy involved diminishing the role of individualism in art and creative writing.

In the mass media, socialist realism involved staunch support to the current political line, the suppression of conflicting opinions, and the portrayal of the worst aspects of life under capitalism. The class struggle was given a prominent place in the content of the media. Differences over policy in the USSR, inadequacies and shortages of Soviet life, let alone oppression and illegality, were taboo topics. The media sought to portray a homogeneous society based on social harmony. Heroes were positive, imbued with simplistic socialist goals. A black-and-white world was depicted: all things Soviet and Communist were good and all things capitalist, imperialist, and American were bad.

This led to an unquestioning and positive portrayal of all actions and policies of the Soviet government. No debate over alternative positions or opinions, even within the socialist bloc, was allowed. When people with different points of view aired their opinions they were repressed. The media presented a one-sided government-sponsored set of views. A consequence of this policy was that the "creative critical intelligentsia" was replaced by loyal socialist Party-minded activists. Dissident opinions and views uncongenial to the authorities were either pushed underground and disseminated in *samizdat* (illegally printed critical literature) or surfaced in allegorical writings.

A major watershed may be detected under Khrushchev, when a reappraisal of the Stalin years took place. Work critical of the Stalin period, mainly in the field of literature, was published and had a wide circulation. Dudintsev's novel *Not by Bread Alone* was published in 1956, and prison camp life was portrayed by Solzhenitsyn in *One Day in the Life of Ivan Denisovich*. In the late 1950s social scientists were able to take a slightly more detached view of Soviet reality and numerous surveys of "empirical sociological research" were published. Critical opinions were raised in intellectual and other circles: important debates on a wide range of social and political themes — elections, the role of markets, incentives at work — took place between elites.

Academics made acquaintance with intellectual developments in the West. The works of J. K. Galbraith, Walt Rostow, and Talcott Parsons were selectively translated. Excerpts from Western fiction were also made available in Russian in specialist Soviet journals such as *Foreign Literature*. Classical works of a nonsocialist character were published — the works of Tolstoy and novels of Bulgakov for instance. Western films, such as *Emmanuelle* and James Bond thrillers were shown to restricted audiences. One could pick up Western newspapers, such as *The Times*, on selected public newsstands, although they were rare.

All these sources, however, were restricted and limited in scope: either they were made available to closed circles of specialists, for example in the cinema industry or the Academy of Sciences, or they were printed in very small numbers and made accessible to specialist audiences. The mass media still presented a solid undifferentiated face of official opinion.

Under Khrushchev, these developments represented a slight thaw in Soviet intellectual life rather than the creation of a new mold. The Department of Propaganda (since 1988, the Commission on Ideology) of the Central Committee, headed by a secretary, usually a member of the Politburo, decided the Party line. The mass media, at least as far as political substance was concerned, had changed little. The content of all books sold through public networks (with the exclusion of some works emanating from the Academy of Sciences presses), radio, magazines, and films was censored: the censor's number appeared on book jackets. Vladimirov (1973) has estimated that in the early 1970s, some seventy thousand people were employed in censorship. One example of the ubiquitous control of the censors is their treatment of Klimov's film *Rasputin*. On the first reading by the censors the film received 169 suggestions for improvement; it went through six subsequent readings by thirty people. Klimov's film, however, did not please the authorities and although completed in 1975, it was not shown in the USSR until 1985.

Ideological control was maintained under Brezhnev but with some important developments. News coverage was selective. Those items which were thought to develop a "socialist consciousness" were reported and "negative phenomena" were ignored. Hence Soviet disasters, interpersonal conflict, crime, and violence were not covered in the press or on television. Those events that portrayed the desired image of the future were given prominence: economic achievements, fulfillment of the economic plan, discussion of ways of improving productivity and quality of work, Soviet achievement in space and in sport were highlighted. Sensationalism and sex were taboo. Unlike the West, "bad news" was not regarded as "good" news — unless, of course, the sufferers were the Western capitalist states. Knowledge of unrest in Eastern Europe, such as the rise of Solidarity in Poland, or the unfolding of reform movements under Dubcek in Czechoslovakia, and of Soviet participation in the civil war in Afghanistan were either not reported at all, or portrayed in a way that would not imply any criticism of inadequacy in Soviet policy.

Many aspects of internal Soviet life were regarded as state secrets. No comprehensive information was published on crime, suicide, accidents, structural inadequacies in government services, the extent of poverty, public catastrophes (such as air crashes), and certainly no criticism of the policies or personal deficiencies of the political leadership was allowed.

But state control was not uniform, many different organizations and institutions had the responsibility for media: Party organizations, government departments, professional associations, local government organs, and voluntary associations (such as the churches) published their own journals and books. While the Party sought to maintain control, it proved difficult to maintain consistency and differences of opinion over what was and what was not a "socialist approach" often occurred. In some of the national republics in particular censorship was less stringent. In Georgia, for example, films were passed for exhibition that would not have been allowed in the Russian republic.

There is some evidence of greater "within system" criticism in the mass press. Jerry Hough (1977: chapter 9) has analyzed *Pravda* and *Izvestiya* and has shown that critical articles and letters calling for improvement of the work of people and institutions increased considerably between 1951 and 1971. Hough points out that much criticism appeared in the press during the 1970s in the

> name of perfecting socialism, democracy, the federal system or social justice ... [Soviet citizens] can propose economic changes that would move the Soviet Union well towards market socialism, political changes that would ... increase the impact of public opinion upon governmental decisions, and social change that would substantially improve the lot of the disadvantaged (197).

These articles contained none of the pointed criticism of the late 1980s, but awareness that such views were published is important for understanding the sources of change that occurred under Gorbachev.

A study of Soviet emigrés to the United States conducted in the 1980s found that 86.2 percent of the respondents read papers. Newspapers were read mainly for news whereas television was watched more for entertainment and 87.9 percent of the respondents looked at variety shows (Zimmerman 1987: 339).

Transformation also gradually took place in the less political aspects of mass culture. Western jazz, rock and roll, and popular dances such as the twist, were heard on the radio and shown on television and film and became absorbed as accepted parts of Soviet life.

The major source of such "Westernization" of Soviet culture was increasing penetration by the Western media, particularly radio, and the spread of Western images through the Eastern European socialist states. The superior development in the West of popular mass entertainment, fashion, and a consumer market was a huge and unstoppable attraction to young people in the USSR. Western jeans and pop became symbols of modernity. The availability of tape recorders made possible copying of all Western "pop" culture.

There are, however, severe limits to the provision of alternative media not sanctioned by the authorities. As noted above, video cassette recorders are in very short supply and viewing has yet to reach a mass market. But the films of Bruce Lee, Emmanuelle, and even Rambo are available to small audiences through contraband tapes. These films may command audiences at many of the private clubs that have grown up in the mid-1980s. Straight pop videos are displayed for the general public at some of the cooperative restaurants that have sprung up. Yet the production and duplication of films and videos and their rental and public showing are not a legitimate form of cooperative activity.

The foreign radio stations — Radio Liberty, Voice of America, and the BBC — are major sources of nonauthorized information. Jamming of Western Russian language programs (English-language ones have often escaped) has been intermittent; though at times of crisis or during the worsening of East-West relations jamming has increased. Since 1987, however, the practice has been abolished.

Photocopiers also give the opportunity to reprint forbidden books and articles, but in practice such equipment has been kept under strict control. Illicit photocopied materials have reached an influential but not a mass market. In addition to the "official" press, *samizdat* (illegally printed critical literature) circulated particularly among the intelligentsia. The study by Zimmerman (1987: 341) found that 44.7 percent of high-level professionals, 40.8 percent of political leaders and 29.9 percent of the sample as a whole has read *samizdat*. Such publications included political protest pamphlets, banned novels, political critiques of the Soviet system, and writing highlighting the plight of religious, political, and national dissenters and political prisoners. Between 1960 and 1980 some five thousand such items reached the West. (A depository is held by Radio Liberty/Radio Free Europe in Munich.)

According to Vera Tolz, a researcher at Radio Liberty, the number of unofficial publications in the USSR, even under perestroika, has increased. Unlike the activities of independent groups, unofficial publications are not discussed in the official press. Recognizing such journals and papers as the organs of those independent groups seeking to become "opposition parties" would undermine the hegemony of the Communist Party. This position has been reversed by Eltsin in the Fall of 1991.

Such developments lead to four conclusions concerning the originators, mode, and effects of media in the USSR. First, the originators of communication have never been consistent in their interpretation of *partiynost* (the Party line). Second, an analysis of the media must include the influence of messages emanating from outside through such mass communications as Voice of America, Radio Liberty, and the BBC. Even though relatively few people may listen directly to these broadcasts, those who do act as "opinion leaders" and retransmit messages to a much wider population. Third, unless the message of the media corresponds to people's experience and perception, it is not believed by the recipients. They then turn to other sources — foreign broadcasts and rumor become major sources of belief and "official propaganda" then becomes seen for what it is. Fourth, individuals have psychic needs for satisfaction and enjoyment that the mass media attempts to meet, but the media cannot impose their own definition on such needs. The concessions made to Western "pop" culture under Khrushchev and Brezhnev are indications that the channels of communication must bow to public demand or else they will lose their effectiveness. In the political sphere, greater freedom had to wait until Gorbachev's arrival on the political scene.

As a medium of political information (and control) the Soviet mass media were becoming ineffective in the late Brezhnev period. While it must be noted that communication was becoming more open and differentiated, this was more in spite of the regime than because of the political leadership. The authorities gave way, often grudgingly, to demands made by various groups. The availability of information, especially about foreign countries and international politics, and the sources of views were greatly restricted when compared to Western liberal democracies. Under Gorbachev, the system has changed considerably. The Soviet Media, particularly television, has been saturated with Western programmes.

CHANGES IN THE MEDIA UNDER PERESTROIKA

Glasnost' (openness or public criticism) has led to a major change in the forms of initiation, content, and effects of mass communications. In essence the system of media control has moved from being one of administrative regulation to a more market-like system in which both the initiators of messages and the recipients have had much greater influence over the content of programs. Although television and radio are financed directly by the government, and come under the control of a state committee of television and radio (*Gosteleradio*)* controllers and program executives have been brought into contact with the public through many public participation programs. Heads of music have been questioned about the alleged lack of "heavy metal" programs, the inadequate presentation

* In February 1991, this body was renamed the State Television and Radio Broadcasting Corporation.

of regional folk music and culture, and the domination of Moscow in program production. (Before the advent of Gorbachev to the leadership, only 15 percent of television programs were produced by local studios.)

The Soviet media are trying to move from a secrecy culture to an information culture, from administrative regulation of information to self-regulation. This has involved a severe reduction in the bureaucratic control and tutelage of Party officials.

The organization of the media, moreover, has not changed radically. Producers are not geared towards profit maximization. Television, radio, and the press are not dependent on advertising revenue, though advertisements are beginning to appear in the press and television: the local press carries notices of entertainments, but there is only exceptionally advertising of commodities; coverage of international sporting events carries advertising in the form of visual perimeter displays; television has no "commercials." The press is financed either from sales of newspapers, or by the institutions that support particular papers. Television and radio are financed by the state budget (like some European broadcasting corporations). The Party and other institutions have had various forms of publications under their jurisdiction. The newspaper *Pravda* came under the supervision of the Central Committee of the Communist Party. *Moscow News*, one of the more outspoken papers, was the organ of the Association of Friendship Societies and the Novosti Press Agency.

Under Gorbachev, the editors and other executive personnel have been given much greater independence to publish and transmit what they think is of interest and importance to the people with far fewer restraints placed on the content of the media. Radical changes were instituted on Eltsin's authority in September 1991. The Party presses were "destatized", some were closed down and others were run by collectives.

Censorship

The formal censorship has been carried out by *glavlit* (Chief Directorate of the USSR Council of Ministers for Safeguarding State Secrets in the Press) whose activity has been much reduced since 1986. *Glavlit's* task has been to restrict information and opinion in certain areas:

> using the press for the purpose of undermining or eliminating the socialist
> system established in the Soviet Union, for the propaganda of war, the ad-
> vocacy of racial or national exclusivity, of hatred and violence on national,
> religious or other grounds, the intention to do damage to the country's sec-
> urity interests, defense capacity and social system, or for the publication

of material not compatible with the requirements of social morality and the protection of public health. (Interview — the first ever — of the head of *Glavlit* — reported in *Izvestiya*, 3 November 1988.)

These restrictions included military and state secrets (which were not defined) and the usual exclusion of pornography.

The head of *Glavlit* stated in 1988 that the Directorate was adjusting its policy in a society that was moving from a secrecy culture to an information culture. Its current policy is to reduce the level of censorship. Since 1985 the list of censored items has been reduced by one third and most literary publications have been excluded from censorship. Library shelves have been restocked with books that were previously put in special stocks and were unavailable to the general reader. It has been reported that only 451 titles are now put in the special section of "reserved books". *Glavlit* declared in July 1990 that censorship was abolished, the office remaining open to check foreign literature.

Receipt of foreign publications through the post has been liberalized. Western newspapers, including the *International Herald Tribune*, the *Guardian* (London), and *Le Monde* are to be made available at newspaper kiosks. Restrictions on foreign literature will in the future be "a very rare exception." A law on the press — a kind of freedom of information act — will define the principles and methods under which *Glavlit* will work in the future.

The supply of publications has been more responsive to demand. The print runs of popular (and more radical) papers have increased. Books that do not sell are curtailed. This is part of the general economic strategy of *khozraschet*, which calls for the balancing of income and expenditure on all items on sale.

As in other forms of media, many previously banned books are now printed. The works of Nekrasov and Pasternak (including *Dr. Zhivago*) have been published. One of the founders of the Soviet Human Rights movement, Yuri Daniel, sentenced in 1966 to five years imprisonment for publishing his works abroad, had some of his poems printed in *Ogonek*. Extracts from Orwell's *1984* have been published both in Ukrainian and in Russian (in *Literaturnaya Gazeta*). Translations of *Animal Farm* were published in 1988 in Estonian and Latvian and chapters in Russian have been published in *Nedelya* (the supplement to *Izvestiya*). Koestler's *Darkness at Noon* has been published in the journal *Neva*. Another satirical novel by the Russian Evgeni Zamyatin, *My (We)*, which portrays a totalitarian state, has also come out in book form. The publication of these works is significant because they cast in doubt not only the achievements of the October Revolution but also the socialist system itself.

This greater openness has been accompanied by the rehabilitation of many previously vilified writers. The Writers' Union has readmitted posthumously Boris Pasternak and many other writers who had been jailed for political dissent.

Limits, however, have been imposed. The journal *Novy Mir* had hoped to publish the works of Solzhenitsyn, but copies of its November 1988 edition announcing its plans to do so were withdrawn. In July 1988 Party Secretary Yakovlev announced that

> the shift in consciousness towards democratic thinking ... [had] also shed light on the petit bourgeois mentality dictated by individualism, egocentrism and banal egotism. ... Attempts to kindle emotions, to heat passions, to sow national or social suspicion, and to cause different social groups to collide, scarcely fit into the process of democratization.

Party Secretary Medvcdev announced in November 1988 that works such as *The Gulag Archipelago* and *Lenin in Zurich* would not be published and emphasized that "radical attacks on the Soviet political system, on our attitude to world history and the revolution, and on Vladimir Ilyich Lenin" would not be published.

The Ideology Commission (and Department) of the Central Committee plays a crucial role in the definition of what information, views, and opinions are deemed to be in the public interest. This function operates not primarily through a system of censors but through editors responding to the pressure from this department (and its executive bodies in the Party apparatus). Gorbachev sometimes admonished editors for their negative and anti-perestroika writings. Glasnost' is not complete: in the words of Soviet journalist Alexander Bovin, there is "half glasnost'," or more likely, "quarter glasnost'." "[O]ur glasnot' is still conditioned and fully dependent on the authorities' frame of mind." (*Moscow News*, 7 May 1989.)

Certain topics have been taboo: exposés of the personal lives of political leaders, unless they are officially disgraced; criticism of Gorbachev (though *Moscow News* in 1990 called for his resignation as general secretary of the CPSU); political prisoners; and other happenings of a more temporal character — including catastrophes such as the Chernobyl explosion (see below) and the suppression by troops of demonstrations in Tbilisi (Georgia) in 1989. There was an embargo on the discussion of the means of election of deputies to the Supreme Soviet following the elections to the Congress of People's Deputies in 1989.

Another revealing cxample has been the treatment of Eltsin by the press. Following his dismissal from his posts as first secretary to the Moscow Party Committee and candidate member of the Politburo, there was a ban on discussion of his case. His criticisms of Raisa Gorbachev and of Gorbachev have not found favor and either have not been reported or have only been mentioned in obscure Soviet sources.

Eltsin appeared, however, before the cameras of the BBC, CBS, and ABC when he criticized his opponent, Ligachev. At the Party Conference in July 1988 he said that he had given an interview with *Moscow News* but, like the two-hour interview with the journal *Ogonek*, it was not published because "publication had not been authorized." The foreign news services, Eltsin said, had been chosen for him by the State Committee for Television and Radio.

In response the editor of *Ogonek* replied that Eltsin had made too many personal remarks about members of the Central Committee and had called for the resignation of various officials. Such calls would have incurred the right of reply by the officials and Eltsin had refused to revise the passages.

It has been reported that Eltsin and other Soviet people have been critical about the public presentation of Mrs. Gorbachev, but none of this kind of glasnost' has been the subject of public comment in the media.

Press coverage of him continued to be unfavorable during his trip to the United States in 1989. *Pravda* printed a profile from an Italian newspaper that recounted his excessive drinking habits. This was followed by other adverse accounts of his private life. Following an exposure of his alleged behavior in the Supreme Soviet in 1989, he publicly claimed that Gorbachev had conducted a campaign against him aimed to "remove him from the political struggle". In February 1991, Eltsin (as President of the RSFSR) accused Goltelradio of bias and of refusing him live air time. As with politicians everywhere, however, bad news is good news and Eltsin has remained unscathed. In February 1991 in a TV interview, much to the consternation of his opponents, he attacked Gorbachev's dictatorial methods and called for his resignation.

Media Coverage and the West

Since the advent of glasnost' television and radio broadcasts and news programs have become more open. "East−West Bridges" have been televised with spontaneous questions asked by studio audiences in the United States and the USSR. Foreign statespersons in the shape of Presidents Mitterrand and Reagan and Prime Minister Thatcher have been given much air time to pontificate on politics and life in general. The American Phil Donahue and his British counterpart, Jimmy Saville, have conducted talk show programs concurrently on Western and Soviet media. In 1988 it was agreed that in Lithuania Christmas and Easter church services would be broadcast.

It may be surprising for Western readers to learn that even before perestroika news about the West played a prominent part in the Soviet mass media. Gayle Hollander, writing in 1972, found that the newspaper *Pravda* devoted 44 percent of its international stories to Western countries, particularly the United States, and only 31 percent to its own socialist allies. A consequence of the biased coverage of capitalist countries, noted above, is an insatiable thirst for knowledge about happenings in the West, whereas coverage of the Third World and the socialist states generates much less interest.

Even negative coverage does not have a negative effect: portrayal of striking U.S. steel workers or British miners shows them driving to the strikes in their own cars and living in homes — conditions far superior to those enjoyed by the Soviets. It is these latter aspects of Western life that are noted, whereas the political struggle is rejected as "Soviet Propaganda." As one Soviet academic put it to me: "American workers on strike get more pay than do Soviet workers in jobs." Even condemnatory accounts of British football hooligans have been interpreted positively by some Soviet *fanaty* (groups following a football team) who have begun to copy their excesses.

Since perestroika, coverage of Western life has become more even and many American popular films have been shown to a mass cinema market. Western classics (such as *Spartacus*) have been shown on the big screen. And Dustin Hoffman's *Tootsie* was showing in Leningrad at the same time as in Birmingham, England. On Soviet television popular Western films are rarely shown, although British nature films often appear. In addition, news and sports clips are often relayed, as are major sporting events held in the West. In the late 1980s American pop stars began to make an appearance — Diana Ross arrived in 1989.

The incidence of English language has increased: words such as *esteblishment*, *middeli* (middle class people), *plyuralizm*, as well as *uikend* (weekend), *dziny* (jeans), *andergraund*, and the international words *striptiz* and *videokasety* have come into general use. Latin script is used to give distinction to clothes, slogans on cars, as well as to name shops and garments. Little pornography is available; newspaper "pin-ups" and sexy stories are not common currency; what is available can be bought on street corners and underground passages in the main cities.

Entertainment and escapism are major functions of all mass communications. Programs of light entertainment, light music, quiz programs, and song competitions are becoming more frequent on Soviet television. However, such coverage is not comparable to Anglo-American television.

Mickiewicz's study (1988: 150—54) of *Vremya* programs found that 41 percent of the week's programs were devoted to public affairs and news. Entertainment accounted for 48 percent: 29 percent of total airtime is taken up with films; music, (classical and pop), and arts programs took up 15 percent of the time, sports 4 percent, children's programs 8 percent, and science and travel 3 percent.

As we noted earlier, it is probable that there are very much higher audience ratings for entertainment and variety programs than for news and public affairs. Observation in the Soviet Union by the present author showed that large crowds gathered around public screens when variety shows were broadcast, though this was not the case for news programs.

Nevertheless, there are still important differences between the Soviets and the West in the content of media. Ellen Mickiewicz (1988) has compared the content of television news in the United States (ABC) and the USSR (*Vremya*) using five months of coverage — three months in 1984 and two in 1985. News subjects that aired for more than one percent of the news program are shown in Table 9.1.

There are some striking contrasts: political and economic news is given much more prominence in the USSR. Economic progress, problems, and issues come to 18 percent of the time in the *Vremya* programs but only make up 6 percent of ABC. Government policy had eight times the amount of reporting in the USSR, and "official visits" (by foreign statespersons) took 14 percent of the time compared to 2 percent in the United States. ABC News compared with *Vremya* had three times more coverage of elections, eight times more reporting on terrorism, eleven times more on science and health, eight times more on disaster and accidents, and seven times more coverage of crime.

Mickiewicz further points out that reporting of foreign countries by *Vremya* is better than that in the United States.

> [T]he United States and its allies are far more central to the Soviet news than is the Soviet Union and its Warsaw Pact Allies to the American news. [The study shows] the centrality of America and the strong interest in the countries of Western Europe. ... Even those Western European countries not in NATO are of greater interest to the Soviet Union than they are to the United States. The regions of the Monroe Doctrine are also greater claimants of attention in the Soviet news, which devotes a larger share of its program to South America and the Caribbean. Central America is of greater interest to ABC than to *Vremya*, but not much. A good deal of Africa is blank for ABC news, and Asia receives only half the attention it does on *Vremya* (1987: 97—98).

Soviet news coverage has become more prompt as a result of two incidents that pointed to the dangers of not reporting news in a timely

Table 9.1
Selected Primary Newstime Subjects on U.S. and Soviet Television
(percentage of newstime*)

	VREMYA	*ABC*
Government policy	8	1
Elections	3	9
National ceremony	6	1
International negotiations	1	2
International meetings (intergovernmental organization)	3	1
International meetings (nongovernmental organization)	2	—
Official visits	14	2
Formal diplomacy	1	2
Arms control	2	2
Operations of party organizations	8	—
Terrorism	1	8
Military issues	1	4
Intelligence/spying	—	3
Space achievements	3	2
Science/health	1	11
Media	4	1
Economic progress	17	1
Economic problems	1	2
Economic issues (no evaluation)	—	3
Disaster/accident	1	8
Nature/environment	—	2
Crime	1	7
Sports	—	3
Arts	3	2
Total newstime (percent)	81	77

Source: Mickiewicz 1988: 109.
* Over 1 percent for at least one news program.

fashion. When the Chernobyl nuclear reactor exploded and caused serious pollution the Soviet public was not given knowledge of this disaster for several days and only after the event had been monitored in the West. A consequence of the news blackout was that valuable time was lost in controlling the effects of toxic nuclear waste and human life was lost unnecessarily. There was also a delay in reporting on the flight of the German aviator Rust, who piloted a biplane from Finland undetected and landed in Red Square, Moscow. News of both of these happenings was learned from foreign sources. This kind of nonreporting weakened the credibility of the news media. A comparable incident would be learning from Radio Moscow of armed Cubans parachuting to the grounds of the White House.

News coverage has changed somewhat under Gorbachev. The trial of the perpetrators of the Chernobyl events was shown on television and has been followed by prompt coverage of other incidents — the hijacking of Soviet aircraft and train derailments have been reported prominently in the press. While television has become a leader in the glasnost' policy and support of the leadership's policy of perestroika, this did not apply to the suppression of riots in Tbilisi in 1989, which was covered more adequately by Voice of America. The resignation of Shevardnadze as Foreign Minister was not covered as he had criticized the tendencies to autocracy under Gorbachev. But *Moscow News* in November 1990 published a letter calling for Gorbachev to give up his post as General Secretary of the Party.

Investigative journalism has always been claimed to be a major function of the press, and it has increased under perestroika. Regular programs spotlight the problems of speculation, bribery, corruption, national re-lations, ethnic identity, and environmental issues. Leading officials are in-terviewed and publicly criticized. The lid has been lifted off corruption and bribery of leading officials. In July 1988, for example, *Sotsialisticheskaya Industriya* declared that a Soviet-owned Swiss bank that had gone bank-rupt had used funds to give gifts to top Moscow officials. The reevaluation of the period of Stalin's rule has been the subject of many programs and press features.

A widening of reportage of other unsavory aspects of Soviet life has also occurred. Soviet television has covered narcotics, alcohol, and pro-stitution. And press articles have dealt with the dangers of AIDS, the extent of suicide, and other social pathologies. Hooliganism, such as destruction of property by Moscow Dynamo football supporters, has been the subject of much media discussion.

Press coverage of internal political debate has broadened to include the discussion of deficiencies of goods and services, the market, incen-tives, economic practice in the West, poverty, income differentials, the Afghan war, comparative election procedures, and interviews with Western political leaders. In 1989, in an opinion poll carried out by the Institute of Public Opinion Research, Margaret Thatcher was voted the "woman of the year" and Ronald Reagan followed Gorbachev as "man of the year."

CONCLUSIONS

In the early period of glasnost' in the USSR restraints on information flow were lifted: the media had a disruptive effect on public opinion. Even taxi drivers would comment negatively on the "anti-Sovietism" of television and papers like *Moscow News*.

The greater coverage of news, the debunking of previous Soviet practices, the delegitimation of people in authority roles, and the greater public attention given to the more seamy side of Soviet life have probably not only led to higher expectations on the part of many groups but also have weakened seriously the ideological cement of Soviet society. Rather than defining a united homogeneous socialist society, socialist pluralism has become the watchword of the Soviet authorities. The totalitarian model of manipulative control from the top does not account for the variety found in the Soviet media today.

While censorship has been reduced, it has not been abolished. State control persists although it is less oppressive and more liberal than in the past. Pressure is still put on editors who are told what they should not criticize. Relying more on self-censorship, editors and publishing houses seek to promote the policies that support perestroika and exclude views that oppose it, but in this operation they have been guided by the ideological apparatus of the Party. Despite these caveats, the mass media in the Soviet Union in the early 1990s is a vibrant and open mechanism for the discussion of Soviet and world affairs and portray a pluralism of views unknown in that country before Gorbachev. While the central authorities attempted to secure media favorable to the Gorbachev leadership, in practice a pluralistic set of originators of papers and journals has grown in the early 1990s. This has effectively undermined the authorities' attempts at media control. This tendency concerned the coup leaders of August 1991: they immediately attempted to restrict the media to official channels and they asserted control over television, press and radio.

Chapter 10

THE STATE OF WELFARE
Pensions and the Aged, Housing, and Health

In earlier chapters we have seen that in modern industrial societies, including the Soviet Union, social control is ensured by the coercive apparatus of the state, by consent that may be achieved through forms of participation by the citizen or through the autonomy afforded by civil society. Here we shall study yet another form of social control. State provision of goods and services for meeting human needs also may exert powerful forces for integration, solidarity, and tension management.

In the first chapter of this book I pointed out that the Soviet form of society, even as it arose under Stalin, exerted a great influence and received support not only in the USSR but also in the West. The appeal of communism, I pointed out, had to do with the fact that socialist society was one in which human needs were satisfied through state provision. In this chapter we shall turn to consider the assumptions that have guided the evolution of the welfare state, the ways they have been met, and how a recalibration of the relations between the state and the individual has influenced the provision of welfare.

THE WELFARE STATE

The Soviet Union claims to be a socialist society building communism. All socialists — Soviet and non-Soviet alike — believe that the fulfillment of human needs should be the major objective of social policy. The organizing principles of a Communist society are, as Marx put it, "from each person to give according to ability, to each to receive according to need."

A socialist society is one of equality, which implies that each individual is given equal consideration. It should be noted that these objectives are more aspirations on the part of socialists, more a normative maxim of how a society ought to be organized, rather than a statement of how any existing society is arranged. A communist society is a goal — a classless society of equals; whereas a socialist society is a lower stage along the evolution towards communism — there is an aspiration for communism but many imperfections continue.

Socialists would argue that this lack of fit between aspiration and reality is due on the one hand to the impossibility of people being able to realize their potential given existing circumstances: the political and social environment stultifies development, the number of jobs is not only inadequate but wage labor often lacks self-fulfillment for the employee; education is limited in content to economistic needs and is not able to draw out the individuals' abilities to their utmost. On the other hand, given the resources available in modern society, people's needs are too numerous to be met in full. Some societies are not able to fulfill the physical needs of shelter and food while even the more advanced ones have insufficient resources to satisfy everyone's need for medical treatment and security, let alone all people's desires for consumer durables such as cars.

Socialists, however, are optimistic: they believe that with economic development the material means to develop abilities and to meet needs will increase and greater equality will ensue. A prime role should be played by social policy in consciously directing resources to meet human needs.

Nonsocialists are more pessimistic about human nature; they stress that self-gratification is a characteristic of human nature and that incentives (particularly material ones) are necessary to make people work. The idea that "needs" can even in principle be fulfilled is mistaken: human needs, it is contended, are infinite, as human societies develop human needs multiply. Further, it is impossible and impracticable to try to meet all needs. Non-socialists regard inequality of ability and unequal satisfaction of needs as part of the human condition: freedom to excel and to become unequal is the catchword. Individual striving and the flourishing of inequality is necessary to maintain growth and to further progress. The objective of government, from the conservative viewpoint, should be to maintain a competitive economy, to encourage individualism and entrepreneurship, and to reward enterprise: desert rather than need is the organizing principle.

From this perspective, social policy is devised to allow the individual a great deal of freedom while state activity provides only a minimum of services — collective security (defense policy) and public works — and care for a residual part of the population (the old and disabled) who are unable to cope.

In practice, however, in all industrial societies the state plays an increasing role in the provision of welfare. The "welfare state" is not a monopoly of socialists. Bismarck's Germany provided national insurance in the nineteenth century. Margaret Thatcher, a high priestess of monetarism, competition and market forces, sought to preserve the British National Health Service, albeit in a more competitive and cost-effective form.

In Russia even before the advent of the Bolsheviks there has been a tradition of state provision. With the freeing of the Russian serfs in 1861 responsibility for their welfare fell principally to the government. The local councils (or *zemstvos*, as they were then called) provided welfare, education, and public health: this was a public service, provided free or for a nominal charge. The Health and Accident Insurance Act was financed by employer and employee contributions. Benefits were often linked to the number and level of contributions made.

In the United States where liberal philosophy emphasizes the individual's responsibility to assure privately against misfortune and for welfare, contributory schemes are encouraged whereby the employee and the employer pay life and health insurance.

In Europe's welfare states government schemes are obligatory — they are financed through compulsory deductions from one's salary, which in some cases finances insurance schemes.

Welfare legislation has been enacted by all modern industrial states. Government intentions have not only been motivated by an altruistic concern for the poor, they have also sought to develop human capital and to defuse political unrest: in this way they have performed tension management and helped social integration.

SOVIET WELFARE PROVISION

Soviet leaders have recognized the limitations on the government's ability to fulfill the needs of the population. Since the time of Stalin, state socialist societies have amended Marx's principle to read: "From each according to ability, to each according to work." The provision of work by the state and the citizen's obligation to work are keystones in social policy. These organizing principles recognize that people have different abilities, that work is differentiated (some is more difficult and arduous than other), and also that people should be rewarded by desert — in terms of qualifications and effort — rather than because of need. As we have noted in chapter 5, socialist justice involves the distribution of rewards according to the contribution of people to society. Although this principle is being emphasized under perestroika, it is important to understand that the tradition of social "justice" goes back to Stalin. The difference is that under perestroika such social "justice" is determined more by the market, whereas under Stalin reward was more administratively fixed.

Determining the value and thus the reward for one's "contribution" to society presents a problem. In a market system complex bargaining between employers and employees (not always to the satisfaction of each side) gives rise to a hierarchy of incomes. In a government-administered system sets of people in the apparatus fix wages (or at least part of them) — not always to the satisfaction of those who receive them. The maxim of "reward according to one's work" is open to different and conflicting interpretations, and fixing the level of wages becomes a site of struggle between those groups which seek to legitimate wide differentials to encourage more effort and innovation and those which claim that collective effort calls for low differentials, cooperation, and social solidarity. The former group places greater value on the contribution of managerial/executive/innovative skills, the latter on the need for physical labor and reward for unpleasant and manually exacting work. We have discussed some of these views above in chapter 5. As we noted earlier, wages and differentials in living standards have become an established part of Soviet society.

The idea of a progression to a society based on the fulfillment of needs has been recognized by socialists and, realizing that the market does not recognize need, they have given the state a major role in the provision of collective welfare. Unlike the ethic of capitalism, which is based on possessive individualism, the ethic of socialism is collectivist and involves redistribution. The state attempts to distribute resources to meet what it believes the public needs; it suppresses individual rewards when these militate against defined collective needs. The welfare state intervenes in the operation of the economy and in civil society to secure the well-being of the citizens as a whole. Social welfare schemes are often "non-contributory" — there are no deductions from individual pay packets for insurance — instead this is done collectively by the government's control of resources.

Soviet-type societies before the reforms of the 1970s and 1980s were state socialist societies. The state attempted to suppress the individualism of the market and took responsibility for the provision of employment and comprehensive social services. The operation of what was left of the market in the economy did not distribute resources according to demand and supply; rather the state collectively allocated resources in line with the rulers' conception of needs.

In all state socialist societies the state sector has taken on a massive role in the provision of welfare services: housing, education, health, and social security. The 1977 Constitution of the USSR guarantees to the citizen of the USSR the right to work, health care, security in old age, and housing. A service is provided by the state and is made available to the public either through cash benefits (disability pension, for instance) or in "kind" (educational and medical services provided free to the public). In principle, people who are sick receive medication according to their illness and not their ability to pay; similarly, educational services are delivered according to the person's ability to benefit. One exception is the area of old age pensions, which are allocated on the basis of the number and level of contributions paid during employment. This is legitimated in terms of a person's contribution "according to work": those who have an incomplete record of paid employment or have had relatively low wages receive lower pensions.

Until the leadership of Gorbachev, the administrative capacity of the state was the major resource both for industrial development and social provision. Autonomous private formations in civil society were weak — there were no charitable institutions, such as the Salvation Army or private insurance schemes, for example. Poverty, it was believed, was largely eliminated through the provision of paid labor for all citizens. The government owned the means of production and all educational and health institutions were owned and controlled by the state.

Somewhat exceptional is the existence of a large private housing stock in the countryside, although the land on which houses stand has been nationalized. The control and certification of professionals — doctors, teachers, lawyers — is the prerogative of a government agency. Health insurance is not a private concern but a state function and private education and medical care were only available at the fringes, that is, in the provision of private tutoring and private medical consultation.

The objective of state legislation was to provide a comprehensive mass facility. By the early 1970s the Soviet social security system covered all industries and social groups, although until 1964 collective farmers were covered only through their own "mutual aid" schemes. Benefits related to earnings were available to all employees through old age and disablement pensions, illness and maternity benefits; child benefit was payable to all, irrespective of employment record.

Expenditure on sociocultural activity and science in the USSR in 1986 amounted to 28 percent of the national income; this figure includes expenditures on the All-Union (Federal), state, cooperative, enterprise, and collective farm accounts. The major welfare expenditures are shown in Table 10.1.

Table 10.1
Distribution of Welfare Expenditure (including Science) in
the USSR, 1986 (percent of total expenditure)

Education		24
Science		17.7
Health and Physical Recreation		14
Social Security and Insurance		39.5
Of which, Pensions	29.5	
grants and allowances	8.7	
Others		4.8
Total		100

Note: The total budget in 1986 was 166.7 billion.
Source: Derived from *Narkhoz za 70 let* (1987): 632.

Imperfections in Welfare Allocation

In practice not all people's needs have been met by the Soviet welfare
state. As noted above, resources have been inadequate to meet needs
and a form of administrative allocation has taken place giving some
people managing the state apparatus enormous powers. Government
agencies have had to work out policies to allocate resources between
different client groups. This has led either to arbitrariness or to administratively distributed privilege. Lack of public confidence in the way
provision is carried out has ensued. Public provision of services means
public control of that provision. In an altruistic society such control is
exercised for the benefit of the public. The bureaucratic control needed
to effect the distribution of benefits, however, leads to a displacement of
public goals by which many of those holding the power to distribute
actually benefit.

The reforms of Gorbachev have sought to redress grievances against
administrative malpractice by increasing the role of the market. As he put
it in his speech to the Nineteenth Party Conference,

We want to strengthen the guarantees of the individual's social and economic
rights, but to this end, corresponding changes in economic and political
conditions are necessary. ... The social benefits received from society and
the attitude toward labor activity are coupled in an inseparable way. ...
Here is displayed again the importance of economic-accountability principles in running the economy, principles that make it possible to link not
only earnings but also the satisfaction of social requirements to the labor
contribution of the individual and of every collective.

It would be erroneous to think of the Soviet state "putting into practice" the socialist norms defined above. In the historical development of the USSR the ideology of Marxism-Leninism was one important formative influence; also important, however, were the traditional value patterns, practices, and the requirements of the economy.

From the time of the consolidation of power under Lenin to the present the Soviet Union has been an economically developing country. After political survival, industrialization and economic growth have been the paramount goals of policy makers. It is in this context that the Soviet state has pursued its social policy. In many respects it shares assumptions similar to those of advanced Western capitalist societies. The Soviet state is concerned with increasing the size and health of the population, inculcating norms of hard work, and teaching students skills that are necessary for the advance of the economy. A comprehensive health care system, employment-linked social security benefits, and a system of polytechnical education all may be said to function in support of the needs of the economy. Employers in all industrial societies prefer a well-fed, healthy, motivated, and well-educated work force.

Functions of Social Policy

One might distinguish, then, between different functions of social policy. On the one hand the provision of certain types of collective welfare, for example, vocational education, are necessary to further development of the economic base of society; on the other hand, collective welfare provisions, such as health and primary education, enhance labor productivity. Social security may help maintain social cohesion and solidarity, as well as give legitimacy to the state: income maintenance in misfortune and old age leads to a politically contented population. Hence the welfare state is supportive of a social order and social provision is made not only by socialist and social-democratic regimes but also by conservatives and liberals. If one is cynical, one may regard such expenditure as a necessary "expense" of the ruling groups to maintain their own power.

Differences arise over the incidence of various types of policies and over sources of finance. One major contrast between state socialist and capitalist economies is policy concerning the provision of paid employment. The Soviet government has accepted the responsibility to maintain all able-bodied persons in work. By giving all people a job and the wages that go with it, income maintenance and social security measures to alleviate poverty and unemployment are made redundant. (For actual levels of unemployment, see chapter 2.) Since the proclamation of a full-employment economy in the USSR in 1930, unemployment benefit has not been available. (But employees have insurance pay for illness or other legitimate absence from work.) The place of work and employment duration have become a crucial determinant of the level of welfare benefits.

Interventionist welfare states everywhere to a large extent function in support of the economy, though they are often legitimated by politicians in terms of public altruism and individual concern. Not all welfare activities, however, may be interpreted as contributing to the reproduction or efficiency of an economic and political system. Some provisions are forms of collective consumption provided by the state either free or for a nominal sum, for example, there are free lending libraries, municipal orchestras, parks, allotments, sports and day care facilities, together with the services provided for the needy and weak, which are the substance of a socialist conception of welfare. Meeting needs through public expenditure, however, may reduce and undermine the allocation of resources to renew and develop the economy. This issue is at the root of the struggle between various social groups over the allocation of resources and the scale of the welfare budget.

Demands for care and treatment may reach such a scale that the process of capital accumulation may be threatened. Once again laissez-faire critics argue that the greater the security and social provision, the less is the incentive for individual effort. Laissez-faire ideologists would argue that after a certain minimum level of "basic" facilities have been collectively provided, it is the responsibility of individuals to allocate income for their own welfare.

More libertarian socialists, too, point to the control function of the welfare state. As we noted in chapter 1, *Brave New World* is a faulted utopia because people in it lack choice and freedom of decision. The satisfaction of human needs requires more than adequate provision of social services. In all modern societies, administrative systems are themselves forms of control over consumers and the employees in the public sector. Employees are confronted by a single employer and consumers have no choice of service if they are disgruntled with state provision.

These points of view, which have been well rehearsed in controversy between republicans and democrats in the United States and conservative and socialist parties in Europe, are now also bones of contention in the USSR. To understand how and why policy has changed we shall examine the salient features of welfare provision in the Soviet Union and the problems to which these have given rise.

Work Under Socialism

For Marxists and socialists work is a primary human need. In a well-known passage in *The German Ideology* Marx pointed out: "The first historical act is ... production of material life itself. This is indeed ... a fundamental condition of all history, which today, as thousands of years ago, must be accomplished every day and every hour merely in order to sustain human life."

Work not only meets human needs through the production and subsequent consumption of goods and services but it fulfills a social need on the part of the worker. Western writers on work and employment also recognize the social and psychological significance of employment and the harm that may result from unemployment. Jahoda (1982) has defined four functions pertaining to employment: the provision of income, the conferment of social status and position to the employee and immediate kin, the provision of an activity to occupy and divide the day, and the making of an environment in which social intercourse may be enjoyed.

As we noted in chapter 2, the Soviet state has attempted to provide full employment for all of the able-bodied population. The 1977 Constitution, moreover, recognizes the right of the individual to a choice of trade or profession. This recognition signals a development in the Soviet conception of work under "mature socialism." Individual satisfaction in and with work was acknowledged as having great importance to policy makers. We may point then to a tension in Soviet society between the economic requirements of the economy and the aspirations of many people. The provision of work is a traditional social goal (both for the individual and the society of which he or she is a part) and has to be reconciled with the aspirations for different types of work expressed by individuals.

Soviet policy makers, therefore, are constrained by ideological objectives that have not been adopted by governments under capitalism: the provision of work for all the population, and the requirement to give opportunities to people to find satisfaction in work. Capitalist governments take a narrower view of employment. The market may call for levels of unemployment as an incentive to efficiency, but the role of government in market economies is to provide income support for the unemployed and family dependents. By the same token, workers who do not find employment in the USSR would be destitute, whereas under modern capitalism their basic minimum needs are usually met.

We may emphasize here a major consequence of the Soviet welfare state. Benefits are linked to employment and earnings. The system encourages people to work instead of providing facilities to meet basic needs. Hence the logic of the system is that people who have inadequate work records (not only the feckless, but heads of single parent families, the old and the handicapped) may live in poverty. (See chapter 5 above for a discussion of poverty.)

Pensions and the Aged

Pensions in old age are the most costly single part of income maintenance provision. (See Table 10.1.) The number of elderly pensioners has risen from 5.4 million in 1960, to 24 million in 1970, to 34 million in 1980, and 40.5 million in 1986. In the mid-1980s pensioners of all kinds came to 19.8 percent of the population (13.8 percent in 1966). The minimum age of retirement in the USSR is much lower than in Western capitalist countries: sixty years for men and fifty-five for women. In the West the statutory age is usually sixty-five, in some countries it is five years earlier for women than men. In sweated labor jobs — mining and furnaces — men may retire at the age of fifty; some other heavy labor occupations qualify for retirement at fifty-five for men and fifty for women. The qualifying work period for receiving a full pension is twenty-five years employment for a man and twenty years for a woman; for a minimum pension, the qualifying period is five years. Other benefits accrue to women who have reared five or more children and have worked fifteen years — they can retire at fifty. The blind can take full pension ten years early if they have worked fifteen years (for men), and ten years (for women).

Since October 1989, pensioners may continue working and draw a full pension. (Before that date, total income could not exceed 150 rubles per month for government employees and 300 per month for engineering-technical workers.) In the early 1980s, 32 percent of pensioners continued to work. The average pension received for manual and nonmanual workers qualifying was 83.7 rubles a month, for collective farmers it was 53.1 rubles. By comparison, the average wage for manual and nonmanual workers in 1986 was 195.6 rubles per month (for more details see Trehub 1987: 25). Dependents such as nonemployed wives or children raise pensions by 10 percent for one dependent and 15 percent for two or more. Pensions are not linked to inflation or increases in the standard of living and they are not taxed.

The old are a particularly vulnerable part of the population. This is particularly so in a society where private wealth has been nationalized and where work is the only source of income. The provision of pensions on the scale of the Soviet Union has undoubtedly provided comprehensive security for the urban population in old age. Rates of between

55 percent to 85 percent of previous income are generous when compared to noncontributory schemes in other countries.

The provision of pensions, however, does suffer from serious inadequacies. Soviet sources estimate that 70 to 75 rubles per month is a minimum material security level. This figure would place many low-paid workers, particularly those on collective farms and those with incomplete qualifying work periods, below the poverty level. It is not surprising, then, that pensioners form the largest groups of people in poverty. Without detailed studies one can only guess at the extent of the problem. An article in the Soviet press (*Sotsialisticheskaya Industriya*, 1 June 1988) found that the majority of single elderly people who retired in the 1960s live in poverty. A fairly cautious estimate would put a quarter of the elderly at the poverty level. As we noted in chapter 5, some one-fifth of the Soviet population lives around the poverty level, with incomes below 70 rubles per month. Data published in 1989 showed that 40.7 percent of pensioners received pensions below 60 rubles per month: 85 percent of collective farmers on pension were in this category.

Although minimum pensions have risen regularly by government decree, it is unlikely that the increased minimum takes account of inflation and the rising standard of living enjoyed by those who are employed. Average pensions (for all types of pensioners) have risen regularly in money terms as follows: 1970, 34.4 Rs; 1980, 57.2 Rs; 1987, 78.1 Rs. If the differences in pensions are expressed as a proportion of average salary, pensions have fallen from 45.9 percent in 1970 to 26.3 percent in 1987. In October 1989 rises in pension rates secured a common minimum monthly payment for workers and collective farmers of 70 rubles per month. Invalids also received increases to a minimum of 85 rubles for the most severely disabled and 70 rubles for the next category.

Current schemes provide poor coverage for dependents who are not employed or who have incomplete contributory years. At root, the weakness of the scheme is that pension according to work record is not commensurate with need. The growing "marketization" of the Soviet economy will probably lead to a worsening position of the pensioner as fewer resources will be made available for transfer payments. This will be exacerbated by a rise in the number of pensioners. It seems likely that the age of retirement may be raised in line with that of capitalist societies and that employees may be encouraged to provide for retirement out of their own income. Supplementary pensions since 1988 may be purchased out of income and give greater pension payments on retirement. This again will lead to greater differentials between different categories of old age pensioners.

Housing

Housing is such an important component of one's social security that most welfare states provide minimum levels of shelter for the homeless and subsidized homes for the poor. In state socialist societies this principle is taken one step further: the state recognizes the citizen's right to housing and seeks to provide it.

Article 44 of the Constitution of the USSR recognizes that its citizens have a right to housing.

> This right is ensured by the development and upkeep of state and socially-owned housing; by assistance for cooperative and individual home building; by fair distribution, under public control, of the housing that becomes available through fulfillment of the program of building well-appointed dwellings, and by low rents and low charges for utility services.

Whereas the market is not regarded as an appropriate means to meet needs, in practice elements of market relations and administrative influence enter into housing allocation and the fulfillment of needs is partial.

The provision of living accommodation has much wider social implications than simply a place to live. The arrangement of housing stock may facilitate different types of family groupings. The location of housing in relation to other uses of space — production, retail trade, and leisure use — also has an important effect on the quality of life. These wider implications may only be touched on here.

In the development of the USSR under Stalin housing had a low priority. Standards of accommodation were poorer than in Western Europe even before the revolution and they were exacerbated by the neglect of house building during the period of rapid industrialization in the 1930s. Housing construction accounted for only 8 percent of total investment in the Third Five Year Plan (1937−42). In the industrialization period the emphasis was on investment in the economy; and in the welfare sector, education and health were given priority. Hence the suppression of the market led to less house building than would otherwise have been the case. The stock of accommodation was further depleted by some 25 percent during the Second World War.

It was only under Khrushchev that a massive housing drive was undertaken. Investment in housing rose to a peak of 23 percent of all capital investment in the period of the Sixth Five Year Plan (1956−60). Since the 1960s over ten million apartments have been constructed per year, though the proportion of capital investment has fallen — it was 15 percent in the Eleventh Five Year Plan (1981−85).

The average size of dwellings has risen from 8.9 square metres in 1960 to 14.9 square metres in 1986. Total building has increased since 1956: in the Sixth Five Year Plan (1956–60) 474 million square metres were constructed, the figure rose to 552 in the Eleventh Five Year Plan (1981–85). In 1986, some 85 percent of urban families lived in self-contained flats.

Despite these advances, a housing shortage remains. Trehub has estimated that over nine million families lived in communal flats sharing kitchens and bathrooms in the mid-1980s (1987: 29). The lack of a market in property means that existing facilities are not efficiently used and young families entering the housing market have to share accommodation. This, in turn, becomes a factor in marriage breakup and the postponement of the start of a family. The goal of the Party's program adopted in 1986, is to achieve a separate dwelling "for each family" by the year 2000.

Housing stock and urban arrangements do not differ greatly in conception from those of Western European countries. Alternatives of communal living with shared facilities were advocated by some left-wing Communists during the 1920s, but these suggestions were not influential: the majority of housing is arranged in self-contained family units. In 1981–85, the two-room self-contained (plus utilities) apartment was the most commonly constructed dwelling (38 percent of flats in the state sector) followed by three-room dwellings (36 percent). The living room usually doubles as a bedroom at night. The average amount of room space is less than that of industrialized Western European countries and much less than that of the United States, though it is more equitably distributed. Even the privileged groups in the USSR live in small flats.

A major traditional divide in the USSR as in other developing societies is the difference in standards between town and country. The urbanization of the USSR has led to the mushrooming of towns and has increased the strain on the urban housing stock. This has been exacerbated by the provision of services — shops, cinemas, hospitals, and higher education — in the large towns, making them attractive as areas of residence. In order to prevent the growth of shanty towns, the authorities have limited residence rights to people with a *propiska*, or authority to live in a given area. This has limited urban sprawl, but has led to long-distance commuting and to settlements of migrating workers on the periphery of large towns. The policy for meeting the needs for work and choice of occupation is geared to the development of industry in the localities, but in practice great differences continue between geographical areas and between town and country.

Housing construction and ownership has three different institutional forms in the USSR: public (*gosudarstvennye*), cooperative, and private ownership (*lichnaya sobstvennost'*). Public housing accounts for the bulk of new construction (6.6 million flats in 1981–86), followed by the co-operatives (580,000 1981–86). Of the total housing stock, in 1986 40 percent (measured in living space) was in private ownership. In the countryside this constituted the predominant form of housing (1,093 million square metres out of a total 1,550 million square metres).

The cooperative sector is relatively small — less than 10 percent of new public housing. Cooperative housing is larger and of better quality than public housing. In the countryside, collective farmers (often with the help of the farm) build their own houses.

Since the 1950s high rise flats have been the most typical form of urban public and cooperative construction. The *mikrorayon* (microdistrict) was a kind of council house (municipally owned) estate of high-rise dwellings served by communal gardens, shops, polyclinic, schools, and child care facilities. The conception of urban living was to build self-contained living and leisure areas or estates spatially separated from industrial production. In practice, however, the social infrastructure was given a low priority and many estates lacked (and lack) facilities. Public transport was irregular and journeys to work were long. "Public sector" housing is built either by local authorities (Soviets) or by enterprises who naturally favor their own employees.

A major difference between "public sector" housing in the USSR and market and public housing in the West is that rents are low and do not even reflect costs of construction. Fixed by law in 1928 and unaltered until the mid-1980s, living space is charged at 13 kopecks per square metre per month. (Note: 100 kopecks=one ruble.) This gives a rental of 6 rubles 65 kopecks per month for the average sized flat in 1986. (Soviet sources reckon rent accounts for some 3 percent of household expenditure.)

The availability of utilities reflects the age of the housing stock. The older wooden dwellings in the countryside usually lack running water, central heating, indoor toilets, and sewerage. In the urban public and cooperative apartments in 1986 over 92 percent had running water, 89 percent central heating, and 72 percent hot water. Costs of utilities are very low, and in total are not much more than rents. The entire outgoings (rent, gas, and electricity) of a new three-room flat (plus kitchen and bathroom) in Moscow came to 25 rubles per month in 1988.

Allocation of Housing
Housing is allocated initially by administrative determination of need in the public sector, by ability to pay in the cooperative, and in the private sector access is determined through inheritance, purchase, or by reward in the collective farm. In the public sector, housing is built and administered by local authorities (this accounts for about 40 percent of the stock) and

the bulk of the remainder by factories and trade union committees. The local authority allocates new housing according to "need," which is determined by a number of criteria including adequacy of existing accommodation, length of time on the list, size of family, the existence of handicap or disability. Availability and size of apartment may also be influenced by the status of the applicant — those requiring a work space at home — writers, executives, lecturers — may be allocated a larger flat. Exchanges of accommodations may be afforded by mutual consent between the parties subject to the exchange meeting their needs. When circumstances change, the administrative authority may relocate residents subject to their approval. Children have the right to "inherit" their parents' housing.

Special occupations, such as the police and medical personnel, may be given priority — as may be notable employees, such as football stars or exemplary workers. In more intangible ways housing is allocated to people with good work records and high levels of public participation. Preference is not only afforded to specific occupations, housing resources also may be allocated to ministries to encourage the development of particular projects or services. The unequal allocation of resources to factories results in low priority industries having fewer funds available for house building than do high priority ones.

Administrative allocation is open to corruption through the bribery of housing officials and "exchanges" of public sector housing may be accompanied by illegal monetary payments. People with influence in the community may circumvent the queue. In addition, for the top elites — writers and political notables — special housing in the form of summer houses (*dachas*) is available. The availability of housing to employees of factories relies on similar principles.

The cooperative sector is financed by groups of consumers. Cooperative housing is often organized by work places or by groups of potential residents in urban areas, with a high concentration in Moscow and Leningrad. The cooperative finances and maintains the apartments. Costs are considerable and much higher than public sector rents: a three-room apartment would cost some 15,000 rubles and a down payment would amount to about 4,500 rubles (30 percent). Mortgage repayments are made over a twenty-year period and rates of interest payable on government loans are very low (0.5 percent). These sums are small compared to Western real estate, but in a country with an average income of 196 rubles in 1986, cooperative housing is an alternative for the richer groups.

Most of the private dwellings are located in the countryside. Their owners and their heirs have a right to the use of the property in perpetuity. Such houses may also be sold. The existence of this large rural stock is the reason why there is little demand for cooperatives in the countryside.

Private dwellings cannot be built in towns with over 100,000 inhabitants, and no family may own more than one house suitable for regular occupation — the amount of living space for any family is limited to a maximum of 60 square metres.

Housing in the USSR has many contradictory features. Under Stalin, housing was not a priority need and the welfare of the population suffered. Since the time of Khrushchev the provision of a mass urban housing stock has been an achievement of the central planners and compares favorably (given the shortage of resources) with the council housing provided for the urban proletariat in England in the early twentieth century. Many inadequacies and shortages remain and the government under Gorbachev has called for renewed efforts to solve the housing shortage. However, one should not adopt too pessimistic an attitude towards the dissatisfaction of housing needs. The study of Soviet emigrants to the United States in the early 1980s found that two-thirds of the sample questioned regarded housing as satisfactory; indeed it was the most favorably evaluated aspect of the standard of living in the USSR. Those who had managed to find accommodation were satisfied with it, whereas the younger emigrants who were disfavored by the allocation system were the least contented (Millar and Clayton 1987: 39–42).

The administrative allocation of housing leads to some injustices. Political influence over housing allocation may lead to distortions. But control over the housing market has minimized the availability of large units for small families and the housing stock is undeniably more equally distributed than under capitalism, although the standards of housing are much worse than in Western Europe and the United States.

The institutional division of housing stock gives rise to many inequalities. The economic development of certain industries and their employees' privileged access to housing has infringed the needs of other workers in low-priority sectors. The supply of cheap and highly subsidized housing initially had an equalizing effect. With the growth of incomes, however, and the massive housing stock, a low rent policy creates its own problems. It leads to inertia in the housing market. The large stock of often poorly constructed buildings needs upkeep and repair. This is a charge on public funds, which has not been forthcoming. Public sector housing has been neglected and underfinanced.

Unless the state budget grows considerably in size, it is likely that rents will rise. "Shortage" is a relative concept; in any society with rents as low as those in the Soviet Union there would be an indefinite housing shortage. Raising rents will reduce the number of flats demanded and may lead to a movement of residents from larger to smaller premises thereby increasing the supply of housing.

Perestroika and Housing

Under perestroika access to the housing stock will change. The provision of state housing has been traditionally part of the process of productive investment. It has been closely linked to industrial priorities and has been a device to reward and discipline labor; meeting social needs was a minor consideration. The greater wealth of the Soviet Union is leading to a more individualized and consumption-oriented society. People want more choice in the disposition of income and housing is one important area of consumer satisfaction. To allow greater social differentiation to take place, it is likely that housing will become a marketable commodity.

In February 1988 industrial enterprises were given the right to sell units from their own housing stock and in 1990/91 many local Soviets resolved to sell or even give tenants their homes. By increasing owners' repair costs this practice will push up expenses, reduce the losses currently incurred in state budgets and use up disposable income. It seems likely that the cooperative and private sector will develop at the cost of public housing.

The "injustice" of privileged people having access to a special fund of housing is likely to be replaced by a market system in which they may have to buy their privileges. The rise of a rich business class with money from trade in the services sector will probably lead to a greater demand for private housing. The constitutional right to "fair distribution of housing under public control" will increasingly be replaced by distribution according to ability to pay. This will not be achieved overnight. The public mentality, as in other Western welfare states, is to regard housing (like health) as a universal human need that should not be determined by people's ability to pay.

A likely compromise has been suggested by Zaslavskaya and one of the leading economic reformers, Aganbegyan. They consider that a minimum housing standard should be subsidized, but that living space above this standard should be priced at market rates. A great advantage of market pricing of housing, from an economic point of view, is that the surplus of money would be mopped up in house purchase and inflationary tendencies would be curbed.

Health and Health Care

Social welfare policies have three aspects: the provision of social capital, enhancing the legitimacy of the state, and fulfilling individual needs. The public provision of health care covers all three functions. The development of an industrial system requires a fit, healthy, and reliable work force. Ideologically, socialism has put much emphasis on the collective power of the state to provide a comprehensive and mass health care system. Only socialism, it is often contended, can meet all people's needs; under capitalism, health is "business" and neglects the poor to the advantage of the rich.

The major principles of health care were enunciated by the Commissariat for Health in 1918. Health care was to be the responsibility of the state, it should be provided free of charge, and the proletariat should have preferential treatment; the system should be centralized and uniform and should involve citizen participation with an emphasis on preventative medicine. According to Article 42 of the Constitution of the USSR of 1977,

> Citizens of the USSR have the right to health protection. This right is ensured by free, qualified medical care provided by state health institutions; by extension of the network of therapeutic and health-building institutions; by the development and improvement of safety and hygiene in industry; by carrying out broad prophylactic measures; by measures to improve the environment; by special care for the health of the rising generation, including the prohibition of child labor, excluding work done by children as part of the school curriculum; and by developing research to prevent and reduce the incidence of disease and ensure citizens a long and active life.

As we have seen many constitutional objectives are only partly fulfilled, and in practice people's health requirements also are not met by the services provided. Until the Brezhnev administration, the Soviet health service was held in high esteem by many foreign specialists who emphasized the tremendous strides taken in the field of public health and medicine. As Mark Field put it in 1967,

> Soviet socialized medicine has been one of the more impressive and positive achievements of the Soviet regime, and has probably met with the approval of the vast majority of the population. ... [T]he challenge imposed by Soviet socialized medicine to the West and particularly to the United States, is imposing. (Field 1967: 202–203)

Under Brezhnev and particularly under Gorbachev, the health service has come under criticism and has been seriously faulted in terms of the quality of its service. The successes may be measured against the provision of a mass rudimentary health service developed under Stalin. Its current failures are due to unevenness in provision, inadequacies in supply and training, higher levels of expectations, and a changing pattern of illness.

The recognition of deficiencies in health service provision was strikingly brought home to the Soviet public by the speech of the Soviet Minister of Health, Chazov, to the Nineteenth Party Conference:

We have become proud of the national health system; but we have been silent about the fact that by level of infant mortality we were in the fiftieth place in the world after Mauritius and Barbados. We were proud that we had more doctors and hospitals than any other country in the world, but we were silent on the fact that by average figures of life expectancy we occupy 32nd place in the world. The Uzbek writer Sharif Rashidov wrote about happy children of a blossoming republic, but the leader of the Communist Party of Uzbekistan, Sh. Rashidov, did exactly nothing for saving the thirty-three thousand children who died every year not surviving up to one year of age. They squandered and embezzled milliards of rubles in the republic, but 46 percent of the hospitals were accommodated in buildings which did not answer minimum sanitary hygienic demands.

The nationalized state health service has pioneered mass public provision, but it has been unable to meet the demands of patients and has fallen back in the provision of medical care. In Russia in 1917 health conditions were centuries behind Western European societies. On this topic Lenin coined the phrase, "Either the lice will defeat socialism or socialism will defeat the lice." The Soviet health service succeeded in defeating the lice, but we shall discover that it has not lived up to the expectations generated for high quality health treatment in an advanced industrial society. We shall first consider, objectively, the changes that have taken place in Soviet health provision and then make some evaluations.

The improvement in health care provision can be measured by the increase in the number of doctors, as shown on Table 10.2. This table illustrates the rapid development of health services in terms of the increase in physicians over time and also the variation between republics. The Central Asian republics are more backward and the Baltic ones are better endowed. The Soviet Union claims to have the highest proportion of qualified physicians per capita in the world (42.7 per 10,000 population).

Table 10.2
Growth in Number of Physicians, 1913—86

	1913	1940	1986	1913	1940	1986
		(in thousands)		(per ten thousand of the population)		
USSR	28.1	155.3	1201.7	1.8	7.9	42.7
Russian Republic	15.9	90.8	663.5	1.8	8.2	45.7
Uzbekistan	0.14	3.2	64.9	0.3	4.7	34.1
Tadzhikistan	0.02	0.6	12.9	0.2	4.1	26.9
Latvia	0.6	2.5	12.8	2.6	13.2	48.8

Source: Data from *Narkhoz za 70 let* (1987): 20.

Comparative figures for the West are 25.7 for the United States (1983), 30.1 in West Germany (1985), and 18.2 in Great Britain (1977).

Average life expectancy has risen from 32 years in 1896—97 to 67 in 1955—56, and 70 in 1968—69; it dropped to 67.9 in 1978—79 and recovered to 69.8 in 1986. These figures are illustrated in Figure 10.1, which also shows comparative figures for the United States and the United Kingdom in 1986.

Similar changes may be observed in the infant mortality rate, that is, deaths of infants under one year of age. This rate fell steadily from 181.5 per thousand live births in 1940, to 80.7 in 1950, and 24.7 in 1970; it rose to peak at 31.4 in 1976, and has fallen steadily since, reaching 27.3 in 1980 and 25.4 in 1987. By way of comparison, the infant mortality rate of the United States has fallen from 20 in 1970 to 10 in 1986; Britain's figure was 9 in the latter year. Significant differences may again be observed between republics: in the Russian Republic, the infant mortality rate fell from 23 in 1970 to 19.4 in 1987; in Lithuania from 19.4 to 12.3; but in Uzbekistan the figures rose from 31 to 45.9, and in Turkmenistan from 46.1 to 56.4. Figure 10.2 illustrates that the rise in infant mortality in the USSR was largely a result of large increases in the rates of the Central

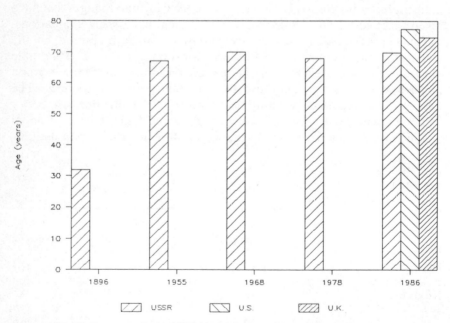

Figure 10.1 Life Expectancy in the USSR, United States, and United Kingdom

Source: Based on data from *Narkhoz v 1987g.* (Moscow 1988).

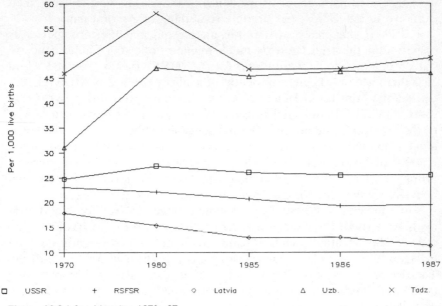

Figure 10.2 Infant Mortality, 1970–87

Source: Based on data from *Narkhoz v 1987g.* (Moscow 1988).

Asian republics (shown by the data for Tadzhikistan and Uzbekistan on the graph) which were not outweighed by the slight decline in the RSFSR and the European republics. In 1989 infant mortality in the USSR fell to 22.6.

The incidence of infectious diseases has shown a steady fall. Typhoid and paratyphoid fell from 62 cases per 100,000 of the population in 1940 to 22 in 1960, and 5 in 1986; the incidence of polio rose from 0.65 in 1940 to 3.3 in 1960, and dropped to 0.06 in 1986; whooping cough dropped from 256 in 1960 to 16 in 1970, 5 in 1980, 19.4 in 1985 and 6.3 in 1986. These figures, however, are still much higher than advanced Western countries — in the United States, for instance, incidence is between 4 and 10 times less.

Unlike in the West, AIDS is a negligible health risk: in 1987 there were only 22 people diagnosed as carriers, and in 1988 only four Soviet citizens suffered from it compared with 40,000 in the United States (in addition there were 83 carriers in 1988). In October 1988 the first death of a Russian from AIDS was reported in the USSR. She was a prostitute from Leningrad who had been incorrectly diagnosed and it was not until after her death that AIDS was confirmed. Public discussion of AIDS led to exaggerated fears about its incidence in the USSR, and "Speed" as it is known in the USSR, has become something of a moral panic.

It is likely that many carriers are undetected and Western specialists suspect that the true figure is much higher. Following public concern, sixteen million people were tested for the AIDS virus in 1988−89. Until 1988 there had only been three deaths officially registered as AIDS related. In 1989 the Minister of Health reported that there were 142 active AIDS cases, and 271 HIV-infected citizens. Many more cases have been caused by the use of infected needles, but incidence in unlikely to reach the levels attained in the West because intravenous drug users are not very common. Homosexuality is a criminal offense, punishable by up to five years in prison. This has the effect of keeping down the level of homosexual behavior by marginalizing a "gay" lifestyle.

While infectious diseases have declined, degenerative illness and accidents have risen: the incidence of heart disease and cancer has increased considerably; deaths from heart and circulatory diseases nearly doubled between 1965 and 1986. Influenza and pneumonia have also risen seriously. The rise in degenerative illness and death is also influenced by the aging of the population. The greater urbanization and faster tempo of life have given rise to stress and pollution. Smoking has led to more cancer deaths, and fatalities due to pulmonary diseases quintupled between 1960 and 1979 (Feshbach 1985: 11).

Accidents and injuries have increased. Safeguards against injury are less effective in Soviet industry than in the West. Road accidents have spiralled upward. High alcohol consumption (discussed later) has contributed significantly to the accident rate, particularly road accidents.

These figures illustrate trends in the Soviet Health Service: there has been a major improvement in health in the fifty-year period spanning from 1920 to 1970, thereafter betterment increased only slightly; in some cases little progress occurred and a significant residual of ill-health persisted. There has also been a shift in the type of illness: infectious diseases are being replaced by degenerative illness and accidents. While the gap between the USSR and other advanced countries narrowed in the earlier period, since 1970 it has not.

In the West, the worsening health situation in the USSR has been somewhat sensationalized in the press. Nick Eberstadt, writing in the *New York Review of Books* (19 February 1981), remarked, "There can be no mistaking it: the Soviet Union is in the grip of a devastating health crisis." The underlying factors leading to a rise in the infant mortality rate are the prevalence of abortions, the breakup of the family, the high female labor participation rate, poor diet, inadequate public sanitation, and insufficient medical supplies.

One should also take into account other factors that influence the figures we use to measure the quality of health care. Part of the recorded increase in morbidity and disease is due to better statistical recording consequent on hospitalization in the Central Asian republics. This point has been made convincingly by Jones and Grupp (1983). A higher infant mortality rate may also be a consequence of a reduction in prenatal loss and spontaneous abortion, given improvements in prenatal care. For these reasons it is somewhat disingenuous of the Soviet Minister of Health to put the Soviet Union after Barbados in this respect, as reporting of infant deaths in Barbados is incomplete.

However, it must be acknowledged that a decline in medical care has occurred. A judicious conclusion by one of the West's leading authorities is that "about one quarter of the rise [in infant mortality rates] was a statistical artifact" [due to improved recording], the remainder may be accounted for by regional shifts in births (this is, proportionally more in traditional areas of higher birth rates) and a deterioration in health conditions (Field 1986). The eradication of these inadequacies has been the objective of reform under Gorbachev to which we shall return later.

Health Service Provision
Differences in health service endowments of regional areas qualify the fulfillment of one of the goals of the health service noted at the beginning of this section: the system is not centralized but organized through republican health ministries. Another exception to universal provision has to do with the provision of health services by ministries outside the Ministry of Health. These employ approximately 12 percent of the physicians (Ryan 1978: 15) and come under the wing of the ministries of transport, defense, civil aviation, security (KGB) and others, including the Academy of Sciences and the Ministry of Foreign Affairs. These divisions in the provision of health care may be traced back to prerevolutionary days when the bulk of provision was carried out by the local authorities and an occupational service was in embryonic form.

On the basis of occupational and regional access to health resources C. M. Davis has divided the Soviet population into three principal access groups representing various degrees of inequality of service. The top group represents about 25 percent of the Soviet population and has high standard facilities. Of this group about one million people (0.4 percent of the population) have access to "elite" (for example, Kremlin clinic) facilities; just over 24 percent use the departmental and capital city services. Another group, 24 percent of the population, has decent services in the industrial or provincial city facilities. The remainder, just over half of the population (129.4 million), is served by the rural subsystem and has a low-quality service (Davis 1988: 129).

Inequality of access to medical treatment occurs in all societies: under capitalism, the private sector of health provision gives a better service to the rich than to the poor. Rationing is by price, so there are no shortages or queues for those who can afford treatment. The poor remain untreated or have inferior service in the public sector.

In administered societies, the delivery of health care is received by those best placed in the administrative system to receive it. But the greatest inadequacies are between geographical areas. The provision of health services is much worse in the countryside than in the towns, Soviet republics with a rural population have poorer services than do urban republics. As noted earlier, the Central Asian republics are more poorly endowed than the European ones. The location of prestigious hospitals in urban centers favors the middle class intelligentsia who have sufficient knowledge and connections to secure entry. Davis has estimated that "only about two-thirds of cases of illness in cities and one-third in rural areas were presented to the medical system for treatment by doctors" (1987: 316). As the population becomes more educated and demanding the proportion will rise.

A second source of inequality is in the access to health services provided by various ministries, such as the railways, civil aviation, and the KGB. It seems likely that the executive and technical staff may fare better than the unskilled manuals. But this is not universally the case: the mining industry is well endowed. A distinction may be made between workers who have been regarded as more essential to meet the needs of the economy than others. Health care in these cases may be regarded as an investment in human capital.

Although "private practice" as in the United States and Europe has never been strong in Russia, there has remained a small private sector of physicians and "self-financing" clinics. These charge a fee for service, usually for consultation. Michael Kaser (1976: 64) estimated that in the 1970s there were only 130 such clinics in the USSR. Their number has increased since the 1970s reaching 570 health establishments in 1987. Only a small part of the profits of polyclinics remain with them, the remainder go to the Ministry of Health. These clinics provide a "second opinion," greater privacy (for example, for sexually transmitted diseases or abortions), and patients may also have immediate treatment with a known specialist. Fee-paying services are likely to increase in future.

Such provision, although growing in scale, is relatively insignificant compared to the service provided by the state system. Here the services of physicians and hospital care are free of direct charges to the patient. Other charges, however, are made. Out-patients have to pay the costs of medicines prescribed, but such charges are low: a prescription for antibiotics would range from 50 kopeck to 2 rubles (exceptionally foreign antibiotics might cost 5 rubles). Most medicines on display in cases in drug stores in the USSR in 1988 were priced under 2 rubles. In-patients are not charged for drugs. Dental and ophthalmic services are subject to payment by patients. Also convalescence at sanatoria and health resorts is subject to a fee. Small charges are made for abortions that are not performed on medical grounds. Some exceptions may be noted: drugs for communicable diseases (tuberculosis, venereal diseases) are free; children under the age of one year also have free medicine; there are reduced rates or free services for army veterans and certain groups of pensioners.

Although charges are not made by the health service, the practice of tipping for services (or expected service) is widespread. As a consequence of the low pay of all personnel in the medical profession, such payments are now expected and are given to physicians, nurses, and orderlies.

The medical profession has had little independent authority. Administrative control is ubiquitous. Unlike in the West where medical practitioners and specialists are able to secure well-paid jobs with expensive equipment, this is not the case in the USSR. After the revolution medicine was regarded as a privileged occupation and an attempt was made to lower doctors' status — pay was reduced to levels of industrial workers and has remained so. It must be borne in mind, however, that "private practice" had not flourished in prerevolutionary Russia. By far the majority of physicians were in state employment, and all "independent professions" were weak under the Tsars. The idea of state-sponsored medicine with government-employed medical personnel predates the Bolshevik regime.

The aspiration to public participation in health care has not been fulfilled. The Soviet health care system is highly bureaucratized and specialized. Health care requires a "scientific approach" to the cure of disease, leaving little role for public participation and patient control of the health service. Facilities are provided at polyclinics organized on a neighbourhood and factory basis. Here doctors specialize in various aspects of health. There has been no "family doctor" type of services although current policy plans to revive this service. Cases are referred to hospitals, which, as in the West, are becoming a dominant institution in the provision of health. The patient is a passive recipient of health care, usually having little or no choice over doctor or treatment.

There has been an improvement in the health service provision: out-patient visits to medical practitioners have risen from 8 per capita in 1970 to 11.4 in 1985, and hospitalization from 21.5 in 1970 to 25.1 in 1985 (Davis 1987).

In Western societies expenditure on health care has tended to rise at a higher rate than that of gross national product. In the welfare states, governments have responded to public demand by increasing health provision, and in the United States people have been willing to contribute a higher proportion of their income to insurance to secure good health care. On the supply side, in the West, the cost of medical provision has soared as a result of the advent of expensive and possibly exorbitant high-tech medical treatment and steep medical fees.

In the USSR, costs have been kept down. In 1980, for example, the cost to the state of maintaining and treating patients in the surgical ward of a cancer hospital was only 10.49 rubles: 1.98 rubles for wages, depreciation of fixed assets, and instruments; 1.35 rubles for food, 1.27 rubles for medicines; 5.89 rubles for indirect costs (data cited by Feshbach 1985: 9). While the total expenditure on health care has increased in ruble terms from 0.9 milliards (1000 million) in 1940, to 4.8 in 1960, 9.3 in 1970, 14.8 in 1980, and 18.0 in 1986, as a proportion of government expenditure, health (and physical culture) has declined. The percentage figures for the above years are: 5.17 percent (1940), 6.56 percent (1960), 6.01 percent (1970), 5.02 percent (1980), and 4.31 percent (1986) (*Narkhoz za 70 let* 1987: 629). Sources in addition to the state budget — for example, trade union support, fees for service — in the 1980s increased health expenditure by another 25 percent (Davis 1987: 317), and such payments have been rising. When this additional spending has been taken into account, health expenditure as a proportion of national income has fallen modestly from 4.1 percent in 1970 to 3.9 percent in 1985; and per capita expenditure per year has risen from 48 rubles to 81 rubles between these dates (Davis 1987: 317). By way of comparison, total (public and private) health service provision in the mid-1980s in Britain was 5.9 percent of GNP, in West Germany it was 8.1 percent and in the United States health expenditure amounted to some 12 percent (this is largely due to the inflated cost of high-tech medicine, and extortionate medical fees).

Health care costs have been held down because salaries of medical personnel are low, the cost of medicines is subject to state control, and investment and development costs are not passed on to the consumer.

In relation to meeting need, the Soviet health service has had many shortcomings. One should not be self-righteous about such inadequacies, because not even the richest capitalist states have fulfilled all the health needs of the population. In the Soviet Union, however, the slow improvement in health care has not kept pace either with people's expectations or with the changing medical requirements of the population. Inadequacies are publicly voiced concerning the low quality of medical practice, the acute shortages of medicines and appliances, the poor food, conditions, and secondary infection in hospitals, as well as the lack of proper buildings and modern equipment. Bureaucratic procedures, waste, and incompetence have been the subject of discussion in the professional medical press.

Lists of "deficit" medicines are regularly issued and they are not pre-scribed by physicians. Davis reports that in 1975 in one region of the USSR there were 330 medical goods on the *defektura* (a list of deficit goods); in the mid-1980s production enterprises fulfilled orders of the Ministry of Health only by 70 to 75 percent (data cited by Davis 1987: 320).

In the Soviet press shortages of all kinds of medical commodities from bandages to throat lozenges have been reported. In a more satirical vein, a recent letter to *Meditsinskaya Gazeta* sums up the situation as follows:

> For already a year now, condoms have not appeared in the pharmacists shops in L'vov, as a result of which my wife and I have become the victims of an unplanned pregnancy. In Belorussia it is impossible to buy these articles. A black market has occurred and the price has jumped a hundred fold. [L]ast year when the newspapers gave more attention to the questions of AIDS, our men began to prick up their ears and ... condoms instantly disappeared from the counters.

Minister of Health Chazov complained about the shortage of medicines at the Nineteenth Party Conference in 1988: "I would like to ask the comrades from Gosplan: what is more important to buy from abroad — labels for the food industry, plastic bags, cigarettes filters and cosmetics, or medicines to save the lives of sick people?"

Such shortages have led to a second economy in medical supplies generally and illegal expropriation of hospital supplies. "Deficits" of commodities have affected the whole range of medical supplies including bed linen, medicine, and instruments, and has led to bribery by patients seeking services.

Despite the inadequacies noted above, the provision of free medical care is popular. Soviet emigrants to the United States interviewed in the 1980s were found to express most support for the free health service and this was also found to be the case with the earlier batch of emigrants of the 1950s (Silver 1987: 111). It is not surprising, then, that there has been much popular opposition in the USSR to the widening of "fee for service" payments in the health service.

The Health Environment
Good health is not only achieved through the provision of medicines but also is shaped by the environment. The provision of food, exercise, leisure, and housing contributes to the state of a population's health. Pollution, overwork, psychological stress, and drug abuse are factors leading to illness. The recent decline in Soviet health standards noted

above may be due to changing environmental conditions as much as inadequacies in the organization of formal health services.

The aging of the population is one obvious cause of the increase in the death rate. The cohort entering the termination ages of over sixty years in 1985 was fifteen years old, or under, in 1940 and did not suffer the high death rate of the Second World War, though it did suffer its effects — poor food, adverse living conditions, and high stress. The older cohorts lost high proportions of men in battle, which seriously depleted the over-sixty age cohort from the 1960s to the 1980s. The death rate in future will naturally rise as those who were children in the Second World War come to maturity. The war was a time of great stress, and as a result the present stock of older people is likely to be in greater need of health service provision as the conditions of old age adversely affect them. The death rate is likely to be higher because of the poorer health of this cohort.

Diet is an important determinant of health. While undoubtedly the supply and distribution of food has improved (see Figure 2.6, chapter 2) shortages and severe inadequacies confront the Soviet consumer. As noted in Table 10.3, average per capita consumption has risen steadily since 1960. However, the balance of diet is inadequate. Even by Soviet desired norms, there are considerable inadequacies in the consumption of meat, milk, vegetables, and fruit, which give rise particularly to vitamin deficiency.

Psychological satisfaction with life has an effect on well-being. Alcoholism and drug dependency may be reactions to social alienation. Such dependency may be caused by inadequate child raising practices: problems

Table 10.3

Consumption and Norms of Selected Food Products in the USSR (kilos)

| | (Consumption per capita) | | | Norm for balanced diet |
	1960	1980	1986	
Meat and meat products	39.50	57.60	62.40	82.00
Milk and milk products	240.00	314.00	333.00	405.00
Eggs (number)	118.00	239.00	268.00	292.00
Fish and fish products	9.90	17.60	18.60	18.20
Sugar	28.00	44.40	44.00	40.00
Vegetable oil	5.30	8.80	9.80	9.10
Potatoes	143.00	109.00	107.00	110.00
Vegetables and melons	70.00	97.00	102.00	130.00
Fruit and berries	22.00	38.00	56.00	91.00
Bread products	164.00	138.00	132.00	115.00

Source: Narkhoz za 70 let (1987): 470. Final column from Trehub 1989: 23.

can arise in a small family when a very high male/female employment rate leads to inadequate socialization of the child. Rapid urbanization and an inadequate social infrastructure of leisure services also lead to dissatisfaction, which may be expressed in alcohol abuse.

The Soviet Union is confronted with problems similar to those of the West: the Minister of Health reported in 1987 that 104 Soviet cities suffer from air pollution. In Alma Ata (Kazakhstan), the official limit of air pollutants is regularly exceeded by from two to ten times. Smoking is widespread and notable increases have taken place in its incidence on the part of women. Motor transport has multiplied giving rise to pollution and accidents. Unlike in the West, there is little concern for potential accidents: machinery is not well guarded and hazards remain around public works. There are few, if any, lifeguards at public swimming places. Many public catastrophes occurred in the late 1980s, and the authorities were badly prepared to deal with them, which illustrates an outlook that pays little attention to personal security.

Annually some 60,000 people commit suicide giving in 1989 a rate of 21 per 100,000 of the population — a figure comparable with West Germany (20.5) and France (about 24), although the rates in the United States and Britain are lower (12.2 and 8.6 respectively). As in the West, more men commit suicide than women. (These statistics may be unreliable, as the definition of "suicide" is culturally determined.) There were 28,000 murders in 1989: 10 per 100,000 of the population.

Drug Addiction and Alcoholism
While drug addiction is considerably less than in the West, it is increasingly a cause for concern in the USSR. In 1984 there were 75,000 registered drug users and in 1987, 40,000 offenses were committed by drug addicts. By 1988 the number of addicts had grown to 4.4 million, though this figure included chronic alcoholics. In one survey of Moscow school children it was found that 9 percent had tried drugs at least once. A study of drug abusers conducted in the Georgian Republic in 1984−85 found that 92 percent were men; 44.5 percent were single, and 81 percent were in the 20−34 age group. Over 63 percent of the respondents were manual workers, very few were professionals, 40 percent of their fathers and 31.8 percent of their mothers were also working class, and a good proportion (about a fifth) had come from nonmanual backgrounds.

The source of the narcotics is the Transcaucasian republics and Moldavia. The most frequently used drug was hashish (84 percent), followed by morphia (47 percent), opium (44 percent), and cocaine (12 percent). By far the most frequently mentioned motive for using drugs was the desire to experience "euphoria."

Consumption of alcohol has been one form of sustenance traditionally enjoyed to excess by Russians. Western analysts have estimated that the consumption of alcohol was 16 litres per year per capita of the population aged over 15 years. Since 1955 consumption had risen by two and a half times. While other European countries such as France and Italy consumed even more per capita (18–20 litres), mainly wine was consumed and it was accompanied by food.

Drinking alcohol varies significantly between nationalities. Taking as an index the number of deaths directly linked to alcohol, the figures in 1980 ranged from 26.4 (per 100,000 of the population) in the RSFSR, 25.9 in Lithuania, 21.2 in Estonia, 18.8 in Latvia, 16.8 in the Ukraine to 1.0 in Armenia, 1.5 in Uzbekistan, 1.9 in Azerbayjan and Tajikistan. Even allowing for biases in the collection of statistics and for the larger under fifteen-year-old population in the Central Asian republics, it is clear that heavy drinking is a phenomenon of Russians and the Baltic nationalities.

It is only in advanced urban-industrial societies that such levels of liquor consumption are considered to be a form of "abuse" and governments take measures to curtail or prevent such levels of drinking. In peasant societies, such as Russia before 1917, heavy drinking and brawling were socially unpleasant but their effects were not significant economically. The interdependence of workers and the importance of raising labor productivity has led to concern over excessive alcohol consumption because alcoholism leads to poor quality of work, mistakes, accidents, and absenteeism. Deaths from acute alcohol poisoning in the USSR in the late 1970s have been estimated by Treml to be as high as 19.5 per 100,000 of the population (1987: 299). Drinking impacts on other phenomena: drunken drivers caused about 14,000 traffic deaths per year and 60,000 serious injuries. Also a high proportion of crime and domestic violence is associated with excessive drinking. Feast days have always been associated in Russia with drunken brawls.

One must be somewhat circumspect in reading accounts of the extent of the effects of alcohol "abuse" — suicide, the spread of venereal disease, mental illness, and congenital birth defects are not "caused" to any great degree by drinking alcohol to excess. Many people in the West as in the Soviet Union adopt a puritanical morality and even punitive vindictiveness towards moderate drinkers, let alone alcoholics.

Early in 1986 an All-Union Temperance Society was formed, which claimed 14 million members in July 1987. Its objective is to create an atmosphere of moral intolerance towards drinking. It goes much deeper than combatting alcoholism: it agitates for alcohol-free weddings, parties, and feast days. In November 1988 an Alcoholics Anonymous Association was founded and it was reported that 4.6 million people were receiving treatment for some form of alcoholism in the USSR.

Under Khrushchev anti-alcohol campaigns were launched that precluded Party functionaries from public drinking, emphasized the greater socialist morality of temperance (excepted was the consumption of light wines with food), reduced the outlets for vodka sales, raised the price and restricted the hours of sale of alcohol. Such measures, however, were ineffective and the consumption of illegally brewed liquor rose.

One of the first policies of the Gorbachev leadership, backed strongly by teetotaler, Ligachev, was an anti-alcoholism campaign, which was part of the strategy of discipline and control. As under Khrushchev, the outlets for sale were restricted and in addition the hours of trade were curtailed to the hours between two and seven p.m. The legitimate production of vodka was reduced. Legal constraints were increased: the sale and consumption of alcohol was forbidden to people under twenty-one (though citizenship is attained at eighteen years), penalties for drunkenness were doubled and even tripled, and prices were hiked up by 50 percent.

Unlike earlier campaigns, Gorbachev's policies bit hard. State production of alcohol fell by 50 percent between 1980 and 1987. Vodka was particularly restricted and many wine factories were required to change over from wine production to soft drinks. Queues at liquor shops became longer, restaurants became "dry," the new cooperative cafes were unlicensed and served only mineral water. As compensation, the production of home distilleries grew and sugar became scarce. In 1988 it was reported that prior to the campaign the consumption of homemade liquor accounted for a third of alcohol consumed; after the campaign, it reached two-thirds. Alcoholics also switched to other fluids containing alcohol such as antifreeze and metal polish.

The Soviet authorities have contended that initially the campaign was a success. The number of drunks in the streets has visibly declined. It is claimed that deaths directly linked to alcoholism have fallen from 19 per 100,000 in 1980 to 8.3 in 1986. Other reports claim that traffic accidents caused by drunks are down by a fifth, and loss of time through absenteeism has dropped 33 percent. These assertions should not be taken at their face value. Street offenses may have moved indoors and other reductions may reflect changes in recording. The widespread rise of home brewing (*samogon*) often with inferior materials and the increase in alcohol substitutes compensates for the decline in state production.

Even more open to question is the Victorian abstemiousness of the policy. The pleasure of moderate drinkers has been denied them. The policy became counterproductive — desperate alcoholics usually find ways to assuage their thirst, while moderate drinkers, who are by far the majority, resent incursions into their freedom by the political leadership.

Alcoholism is a cultural phenomenon that is rooted in peasant mores, but it takes on a new form as an escape from the tensions and demands of a modernizing industrial society. The provision of more recreational facilities, sports clubs, "do-it-yourself" materials, and leisure centers have been advocated by the authorities to provide alternative outlets for drug users and alcoholics. Such provisions, I believe, will not solve the problem — they have little appeal to those who have failed and become dropouts. Repainting one's house or fixing the car is hardly a substitute for the kind of "euphoria" provided in a narcotics den. Without being too pessimistic, it is likely that a cost of the growing competitiveness of Soviet society will be a group of people who turn to alcohol and drugs for pleasure.

In the autumn of 1988 the anti-alcoholism drive was relaxed, the supply of vodka restored, and deliveries of spirits were resumed both to the shops and to restaurants (except to the cooperatives). A Central Committee resolution conceded that the shortage of alcohol had led to long queues, a rise in home brewing, speculation in spirits, and drug addiction. Home brewing caused shortages in sugar and confectionery.

The pursuit of such a strict anti-alcoholism campaign so early in the period of the Gorbachev leadership represented a psychological strategy. Because the campaign against drinking affected a large proportion of the population it brought home to all citizens that the new leadership expected a higher level of discipline from everybody: changes were required in the "human factor" (people's motivations and work habits) for perestroika to be successful. The campaign was also a means to exert control, to strengthen and enforce legality. Its short-term effects were probably successful but in the longer term they were less so.

Health and Perestroika
No less than coercion and participation, welfare services contribute to social integration and in the Soviet Union have contributed to the legitimation of the regime. Social policy involves the state playing a major role as provider of services. Levels of employment, education, health, and housing have been taken out of the market and provided to meet needs.

The present political leadership is confronted with growing public demands for improvement of the health service and Gorbachev at the Twenty-Seventh Congress pledged that he would find "considerable funds" to finance the improvements necessary. The political leadership has adopted a number of strategies to improve the health service, including replacing personnel and introducing measures to make the service less supply driven and more patient responsive.

As in other spheres, changes have been made with the replacement of top personnel. In the fifteen months beginning in November 1985, at least a dozen top administrators at deputy minister level and above were replaced and the medical supply industries were reorganized (see Davis 1987: 327–30). It is planned that outpatient and hospital provision will grow, and that salaries of medical personnel will increase.

Discussions in the medical press call for a reduction in the length of time patients remain in hospital and the revival of the "family practitioner" has been advocated by the minister of health. Innovations are being introduced in the funding of services that will lead to greater consumer choice and more differentiation of physicians' incomes.

The criterion of willingness and ability to pay will be strengthened. As in other parts of the economy, "value for money" will become a major criterion of supply of service and a greater cost consciousness will be fostered. Resistance to the introduction of the price mechanism and "fees for service" is great. As in other welfare states, the provision of a health service on the basis of need is often at variance with the requirement of ability to pay. Popular support for a public "free" health service is widespread, and as we have noted has been advocated by a majority even of Soviet emigrés to the United States. However, the difficulty of finding more resources from the budget in the face of widespread public demand and a deteriorating health environment has led the government to favor "self-financing" schemes outside of the national health service provision. In 1987 only 1.3 rubles per head of the population was expended on private medical expenditure; this is planned to rise to 3.7 rubles by the end of the Thirteenth Five Year Plan (1995).

The expansion of fee-for-service polyclinics is a major step in the direction of a client-based health service. As noted above, in 1987 there were 570 "independent self-supporting health establishments," these were made up of 10,000 departments and surgeries. They are to be expanded in the fields of dentistry, cosmetics, massage, sexual (reproductive), drug addiction, abortion services, and acupuncture. Home services on a paid basis are to be introduced, as are fee-paying hotels for outpatients. Nursing facilities for the elderly, invalids, and the chronically sick are to be introduced. At present such clinics are part of the state system and personnel are on the government payroll. A high proportion of fees are not kept in the "self-financing" institutions but are transferred into the state budget. Charges are low: in a survey in 1986 in Moscow, 73 percent of patients paid under 5 rubles for the service they obtained. This survey found that most patients would be prepared to pay more. Also it has been discovered that demand for such fee-paying services exceeds supply — the same survey found that in Moscow over a ten year period a third of people seeking help from such clinics were not able to receive it, waiting lists at some clinics were from a week to two months. Policy is undoubtedly moving in the direction of widening such pay-clinics. This is part of the general strategy of making services reflect costs and giving money greater value. It also moves considerably away from a "supply-dominated" system to one wherein greater influence is given to the consumers of services.

An extension of the fee-for-service polyclinic is the development of "cooperative" medical services. These are modelled on the pattern of private enterprise in other trades and services, such as car repair agencies and cafes. The Ministry of Health of the USSR in 1988 recommended the establishment of cooperatives in the fields of stomatology (disease of the mouth), denture production, restorative treatment (physiotherapy, massage, manipulation), cosmetic treatment, home and hospital care, contraceptive advice, and the production of specialist physical aids and equipment. It is not recommended that cooperatives deal with cancer, venereal disease, drug addiction, pregnancy, invasive investigations, surgery, and abortions. Creating these additional services is regarded by the Ministry of Health as a means of meeting part of the projected fivefold growth of paid medical services by the year 2000.

This kind of private practice is welcomed by many as a valuable form of competition to the national health service. As a correspondent to *Meditsinskaya Gazeta* in May 1988 has put it, "[P]erhaps competition of cooperatives with polyclinics will make the latter pull themselves together. . . . One thing is clear — breaking the monopoly of medical care is for the good of the population."

More important than the introduction of alternative fee-paying provision, however, are the changes being introduced in the national health service itself. Here there is to be a change from the more specialized medical services provided at polyclinics to the "family doctor" who is concerned with a range of functions and cares for a population of from 1,200 to 1,400 people. The Minister of Health promised in 1988 that future medical students would be trained with these functions in mind.

The financing of polyclinics will also lead to other changes in services. Briefly, the idea is that polyclinics will be given a budget that they will use to buy services for patients. The clinic can provide treatment itself or buy the services from other health units. Hospitals therefore have incentives to provide services economically because they have to compete for clients from polyclinics. Other services, such as ambulances and diagnosis and health centers also come under this scheme. Savings effected by polyclinics may be used to increase the pay of medical workers at the clinics or to improve services. The objective here is to make the health service more cost effective. In practice this policy has resulted in a reduction in treatment times in hospitals and greater differentiation between staff at the clinics. The scheme is similar in character to that introduced in the British Health Service under Margaret Thatcher.

In Western societies (and in Russia before the revolution) charity provides resources for the people's welfare. Numerous associations from the Red Cross to organizations for the mentally handicapped and those with multiple sclerosis provide facilities, personal services, and funds for research. Until the advent of the Gorbachev leadership, charitable and self-help activity hardly existed. This has changed in many spheres. In the field of health care a Soviet Fund for Health and Charity was set up in April 1988. It was composed of a wide range of organizations including the Press Agency *Novosti*, the All-Union Central Council of Trade Unions, Societies for the Blind and Deaf, and numerous ministries including those of Health and Finance. The fund is to be financed from voluntary donations from individuals and associations. Such sums are to be used for a wide range of health related activities: helping families, supporting anti-alcohol campaigns, financing associations such as the Red Cross and Red Crescent. Volunteers, including those from the churches, are to be allowed to help in hospitals. While this charitable form of health provision is only in embryo form in the early 1990s, it is likely that such charitable activities will increase, providing yet another element in the pluralistic form of health and social provision. All these measures will move health service away from administrative direction and control towards the market system.

Current policy is to bring the allocation of welfare provision more in line with what people are prepared to do with their earnings, to increase client choice, and to enhance the role of the market. It is likely that the health care service will include more services on a fee principle. An increase in cooperative (private enterprise) activities will be encouraged. The development of the market will give money value, provide an incentive for work, and give clients a greater say and more choice in the provision of services. It is unlikely, however, to equalize facilities or help the needs of the poor.

Selected Bibliography for Part Three

The general journals listed in the references to Part One are also relevant to this section. See also the note there on sources of statistical data.

Soviet education is widely covered in the West in translation, the series *Soviet Education* published by M. E. Sharpe contains useful extracts from the Soviet pedagogical literature, including major documents and the main speeches of Soviet leaders on education. Other journals are: *East—West Education* and *Comparative Education Review*. *Soviet Education*

Study Bulletin contains up-to-date information and bibliographies on Soviet education and is useful for the specialist. *Glasnost'* (New York: Center for Democracy) is the English language edition of "independent social forces" in the Soviet Union, edited by the dissident Sergei Grigoryants; it features a wide range of *samizdat* articles.

Andrusz, G. D. 1984. *Housing and Urban Development in the USSR.* London: Macmillan.

Bialer, S. 1988. "'New Thinking' and Soviet Foreign Policy." *Survival* 30, no. 4 (July/August): 291−309.

Binns, C. A. P. 1979. "The Changing Face of Power: Revolution and Accommodation in the Development of the Soviet Ceremonial System," Part One. *Man* 14 (4): 585−606.

————1980. "The Changing Face of Power: Revolution and Accommodation in the Development of the Soviet Ceremonial System," Part Two. *Man* 15 (1): 170−87.

Bloch, S. and P. Reddaway. 1978. *Psychiatric Terror: How Soviet Psychiatry Is Used to Suppress Dissent.* London: Future Publications.

Bohr, A. 1988. "Self-Immolation Among Central Asian Women." *Radio Liberty Research* 126: 88.

Bronfenbrenner, U. 1971. *Two Worlds of Childhood.* London: Allen and Unwin.

Conner, W. D. 1986. "Social Policy under Gorbachev." *Problems Of Communism* 35 (August): 31−46.

Cooper, J. 1988. "Industry and Higher Education under Gorbachev." *Industry and Higher Education* (December): 217−22.

Cushman, T. O. 1988. "Ritual and Conformity in Soviet Society." *The Journal of Communist Studies* 4, no. 2 (June): 162−80.

Davis, C. M. 1987. "Developments in the Health Sector of the Soviet Economy, 1970−90." In *Gorbachev's Economic Plans.* vol. 2, Joint Economic Committee. Washington, D.C.: Government Printing Office.

————1988. "The Organization and Performance of the Contemporary Soviet Health Service." In *State and Welfare USA/USSR*, ed. G. W. Lapidus and G. E. Swanson. Berkeley, Calif.: Institute of International Studies.

————1989. "The Soviet Health System: A National Health Service in a Socialist Society." In *Success and Crisis in National Health Systems*, ed. Mark Field. London: Tavistock.

Dunstan, J. 1987. "Equalization and Differentiation in the Soviet School 1958−1985: A Curriculum Approach." In *Soviet Education under Scrutiny*, ed. J. Dunstan. Glasgow: Jordanhill, 32−69.

Eberstadt, N. 1988. *The Poverty of Communism.* New Brunswick and Oxford: Transaction Books. Considers Soviet Union and other socialist states. Refutes the idea that sacrifice of liberty has led to abolition of poverty.

Feshbach, M. 1985. "Health in the USSR-Organization, Trends, and Ethics." Paper presented at International Colloquium, Bad Homburg, West Germany.

Field, M. 1967. *Soviet Socialized Medicine.* New York: The Free Press.

————1986. "Soviet Infant Mortality: A Mystery Story." In *Advances in International Maternal and Child Health*, vol. 6, ed. D. B. Jelliffe and E. F. P. Jelliffe. Oxford: Clarendon Press 1986, 25−65.

George, V. and N. Manning. 1980. *Socialism, Social Welfare and the Soviet Union.* London and Boston: Routledge.

Golod, S. I. 1988. "Prostitutsiya v kontekste izmeniya polovy morali." *Sotsiologicheskie issledovaniya*, no. 2: 65−70.

Gorbachev, M. S. 1987. *Perestroika: New Thinking for Our Country and the World.* London: Collins.

Hollander, Gayle D. 1972. *Soviet Political Indoctrination.* New York: Praeger.

Hough, J. 1977. *The Soviet Union and Social Science Theory.* Cambridge, Mass.: Harvard University Press.

————1979. "Thinking about Thinking about Dissent." *Studies in Comparative Communism* 12: 1–2.

"How Soviet Censorship is Easing Up," (Interview with the Director of the USSR Chief Administration for the Protection of State Secrets in the Press, *Izvestiya*, 3 Nov 1988), *Current Digest of the Soviet Press* 15 (44): 1–6.

Inkeles, A. and R. A. Bauer. 1959. *The Soviet Citizen*. Cambridge, Mass.: Harvard University Press.

Jahoda, M. 1982. *Employment and Unemployment: A Social-Psychological Analysis*. Cambridge and New York: Cambridge University Press.

Jones, E. and F. W. Grupp. 1983. "Infant Mortality Trends in the Soviet Union." *Population and Development Review* 9: 213–46.

Jones, T. Anthony. 1989. "Social Deviance and Social Problems." *Soviet Sociology* 27, no. 4. Contains translations of Soviet articles on drunkenness, suicide, prostitution, and youth.

Kaser, M. 1976. *Health Care in the Soviet Union and Eastern Europe*. London: Croom Helm.

Kerr, S. T. 1988. "The Soviet Reform of Higher Education." *The Review of Higher Education* 11, no. 3 (Spring): 215–46.

Knaus, W. 1982. *Inside Russian Medicine*. New York: Everest House.

Lampert, N. 1988a. "The Dilemmas of *Glasnost*". In ed. W. Joyce, H. Tickten and S. White, "Gorbachev and Gorbachevism." Special issue of *The Journal of Communist Studies* 4, no. 4 (December): 48–63.

Lane C. 1984. "Legitimacy and Power in the Soviet Union through Socialist Ritual." *British Journal of Political Science* 14: 207–17.

Lane, C. 1981. *The Rites of Rulers: Ritual in Industrial Society*. Cambridge: Cambridge University Press.

Lane, D. 1985. *State and Politics in the USSR*. Oxford: Blackwell; New York: New York University Press.

Lapidus, G. W. and G. E. Swanson, eds. 1988. *State and Welfare USA/USSR: Contemporary Policy and Practice*. Berkeley: University of California Press.

Mason, D. S. and S. Sydorenko. 1990. "Perestroyka, Social Justice and Soviet Public Opinion." *Problems of Communism* vol. 39, no. 6 (November/December): 34–44.

Matthews, M. 1982. *Education in the Soviet Union: Policies and Institutions Since Stalin*. London: Allen and Unwin. Comprehensive overview of Soviet education under Khrushchev and Brezhnev.

Mickiewicz, Ellen. 1981. *Media and the Russian Public*. New York: Praeger.

————1988a. "Changes in the Media Under Gorbachev: The Case of Television." In ed. W. Joyce, H. Tickten, and S. White, "Gorbachev and Gorbachevism." Special issue of *The Journal of Communist Studies* 4, no. 4 (December): 35–47.

————1988b. *Split Signals: Television and Politics in the Soviet Union*. New York: Oxford University Press. A major comparative study of Soviet and American television.

Mickiewicz, Ellen and Gregory Haley. 1987. "Soviet and American News: Week of Intensive Interaction." *Slavic Review* 2 (15) (Summer): 214–28.

Millar J. R. and Elizabeth Clayton. 1987. "Quality of Life: Subjective Measures of Relative Satisfaction." In *Politics, Work and Daily Life in the USSR*, ed. J. R. Millar. New York: Cambridge University Press, 39–42.

Muckle, James. 1988. *A Guide to the Soviet Curriculum*. London: Croom Helm, 19.

Porket, J. L. 1983. "Income Maintenance for the Soviet Aged." *Ageing and Society* 3, part 3 (November): 301–23.

Pravda, A. 1982. "Is there a Soviet Working Class?" *Problems of Communism* 31, no. 6 (November–December): 1–24.

Riordan, J., ed. 1988. *Soviet Education: The Gifted and the Handicapped*. London: Routledge.

Has articles on special schools for the gifted by J. Dunstan; and on schools for the handicapped, by Andrew Sutton and A. Suddaby; a chapter on the deaf-blind by M. Lammbert; and articles on sport schools by J. Riordan.

Ryan, M. 1978. *The Organization of Soviet Medical Care*. London: Martin Robertson.

Sakharov, A. 1968. *Reflections on Progress, Co-existence and Intellectual Freedom*. London: André Deutsch.

Scanlon, J. P. 1988. "Reforms and Civil Society in the USSR." *Problems of Communism* 37, no. 2 (March–April): 41–46.

Schlapentokh, V. 1989. *Public and Private Life of the Soviet People*. New York and Oxford: Oxford University Press.

Silver, B. D. 1987. "Political Beliefs of Soviet Citizens: Sources of Support for Regime Norms." In *Politics, Work and Daily Life in the USSR*, ed. J. R. Millar, 100–41.

Soviet Education. "Reformulating the Educational Reform," is the title of two issues containing articles on perestroika. Vol. 31, no. 2 (February 1989) and no. 3 (March 1989).

Tokes, R. L. 1975. *Dissent in the USSR: Politics, Ideology and People*. Baltimore, Md.: Johns Hopkins University Press. Good overview of the dissident movement and its suppression in the sixties and early seventies.

Tomiak, J. J., ed. 1986. *Western Perspectives on Soviet Education in the 1980s*. London: Macmillan.

Trehub, A. 1987. "Social and Economic Rights—the Soviet Union." *Survey* 29, no. 4.

———1989. "Growing Alarm about AIDS in the Soviet Union." Radio Liberty, *Report on the USSR* 1, no. 14 (7 April): 3–5.

———1989. "The Congress of People's Deputies on Poverty." Radio Liberty, *Report on the USSR* 1, no. 24 (16 June): 5–9.

Treml, V. G. 1987. "Gorbachev's Anti-drinking Campaign: A 'Noble Experiment' or an Exercise in Futility?" Washington D.C.: Joint Economic Committee, *Gorbachev's Economic Needs*, vol. 2, 297–311.

Vladimirov, L. 1973. "*Glavlit*: How the Soviet Censor Works." *Index*, (1973).

Yanov, A. 1988. "Russian Nationalism as the Ideology of Counterreform." In *Russian Nationalism Today*, Radio Liberty, Special Edition (December) 43–52.

Zajda, J. I. 1980. *Education in the USSR*. Oxford: Pergamon.

Zimmerman, W. 1987. "Mobilized Participation and the Nature of the Soviet Dictatorship." In *Politics, Work and Daily Life in the USSR: A Survey of Former Soviet Citizens*, ed. J. R. Millar. Cambridge, 1980: 332–53.

Part Four

CONCLUSIONS

Chapter 11

PERESTROIKA

New Beginnings

> *A spectre is haunting Europe — the spectre of Communism. All the Powers of old Europe have entered into a holy alliance to exorcise this spectre: Pope and Tsar, Metternich and Guizot, French Radicals and German police-spies.*
>
> *Where is that party in opposition that has not been decried as Communistic by its opponents in power? Where the Opposition that has not hurled back the branding reproach of Communism, against the more advanced opposition parties, as well as against its reactionary adversaries?*
>
> — *K. Marx and F. Engels*

This quotation from *Manifesto of the Communist Party* published in 1848 has to be amended in at least two respects at the end of the twentieth century.

First, the "spectre of Communism" has been translated into a worldwide movement. Self-styled Communist states have spread from Russia and Eastern Europe to include not only China and Cuba but also some thirty states of "Marxist orientation" in Africa, Asia, and Latin America. The opposition to the expansion of Communism has led to unprecedented military and political confrontation between the major capitalist powers and the supporters of Communism: wars have occurred in Korea, Malaya, Vietnam, and Nicaragua. The "spectre of communism" has haunted the world. There have been six characteristics of the Soviet Union that have been associated with its model of Communism and have defined it as a socialist state: the goal of a classless society, a planned economy based on public ownership, democratic centralism in politics and economics, the international fraternity of the working class and oppressed peoples, a quest for social equality as opposed to freedom, and the leading role of the Communist Party.

Second, capitalism has fought back and one might equally argue that

375

in the 1990s the "spectre of capitalism" has overburdened Communism. During the earlier history of Communist states — the consolidation of revolution, then the period of "socialist development and industrialization" — Communist ways of doing things seemed to be ascendant and the West was on the defensive. Since the 1960s, the optimism of the Communists has been on the wane. The six traditional characteristics of Communist systems noted above have been abandoned by the Soviet leadership. Comparisons with the advanced countries of the West have shown inadequacies in human rights and political participation; economic growth has declined significantly and developments in the cultural sphere (and mass leisure) have not kept pace with the aspirations of the younger generation. The countries of Eastern Europe, China, and finally the Soviet Union have abandoned the methods and structures developed in the USSR under Lenin and Stalin. They have looked for inspiration to the experience and practice of Western capitalist states.

The epoch that began with the Russian Revolution of 1917 has come to an end under the leadership of Gorbachev. No longer is the Soviet Union held up as the image of the future. Many of the criticisms of the nature of Soviet democracy and the form of centralized control that were earlier expressed by the Trotskyite opposition, the social democrats in the West, as well as the press and leaders of the capitalist states, are now endorsed by the authorities of the Soviet state.

In the first chapter I pointed to the changing and declining fortunes of the Soviet Union in the international political order. Under Gorbachev, major turns in policy have occurred, seeking to bring about a new alignment in international affairs. In essence the Soviet Union has sought to relinquish the mantle of leader of an ascendant Communist bloc against the principal capitalist states. It has carried out a significant withdrawal from Eastern Europe, it has disengaged from intervention in Afghanistan, and has taken a more conciliatory attitude in Third World conflicts. Soviet hegemony in Eastern Europe has been abandoned in favor of a multiple party system and popularly elected non-Communist governments. The Soviet leadership has sought a less "ideological" policy with respect to the West and more accommodation in an "interdependent" world with more integrated economies. In a less threatening international climate, the Soviet Union has reduced its spending on armaments to the advantage of domestic production. Hence, by modifying the aspirations of the Soviet leadership, Gorbachev has resolved some of the problems that confronted his predecessors.

The Gorbachev leadership, however, regarded its reforms in the USSR as a development of socialism, a "modernization," as it were, of socialism to bring it up to date in the modern epoch. The policy of perestroika has involved the dismantling of the centrally controlled, state-owned economy and a move to a market with competing enterprises and private ownership of assets. However, in the foreseeable future the state will retain a considerable stake in planning and ownership; the mixed economy will be biased towards the government sector and key economic categories will be controlled.

The proposals of the reform movement have lead to contradictions within Soviet society concerning the nature and extent of the changes. There has undoubtedly been a significant recasting of the organizing principles of socialist society. Post-Communist states have moved away from the centralized plan to greater use of market forces, from collective solidarity to individualism, and from a primacy on politics to a greater role for economics. The centralized forms of control are to be superseded by greater devolution and by a more "pluralistic" political system. Ideas of a classless society and a hegemonic Communist Party leading the working class to a world order of communism have been completely repudiated. The resulting ideological vacuum is being filled by an individualized consumerist mentality and a revival of traditional national and religious values. Freedom rather than equality is becoming a dominant goal. The organizing principles of a Party-led society governed by a centrally devised plan have been replaced by increasing inequality, market exchanges, and a greater emphasis on the profit motive. There is coming about a convergence in the operating rules of capitalist and post-Communist states with the latter moving towards the practices and procedures of the former.

These developments are illustrated in Table 11.1, which shows the organizing principles of the Soviet state as understood by those steeped in the tradition of Soviet Marxism-Leninism and the leaders of the reform movement. These points have been detailed in the earlier chapters of this book and will only be briefly outlined here.

Table 11.1
Value Axes of Socialist Traditionalists and Socialist Reformers

Function	Socialist Traditionalist	Policy Socialist Reformer	Likely Outcomes
Efficiency	Planning	Market	Mixed economy
Effectiveness	Centralism	Pluralistic democracy	Controlled democracy
Control	Class Politics	Law	Law governed
Integration	Public	Private	Mixed
Gratification	Work	Consumption	Consumption

Economic reformers in socialist states have consistently focused on the market as a means of attaining efficiency. This applies particularly to the exchange of commodities in the retail market, transactions between production enterprises, as well as those on the world market. There are contradictions in this policy, particularly between the ideological objectives of socialism, which are still cherished by many of the leaders, and the results of market operation. Using wages as material incentives will only be effective if income can be realized through consumption. Consumer demand, in turn, will stimulate production to respond to the distribution of incomes — and will favor production of goods for the rich (who can afford to pay for them) rather than for the poor. Differentials will increase, economic inequality will rise, reflected in differences between regions of the country and levels of personal income.

The system will become increasingly driven by preferences expressed through the market rather than state redistribution of goods and services. A value change has taken place here. A finding of the Harvard project on Soviet refugees conducted in the 1950s was that welfare institutions "form the cornerstone of the type of society they would like to live in." (Inkeles and Bauer 1959: 236). This preference does not hold in the 1980s and early 1990s when client and consumer preference has been demanded by the radicalized reform movement.

Rewarding workers who work well is one side of the coin, penalizing those who do not is the other. Many economists in the USSR have advocated less job security and some have urged the use of unemployment as a stimulus to labor productivity. The rate of unemployment in 1991 rose rapidly to 10 percent. As the reforms begin to bite it will inevitably rise. No Western advanced capitalist country, even among those with a mixed economy, has succeeded in providing full employment, and unemployment inevitably falls on the groups least able to bear the cost. The recently formed Society for the Disabled, for example, has argued for a quota of 2 percent of jobs to be reserved for disabled people. This, it claims, is justified because khozraschet (economic accounting) was the "most commonly cited reason for refusing someone a job." When unemployment bites it will affect the poorer groups of the population. It is here that the more moderate reformers around Gorbachev, seeking to maintain a large public sector and a "welfare state", might gather public support. A social-democratic policy along traditional Western European lines should have more resonance under Soviet conditions than a move to economic liberalism along Thatcherite lines.

A distinguishing feature of the reforms enacted in Eastern Europe and in the USSR under Gorbachev have been in the political sphere. This is a necessary condition to ensure economic change. Established political groups would not be too worried about an economic reform that does not affect their interests and power. The reforms of the political system undoubtedly give greater influence to the market and reduce the power of the center. Thus it is there that opposition to reform has been greatest.

The types of political control ("politics in command") characteristic of the periods of revolution and development are no longer appropriate in a complex economy with a more differentiated population. The movement to a law-governed state is intended to ensure an acceptable and enduring social equilibrium. Here, again, the existing power of the state security services (KGB) has come into conflict with certain elements of the reforms.

Integration through public forms of solidarity, not only public ownership but also symbolic forms of ritual and ceremony, was more appropriate to fuse people in a rapidly urbanizing and industrializing society than it is in one already differentiated and developed. However, the individualism of capitalist society is usually enclosed in a shell of solidarity provided by ideology and rights to private property. As the explicit socialist ideology of traditional Marxism-Leninism evaporates, the vacuum is likely to be filled by goals of individual striving for status through consumption styles. Alternatively, attachments to more traditional symbols and values such as nationalism and religion are powerful alternative integrating ideologies for the groups concerned. Nationalist sentiment is clearly disruptive to the unity of the USSR and is a consequence not only of objective inequalities and historical enmities but also is due to the weakening of Soviet ideological controls.

Finally, the notion of work as a socially valued activity has been replaced by the greater need for employment to receive money. Money and the things that money will buy are increasingly becoming major motivating principles of activity in the USSR as it moves towards becoming a consumer society.

The "likely outcomes" column indicates that there will not be a complete change in the ordering of activities or in the way that the USSR is organized; rather there will be a shift in organizing principles and a mixture of the traditional system and new elements. There will be a greater role for the political and economic market, individualism, law, and consumption.

BECOMING MODERN

How does one evaluate the significance of these changes? Unlike the reasoning of those who take a totalitarian line of explanation, the approach adopted here views the radical reforms introduced in the 1980s as having their roots in the maturation of Soviet society. The political style and market orientation of perestroika are visible effects of the process of "becoming modern." A silent social revolution has been in progress in the Soviet Union since the death of Stalin. The social changes underlying this transition are irreversible and are the key to the understanding of the contemporary USSR.

The Soviet Union is a rapidly changing society. It cannot be described in a static manner. Western writers adopting the approach of totalitarianism see changes in society as emanating from the political will of a ruling elite. This line of reasoning, however, can neither explain the major differences that have occurred between diverse political factions nor the significant changes between state and society that have occurred under perestroika.

While one must concede that the technological backwardness of the socialist states and the changing constellation of world forces are factors that have impelled modification in the USSR, internal thrusts are the most decisive. While there are obviously significant constraints on individual liberty in the USSR, the changes we have discussed in this book lead one to observe that a shift is occurring towards greater individualization. The Party's monopoly of power has gone and its legality is under threat.

Both the causes and repercussions of the political changes taking place under Gorbachev must be taken into account to comprehend the course of perestroika. While the early period of reform was primarily concerned with instigating changes in the economy, with the passage of time, public criticism and new ways of thinking and acting have spread and have been adopted generally in the conduct of affairs. Under Gorbachev, many of the "sacred" tenets of communism as understood under Stalin and adopted in Soviet-type societies have been rejected. Under Gorbachev's leadership before the coup, there was movement towards the industrial ministries being turned into public corporations, rather like British Coal or the nationalized Renault motor corporation. Under Eltsin, it is likely that more privatization will occur following the pattern of Margaret Thatcher. The legitimation of socialist ideology will disappear and a kind of welfare state capitalism is likely to develop.

A sociological analysis has been adopted in this book: it is assumed that changes in social structure influence political style and political outcomes. Adopting a "modernization" rather than a totalitarian or traditional Marxist-Leninist perspective enables one to build a dynamic element into Soviet developments. The effects of industrialization, world communication, education, and urbanization limit the extent of unitary state control. People's expectations change: they aspire to greater participation, develop identities of themselves, and become aware of their own interests.

The approach that considers the USSR to be a totalitarian state fusing all power into one dominant ruling elite fails to distinguish between Party, government executive (including industry, policy, armed forces), and various professional elites such as writers, scientists, and economists. As government becomes more complex it becomes dependent on various groups not only to carry out decisions but also to provide information, policy suggestions, and support. The theory of totalitarianism assumes that "bureaucratic coordination" can be ensured by the top leadership through the hierarchically oligarchic Party apparatus. This must be doubted because organizations have taken on their own relatively autonomous character. State and Party structures have bifurcated (that is, formed separate entities). Being "dedicated to ideology," to Communism, has been vitiated by other forms of group interest and identity. All of the principle leaders in the reform movement have originated and were prominent in the Communist Party of the Soviet Union (Eltsin, Shevardnadze, Yakovlev, Popov, to name but a few).

These interests were recognized by some academic writers in the West long before perestroika. What, then, are the forces for and against perestroika and what are the major divisions within the reform movement?

THE SOCIAL FORCES FOR AND AGAINST PERESTROIKA

At one level, it would be impossible to find people who would admit to being opposed to reform. As Egor Yakovlev, the editor of the reformist *Moscow News*, has put it, "The ideals contained in perestroika are so high that it is practically impossible to speak against them." Precisely. This is why on one occasion Gorbachev received no response when he asked for opponents of perestroika to identify themselves. Perestroika means dissimilar things to different people and they support it, or consider that they support it, for diverse reasons. It includes traditional values such as the statement by Gorbachev that "we are not departing one step from socialism, from Marxism-Leninism" (Plenum on Ideology, February 1988) to views that identify socialism with a mixed economy of the Western type. Perestroika is supported by Nina Andreeva (see chapter 4) who emphasizes traditional socialist morality. Sakharov also advocated under the banner of perestroika a society devised more on the politically pluralist and free enterprise foundations of the West.

This diversity of views may be illustrated by a survey of public opinion conducted in 1989 that defined six specific policy positions on perestroika. The survey does not portray the balance of Soviet attitudes but it helps distinguish the most important trends. As part of the survey respondents were asked about their opinion of political leaders — their favorites and least liked are shown below. (Lenin and Gorbachev universally scored high points and are omitted.)

1. "Pragmatic" Westernizers. These are people who seek a Western-type economic and political system. They admire Reagan and Sakharov and deplore Brezhnev and Stalin.
2. *Obnovlentsy* (People seeking "Renewal.") This group endorses a form of renewal leading to "social justice" — wider differentials based on work and effort and supporting the interests of "ordinary workers." This group particularly supports Eltsin and Fidel Castro; it most dislikes Brezhnev and Stalin.
3. The "Greens." They seek greater environmental and health protection, peace, and disarmament. They support Sakharov, Eltsin, A. N. Yakovlev, Ligachev, and Andropov. At the bottom of their list come Stalin and Brezhnev.
4. *Obyvateli* (the "man in the street" with a mildly negative connotation). This group emphasizes a rising standard of living and material well-being. Andropov, Eltsin, and Castro are the esteemed leaders while Brezhnev and Khrushchev are the least popular.
5. *Gosudarstvenniki*, or supporters of a strong state. Upholders of law and order campaigns, stronger discipline, and a powerful industrial and military state. Stalin, Andropov, Eltsin and Castro are their top leaders whereas Brezhnev, Khrushchev, and Sakharov are the least liked.
6. "Patriots." They support Russian nationalist culture, the family, and tradition. Stalin, Andropov, Eltsin, and Ligachev are highly approved of and Brezhnev, Khrushchev, Sakharov, Reagan, and Yakovlev are unpopular.

Of these positions, groups five (strong state) and six (nationalists) hardly fit into the policy options advocated by Gorbachev's view of perestroika. Indeed, they may be considered to be opposed to it.

We have no adequate survey data on which social strata or institutions may be identified as being in support or opposition to the leadership's policies. (The sampling of the above survey is not representative of the USSR as a whole.) It is likely that any given group or institution will have misgivings about some of the policies and be in support of others.

In Table 11.2 I have attempted to classify the major groups with re-

Table 11.2
Attitudes toward Perestroika by Institutions and Groups

		Aspect of Perestroika		
	Economic	Ideological	Political	International
1. Elites				
Party secretariat	A/F	A/F	A/F	F/A
Security police	F	A	F/A	A
Military, foreign affairs	F/A	A	F/A	A
Industrial state apparatus	A	A	A	I
2. Leading institutions				
Republican party/state apparatus	F/A	F/A	F/A	F/A
Trade unions	A	A	A	I
Academies of Sciences	F/A	F	F	F
Humanistic/social science				
professionals	F/A	F/A	F/A	F
3. Local interests				
Soviets	F	F/A	F/A	I
Industrial managers/executives	F/A	F/I	F/A	I
Party Branches	F/A	F/A	F/A	F
Local Party apparat	A/F	A	A	F
4. Informal Groups				
Greens	A/F	F	F	F
People's Fronts	F	F	F	F
Women's, Friendship, self-help groups	F	F	F	F
5. Social classes				
Manual workers	F/A	A/F	A/F	F
Nonmanual workers	F/A	A/F	A/F	F
Collective farmers	F/A	I	I	F
Private business, cooperatives	F	F	F	F
6. Non-Russian nationalities	F	F	F/A	I

spect to their attitude toward perestroika. The groups and institutions are arranged in a hierarchy with the most powerful at the top and the least at the bottom. Four aspects of perestroika are considered: economic reform (khozraschet), ideological reform, political reform, and new thinking in international relations. The hypothesized attitudes are divided into three choices: F for, A against and I indifferent to the relevant dimension. In some columns, the two letters F and A indicate groups for and against the policy dimension.

It may be hypothesized that much of the initiative for the reform movement came from opinion makers in the following groups: the top Party leadership, the armed forces, the police and security forces, social science professionals, humanitarian and literary intelligentsia, industrial management, skilled manual strata, and national minorities. It should be emphasized that these are large groups with important divisions and reservations about, and opposition to other aspects of the reform strategy. The reasoning behind these classifications is as follows.

The sluggish performance of the economy and the lack of growth of the technological capacity of the USSR to compete with high technology developments in the West has led to concern on the part of the more technologically developed parts of the armed forces. To compete in a modern war one needs more than a lot of men in army great coats, war is increasingly a technological battle. The Soviet Union has lagged behind in electronics and laser technology. The benefits of economic efficiency and an emphasis on technological advance would help modernize the armed forces, especially the air force and rocket weaponry.

Equally good reasons can be put forward as to why people in the armed forces may also oppose reforms. Reliance on market forces and a greater concern with the provision of consumption and a more "open door" to the West would lead to a lessening of the role of the military and a reduction in the military budget. Furthermore, not all the military are committed to high technology and the doctrine which underpins it; conventional forces are an important part of the Soviet defense establishment. *Any* weakening of the armed forces is opposed by the more conventional defense staff and all have misgivings about the pull-out from Eastern Europe.

The security forces under Andropov were an important element in giving the reform movement an impetus. The corruption of the Brezhnev period, the absence of universal application of a common legal code, undermined the authority of the police. Also the corruption and widespread economic crime had its roots in the malfunctioning of the system of economic planning. But the security forces cannot be expected to be wholeheartedly in support of all policies; they have much to lose from a political and ideological point of view. They value a strong military state and are undermined by the political aspects of perestroika; pluralism makes their work more difficult, and glasnost' makes their work open to public scrutiny. The security forces have been involved in repression not only under the Stalin regime, but also have persecuted contemporary dissidents such as Sakharov.

In the economy and the public sector as a whole, the reforms will favor some but they will by the same token adversely affect others. Those who have developed administrative skills over a long period will lose them and the seniority and status that goes with them. The strongest opponents must be among the *apparatchiks* of the central government apparatus. The ministerial apparatus is being diminished in size and importance. Many are losing their jobs as a consequence of decentralization and the more market-orientated system. Hence apart from general considerations of peace, the industrial administrative apparat is strongly opposed to the major features of perestroika.

The policies adopted by the Gorbachev leadership were not hastily put together after the fall of Chernenko, but had been worked out by reform intellectuals under Brezhnev. Social science professionals are in a position to judge comparatively the performance of the economy and social policy against plans and international achievements. The slowdown in the rate of growth and the low level of productivity lead many Soviet economists and management specialists to look to alternative forms of organization, particularly the market as a means of reform. Many of these academics seek a more unequally differentiated system of rewards and social opportunities.

Sociologists and other social planners are aware of the unfulfilled aspirations of many groups in the population and of the injustices that the system of planning has created. While they support new political and ideological policy initiatives advocated by the leadership, their expectations are quite different from those of the economists. Their orientation is more like that of welfare state social scientists in the West. They favor equality and seek curbs on the effects of the operation of the market. Social scientists also are not a homogeneous body. Many have legitimated the Stalinist orthodoxy all their lives and their reputations as well as their intellectual capital may suffer if a reformist strategy is adopted.

The humanistic, literary, and scientific intelligentsia come to the reform program from a different point of view. They seek more independence of individual expression, more freedom, and rights to pursue their own work without state interference. They are opposed to state control and support a market in ideas, an opening up of intellectual life both internally and with the West. Journalists in television and the mass press have been particularly forceful advocates of the reform policy. Having little to gain from the Stalinist form of rule, they are less critical of the reform policy and may wish it to be more radical and proceed more quickly. In the humanities, too, the traditional Soviet outlook is not dead. The views of lecturer Nina Andreeva characterize this group. One must bear in mind that the Party has had its own intelligentsia, which has been brought up on a traditional version of Marxism-Leninism devised in the period since Stalin. The Party intelligentsia not only has had a fundamental ideological stake in traditional ideology, but many may also oppose in principle moves toward the anarchy of the market and its attendant values of consumerism and acquisitiveness. There is a sharp ideological struggle in the USSR.

Industrial management at the level of the enterprise contains many specialists who are aware of the incompetencies of planning, the disproportions between inputs and outputs, and the waste of human and material resources. Efficiency modelled on the Western experience is their expectation. Thus they are drawn to reward on the basis of efficiency and payment according to desert. They believe that differentials should be widened to reward effort and penalties should be applied to sanction incompetence and idleness, including the disciplining of the labor force with a dose of unemployment. For factory managers, for instance, khozraschet will give greater possibilities for initiative and advancement for the successful. The other side of the coin is greater uncertainty, more economic accountability, and a more difficult job. Those who have developed administrative skills in the command economy will probably fear the more uncertain and entrepreneurial environment. People in trade lower down the hierarchy who are able to live on speculation must also fear a move to a more open market system.

The manual working class is divided: the trained and skilled younger workers who are ambitious to earn more and use their skills see opportunity in the economic reforms. There will be greater incentives and differentials will widen, but this will be at the cost of harder work and uncertainty about job security. For the younger better qualified workers job mobility and work flexibility will be less of a problem. The older workers, with little skill and only rudimentary knowledge of production techniques are likely to fare much worse under the economic aspects of perestroika.

The official trade unions have been severely criticized both by the reform leadership and the rank and file workers and will find the new environment much more demanding. There are few immediate advantages for this group under perestroika. Though some may welcome the opportunity to reform and become genuine proponents of workers' interests, trade union officials are opponents of the economic and political aspects of perestroika.

The collective farmers are probably indifferent to the reforms. In recent years their conditions have improved, and proposed leasing arrangements may be regarded with suspicion as they involve uncertainty and possible loss. Many of the younger and more ambitious people have moved from the collective farm. It is unlikely that many who remain are attracted to the political or ideological aspects.

The major national minorities consider the economic and political aspects of perestroika to be in their interests. Policy should give them greater independence and autonomy. But here again one may detect differences of interest between regions. The non-Russian nationalities lodged in elite positions in places such as Kazakhstan and Georgia may resent the leadership's attempt to strengthen legality. Greater concern with efficiency and relative costs will not favor the less developed regions (such as Tadzhikistan), which may receive less transfer payments from the more industrial and developed parts of the USSR. Republics in the Baltic, however, have advocated a more radical perestroika — secession from the USSR.

Despite the differences of interest and expectations of perestroika, there is a constellation of forces, fanned no doubt by the pro-perestroika propaganda campaign, that shares a conviction that the form and process of rule set up in the Stalin period is no longer appropriate and must be replaced. To this extent these people in different constituencies are united. The reformers are held together by sentiments opposing the distortions of the Stalin period, but they have not arrived at a common set of policies on which they are all agreed — and neither have the emergent opposition forces.

One other factor that works to strengthen the reform political leadership is the international perspective and the place of the USSR in the world community. Gorbachev has been immensely successful in the policy of detente and coexistence with the West; he has extricated the USSR with honor from Afghanistan. He has appealed to the deeply held sentiments for peace on the part of the Soviet people. His ability to deal on an equal footing with the Western leaders has had internal repercussions: it has strengthened his political position at home.

One must also bear in mind that the social and institutional groups mentioned above contain a range of opinions. In all groups there are innovators or entrepreneurs of perestroika, supporters, people who stand on the sidelines, and others who passively or actively oppose the changes.

Age, education, and qualification are the basis for the social divisions in support of or opposition to perestroika: the younger, better educated and more highly qualified will gain most from the reforms and are likely to be among its most articulate though not uncritical supporters. There has been a major generational shift (see chapter 7) with the younger people being more individualistic and seeking to fulfill more consumerist needs. These people, moreover, are ascendant groups — the future of the country depends on their active commitment and goodwill.

WHITHER PERESTROIKA?

The effects of perestroika will not be to everybody's liking. The reforms may well lead to greater economic efficiency but will concurrently bring in their wake other distortions and contradictions. Market systems under capitalism have not created equal all-round economic growth, nor have they abolished poverty — even in countries with very high per capita levels of wealth. The market in politics and economics under capitalism has enlarged the area of personal choice and wealth. Market relations are associated often unthinkingly in the minds of the reformers with progress; they are seen as the antidote to everything that is undesirable in Soviet society.

However much markets under capitalism may generate wealth, they do not fulfill other forms of well-being: loyalty, friendship, community, love, cultural services, and public provision in general. Behind claims for the market lurk ideological preferences for freedom over equality, for individualism over collectivism. The more the system encourages efficiency through individual effort, the more it will weaken policies designed to promote equal distribution of resources. As in capitalist societies, greater exposure to the world market will weaken the position of labor but will lead to greater labor productivity. Redistribution of resources through welfare services under state socialism, for all its inefficiencies, had proved relatively progressive and a decline in public welfare expenditure will probably weaken the redistributive policies of the welfare state. Thus the reforms are a wager on the strong. In the short run, the Soviet Union will experience the inefficiencies associated with both the market and the plan. A period of destabilization has characterized the USSR in the early 1990s.

Opposition to Gorbachev has taken many forms. Defense of self interest by the bureaucratic elites and those in managerial positions threatened by market reforms is a major obstacle to be overcome by the reform leadership. In Table 11.2 there is a clustering of "Against" signs in the top elites's bracket. Others are opposed on ideological grounds to the tenets of market socialism. Kosolapov and Andreeva reflect this position. Perestroika delegitimizes the traditional Soviet concept of socialism and its sacred symbols: central planning, Party leadership, and control. Ideological opponents defend an egalitarian version of social justice, opposition to the theory and practice of private enterprise and the rising class of business persons. In its place they espouse the traditional values of Marxism-Leninism and the building of communism through the working class as a political vanguard. They still acknowledge the external threat of capitalism, fear the hostility of the capitalist West, and deplore the role of imperialism on a world scale. The ideological shell of Soviet society, they argue, has been broken by perestroika.

The social support of this group is derived not only from the bureaucracy, which fears displacement as a consequence of marketization, but also from the Workers' Fronts that grew up in 1989. Many workers have been threatened by growing marketization and price rises. The growing levels of crime, inflation, food shortages, internal upheaval and disorder (particularly strikes and interethnic murders), demands for independence and secession from the Baltic republics are evidence of this group's way of thinking that liberalization has gone too far. In the September 1989 plenum of the Central Committee, Ligachev deplored the tendency for some to turn towards capitalism and bourgeois democracy: the introduction of private ownership and a multiparty political system would undermine a socialist system and might lead to a restoration of capitalism.

How far are these fears true? There are clearly such dangers inherent in the forces let loose by the reform movement. Prior to the coup of August 1991, private ownership of the means of production and the employment of labor was extremely limited. Multiple parties can operate under any system of economy: a multiparty system has hardly been found to be a threat to capitalism. Competition of parties can operate within socialism if they accept the ideological parameters of the system and work to further socialist ideals. Hence, one outcome of perestroika (as indicated in Table 11.1) is a mixed economy with private and public ownership containing different forms of socialist ownership relations. A "pluralistic" form of polity, with multiple parties, is not incompatible with a socialist economy if laws proscribe capitalist economic processes. This was the line taken by Gorbachev before the coup.

Until it is replaced by a different and accepted set of organizing principles there will be a period of dislocation, of internal social struggle and strife. The legitimacy of the reformers has not been established — economic conditions in the USSR between 1989 and 1991 worsened. They will have helped to create a legitimacy crisis.

Andreeva, in discussing the position of Gorbachev, has contended that he tries to "sit between two stools." There is a shrewdness in this observation. Gorbachev has maintained some of the rhetoric of traditional Soviet Communism: he has advocated the supremacy of socialism over capitalism and contended that the Soviet system is qualitatively different from the capitalism of the West. He has maintained the vanguard role of the Party. But the tenor of his reforms has been to marketization and to a political order based on pluralism and glasnost'. In order to command support, he has needed to appeal to both factions, and he has sought to perpetuate the traditional appeal of Communism with the modernizing principles of the reformers. In 1990, he "changed stools" and conceded the political monopoly of power of the Communist Party.

Gorbachev, however, has failed both camps. For the traditionalist, he has delegitimized the command system and provided an unacceptable and inadequate alternative in its place. For the reformers, he has appeared too indecisive: Eltsin in September 1989 pointed out that Gorbachev is "an advocate of constant compromise and one cannot win in politics by constant compromises." Gorbachev has failed to carry through the logic of the reforms: when confronted by the Party apparatus, by resistance from the working class, he has moved away from the market mechanism. In the winter of 1990/91, he delayed economic reform to secure stability. He is accused of not moving fast enough and firmly enough towards private property, denationalization and market forms.

Gorbachev has had no alternative but to tread a middle course. The reformers themselves adopt different and contradictory perspectives on perestroika. As I indicated in the first chapter, glasnost' and demokratiya were conceived by the political leadership to be above all means to achieve acceleration (*uskorenie*). Various groups have viewed these principles as ends in themselves. The national minorities particularly have utilized such precepts to legitimate their own interests against the center thereby bringing into disrepute the wider goals of the reform movement. Groups of workers (particularly the miners) have asserted their own interest without respect to the collective interest. A "pluralism of interests" can only be effective in the context of agreement about what constitutes the boundaries of such interests, in terms of the collective interest. Western liberal democracies have had hundreds of years of experience in shaping the balance between the collective, represented by the state, and the individual's actions in civil society. The Soviet Union is currently embarking on this course and it can be expected that divisions and conflict between groups on national, ethnic, regional, social, and political bases will occur as the state works out the extent and means of enforcing its powers.

In the late 1980s and early 1990s, destabilizing elements have become apparent. Three major ingredients for radical change have surfaced: first, widespread dissatisfaction with economic and social conditions; second, ambiguity among the leaders and the lack of a definite plan to overcome the discontent; third, increased political activity among the masses. Could this precipitate a major counterrevolution? For such a major change to occur, however, a fourth factor is needed: a clear political alternative and leaders intent on achieving it. The four conditions were met in August 1991. The leaders of the coup, drawn from the elite of Gorbachev's own government apparatus, attempted to halt the process of democratization, marketization and openness. However, they lacked ideological conviction: rather than a move back to Stalinism, they sought a period of authoritarian rule to stabilize conditions. The command system under Party control had been discredited. If one considers the six characteristics I listed as defining state socialism at the beginning of this chapter, all were repudiated by the leadership of Gorbachev.

The post-coup authority of Eltsin does offer an alternative to the incoherence of Gorbachev. Eltsin and his supporters favour much greater decentralization and more power to the republican elites. They endorse a multi-party system and the destatization of the Communist Party. They advocate a shift in policy towards marketization with various forms of privatization and a greater emphasis on private property. This is a logical development of the ideological, economic, political and organizational demise of state socialism which was carried out by Gorbachev. In this case Ligachev was probably right — perestroika will lead to capitalism. The market is not a neutral institution, but a form of political power just as potent as an administratively-ordered system. In a market system, those with control over productive and organizational assets — form a dominant class over those who lack these attributes.

No serious contender for power could advocate going back to Stalin's or Brezhnev's policies. While some of the achievements of perestroika may be curtailed, many of the changes in economic and political processes discussed in this book are irreversible. Perestroika is not a sudden break with the past. It should be seen as the culmination of an uneven and discontinuous process of development that has been taking place in the USSR since the rise of Khrushchev. There has been a gradual relaxation, an incremental adoption of more openness, and a greater awareness of the inadequacies of the system as it developed under Stalin.

A movement to greater pluralism cannot be achieved quickly and without setbacks. The institutions of democratic control are at an early stage of formation. The public mentality has been shaped by a legacy of political dictatorship going back generations before 1917. It is to be expected that the practices that have made the Soviet Union a world power and have maintained social and political unity since the time of the revolution will not be discredited or destroyed in one fell swoop. In 1990, presidential power gave Gorbachev a level of authority enjoyed by the tsars. Eltsin may yet act like one. The Union has entered a period of instability in which the relations between the center (the Union government) and the republics are being negotiated, in which the forms of ownership and control of assets are being changed. This has lead to a changing balance of forces and to the secession of some republics from the union. The significance of the reform movement is that Russia is finally emerging from centuries of isolation first established by the tsars and perpetuated by the commissars.

Appendix ————————————————————————————————

THE CONSTITUTION (FUNDAMENTAL LAW) OF THE USSR, 1977. (AS AMENDED TO DECEMBER 1990)

The Great October Socialist Revolution, made by the workers and peasants of Russia under the leadership of the Communist Party headed by Lenin, overthrew capitalist and landowner rule, broke the fetters of oppression, established the dictatorship of the proletariat, and created the Soviet state, a new type of state, the basic instrument for defending the gains of the revolution and for building socialism and communism. Humanity thereby began the epoch-making turn from capitalism to socialism.

After achieving victory in the Civil War and repulsing imperialist intervention, the Soviet government carried through far-reaching social and economic transformations, and put an end once and for all to exploitation of man by man, antagonisms between classes, and strife between nationalities. The unification of the Soviet Republics in the Union of Soviet Socialist Republics multiplied the forces and opportunities of the peoples of the country in the building of socialism. Social ownership of the means of production and genuine democracy for the working masses were established. For the first time in the history of mankind a socialist society was created.

The strength of socialism was vividly demonstrated by the immortal feat of the Soviet people and their Armed Forces in achieving their historic victory in the Great Patriotic War.* This victory consolidated the influence and international standing of the Soviet Union and created new opportunities for growth of the forces of socialism, national liberation, democracy and peace throughout the world.

Continuing their creative endeavours, the working people of the Soviet Union have ensured rapid, all-round development of the country and steady improvement of the socialist system. They have consolidated the alliance of the working class, collective-farm peasantry, and people's intelligentsia, and friendship of the nations and nationalities of the USSR. Socio-political and ideological unity of

* i.e. Second World War.

Soviet society, in which the working class is the leading force, has been achieved. The aims of the dictatorship of the proletariat having been fulfilled, the Soviet state has become a state of the whole people.

In the USSR a developed socialist society has been built. At this stage, when socialism is developing on its own foundations, the creative forces of the new system and the advantages of the socialist way of life are becoming increasingly evident, and the working people are more and more widely enjoying the fruits of their great revolutionary gains.

It is a society in which powerful productive forces and progressive science and culture have been created, in which the well-being of the people is constantly rising, and more and more favourable conditions are being provided for the all-round development of the individual.

It is a society of mature socialist social relations, in which, on the basis of the drawing together of all classes and social strata and of the juridical and factual equality of all its nations and nationalities and their fraternal co-operation, a new historical community of people has been formed — the Soviet people.

It is a society of high organizational capacity, ideological commitment, and consciousness of the working people, who are patriots and internationalists.

It is a society in which the law of life is concern of all for the good of each and concern of each for the good of all.

It is a society of true democracy, the political system of which ensures effective management of all public affairs, ever more active participation of the working people in running the state, and the combining of citizens' rights and freedoms with their obligations and responsibility to society.

Developed socialist society is a natural, logical stage on the road to communism.

The supreme goal of the Soviet state is the building of a classless communist society in which there will be public, communist self-government. The main aims of the people's socialist state are: to lay the material and technical foundation of communism, to perfect socialist social relations and transform them into communist relations, to mould the citizen of communist society, to raise the people's living and cultural standards, to safeguard the country's security, and to further the consolidation of peace and development of international co-operation.

The Soviet people, guided by the ideas of scientific communism and true to their revolutionary traditions, relying on the great social, economic, and political gains of socialism, striving for the further development of socialist democracy, taking into account the international position of the USSR as part of the world system of socialism, and conscious of their internationalist responsibility, preserving continuity of the ideas and principles of the first Soviet Constitution of 1918, the 1924 Constitution of the USSR and the 1936 Constitution of the USSR, hereby affirm the principles of the social structure and policy of the USSR, and define the rights, freedoms and obligations of citizens, and the principles of the organization of the socialist state of the whole people, and its aims, and proclaim these in this Constitution.

I. Principles of the Social Structure and Policy of the USSR

Chapter 1: The Political System

Article 1. The Union of Soviet Socialist Republics is a socialist state of the whole people, expressing the will and interests of the workers, peasants, and intelligentsia, the working people of all the nations and nationalities of the country.

Article 2. All power in the USSR belongs to the people.

The people exercise state power through Soviets of People's Deputies, which constitute the political foundation of the USSR.

All other state bodies are under the control of, and accountable to, the Soviets or People's Deputies.

Article 3. The Soviet state is organized and functions on the principle of democratic centralism, namely the electiveness of all bodies of state authority from the lowest to the highest, their accountability to the people, and the obligation of lower bodies to observe the decisions of higher ones. Democratic centralism combines central leadership with local initiative and creative activity and with the responsibility of each state body and official for the work entrusted to them.

Article 4. The Soviet state and all its bodies function on the basis of socialist law, ensure the maintenance of law and order, and safeguard the interests of society and the rights and freedoms of citizens.

State organizations, public organizations and officials shall observe the Constitution of the USSR and Soviet laws.

Article 5. Major matters of state shall be submitted to nationwide discussion and put to a popular vote (referendum).

Article 6. The Communist Party of the Soviet Union and other political parties, as well as trade union, youth and other social organizations and mass movements, participate in the formulation of the policy of the Soviet state and in the administration of the state and social affairs through their representatives elected to the soviets of people's deputies and in other ways.

Article 7. All political parties, social organizations and mass movements, in the exercise of the functions stipulated in their programmes and rules, operate within the framework of the Constitution and Soviet laws.

The formation and operation of parties, organizations and movements having the aim of forcibly changing the Soviet constitutional system and the integrity of the socialist state, undermining its security or kindling social, national or religious strife are not permitted.

Article 8. Work collectives take part in discussing and deciding state and public affairs, in planning production and social development, in training and placing personnel, and in discussing and deciding matters pertaining to the management of enterprises and institutions, the improvement of working and living conditions, and the use of funds allocated both for developing production and for social and cultural purposes and financial incentives.

Work collectives promote socialist emulation, the spread of progressive methods of work, and the strengthening of production discipline, educate their members in the spirit of communist morality, and strive to enhance their political consciousness and raise their cultural level and skills and qualifications.

Article 9. The principal direction in the development of the political system of Soviet society is the extension of socialist democracy, namely ever broader participation of citizens in managing the affairs of society and the state, continuous improvement of the machinery of state, heightening of the activity of public organizations, strengthening of the system of people's control, consolidation of the legal foundations of the functioning of the state and of public life, greater openness and publicity, and constant responsiveness to public opinion.

Chapter 2: The Economic System

Article 10. The economic system of the USSR develops on the basis of ownership by Soviet citizens and collective and state ownership.

The state creates the conditions necessary for the development of diverse forms of ownership and ensures equal protection for them.

The land, its mineral resources, water resources and the plant and animal world in their natural state are the inalienable property of the peoples inhabiting a given territory, are under the jurisdiction of the Soviets of people's deputies and are granted to citizens, enterprises, institutions and organizations for their use.

Article 11. A USSR citizen's property is his personal property and is used to meet material and spiritual needs and carry out autonomous economic activity and other activity that is not banned by law.

Any property for consumption and production purposes acquired out of earned income and on other lawful grounds may be under the ownership of a citizen, with the exception of those forms of property whose acquisition by citizens for their own ownership is not permitted.

In order to pursue peasant and personal subsidiary farming and for other purposes stipulated by law, citizens are entitled to hold land plots in heritable life tenure, and also in use [Russian: *polzovaniye*].

The right of inheritance of a citizen's property is acknowledged and protected by law.

Article 12. Collective property is the property of leaseholding enterprises, collective enterprises, co-operatives, joint-stock companies, economic organizations and other associations. Collective property is created through the transformation, by methods stipulated by law, of state property and through the voluntary amalgamation of the property of citizens and organizations.

Article 13. State property is union-wide property, the property of union republics, and the property of autonomous republics, autonomous oblasts, autonomous okrugs, krays, oblasts and other administrative-territorial units (communal property).

Article 14. The source of the growth of social wealth and of the well-being of the people, and of each individual, is the labour, free from exploitation, of Soviet people.

The state exercises control over the measure of labour and of consumption in accordance with the principle of socialism: "From each according to his ability, to each according to his work". It fixes the rate of taxation on taxable income.

Socially useful work and its results determine a person's status in society. By combining material and moral incentives and encouraging innovation and a creative attitude to work, the state helps transform labour into the prime vital need of every Soviet citizen.

Article 15. The supreme goal of social production under socialism is the fullest possible satisfaction of the people's growing material, and cultural and intellectual requirements.

Relying on the creative initiative of the working people, socialist emulation, and scientific and technological progress, and by improving the forms and methods of economic management, the state ensures growth of the productivity of labour, raising of the efficiency of production and of the quality of work, and dynamic, planned, proportionate development of the economy.

Article 16. The economy of the USSR is an integral economic complex comprising all the elements of social production, distribution, and exchange on its territory.

The economy is managed on the basis of state plans for economic and social development, with due account of the sectoral and territorial principles, and by combining centralized direction with the managerial independence and initiative of individual and amalgamated enterprises and other organizations, for which active use is made of management accounting, profit, cost, and other economic levers and incentives.

Article 17. In the USSR, the law permits individual labour in handicrafts, farming, the provision of services for the public, and other forms of activity based exclusively on the personal work of individual citizens and members of their families. The state makes regulations for such work to ensure that it serves the interests of society.

Article 18. In the interests of the present and future generations, the necessary steps are taken in the USSR to protect and make scientific, rational use of the land and its mineral and water resources, and the plant and animal kingdoms, to preserve the purity of air and water, ensure reproduction of natural wealth, and improve the human environment.

Chapter 3: Social Development and Culture

Article 19. The social basis of the USSR is the unbreakable alliance of the workers, peasants, and intelligentsia.

The state helps enhance the social homogeneity of society, namely the elimination of class differences and of the essential distinctions between town and country and between mental and physical labour, and the all-round development and drawing together of all the nations and nationalities of the USSR.

Article 20. In accordance with the communist ideal — 'The free development of each is the condition of the free development of all' — the state pursues the aim of giving citizens more and more real opportunities to apply their creative energies, abilities, and talents, and to develop their personalities in every way.

Article 21. The state concerns itself with improving working conditions, safety and labour protection and the scientific organization of work, and with reducing and ultimately eliminating all arduous physical labour through comprehensive mechanization and automation of production processes in all branches of the economy.

Article 22. A programme is being consistently implemented in the USSR to convert agricultural work into a variety of industrial work, to extend the network of educational, cultural and medical institutions, and of trade, public catering, service and public utility facilities in rural localities, and transform hamlets and villages into well-planned and well-appointed settlements.

Article 23. The state pursues a steady policy of raising people's pay levels and real incomes through increase in productivity.

In order to satisfy the needs of Soviet people more fully social consumption funds are created. The state, with the broad participation of public organizations and work collectives, ensures the growth and just distribution of these funds.

Article 24. In the USSR, state systems of health protection, social security, trade and public catering, communal services and amenities, and public utilities, operate and are being extended.

The state encourages co-operatives and other public organizations to provide all types of services for the population. It encourages the development of mass physical culture and sport.

Article 25. In the USSR there is a uniform system of public education, which is being constantly improved, that provides general education and vocational training for citizens, serves the communist education and intellectual and physical development of the youth, and trains them for work and social activity.

Article 26. In accordance with society's needs the state provides for planned development of science and the training of scientific personnel and organizes introduction of the results of research in the economy and other spheres of life.

Article 27. The state concerns itself with protecting, augmenting and making extensive use of society's cultural wealth for the moral and aesthetic education of the Soviet people, for raising their cultural level.

In the USSR development of the professional, amateur and folk arts is encouraged in every way.

Chapter 4: Foreign Policy

Article 28. The USSR steadfastly pursues a Leninist policy of peace and stands for strengthening of the security of nations and broad international co-operation.

The foreign policy of the USSR is aimed at ensuring international conditions favourable for building communism in the USSR, safeguarding the state interests of the Soviet Union, consolidating the positions of world socialism, supporting the struggle of peoples for national liberation and social progress, preventing wars of aggression, achieving universal and complete disarmament, and consistently implementing the principle of the peaceful coexistence of states with different social systems.

In the USSR war propaganda is banned.

Article 29. The USSR's relations with other states are based on observance of the following principles: sovereign equality; mutual renunciation of the use or threat of force; inviolability of frontiers; territorial integrity of states; peaceful settlement of disputes; non-intervention in internal affairs; respect for human rights and fundamental freedoms; the equal rights of peoples and their right to decide their own destiny; co-operation among states; and fulfilment in good faith of obligations arising from the generally recognized principles and rules of international law, and from the international treaties signed by the USSR.

Article 30. The USSR, as part of the world system of socialism and of the socialist community, promotes and strengthens friendship, co-operation, and comradely mutual assistance with other socialist countries on the basis of the principle of socialist internationalism, and takes an active part in socialist economic integration and the socialist international division of labour.

Chapter 5: Defence of the Socialist Motherland

Article 31. Defence of the Socialist Motherland is one of the most important functions of the state, and is the concern of the whole people.

In order to defend the gains of socialism, the peaceful labour of the Soviet people, and the sovereignty and territorial integrity of the state, the USSR maintains Armed Forces and has instituted universal military service.

The duty of the Armed Forces of the USSR to the people is to provide reliable defence of the Socialist Motherland and to be in constant combat readiness, guaranteeing that any aggressor is instantly repulsed.

Article 32 The state ensures the security and defence capability of the country, and supplies the Armed Forces of the USSR with everything necessary for that purpose.

The duties of state bodies, public organizations, officials, and citizens in regard to safeguarding the country's security and strengthening its defence capacity are defined by the legislation of the USSR.

II. The State and the Individual

Chapter 6: Citizenship of the USSR, Equality of Citizens' Rights

Article 33. Uniform federal citizenship is established for the USSR. Every citizen of a Union Republic is a citizen of the USSR.

The grounds and procedure for acquiring or forfeiting Soviet citizenship are defined by the Law on Citizenship of the USSR.

When abroad, citizens of the USSR enjoy the protection and assistance of the Soviet state.

Article 34. Citizens of the USSR are equal before the law, without distinction of origin, social or property status, race or nationality, sex, education, language, attitude to religion, type and nature of occupation, domicile, or other status.

The equal rights of citizens of the USSR are guaranteed in all fields of economic, political, social, and cultural life. Benefits to individual categories of citizens are established solely on the basis of the law. No-one in the USSR may enjoy unlawful privilege.

Article 35. Women and men have equal rights in the USSR.

Exercise of these rights is ensured by according women equal access with men to education and vocational and professional training, equal opportunities in employment, remuneration, and promotion, and in social and political, and cultural activity, and by special labour and health protection measures for women; by providing conditions enabling mothers to work; by legal protection, and material and moral support for mothers and children, including paid leaves and other benefits for expectant mothers and mothers, and gradual reduction of working time for mothers with small children.

Article 36. Citizens of the USSR of different races and nationalities have equal rights.

Exercise of these rights is ensured by a policy of all-round development and drawing together of all the nations and nationalities of the USSR, by educating citizens in the spirit of Soviet patriotism and socialist internationalism, and by the possibility to use their native language and the languages of other peoples of the USSR.

Any direct or indirect limitation of the rights of citizens or establishment of direct or indirect privileges on grounds of race or nationality, and any advocacy of racial or national exclusiveness, hostility or contempt, are punishable by law.

Article 37. Citizens of other countries and stateless persons in the USSR are guaranteed the rights and freedoms provided by law, including the right to apply to a court and other state bodies for the protection of their personal, property, family and other rights.

Citizens of other countries and stateless persons, when in the USSR, are obliged to respect the Constitution of the USSR and observe Soviet laws.

Article 38. The USSR grants the right of asylum to foreigners persecuted for defending the interests of the working people and the cause of peace, or for participation in the revolutionary and national-liberation movement, or for progressive social and political, scientific or other creative activity.

Chapter 7: The Basic Rights, Freedoms, and Duties of Citizens of the USSR

Article 39. Citizens of the USSR enjoy in full the social, economic, political and personal rights and freedoms proclaimed and guaranteed by the Constitution of the USSR and by Soviet laws. The socialist system ensures enlargement of the rights and freedoms of citizens and continuous improvement of their living standards as social, economic, and cultural development programmes are fulfilled.

Enjoyment by citizens of their rights and freedoms must not be to the detriment of the interests of society or the state, or infringe the rights of other citizens.

Article 40. Citizens of the USSR have the right to work (that is, to guaranteed employment and pay in accordance with the quantity and quality of their work, and not below the state-established minimum), including the right to choose their trade or profession, type of job and work in accordance with their inclinations, abilities, training and education, with due account of the needs of society.

This right is ensured by the socialist economic system, steady growth of the productive forces, free vocational and professional training, improvement of skills, training in new trades or professions, and development of the systems of vocational guidance and job placement.

Article 41. Citizens of the USSR have the right to rest and leisure.

This right is ensured by the establishment of a working week not exceeding 41 hours for workers and other employees, a shorter working day in a number of trades and industries, and shorter hours for night work; by the provision of paid annual holidays, weekly days of rest, extension of the network of cultural, educational and health-building institutions, and the development on a mass scale of sport, physical culture, and camping and tourism; by the provision of neighbourhood recreational facilities, and of other opportunity for rational use of free time.

The length of collective farmers' working and leisure time is established by their collective farms.

Article 42. Citizens of the USSR have the right to health protection.

This right is ensured by free, qualified medical care provided by state health institutions; by extension of the network of therapeutic and health-building institutions; by the development and improvement of safety and hygiene in industry; by carrying out broad prophylactic measures; by measures to improve the environment; by special care for the health of the rising generation, including prohibition of child labour, excluding the work done by children as part of the school curriculum; and by developing research to prevent and reduce the incidence of disease and ensure citizens a long and active life.

Article 43. Citizens of the USSR have the right to maintenance in old age, in sickness, and in the event of complete or partial disability or loss of the breadwinner.

This right is guaranteed by social insurance of workers and other employees and collective farmers; by allowances for temporary disability; by the provision by the state or by collective farms of retirement pensions, disability pensions, and pensions for loss of the breadwinner; by providing employment for the partially disabled; by care for the elderly and the disabled; and by other forms of social security.

Article 44. Citizens of the USSR have the right to housing.

This right is ensured by the development and upkeep of state and socially-owned housing; by assistance for co-operative and individual house building; by fair distribution, under public control, of the housing that becomes available through fulfilment of the programme of building well-appointed dwellings, and by low rents and low charges for utility services. Citizens of the USSR shall take good care of the housing allocated to them.

Article 45. Citizens of the USSR have the right to education.

This right is ensured by free provision of all forms of education, by the institution of universal, compulsory secondary education, and broad development of vocational, specialized secondary and higher education, in which instruction is oriented toward practical activity and production; by the development of extra-mural, correspondence and evening courses; by the provision of state scholarships and grants and privileges for students; by the free issue of school text-books; by the opportunity to attend a school where teaching is in the native language; and by the provision of facilities for self-education.

Article 46. Citizens of the USSR have the right to enjoy cultural benefits.

This right is ensured by broad access to the cultural treasures of their own land and of the world that are preserved in state and other public collections; by the development and fair distribution of cultural and educational institutions throughout the country; by developing television and radio broadcasting and the publishing of books, newspapers and periodicals, and by extending the free library service; and by expanding cultural exchanges with other countries.

Article 47. Citizens of the USSR, in accordance with the aims of building communism, are guaranteed freedom of scientific, technical, and artistic work. This freedom is ensured by broadening scientific research, encouraging invention and innovation, and developing literature and the arts. The state provides the necessary material conditions for this and support for voluntary societies and unions of workers in the arts, organizes introduction of inventions and innovations in production and other spheres of activity.

The rights of authors, inventors and innovators are protected by the state.

Article 48. Citizens of the USSR have the right to take part in the management and administration of state and public affairs and in the discussion and adoption of laws and measures of All-Union and local significance.

This right is ensured by the opportunity to vote and to be elected to Soviets of People's Deputies and other elective state bodies, to take part in nationwide discussions and referendums, in people's control, in the work of state bodies, public organizations, and local community groups, and in meetings at places of work or residence.

Article 49. Every citizen of the USSR has the right to submit proposals to state bodies and public organizations for improving their activity, and to criticize shortcomings in their work.

Officials are obliged, within established time-limits, to examine citizens' proposals and requests, to reply to them, and to take appropriate action.

Persecution for criticism is prohibited. Persons guilty of such persecution shall be called to account.

Article 50. In accordance with the interests of the people and in order to strengthen and develop the socialist system, citizens of the USSR are guaranteed freedom of speech, of the press, and of assembly, meetings, street processions and demonstrations.

Exercise of these political freedoms is ensured by putting public buildings, streets and squares at the disposal of the working people and their organizations, by broad dissemination of information, and by the opportunity to use the press, television, and radio.

Article 51. USSR citizens have the right to form political parties and social organizations and to participate in mass movements that promote the development of political activeness and independent activity and the satisfaction of their diverse interests.

Social organizations are guaranteed the conditions for the successful fulfillment of their statutory tasks.

Article 52. Citizens of the USSR are guaranteed freedom of conscience, that is, the right to profess or not to profess any religion, and to conduct religious worship or atheistic propaganda. Incitement of hostility or hatred on religious grounds is prohibited.

In the USSR, the church is separated from the state, and the school from the church.

Article 53. The family enjoys the protection of the state.

Marriage is based on the free consent of the woman and the man; the spouses are completely equal in their family relations.

The state helps the family by providing and developing a broad system of childcare institutions, by organizing and improving communal services and public catering, by paying grants on the birth of a child, by providing children's allowances and benefits for large families, and other forms of family allowances and assistance.

Article 54. Citizens of the USSR are guaranteed inviolability of the person. No one may be arrested except by a court decision or on the warrant of a procurator.

Article 55. Citizens of the USSR are guaranteed inviolability of the home. No one may, without lawful grounds, enter a home against the will of those residing in it.

Article 56. The privacy of citizens, and of their correspondence, telephone conversations, and telegraphic communications is protected by law.

Article 57. Respect for the individual and protection of the rights and freedoms of citizens are the duty of all state bodies, public organizations, and officials.

Citizens of the USSR have the right to protection by the courts against encroachments on their honour and reputation, life and health, and personal freedom and property.

Article 58. Citizens of the USSR have the right to lodge a complaint against the actions of officials, state bodies and public bodies. Complaints shall be examined according to the procedure and within the time-limit established by law. Actions by officials that contravene the law or exceed their powers, and infringe the rights of citizens, may be appealed against in a court in the manner prescribed by law.

Citizens of the USSR have the right to compensation for damage resulting from unlawful actions by state organizations and public organizations, or by officials in the performance of their duties.

Article 59. Citizens' exercise of their rights and freedoms is inseparable from the performance of their duties and obligations.

Citizens of the USSR are obliged to observe the Constitution of the USSR and Soviet laws, comply with the standards of socialist conduct, and uphold the honour and dignity of Soviet citizenship.

Article 60. It is the duty of, and a matter of honour for, every able-bodied citizen of the USSR to work conscientiously in his chosen, socially useful occupation, and strictly to observe labour discipline. Evasion of socially useful work is incompatible with the principles of socialist society.

Article 61. Citizens of the USSR are obliged to preserve and protect socialist property. It is the duty of a citizen of the USSR to combat misappropriation and squandering of state and socially-owned property and to make thrifty use of the people's wealth.

Persons encroaching in any way on socialist property shall be punished according to the law.

Article 62. Citizens of the USSR are obliged to safeguard the interests of the Soviet state, and to enhance its power and prestige.

Defence of the Socialist Motherland is the sacred duty of every citizen of the USSR.

Betrayal of the Motherland is the gravest of crimes against the people.

Article 63. Military service in the ranks of the Armed Forces of the USSR is an honourable duty of Soviet citizens.

Article 64. It is the duty of every citizen of the USSR to respect the national dignity of other citizens, and to strengthen friendship of the nations and nationalities of the multinational Soviet state.

Article 65. A citizen of the USSR is obliged to respect the rights and lawful interests of other persons, to be uncompromising toward anti-social behaviour, and to help maintain public order.

Article 66. Citizens of the USSR are obliged to concern themselves with the upbringing of children, to train them for socially useful work, and to raise them as worthy members of socialist society. Children are obliged to care for their parents and help them.

Article 67. Citizens of the USSR are obliged to protect nature and conserve its riches.

Article 68. Concern for the preservation of historical monuments and other cultural values is a duty and obligation of citizens of the USSR.

Article 69. It is the internationalist duty of citizens of the USSR to promote friendship and co-operation with peoples of other lands and help maintain and strengthen world peace.

III. The National—State Structure of the USSR

Chapter 8: The USSR — a Federal State

Article 70. The Union of Soviet Socialist Republics is an integral, federal, multinational state formed on the principle of socialist federalism as a result of the free self-determination of nations and the voluntary association of equal Soviet Socialist Republics.

The USSR embodies the state unity of the Soviet people and draws all its nations and nationalities together for the purpose of jointly building communism.

Article 71. The Union of Soviet Socialist Republics unites:
the Russian Soviet Federative Socialist Republic,
the Ukrainian Soviet Socialist Republic,
the Byelorussian Soviet Socialist Republic,
the Uzbek Soviet Socialist Republic,
the Kazakh Soviet Socialist Republic,
the Georgian Soviet Socialist Republic,
the Azerbayjan Soviet Socialist Republic,
the Lithuanian Soviet Socialist Republic,
the Moldavian Soviet Socialist Republic,
the Latvian Soviet Socialist Republic,
the Kirghiz Soviet Socialist Republic,
the Tajik Soviet Socialist Republic,
the Armenian Soviet Socialist Republic,
the Turkmen Soviet Socialist Republic,
the Estonian Soviet Socialist Republic.

Article 72. Each Union Republic shall retain the right freely to secede from the USSR.

Article 73. The jurisdiction of the Union of Soviet Socialist Republics, as represented by its highest bodies of state authority and administration, shall cover:

(1) the admission of new republics to the USSR; endorsement of the formation of new autonomous republics and autonomous regions within Union Republics;

(2) determination of the state boundaries of the USSR and approval of changes in the boundaries between Union Republics;

(3) establishment of the general principles for the organization and functioning of republican and local bodies of state authority and administration;

(4) the ensurance of uniformity of legislative norms throughout the USSR and establishment of the fundamentals of the legislation of the Union of Soviet Socialist Republics and Union Republics;

(5) pursuance of a uniform social and economic policy; direction of the country's economy; determination of the main lines of scientific and technological progress and the general measures for rational exploitation and conservation of natural resources; the drafting and approval of state plans for the economic and social development of the USSR, and endorsement of reports on their fulfilment;

(6) the drafting and approval of the consolidated Budget of the USSR, and endorsement of the report on its execution; management of a single monetary and credit system; determination of the taxes and revenues forming the Budget of the USSR; and the formulation of prices and wages policy;

(7) direction of the sectors of the economy, and of enterprises and amalgamations under Union jurisdiction, and general direction of industries under Union-Republican jurisdiction;

(8) issues of war and peace, defence of the sovereignty of the USSR and safeguarding of its frontiers and territory, and organization of defence; direction of the Armed Forces of the USSR;

(9) state security;

(10) representation of the USSR in international relations; the USSR's relations with other states and with international organizations; establishment of the general procedure for, and co-ordination of, the relations of Union Republics with other states and with international organizations; foreign trade and other forms of external economic activity on the basis of state monopoly;

(11) control over observance of the Constitution of the USSR, and ensurance of conformity of the Constitutions of Union Republics to the Constitution of the USSR;

(12) and settlement of other matters of All-Union importance.

Article 74. The laws of the USSR shall have the same force in all Union Republics. In the event of a discrepancy between a Union Republic law and an All-Union law, the law of the USSR shall prevail.

Article 75. The territory of the Union of Soviet Socialist Republics is a single entity and comprises the territories of the Union Republics.

The sovereignty of the USSR extends throughout its territory.

Chapter 9: The Union Soviet Socialist Republics

Article 76. A Union Republic is a sovereign Soviet socialist state that has united with other Soviet Republics in the Union of Soviet Socialist Republics.

Outside the spheres listed in Article 73 of the Constitution of the USSR, a Union Republic exercises independent Authority on its territory.

A Union Republic shall have its own Constitution conforming to the Constitution of the USSR with the specific features of the Republic being taken into account.

Article 77. A union republic participates in the resolution of questions coming under the jurisdiction of the USSR at the USSR Congress of People's Deputies, the USSR Supreme Soviet, the Presidium of the USSR Supreme Soviet, the Council of the Federation, the USSR Cabinet of Ministers bodies and other bodies of the USSR.

A Union Republic shall ensure comprehensive economic and social development on its territory, facilitate exercise of the powers of the USSR on its territory, and implement the decisions of the highest bodies of state authority and administration of the USSR.

In matters that come within its jurisdiction, a Union Republic shall co-ordinate and control the activity of enterprises, institutions, and organizations subordinate to the Union.

Article 78. The territory of a Union Republic may not be altered without its consent. The boundaries between Union Republics may be altered by mutual agreement of the Republics concerned, subject to ratification by the Union of Soviet Socialist Republics.

Article 79. A Union Republic shall determine its division into territories, regions, areas, and districts, and decide other matters relating to its administrative and territorial structure.

Article 80. A Union Republic has the right to enter into relations with other states, conclude treaties with them, exchange diplomatic and consular representatives, and take part in the work of international organizations.

Article 81. The sovereign rights of Union Republics shall be safeguarded by the USSR.

Chapter 10: The Autonomous Soviet Socialist Republic

· **Article 82.** An autonomous Republic is a constituent part of a Union Republic.
In spheres not within the jurisdiction of the Union of Soviet Socialist Republics and the Union Republic, an Autonomous Republic shall deal independently with matters within its jurisdiction.
An Autonomous Republic shall have its own Constitution conforming to the Constitutions of the USSR and the Union Republic with the specific features of the Autonomous Republic being taken into account.

Article 83. An Autonomous Republic takes part in decision-making through the highest bodies of state authority and administration of the USSR and of the Union Republic respectively, in matters that come within the jurisdiction of the USSR and the Union Republic.
An Autonomous Republic shall ensure comprehensive economic and social development on its territory, facilitate exercise of the powers of the USSR and the Union Republic on its territory, and implement decisions of the highest bodies of state authority and administration of the USSR and the Union Republic.
In matters within its jurisdiction, an Autonomous Republic shall co-ordinate and control the activity of enterprises, institutions, and organizations subordinate to the Union or the Union Republic.

Article 84. The territory of an Autonomous Republic may not be altered without its consent.

Article 85. The Russian Soviet Federative Socialist Republic includes the Bashkir, Buryat, Daghestan, Kabardin-Balkar, Kalmyk, Karelian, Komi, Mari, Mordovian, North Ossetian, Tatar, Tuva, Udmurt, Chechen-Ingush, Chuvash, and Yakut Autonomous Soviet Socialist Republics.
The Uzbek Soviet Socialist Republic includes the Kara-Kalpak Autonomous Soviet Socialist Republic.
The Georgian Soviet Socialist Republic includes the Abkhasian and Adzhar Autonomous Soviet Socialist Republics.
The Azerbayjan Soviet Socialist Republic includes the Nakhichevan Autonomous Soviet Socialist Republic.

Chapter 11: The Autonomous Region and Autonomous Area

Article 86. An Autonomous Region is a constituent part of a Union Republic or Territory. The Law on an Autonomous Region, upon submission by the Soviet of People's Deputies of the Autonomous Region concerned, shall be adopted by the Supreme Soviet of the Union Republic.

Article 87. The Russian Soviet Federative Socialist Republic includes the Adygei, Gorno-Altai, Jewish, Karachai-Circassian, and Khakass Autonomous Regions.

The Georgian Soviet Socialist Republic includes the South Ossetian Autonomous Region.

The Azerbayjan Soviet Socialist Republic includes the Nagorno-Karabakh Autonomous Region.

The Tajik Soviet Socialist Republic includes the Gorno-Badakhshan Autonomous Region.

Article 88. An Autonomous Area is a constituent part of a Territory or Region. The Law on an Autonomous Area shall be adopted by the Supreme Soviet of the Union Republic concerned.

IV. Soviets of People's Deputies and Electoral Procedure

Chapter 12: The System of Soviets of People's Deputies and the Principles of Their Work

Article 89. The soviets of people's deputies — the USSR Congress of People's Deputies and USSR Supreme Soviet, congresses of people's deputies and supreme soviets of union and autonomous republics and soviets of people's deputies of autonomous oblasts and of krays, oblasts and other administrative-territorial units — shall constitute a single system of bodies of state authority.

Article 90. The term of office of soviets of people's deputies shall be five years.

Elections of USSR people's deputies shall be called not later than four months before the expiry of the term of the USSR Congress of People's Deputies.

The timing and procedure for calling elections of people's deputies of union and autonomous republics and to local soviets of people's deputies shall be determined by the laws of union and autonomous republics.

Article 91. The most important matters of union-wide, republican and local significance shall be resolved at sessions of the congresses of people's deputies and sessions of supreme soviets and local soviets of people's deputies or be put to referendums by them.

Supreme soviets of union and autonomous republics shall be elected directly by voters, and in republics where it is envisaged to create congresses — by the congresses of people's deputies.

Soviets of people's deputies shall form committees and standing commissions and shall set up executive and administrative bodies as well as other bodies accountable to them.

Officials elected or appointed by soviets of people's deputies, with the exception of judges, may not hold office for more than two consecutive terms.

Any official can be released from his post early if he fails to perform his official duties properly.

Article 92. The soviets of people's deputies shall form bodies of people's control, combining state control with social control by working people at enterprises, institutions, and organizations.

The bodies of people's control shall verify the fulfilment of the requirements of legislation and state programmes and targets; combat breaches of state discipline, manifestations of parochialism and a departmental approach to the task, thrift-lessness and extravagance, red tape, and bureaucracy, co-ordinate the work of other control bodies and promote the improvement of the structure and work of the state apparatus.

Article 93. The soviets of people's deputies, directly and through the bodies they set up, shall direct all sectors of state, economic and sociocultural development, make decisions, ensure their execution and verify their implementation.

Article 94. The activity of the soviets of people's deputies shall be based on collective, free and business-like discussion and resolution of questions, glasnost', regular accountability of executive and management bodies and other bodies created by the soviets to them and to the population and the wide involvement of citizens in participation in their work.

The soviets of people's deputies and the bodies set up by them shall take account of public opinion, submit the most important matters of state-wide and local significance for discussion by citizens and systematically inform citizens about their work and the decisions taken by them.

Chapter 13: The Electoral System

Article 95. Elections of people's deputies shall be held in single-seat or multi-seat constituencies on the basis of universal, equal and direct suffrage by secret ballot.

Some people's deputies of union and autonomous republics may be elected by public organizations, if this is provided for by the republics' constitutions.

Article 96. Elections of people's deputies from constituencies shall be universal — USSR citizens who have reached the age of 18 shall have the right to vote.

USSR citizens who have reached the age of 21 may be elected USSR people's deputies.

A citizen of the USSR may not be a deputy of more than two soviets of people's deputies simultaneously.

Persons belonging to the USSR Cabinet of Ministers, the councils of ministers of union and autonomous republics, and the executive committees of local soviets, with the exception of the chairmen of these bodies and also leaders of offices, departments and directorates of executive committees of local soviets and judges may not be deputies of the soviet to which they are appointed or elected.

Citizens who are mentally ill and are deemed by the court to be incompetent, and persons confined to places of deprivation of liberty following a court sentence, shall not participate in elections. Persons who are remanded in custody according to procedures laid down by the Code of Criminal Procedure shall not participate in elections.

Any direct or indirect restriction whatsoever of the electoral rights of USSR citizens is impermissible and punishable under the law.

Article 97. Elections of people's deputies from constituencies shall be equal: a voter for each constituency shall have one vote; voters shall participate in elections on an equal basis.

Article 98. Elections of people's deputies from constituencies shall be direct: people's deputies shall be elected by citizens directly.

Article 99. Voting at elections of people's deputies shall be secret: control over voters' exercising of the franchise is not permitted.

Article 100. The right to nominate candidate people's deputies in constituencies shall be vested with work collectives, public organizations, collectives of secondary, specialized and higher educational establishments, voters' meetings at places of residence and servicemen's meetings in military units. Bodies and organizations with the right to nominate candidate people's deputies from public organizations shall be determined by the laws of the USSR and of union and autonomous republics respectively.

The number of candidate people's deputies shall be unlimited. Every participant in an election campaign meeting may propose anyone's nomination including his own for discussion.

Any number of candidates may be included in the ballot papers.

Candidate people's deputies shall participate in the election campaign on an equal footing.

With a view to ensuring equal conditions for every candidate people's deputy, the expenditure associated with the preparation and holding of elections of people's deputies shall be met by the corresponding electoral commission from a single fund created at the state's expense and from voluntary contributions by enterprises, public organizations and citizens.

Article 101. Preparations for elections of people's deputies shall be carried out openly and in an atmosphere of glasnost'.

The holding of elections shall be conducted by electoral commissions consisting of representatives elected by meetings (conferences) of work collectives, public organizations, collectives of secondary, specialized and higher education establishments, voters' meetings at places of residence and servicemen's meetings in military units.

USSR citizens, work collectives, public organizations, collectives of secondary specialized and higher education establishments and servicemen in military units shall be guaranteed the opportunity for free and comprehensive discussion of the political, professional and personal qualities of candidate people's deputies, as well as the right to campaign for or against a candidate at meetings, in the press and on television and radio.

The procedure for holding elections on people's deputies shall be defined by laws of the USSR and of union and autonomous republics.

Article 102. Voters and social organizations shall give mandates to their deputies.

The appropriate soviets of people's deputies shall examine the mandates, take them into account when formulating economic and social development plans and drawing up the budget, and also in preparing resolutions on other matters, organize the fulfilment of mandates and inform citizens about their implementation.

Chapter 14: People's Deputies

Article 103. Deputies are the plenipotentiary representatives of the people in the Soviets of People's Deputies.

In the Soviets, deputies deal with matters relating to state, economic and social and cultural development, organize implementation of the decisions of the Soviets, and exercise control over the work of state bodies, enterprises, institutions and organizations.

In their activity deputies are guided by state-wide interests, take into account the requests of the constituency's population and the expressed interests of the social organisation which has elected them and strive to implement the mandates of the voters and the social organization.

Article 104. Deputies shall exercise their powers without, as a rule, interrupting their production or official activity.

During sessions of congresses of people's deputies and sessions of supreme soviets or local soviets of people's deputies, and also for the exercise of deputy powers in other instances envisaged by the law, deputies shall be released from carrying out their production or official duties and shall be reimbursed for expenses occasioned by their activities as deputies from the funds of the corresponding state or local budget.

Article 105. Deputies shall have the right of inquiry of the appropriate state bodies and officials, which are obliged to respond to the inquiry at a congress of people's deputies or a session of the supreme soviet or local soviet of people's deputies.

Deputies have the right to approach any state or public body, enterprise, institution, or organization on matters arising from their work as deputies and to take part in considering the questions raised by them. The heads of the state or public bodies, enterprises, institutions or organizations concerned are obliged to receive deputies without delay and to consider their proposals within the time-limit established by law.

Article 106. Deputies shall be ensured conditions for the unhampered and effective exercise of their rights and duties.

The immunity of deputies, and other guarantees of their activity as deputies, are defined in the Law on the Status of Deputies and other legislative acts of the USSR and of Union and Autonomous Republics.

Article 107. Deputies shall be obliged to report on their own work and the work of a congress of people's deputies or a supreme soviet or local soviet of people's deputies to the voters, the collectives and social organizations which nominated them to be candidate deputies or to the social organization which elected them.

Deputies who fail to justify the trust of voters or the social organization may be recalled at any time in the legally established manner by a resolution of the majority of voters or the social organization which elected them.

V. Higher Bodies of State Authority and Administration of the USSR

Chapter 15: The USSR Congress of People's Deputies and the USSR Supreme Soviet

Article 108. The higher body of state authority of the USSR shall be the USSR Congress of People's Deputies.

The USSR Congress of People's Deputies is empowered to take up for its examination and decide any matter within the jurisdiction of the USSR.

The following shall be the exclusive prerogative of the USSR Congress of People's Deputies:

(1) The adoption and amendment of the USSR Constitution;

(2) the adoption of resolutions on matters of the national-state structure within the jurisdiction of the USSR;

(3) the definition of the USSR state border; the ratification of changes in the borders between union republics;

(4) the definition of the basic guidelines of USSR domestic and foreign policy;

(5) the ratification of long-term state plans and highly important all-union programmes of economic and social development of the USSR;

(6) the election of the USSR Supreme Soviet and the Chairman of the USSR Supreme Soviet;

(7) the ratification of the Chairman of the USSR Supreme Soviet Court, the USSR Procurator General and the Chairman of the USSR Supreme Arbitration Court on the submission of the Chairman of the USSR Supreme Soviet;

(8) the election of the USSR Committee for Supervision of the Constitution;

(9) the repeal of acts adopted by the USSR Supreme Soviet.

(10) the adoption of resolutions on holding nation-wide polls (referendums).

The USSR Congress of People's Deputies adopts USSR laws and resolutions, upon a vote, by a majority of the total number of USSR people's deputies.

Article 109. The USSR Congress of People's Deputies shall consist of 2,250 deputies who are elected as follows:

750 deputies from territorial constituencies with an equal number of voters;

750 deputies from national-territorial constituencies in accordance with the following norms: 32 deputies from each union republic, 11 deputies from each autonomous republic, five deputies from each autonomous oblast, and one deputy from each autonomous okrug;

750 deputies from all-union social organizations in accordance with the norms laid down by the USSR law on the election of people's deputies.

Article 110. The USSR Congress of People's Deputies shall convene for its first session no later than two months after the elections.

On the representation of the credentials commission electable by it, the USSR Congress of People's Deputies shall resolve to recognize the powers of the deputies, and — in the event of a violation of election legislation — to recognize the invalidity of individual deputies' election.

The USSR Congress of the People's Deputies shall be convened by the USSR Supreme Soviet.

Routine sessions of the USSR Congress of People's Deputies are held at least once a year. Extraordinary sessions shall be convened on the initiative of the USSR Supreme Soviet, on the proposal of one of the USSR Supreme Soviet's chambers, the President of the USSR, or no fewer than one-fifth of the USSR people's deputies, or on the initiative of a union republic in the form of its supreme body of state power.

The first session of the USSR Congress of People's Deputies following the elections shall be chaired by the Chairman of the Central Electoral Commission for the elections of USSR people's deputies and subsequently by the Chairman of the USSR Supreme Soviet.

Article 111. The USSR Supreme Soviet is the standing legislative, administrative and monitoring body of USSR state authority.

The USSR Supreme Soviet shall be elected by secret ballot from among the USSR people's deputies by the USSR Congress of People's Deputies and shall be accountable to the latter.

The USSR Supreme Soviet consists of two chambers: the Soviet of the Union and the Soviet of Nationalities, which are numerically equal. The chambers of the USSR Supreme Soviet shall have equal rights.

The chambers shall be elected at the USSR congress of People's Deputies by a general vote of the deputies. The Soviet of the Union shall be elected from among the USSR people's deputies from the territorial constituencies and the USSR people's deputies from the social organizations — taking into account the number of voters in the union republic or region. The Soviet of Nationalities shall be elected from among the USSR people's deputies from the national-territorial constituencies and the USSR people's deputies from the social organizations in accordance with the following norms: eleven deputies from each union republic, four deputies from each autonomous republic, two deputies from each autonomous oblast, and one deputy from each autonomous okrug.

The USSR Congress of People's Deputies annually renews up to one-fifth of the composition of the Soviet of the Union and Soviet of Nationalities.

Each chamber of the USSR Supreme Soviet shall elect a chairman of the chamber and two deputy chairmen. The Chairmen of the Soviet of the Union and Soviet of Nationalities shall chair the sessions of the corresponding chambers and are in charge of their internal proceedings.

Joint sessions of the chambers shall be chaired by the Chairman of the USSR Supreme Soviet, or the Chairmen of the Soviet of the Union and the Soviet of the Nationalities in turn.

Article 112. The USSR Supreme Soviet shall be convened annually by the Chairman of the USSR Supreme Soviet for regular spring and autumn sessions, each lasting three to four months as a rule.

Extraordinary sessions shall be convened by the Chairman of the USSR Supreme Soviet on his initiative or at the proposal of the President of the USSR, a union republic in the form of its supreme body of state power, or at least one-third of the deputies from either chamber of the USSR Supreme Soviet.

USSR Supreme Soviet sessions shall take the form of separate and joint sittings of the chambers and of sittings of the chambers' permanent commissions and the USSR Supreme Soviet committees held between sessions. A session shall be opened and closed at separate or joint sittings of the chambers.

Upon the expiry of the term of the USSR Congress of People's Deputies, the USSR Supreme Soviet shall retain its powers until the formation of a new composition of the USSR Supreme Soviet by the newly elected USSR Congress of People's Deputies.

Article 113. The USSR Supreme Soviet shall:

(1) schedule elections of USSR people's deputies and ratify the composition of the Central Electoral Commission on elections of USSR people's deputies;

(2) at the proposal of the USSR President form and abolish USSR ministries and other central bodies of state management of the USSR;

(3) on the submission of the USSR President confirm the prime minister, accept or reject at a session the candidacy of members of the USSR Cabinet of Ministers and members of the USSR Security Council and agree to the release of the aforementioned officials from their duties;

(4) elect the USSR Supreme Court, the USSR Supreme Arbitration Court, appoint the USSR Procurator General, ratify the collegium of the USSR Procurator's Office and appoint the Chairman of the USSR Control Chamber;

(5) regularly hear reports by bodies constituted or elected by it or by officials appointed or elected by it;

(6) ensure the uniformity of legislative regulations throughout the territory of the USSR and the union republics;

(7) carry out, within the limits of the competence of the USSR, legislative regulations of the procedure for the exercise of citizens' constitutional rights, freedoms and duties, ownership relations, the organization of the management of the national economy and socio-cultural builiding, the budget and financial system, labour remuneration and pricing, taxation, environmental conservation and the use of natural resources and other relations;

(8) interpret USSR laws;

(9) lay down general principles of the organization and activity of republican and local bodies of state authority and administration; determine the foundations of the legal status of social organizations;

(10) submit for ratification by the USSR Congress of People's Deputies draft long-term state plans and the most important all-union programmes of the USSR's economic and social development; ratify the State Plans of the USSR's Economic and Social Development and the USSR State Budget; monitor progress in the implementation of the plan and budget; ratify reports on their performance; introduce amendments to the plan and budget whenever necessary;

(11) ratify and denounce the USSR's international treaties;

(12) supervise the granting of state loans and economic and other assistance to foreign states, and also the conclusion of agreements on state loans and credits obtained from foreign sources;

(13) determine basic measures in the spheres of defence and of ensuring state security; impose martial law or a state of emergency countrywide, proclaim a state of war in the event of the need to meet international treaty obligations for mutual defence against aggression;

(14) make decisions on the use of contingents of the USSR Armed Forces in the event of the need to meet international treaty obligations for the maintenance of peace and security;

(15) determine military ranks and diplomatic and other special ranks;

(16) institute USSR orders and medals; confer honorary titles of the USSR;

(17) promulgate all-union acts of amnesty;

(18) be empowered to revoke acts of the USSR Cabinet of Ministers if they do not accord with the USSR Constitution and USSR laws;

(19) repeal resolutions and orders by union republican ministers in the event of their not being in keeping with the USSR Constitution and the USSR laws;

(20) in the period between Congresses of the USSR People's Deputies adopt and decision to hold a nationwide vote ('referendum of the USSR');

(21) decide other matters within the jurisdiction of the USSR, apart from other matters which are the exclusive prerogative of the USSR Congress of People's Deputies.

The USSR Supreme Soviet adopts USSR laws and resolutions.

Laws and resolutions adopted by the USSR Supreme Soviet cannot be contrary to laws and other acts adopted by the USSR Congress of People's Deputies.

Article 114. The right to initiate legislation in the USSR Congress of People's Deputies and the USSR Supreme Soviet shall be vested in USSR people's deputies, the Soviet of the Union, the Soviet of the Nationalities, the Chairman of the

USSR Supreme Soviet, permanent commissions of the chambers and committees of the USSR Supreme Soviet, the President of the USSR, the USSR Federation Council, the USSR Committee for the Supervision of the Constitution, union and autonomous republics in the person of their highest bodies of state power, autonomous *oblasts*, autonomous *okrugs*, the USSR Supreme Court, the USSR Procurator General and the USSR Supreme Arbitration Court.

Article 115. Draft laws submitted for examination by the USSR Supreme Soviet shall be discussed by its chambers at separate or joint sittings.

A USSR law shall be deemed adopted if a majority of chamber members votes for it in each chamber of the USSR Supreme Soviet.

Draft laws and other important matters of state life may be submitted for nation-wide discussion following a resolution by the USSR Supreme Soviet adopted either on its own initiative or at the proposal of a union republic in the form of its supreme body of state authority.

Article 116. Each chamber of the USSR Supreme Soviet shall be empowered to examine any matters which are the prerogative of the USSR Supreme Soviet.

The Soviet of the Union shall primarily examine matters of socio-economic development and state building of general importance to the entire country; the rights, freedoms and duties of USSR citizens; USSR foreign policy; the USSR's defence and state security.

The Soviet of Nationalities shall primarily examine matters of ensuring national equality and the interests of nations, nationalities and ethnic groups in combination with the general interests and needs of the Soviet multinational state; improvements to USSR legislation regulations between the nationalities.

Each chamber adopts resolutions on matters within its competence.

Any resolution adopted by one of the chambers, if necessary, shall be remitted to the other chamber and, when approved by it, acquire the force of a USSR Supreme Soviet resolution.

Article 117. In the event of disagreement between the Soviet of the Union and the Soviet of Nationalities, the matter shall be handed over for resolution by a conciliation commission formed by the chambers on the basis of parity, after which the matter shall be re-examined by the Soviet of the Union and Soviet of Nationalities at a joint sitting.

Article 118. A presidium of the USSR Supreme Soviet headed by the Chairman of the USSR Supreme Soviet is set up to organize the work of the USSR Supreme Soviet. The Presidium of the USSR Supreme Soviet includes: the Chairman of the Soviet of the Union and the Soviet of Nationalities, their deputies, the chairman of the standing commissions of the chambers and committees of the USSR Supreme Soviet and other USSR people's deputies — one from each union republic, and also two representatives from autonomous republics and one from autonomous *oblasts* and autonomous *okrugs*.

The Presidium of the USSR Supreme Soviet prepares Congress sessions and

USSR Supreme Soviet session, co-ordinates the activity of the standing commissions of the chambers and committees of the USSR Supreme Soviet and organizes nationwide discussions of USSR draft laws and other most important questions of state life.

The Presidium of the USSR Supreme Soviet ensures the publication in the languages of the union republics of the texts of USSR laws and other acts adopted by the USSR Congress of People's Deputies, the USSR Supreme Soviet, its chambers and the President of the USSR.

Decisions of the Presidium of the USSR Supreme Soviet shall be formulated as resolutions.

Article 119. The Chairman of the USSR Supreme Soviet is elected by the USSR Congress of People's Deputies from among the USSR people's deputies by secret ballot for a term of five years and for not more than two successive terms. He may be recalled by the USSR Congress of People's Deputies at any time by secret ballot.

The Chairman of the USSR Supreme Soviet is accountable to the USSR Congress of People's Deputies and the USSR Supreme Soviet.

The Chairman of the USSR Supreme Soviet issues resolutions on the convocation of USSR Supreme Soviet sessions and instructions on other matters.

Article 120. The Soviet of the Union and Soviet of Nationalities shall elect from among the members of the USSR Supreme Soviet and other USSR people's deputies permanent commissions of the chambers to carry out the drafting of laws and preliminary examination and preparation of matters which are the prerogative of the USSR Supreme Soviet, and also promote the implementation of USSR laws and other resolutions adopted by the USSR Congress of People's Deputies and the USSR Supreme Soviet and monitor the activity of state bodies and organizations.

For the same purposes, the chambers of the USSR Supreme Soviet may set up committees of the USSR Supreme Soviet on the basis of parity.

The USSR Supreme Soviet and each of its chambers, when they deem it necessary, set up investigating, auditing or other commissions on any matter.

Up to one-fifth of the composition of the standing commissions of the chambers and the committees of the USSR Supreme Soviet is renewed annually.

The permanent commissions of the chambers and committees of the USSR Supreme Soviet shall renew annually one-fifth of their membership.

Article 121. Laws and other resolutions of the USSR Congress of People's Deputies and the USSR Supreme Soviet and resolutions of its chambers shall be adopted, as a rule, after preliminary discussion of the drafts by the appropriate permanent commissions of the chambers or committees of the USSR Supreme Soviet.

The appointment and election of officials belonging to the USSR Cabinet of Ministers, the USSR Supreme Arbitration Court, the USSR Procurator's Office collegium and also Chairman of the USSR Control Chamber shall be conducted when the corresponding standing commissions of the USSR Supreme Soviet

Chambers of USSR Supreme Soviet Committees have presented their conclusions.

All state and social bodies organizations and officials must fulfil the requirements of the commissions of the chambers and commissions and committees of the USSR Supreme Soviet and provide them with the necessary material and documents.

The recommendations of commissions and committees shall be subject to compulsory examination by state and social bodies, institutions and organizations. The resulsts of the examination and the measures adopted must be reported to the commissions and committees within the time laid down by them.

Article 122. A USSR people's deputy has the right to submit a question at sessions of the USSR Congress of People's Deputies and sessions of the USSR Supreme Soviet to the USSR Cabinet of Ministers and leaders of other bodies formed or elected by the Supreme Soviet and to the President of the USSR at sessions of the USSR Congress of People's Deputies. A body or official to whom a question is submitted is obliged to given an oral or written answer at the Congress session in question or the USSR Supreme Soviet session in question within no more than three days.

Article 123. USSR people's deputies are entitled to be relieved of the performance of their official or production duties for the period necessary to implement their activity as deputies in the USSR Supreme Soviet, its chambers, commissions and committees, and also among the population.

A USSR people's deputy cannot be subjected to criminal proceedings, be arrested or incur judicially imposed administrative penalties without the consent of the USSR Supreme Soviet or, in the period betweens sessions, without the consent of the Presidium of the USSR Supreme Soviet.

Article 124. The USSR Committee for Supervision of the Constitution shall be elected by the USSR Congress of People's Deputies from the ranks of specialists in the field of politics and law in the form of a chairman, deputy chairman and 25 members of the committee, for each union republic included.

The term of the authority of the persons elected to the USSR Committee for Supervision of the Constitution shall be 10 years.

Persons elected to the USSR Committee for Supervision of the Constitution may not simultaneously be members of bodies whose instruments are under the supervision of the committee.

Upon performance of their duties persons elected to the USSR Committee for Supervision of the Constitution shall be independent and subordinate only to the USSR Constitution.

The USSR Committee for Supervision of the Constitution shall:

(1) at the behest of the USSR Congress of People's Deputies submit to it findings concerning the correspondence to the USSR Constitution of draft laws of the USSR and other instruments submitted for examination by the Congress;

(2) at the proposals of no less than one-fifth of USSR people's deputies, the President of the USSR and the supreme bodies of state power in the union republics, [the Committee for Supervision of the Constitution] submit findings to

the USSR Congress of People's Deputies regarding the correspondence between USSR laws and other acts adopted by the Congress and the USSR Constitution.

On the instructions of the USSR Congress of People's Deputies or on the proposal of the USSR Supreme Soviet, submit findings regarding the correspondence between decrees of the President of the USSR Constitution and USSR laws;

(3) on the instructions of the USSR Congress of People's Deputies or at the proposal of the USSR Supreme Soviet, the President of the USSR, the Chairman of the USSR Supreme Soviet or the supreme bodies of state power in the union republics, submit findings to the USSR Congress of People's Deputies or the USSR Supreme Soviet regarding the correspondence between union republican constitutions and the USSR Constitution and between union republican laws and USSR laws;

(4) on the instructions of the USSR Congress of People's Deputies or at the proposal of no less than one-fifth of the members of the USSR Supreme Soviet, the President of the USSR, or the supreme bodies of state power in the union republics, submit findings to the USSR Supreme Soviet or the President of the USSR regarding the correspondence between acts adopted by the USSR Supreme Soviet and its chambers and draft acts submitted for consideration by these bodies and the USSR Constitution and USSR laws adopted by the USSR Congress of People's Deputies, and also the correspondence between resolutions and instructions adopted by the USSR Cabinet of Ministers and USSR laws adopted by the USSR Supreme Soviet; on the correspondence between USSR and union republican international treaty and other obligations and the USSR Constitution and USSR laws;

(5) on the instructions of the USSR Congress of People's Deputies or at the proposal of the USSR Supreme Soviet, its chambers, the President of the USSR, the Chairman of the USSR Supreme Soviet, the chambers' standing commissions, USSR Supreme Soviet committees, the USSR Cabinet of Ministers, the supreme bodies of state power in the union republics, the USSR Control Chamber, the USSR Supreme Court, the USSR Procurator General, the USSR Supreme Arbitration Court, all union bodies of public organizations or the USSR Academy of Sciences, submit findings, regarding the correspondence between normative legal acts adopted by other state bodies and public organizations to which supervision by the Procurator's Office does not apply under the USSR Constitution and the USSR laws.

Article 125. The USSR Congress of People's Deputies and the USSR Supreme Soviet monitor the activity of all their subordinate state bodies.

The USSR Supreme Soviet shall guide the activity of the USSR Control Chamber and periodically hear its reports on the results of monitoring the receipt and expenditure of resources from the union budget and of the use of all-union property.

The organization and procedure of work of the USSR Control Chamber shall be determined by USSR law.

Article 126. The procedure of work of the USSR Congress of People's Deputies, the USSR Supreme Soviet and their bodies shall be determined by the regulations of the USSR Congress of People's Deputies and the USSR Supreme Soviet and by other USSR laws promulgated on the basis of the USSR Constitution.

Chapter 15(1): The President of the USSR

Article 127. The head of the Soviet state — the Union of Soviet Socialist Republics — is the President of the USSR.

Article 127(1). Any citizen of the USSR no younger than 35 and no older than 65 years of age can be elected President of the USSR. The same person can be President of the USSR for no more than two terms.

The President of the USSR is elected by USSR citizens on the basis of universal, equal and direct suffrage by secret ballot for a five-year term. The number of candidates for the post of President of the USSR is not limited. Elections for the President of the USSR are considered valid if at least 50% of voters participated in them.

The candidate who has received over half the votes of voters taking part in the election in the USSR as a whole and in the majority of union republics is deemed to be elected.

The procedure for elections of the President of the USSR is defined by USSR law.

The President of the USSR cannot be a people's deputy.

The person who is President of the USSR can receive wages for that post alone.

Article 127(2). Upon inauguration the President of the USSR swears an oath at a session of the USSR Congress of People's Deputies.

Article 127(3). The President of the USSR

(1) is the guarantor of observance of Soviet citizens' rights and freedoms and of the USSR Constitution and laws;

(2) takes the necessary measures to protect the sovereignty of the USSR and union republics and the country's security and territorial integrity and to implement the principles of the national-state structure of the USSR;

(3) represents the Union of Soviet Socialist Republics inside the country and in international relations;

(4) heads the system of bodies of state management and ensures their collaboration with the supreme bodies of USSR state power;

(5) submits to the USSR Congress of People's Deputies annual reports on the state of the country; briefs the USSR Supreme Soviet on the most important matters of the USSR's domestic and foreign policy;

(6) in the light of the opinion of the Federation Council and in co-ordination with the USSR Supreme Soviet, forms the USSR Cabinet of Ministers, makes changes to its composition and presents to the USSR Supreme Soviet the nomina-

tion for the post of prime minister; and in co-ordination with the USSR Supreme Soviet relieves the prime minister and members of the USSR Cabinet of Ministers of their duties;

(7) submits to the USSR Supreme Soviet candidates for the post of Chairman of the USSR Supreme Court, USSR Procurator General and Chairman of the USSR Supreme Arbitration Court, and then submits these officials to the USSR Congress of People's Deputies for confirmation; makes representations to the USSR Supreme Soviet and the USSR Congress of People's Deputies regarding releasing the aforementioned officials, with the exception of the Chairman of the USSR Supreme Court, from their duties;

(8) signs USSR laws; is entitled within a period of no more than two weeks to refer a law along with his objections back to the USSR Supreme Soviet for repeat discussion and voting. If the USSR Supreme Soviet confirms its earlier decision by two-thirds majority in each chamber, the President of the USSR signs the law;

(9) is entitled to revoke resolutions and ordinances of the USSR Cabinet of Ministers, acts of USSR ministries and other bodies subordinate to it; has the right on questions under USSR jurisdiction to suspend the execution of resolutions or ordinances of republics' councils of ministers in instances where they violate the USSR Constitution and USSR laws;

(9.1) heads the USSR Security Council, which is entrusted with elaborating recommendations on implementing all-union policy in the sphere of the country's defence, maintaining its reliable state, economic and ecological security, eliminating the aftermath of natural disasters and other emergency situations and ensuring stability and law and order in society. The members of the USSR Security Council shall be appointed by the USSR President taking account of the Federation Council's opinion and in co-ordination with the USSR Supreme Soviet.

(10) co-ordinates the activity of state bodies to ensure the defence of the country; is the Supreme Commander-in-Chief of the USSR Armed Forces, appoints and replaces the Supreme Command of the USSR Armed Forces and confers the highest military ranks; appoints the judges of military tribunals;

(11) holds talks and signs the USSR's international treaties; accepts the credentials and letters of recall of diplomatic representatives of foreign states accredited to it; appoints and recalls the USSR's diplomatic representatives in foreign states and in international organizations; confers the highest diplomatic ranks and other special titles;

(12) awards USSR orders and medals and confers USSR honorary titles;

(13) decides questions of admittance to USSR citizenship, withdrawal from it and the deprivation of Soviet citizenship and of the granting of asylum; grants pardons;

(14) declares general or partial mobilization; declares a state of war in the event of military attack on the USSR and immediately refers this question for examination by the USSR Supreme Soviet; declares in the interests of the defence of the USSR and the security of its citizens martial law in particular localities. The procedure for introducing martial law and the regime thereof are determined by the law;

(15) in the interests of safeguarding the security of citizens of the USSR, gives warning of the declaration of a state of emergency in particular localities and, if necessary, introduces it at the request or with the consent of the Presidium of the Supreme Soviet or supreme body of state power of the corresponding union republic. In the absence of such consent, introduces the state of emergency and submits the adopted decision for ratification by the USSR Supreme Soviet without delay. The USSR Supreme Soviet resolution on this question must be adopted by a majority of at least two-thirds of the total number of its members.

In the cases indicated in the first part of this point, can introduce temporary presidential rule while observing the sovereignty and territorial integrity of the union republic.

The regime for a state of emergency and also for presidential rule is laid down by law;

(16) in the event of disagreements between the Soviet of the Union and Soviet of Nationalities of the USSR Supreme Soviet that cannot be eliminated via the procedure envisaged by Article 117 of the USSR Constitution, the President of the USSR examines the contentious issue with a view to formulating an acceptable solution. If it is not possible to reach consensus and there is a threat of disruption to the normal activity of the USSR's supreme bodies of state power and management, the President can submit to the USSR Congress of people's deputies a proposal regarding the election of a new USSR Supreme Soviet.

Article 127(4). The candidate USSR President shall nominate a Vice President of the USSR who shall be elected together with him. On the instructions of the USSR President the USSR Vice President exercises certain of the President's powers and takes the USSR President's place when the latter is absent and unable to perform his own duties.

Article 127(5). The President of the USSR on the basis of and in execution of the USSR Constitution and USSR laws, issues decrees that are binding throughout the territory of the country.

Article 127(6). The President of the USSR has the right of inviolability and may only be replaced by the USSR Congress of People's Deputies in the event of his violating the USSR Constitution or USSR laws. This decision is made by the USSR Congress of People's Deputies on the initiative of the Congress itself or of the USSR Supreme Soviet by a majority of at least two-thirds of the total number of deputies, taking into account the findings of the USSR Committee for Supervision of the Constitution.

Article 127(7). If the President of the USSR is for any reason unable to continue to execute his duties, until the election of a new President, his powers are transferred to the Vice President of the USSR or, if that is not possible, to the Chairman of the USSR Supreme Soviet. In this case the election of a new President of the USSR must take place within three months.

Chapter 15 (2). Federation Council

Article 127(8). The USSR President heads the Federation Council which shall include the USSR Vice President and the presidents (supreme state officials) of the republics. The supreme state officials of the autonomous oblasts and autonomous okrugs are entitled to participate in sittings of the Federation Council with the right to a vote on questions affecting their interests.

On the basis of USSR domestic and foreign policy guidelines laid down by the USSR Congress of People's Deputies, the Federation Council co-ordinates the activity of the supreme bodies of state management of the union and the republics, monitors the observance of the union treaty, determines measures to implement the Soviet state's nationalities policy, ensures the republics' participation in the solution of questions of all-union significance and adopts recommendations on the solution of disputes and the settlement of conflict situations in interethnic relations.

Questions affecting the interests of peoples without their own national-state entities shall be examined at the Federation Council with the participation of those peoples' representatives.

Article 127(9). A member of the Federation Council is the supreme state official of a republic, representing and defending its sovereignty and legitimate interests, and takes part in the solution of all questions submitted for the Federation Council's examination.

A member of the Federation Council ensures the implementation of Federation Council decisions in the corresponding republic; monitors the execution of those decisions; receives all necessary information from union bodies and officials; may protest against decisions of union bodies of state management which infringe the legally-established rights of the republic; and on the instructions of the USSR President represents the USSR abroad and exercises other powers.

Article 127(10). Decisions of the Federation Council are adopted by a majority of not less than two-thirds of the votes and are enacted by USSR presidential decrees.

The Chairman of the USSR Supreme Soviet may participate in sessions of the Federation Council.

Chapter 16. The Cabinet of Ministers of the USSR

Article 128. The Cabinet of Ministers of the USSR, i.e. the Government, is the executive and administrative body of the USSR, and is subordinate to the USSR President.

Article 129. The USSR Cabinet of Ministers consists of the prime minister, his deputies and ministers of the USSR.

The structure of the USSR Cabinet of Ministers is determined by the USSR Supreme Soviet at the suggestion of the USSR President.

Heads of the republic governments may participate in the work of the USSR Cabinet of Ministers with the right to vote.

Article 130. The USSR Cabinet of Ministers is responsible to the USSR President and the USSR Supreme Soviet.

The newly-formed USSR Cabinet of Ministers submits a programme of forthcoming activity for the duration of its powers to the USSR Supreme Soviet for examination.

At least once a year the USSR Cabinet of Ministers reports back to the USSR Supreme Soviet on its works.

The USSR Supreme Soviet may pass a vote of no-confidence in the USSR Cabinet of Ministers which entails its resignation. A resolution on this question is adopted by a majority of votes from at least two-thirds of the total number of members of the USSR Supreme Soviet.

Article 131. The USSR Cabinet of Ministers is competent to resolve questions of state management under the USSR's jurisdiction since, according to the USSR Constitution, they do not fall within the competence of the USSR Congress of People's Deputies, the USSR Supreme Soviet and the Federation Council.

Article 132. The USSR Cabinet of Ministers ensures:

the implementation, jointly with the republics, of a unified financial, credit and monetary policy based on a common currency; the compilation and implementation of the union budget; the implementation of all-union economic programs; the creation of inter-republican development funds and funds for the elimination of the aftermath of natural disasters and catastrophes;

the management, jointly with the republics, of the country's unified fuel and energy system and transport system; the management of defence enterprises, space research and the union communications, information, meterological, geodetic, cartographic, geological, metrological and standardization systems; the implementation of a concerted policy in the sphere of nature conservation, ecological safety and use of natural resources;

the implementation, jointly with the republics, of all-union programs for food, health protection, social security, the population's employment, care for mother and child, culture and education, basic scientific research and the encouragement of scientific and technical progress;

the adoption of measures to ensure the country's defence and state security;

the realization of USSR foreign policy, the regulation of the USSR's foreign economic activity, the co-ordination of the republics' foreign policy and foreign economic activity and customs matters;

the implementation of measures agreed with the republics to ensure legality and citizens' rights and freedoms, to protect property and public order and to fight crime.

Article 133. On the basis of and in execution of USSR laws and other decisions of the USSR Congress of People's Deputies and the USSR Supreme Soviet and USSR presidential decrees, the USSR Cabinet of Ministers promulgates resolutions and ordinances and verifies their execution. Resolutions and ordinances of the USSR Cabinet of Ministers are mandatory for execution throughout the USSR's territory.

Article 134. Deleted.

Article 135. The USSR Cabinet of Ministers unites and directs the work of USSR ministries and other bodies subordinate to it.

Collegiums, which include, ex officio, the leaders of the republics' corresponding bodies, are created in ministries and other central bodies of USSR state management to co-ordinate the resolution of questions of state management.

Article 136. The competence of the USSR Cabinet of Ministers, its operating procedure, relations with other state bodies and also the list of ministries and other central bodies of USSR state management are defined in USSR law.

VI. Basic Principles of the Structure of the Bodies of State Authority and Administration in Union Republics

Chapter 17: Higher Bodies of State Authority and Administration of a Union Republic

Article 137. The highest bodies of state authority in union republics shall be the union republic supreme soviets and in union republics where it is envisaged to create congresses, the congresses of people's deputies.

Article 138. The powers, composition and standing orders of the highest bodies of state authority in union republics shall be determined by the constitutions and laws of the union republics.

Article 139. The Supreme Soviet of a Union Republic shall form a Council of Ministers of the Union Republic, i.e. the Government of that Republic, which shall be the highest executive and administrative body of state authority in the Republic.

The council of ministers of a union republic shall be responsible to the congress of people's deputies and the supreme soviet of the union republic and accountable to them.

Article 140. The Council of Ministers of a Union Republic issues decisions and ordinances on the basis of, and in pursuance of, the legislative acts of the USSR and of the Union Republic, and of acts of the USSR President and of the USSR Cabinet of Ministers, and shall organize and verify their execution.

Article 141. The Council of Ministers of a Union Republic has the right to suspend the execution of decisions and ordinances of the Councils of Ministers of Autonomous Republics, to rescind the decisions and orders of the Executive Committees of Soviets of People's Deputies of Territories, Regions, and cities (i.e. cities under Republic jurisdiction) and of Autonomous Regions, and in Union Republics not divided into regions, of the Executive Committees of district and corresponding city Soviets of People's Deputies.

Article 142. The Council of Ministers of a Union Republic shall co-ordinate and direct the work of the Union-Republican and Republican ministries and of state committees of the Union Republic, and other bodies under its jurisdiction.

The Union-Republican ministries and state committees of a Union Republic shall direct the branches of administration entrusted to them, or exercise inter-branch control, and shall be subordinate to both the Council of Ministers of the Union Republic and the corresponding Union-Republican ministry or state committee of the USSR.

Republican ministries and state committees shall direct the branches of administration entrusted to them, or exercise inter-branch control, and shall be subordinate to the Council of Ministers of the Union Republic.

Chapter 18: Higher Bodies of State Authority and Administration of an Autonomous Republic

Article 143. The highest bodies of state authority in autonomous republics shall be the autonomous republic supreme soviets, and in autonomous republics where it is envisaged to create congresses, the congresses of people's deputies.

Article 144. The supreme soviet of an autonomous republic shall form a council of ministers of the autonomous republic — the autonomous republic's government — as the highest executive and administrative body of state authority in the autonomous republic.

Chapter 19: Local Bodies of State Authority and Administration

Article 145. The bodies of state authority in autonomous oblasts, autonomous okrugs, krays, oblasts, rayons, towns, urban rayons, settlements, rural population centres and other administrative-territorial units, constituted in conformity with the laws of union and autonomous republics, shall be the corresponding soviets of people's deputies.

In the system of local self-management bodies of territorial public self-management, citizens' assemblies and other forms of direct democracy may operate in addition to local soviets of people's deputies, in accordance with the republics' legislation.

Article 146. Local Soviets of People's Deputies shall deal with all matters of local significance in accordance with the interests of the whole state and of the citizens residing in the area under their jurisdiction, implement decisions of higher bodies of state authority, guide the work of lower Soviets of People's Deputies, take part in the discussion of matters of Republican and All-Union significance, and submit their proposals concerning them.

Local Soviets of People's Deputies shall direct state, economic, social and cultural development within their territory; endorse plans of economic and social development and the local budget; exercise general guidance over state bodies, enterprises, institutions and organizations subordinate to them; ensure observance of the laws, maintenance of law and order, and protection of citizens' rights, and help strengthen the country's defence capacity.

Article 147. Within their powers, local Soviets of People's Deputies shall ensure the comprehensive, all-round economic and social development of their area; exercise control over the observance of legislation by enterprises, institutions and organizations subordinate to higher authorities and located in this area; and co-ordinate and supervise their activity as regards land use, nature conservation, building, employment of manpower, production of consumer goods, and social, cultural, communal and other services and amenities for the public.

Article 148. Local Soviets of People's Deputies shall decide matters within the powers accorded them by the legislation of the USSR and of the appropriate Union Republic and Autonomous Republic. Their decisions shall be binding on all enterprises, institutions, and organizations located in their area and on officials and citizens.

Article 149. The executive and administrative bodies of local soviets of people's deputies are the executive committees or other bodies elected by the local soviets of people's deputies.

At least once a year the executive and administrative bodies of local soviets report back to the soviets which elected them, as well as at meetings of work collectives and at citizens' places of residence.

Article 150. The executive and administrative bodies of local soviets of people's deputies are obliged to fulfil the laws, USSR presidential decrees and other acts of the supreme bodies of state power and management in the USSR and the republics adopted within the bounds of their competence.

The executive and administrative bodies of local soviets are directly subordinate both to the soviet which elected them and to the higher executive and administrative body.

VII. Justice, Arbitration, and Procurator's Office Supervision

Chapter 20: The Courts

Article 151. In the USSR justice is administered only by the courts.

In the USSR there are the following courts: the Supreme Court of the USSR, the Supreme Courts of Union Republics, the Supreme Courts of Autonomous Republics, Territorial, Regional, and city courts, courts of Autonomous Regions, courts of Autonomous Areas, district (city) people's courts and military tribunals in the Armed Forces.

Article 152. All courts in the USSR are constituted on the principle of the electivity of judges and lay assessors with the exception of the judges of military triburals.

People's judges of rayon (town) people's courts and the judges of kray, oblast and town courts shall be elected by corresponding superior soviets of people's deputies.

Judges of the USSR supreme court, the supreme courts of union and autonomous republics and the courts of autonomous oblasts and autonomous okrugs shall be elected by, respectively, the USSR supreme soviet, the supreme soviets of the union and autonomous republics and the soviets of people's deputies of autonomous oblasts and autonomous okrugs.

Lay assessors of rayon (town) people's courts shall be elected by open ballot at meetings of citizens held at their place of residence or work and the people's assessors of superior courts shall be elected by the corresponding soviets of people's deputies.

Judges of military tribunals shall be appointed by the President of the USSR and lay assessors by servicemen's meetings by open ballot.

Judges of all courts shall be elected for a term of 10 years. Lay assessors of all courts shall be elected for a term of five years.

Judges and lay assessors may be recalled in accordance with the legally established procedure.

Article 153. The USSR Supreme Court is the supreme judicial body in the USSR and supervises the judicial activity of USSR courts and of union republican courts within the parameters laid down by the law.

The USSR Supreme Court shall consist of a Chairman, his deputies, members and lay assessors. Chairmen of union republican supreme courts shall be ex officio members of the USSR Supreme Court.

The organization and procedure of work of the USSR Supreme Court shall be determined by the Law on the USSR Supreme Court.

Article 154. The hearing of civil and criminal cases in all courts is collegial; in courts of first instance cases are heard with the participation of people's assessors. In the administration of justice people's assessors have all the rights of a judge.

Article 155. Judges and lay assessors shall be independent and subordinate only to the law.

Conditions shall be provided for judges and lay assessors to exercise their rights and duties effectively without hindrance. Any interference in the activity of judges and lay assessors in the administration of justice is inadmissible and entails legal responsibility.

The immunity of judges and lay assessors and other guarantees of their independence shall be laid down in the Law on the Status of Judges in the USSR and other USSR and union republican legislative acts.

Article 156. Justice is administered in the USSR on the principle of the equality of citizens before the law and the court.

Article 157. Proceedings in all courts shall be open to the public. Hearings in camera are only allowed in cases provided for by law, with observance of all the rules of judicial procedure.

Article 158. A defendant in a criminal action is guaranteed the right to legal assistance.

Article 159. Judicial proceedings shall be conducted in the language of the Union Republic, Autonomous Republic, Autonomous Region, or Autonomous Area, or in the language spoken by the majority of the people in the locality. Persons participating in court proceedings, who do not know the language in which they are being conducted, shall be ensured the right to become fully acquainted with the materials in the case; the services of an interpreter during the proceedings; and the right to address the court in their own language.

Article 160. No one may be adjudged guilty of a crime and subjected to punishment as a criminal except by the sentence of a court and in conformity with the law.

Article 161. Colleges of advocates are available to give legal assistance to citizens and organizations. In cases provided for by legislation citizens shall be given legal assistance free of charge.

The organization and procedure of the bar are determined by legislation of the USSR and Union Republics.

Article 162. Representatives of public organizations and of work collectives may take part in civil and criminal proceedings.

Article 163. Economic disputes in the USSR are resolved by the USSR Supreme Court of Arbitration and by the bodies created in the republics in accordance with their laws for the resolution of economic disputes.

No bodies, organizations or officials are permitted to interfere in the judges' activities in resolving disputes.

The organization and operating procedure of the USSR Supreme Court of Arbitration are defined in USSR law.

Chapter 21: The Procurator's Office

Article 164. The precise and uniform execution of USSR laws by all ministries and other bodies of state management, enterprises, establishments, organizations, local soviets of people's deputies, their organizations and mass movements, officials and also citizens is supervised by the USSR Procurator General, the union republic procurators and the procurators subordinate to them.

Article 165. The USSR Procurator General shall be responsible to the USSR Congress of People's Deputies and the USSR Supreme Soviet and accountable to them.

Article 166. Republican procurators are appointed by the republics' supreme bodies of state power in agreement with the USSR Procurator General and are subordinate to them. In their activity in supervising the execution of USSR laws, the republican procurators are also subordinate to the USSR Procurator General.

Article 167. The Procurator-General of the USSR shall be empowered for a period of five years.

Article 168. The agencies of the Procurator's Office exercise their powers independently of all local bodies.

The organization and procedure of the agencies of the Procurator's Office are defined in USSR and union republican legislation.

VIII. The Emblem, Flag, Anthem, and Capital of the USSR

Article 169. The State Emblem of the Union of Soviet Socialist Republics is a hammer and sickle on a globe depicted in the rays of the sun and framed by ears of wheat, with the inscription 'Workers of All Countries, Unite!' in the languages of the Union Republics. At the top of the Emblem is a five-pointed star.

Article 170. The State Flag of the Union of Soviet Socialist Republics is a rectangle of red cloth with a hammer and sickle depicted in gold in the upper corner next to the staff and with a five-pointed red star edged in gold above them. The ratio of the width of the flag to its length is 1:2.

Article 171. The State Anthem of the Union of Soviet Socialist Republics is approved by the Presidium of the Supreme Soviet of the USSR.

Article 172. The Capital of the Union of Soviet Socialist Republics is the city of Moscow.

IX. The Legal Force of the Constitution of the USSR and Procedure for Amending the Constitution

Article 173. The Constitution of the USSR shall have supreme legal force. All laws and other acts of state bodies shall be promulgated on the basis of and in conformity with it.

Article 174. Amendment of the USSR Constitution shall take place by a resolution of the USSR Congress of People's Deputies adopted by a majority of at least two-thirds of the total number of people's deputies of the USSR.

ABOUT THE AUTHOR

David Lane is currently Fellow of Emmanuel College, Cambridge and University Lecturer in Sociology. Previously he was Professor of Sociology at the University of Birmingham and a member of the Centre for Russian and East European Studies there. He was a doctoral student at the University of Oxford and has been on the faculty of the University of Essex. He has also been a visiting professor at Cornell University and Graz University (Austria) and has held short-term research grants at the Kennan Institute in Washington, D.C. He has travelled in all the Eastern European countries (except Albania), and has visited the USSR on more than twenty occasions. Professor Lane's publications include *Politics and Society in the USSR* (1970) and most recently *Soviet Labour and the Ethic of Communism: Employment and the Labour Process in the USSR* (1987) and *Political Power and Elites in the USSR* (1988).

INDEX

Note: 'coup' refers to the attempted coup of August 1991.

437